MICROPROCESSORS AND SMALL DIGITAL COMPUTER SYSTEMS FOR ENGINEERS AND SCIENTISTS

MICROPROCESSORS AND SMALL DIGITAL COMPUTER SYSTEMS FOR ENGINEERS AND SCIENTISTS

GRANINO A. KORN, Ph.D.

Professor of Electrical Engineering
The University of Arizona
Tucson, Arizona

McGRAW-HILL BOOK COMPANY

New York   St. Louis   San Francisco   Auckland   Bogotá
Düsseldorf   Johannesburg   London   Madrid   Mexico
Montreal   New Delhi   Panama   Paris   São Paulo
Singapore   Sydney   Tokyo   Toronto

Library of Congress Cataloging in Publication Data

Korn, Granino Arthur, date.
 Microprocessors and small digital computer systems for engineers and scientists.

 Edition for 1973 published under title: Minicom-
puters for engineers and scientists.
 Bibliography: p.
 Includes index.
 1. Miniature computers. 2. Microcomputers.
3. Microprocessors. I. Title.
QA76.5.K67   1977   001.6′4′044   77-492
ISBN 0-07-035367-0

1234567890   DODO   786543210987

The editors for this book were Tyler G. Hicks and Lester Strong,
and the production supervisor was Teresa F. Leaden.

Printed and bound by R. R. Donnelley & Sons Company.

The previous edition of this book was published under the title
Minicomputers for Engineers and Scientists.

CONTENTS

PREFACE

Microcomputers represent a very remarkable achievement of engineering ingenuity and industrial know-how at their best. *Microprocessors,* i.e., large-scale-integrated-circuit computer processors can be inexpensively produced by *millions* to serve as exceptionally versatile system components in an ever-increasing number of applications. Special-purpose design and redesign is replaced by relatively simple programming and reprogramming. *Microcomputers* are digital computers using microprocessor central-processor logic. This definition includes almost all new *minicomputers,* an only roughly defined term for a small digital computer capable, at least in principle, of stand-alone operation (Chaps. 1 and 7). Small digital computers have quickly retraced the entire development history of larger computers and now duplicate most of their hardware and software features, including floating-point arithmetic, direct memory access, and advanced languages and operating systems. Micro/minicomputers, then, will serve not only as system components but also as end-user machines with enough computing power to free researchers and engineers from bondage to a computer-center bureaucracy.

This book, a largely rewritten and enlarged new edition of my book *Minicomputers for Engineers and Scientists,* attempts to introduce engineers and scientists to microprocessors, microcomputers, and minicomputation. Each chapter pinpoints important features of hardware, programming, and interface design. I hope that the book will help readers to understand the manufacturers' literature and to make informed choices of microprocessors, minicomputers, peripherals, and application areas, and thus to realize the exceptional possibilities of the new digital techniques.

The first chapter is an introduction to the computer's role as a *pro-*

grammed information transducer, and to its *data representations, codes, logic,* and *basic arithmetic.* Modern *integrated-circuit families* used for microprocessor logic and memory are reviewed and compared, and the reader is introduced to *read-only memory* and *programmed-logic arrays.* This chapter is intended to make the book self-sufficient, but even engineers familiar with digital computation will find the tabulated information on number systems, data-word formats, and logic circuits useful for reference. As throughout the book, *compact presentation of reference material in the form of boxed tables has made it possible to present a respectable amount of such information without cluttering the text.*

Chapter 2 discusses processor operation and presents a thorough discussion of *instruction sets* and *addressing modes.* Instructions are discussed with emphasis on their effect on programs and software, a necessary viewpoint for reasonable comparison of different computer systems. Separate sections describe *stack operations, subroutine linkage, memory mapping,* and horizontal and vertical *microprogramming.*

Chapter 3 shows how the instructions and addressing modes introduced in Chap. 2 are used in *machine-language* and *assembly-language programs.* This chapter introduces *assembler operation, program documentation, branching and flow charts, arrays, loops, stacks, table lookup,* and *return-address storage* and *data passing* for modern *reentrant subroutines.* I strongly believe that some knowledge of these concepts is vital even for computer users who will never program in assembly language, if they are to make intelligent choices of computer architectures and instruction sets. Chapter 2 further discusses *linking and relocation of programs* and the use of *asembly-language macros for instruction-set emulation and for writing simple applications-oriented languages,* such as block-diagram languages, which can greatly simplify microcomputer programming. The chapter closes with examples of *programmed logic, counting, delay, and arithmetic routines for microprocessors.*

The most important feature of a small digital computer is its ability to interact inexpensively with devices in the outside world. Chapter 4 presents what is probably the most extensive currently available description of *micro/minicomputer interface systems, including program-controlled interfaces for synchronous and asynchronous bus systems, priority-interrupt systems and their status-saving programs, context switching, and direct access.* This chapter highlights the impressive simplicity of interface design with off-the-shelf interface-logic cards and I/O-port chips and discusses *parallel/serial conversion* for communications interfaces, *graphic-display interfacing,* and *CAMAC* and *Hewlett-Packard-type instrumentation-bus systems.*

Chapter 5 introduces the reader to micro/minicomputer *control-panel operations, peripherals, mass storage,* and *system software* and will serve as a helpful introduction to the manufacturer's manuals on the latter subject. Several sections discuss *input/output software* for file access, *input/output macros*, and *device-independent input/output*. I have emphasized the power of modern *disk operating systems* for general-purpose minicomputation, and included discussions of *cathode-ray-tube keyboard terminals, on-line editing, and debugging*. Five sections describe single-user and multiuser *real-time operating systems*, including the problems of *task scheduling, resource allocation, intertask communication*, and *software overhead*. This is followed by a brief discussion of *higher-order languages*, both for minicomputers and for microcomputers. The chapter closes with three sections on *microcomputer program preparation and system development*, including descriptions of simple and advanced *microcomputer prototyping systems, cross translation, and microcomputer program emulation*.

Chapter 6 deals with *microcomputer systems and design decisions*. The introductory sections present the vital *cost equation* governing the *allocation of hardware versus programming expenditures*. *Microprocessors, memories, I/O ports*, and *bus systems* are then discussed as system components. The bulk of Chap. 6 describes and compares architectures, advantages, and disadvantages of different microcomputer instruction sets, addressing modes, and I/O structures. Microprocessors described in some detail are *Intel 4040 and 8080A, Motorola 6800, MOS Technology 650X, Zilog Z-80, Signetics 2650, Fairchild F-8, RCA CDP 1802, Scientific Micro Systems SMS 300, Digital Equipment PDP-8/Intersil 6100, National Semiconductor SC/MP and PACE, General Instruments CP 1600, and Western Digital MCP 1600*. Numerous tables list and compare specifications and instruction sets. A separate subchapter deals with *bit-sliced microprocessors* and describes processor designs and microprogram control for *Monolithic Memories, Advanced Microsystems, Intel*, and *Motorola* products; Texas Instruments processors are discussed in Chap. 7.

Chapter 7 deals with *minicomputer-system selection* and presents a critical discussion of the principal *micro/minicomputer families* in the light of the writer's consulting practice in this field. Successive sections discuss *Hewlett-Packard, General Automation, Interdata, Data General, Digital Equipment Corporation, Varian, Honeywell*, and *Texas Instruments* families of micro/minicomputers. Special emphasis is given to the important *Digital Equipment Corporation PDP-11 family*, the *Data General NOVA/ECLIPSE family*, and the new *Honeywell Level 6 and Texas Instruments 990 families*, which incorporate significant architectural innovations as well as LSI processor chips.

Appendices present *sections summarizing features of the BASIC, FORTRAN, and PL-1 languages*, as well as reference tables on *number systems* and *computer codes*.

I am greatly indebted to my colleagues in the computer industry for supplying me with information and reference material for this book which attempts to describe the astonishing success of *their* vision and *their* labor. I would in particular like to thank the following individuals and organizations:

American Microsystems, Inc.
    Santa Clara, California
Computer Operations, Inc.
    Beltsville, Maryland   R. Bushnell
Data General Corporation
    Southboro, Massachusetts   J. Scanlon
Digital Equipment Corporation
    Maynard, Massachusetts   S. A. Kallis
Electronics
    New York, New York   K. Anderson
Fairchild Semiconductor
    Mountain View, California
General Automation, Inc.
    Anaheim, California   S. D. Lane
Hewlett-Packard Corporation
    Cupertino, California
Honeywell Information Systems, Inc.
    Waltham, Massachusetts   Joanne Full
Intel Corporation
    Santa Clara, California
Interdata
    Oceanport, New Jersey   A. Furman
Monolithic Memories, Inc.
    Sunnyvale, California   E. Barnett
Motorola Semiconductor
    Phoenix, Arizona   L. Stern
National Semiconductor Corp.
    Santa Clara, California   C. Signor
Pro-log Corporation
    Monterey, California   E. S. Lee
Tektronix, Inc.
    Beaverton, Oregon   M. Floathe
Three Rivers Corporation
    Pittsburgh, Pennsylvania   V. Fuller
                                        Dr. Teters

Western Digital Corporation
    Newport Beach, California   K. Harlan

I am also grateful to my colleagues and assistants at the Computer Science Research Laboratory of the Electrical Engineering Department of the University of Arizona, for their help.

Tucson, Arizona   GRANINO A. KORN

MICROPROCESSORS AND
SMALL DIGITAL
COMPUTER SYSTEMS
FOR ENGINEERS
AND SCIENTISTS

CHAPTER 1

THE INGREDIENTS OF MINI/ MICROCOMPUTATION

NEW TOOLS OF EXTRAORDINARY POWER

1-1. The Role of Small Computers. If "information" refers to an ability to select *decisions* from classes of available decisions, then a computer is an "information transducer" which transforms given *input decisions* (programs and data, stimuli) into *output decisions* (computed results, responses), as in Fig. 1-1. Actually, many hardware systems and components fit this description (e.g., controllers, servomechanisms, communication systems, displays); we will speak of a **computer** if our hardware was consciously designed to implement a mathematical model.

Inputs and outputs are *physical representations* of (possibly very many) decisions which can select

numbers
alphanumeric character strings

but also, more directly,

instrument or sensor responses
physical operations (switch closings, valve settings)
display signals

In multipurpose computers, inputs include commands (instructions, programs) which determine the computer operation itself. To deal economically with large and changing sets of inputs, outputs, and operations, "sequential" computers reduce complicated operations to *sequences* of

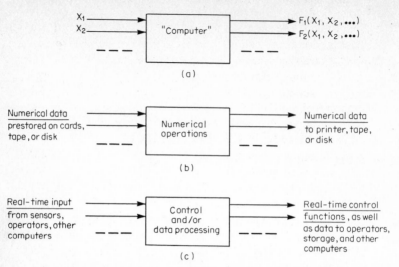

Fig. 1-1. Information processing (*a*), and evolution of real-time computation (*b*), (*c*).

relatively few standard operations (**instruction set**) and provide **memory** to store data awaiting processing or output, intermediate results, and programs awaiting execution (Fig. 1-2).

Professional workers are likely to meet computers in the following roles:

1. **Numerical problem solving and data processing:** This ranges from little slide-rule and calculator jobs to big number-crunching projects and includes design calculations, statistics, genetics calculations, book-

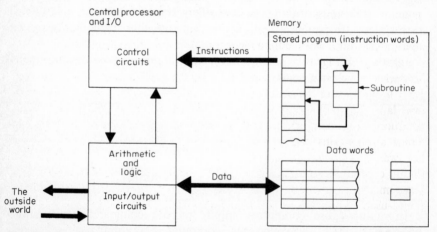

Fig. 1-2. The stored-program computer performs complicated operations by fetching and executing a sequence of simple instructions (program) stored in the computer memory together with intermediate data.

keeping, etc.   The end product may be scientific or clerical *description*, but, in the long run, calculations usually serve for *making decisions*.

2. **Storing, retrieving, sorting, and updating data:** This is by no means restricted to numerical data only.

3. Computer **simulation:** We use the convenient, easy-to-change "live mathematical model" for *experiments* which might be slow, expensive, unsafe, or impossible with the real-world system or situation being simulated.   Computer simulation serves the purposes of design, systems research, education, training, and play; simulation experiments or tests sometimes involve parts of real systems.

4. **"Real-time" or "on-line" computing devices** serve as components of control and instrumentation systems to:
    (*a*) Implement desired mathematical relations between physical variables (e.g., function generation, filtering, prediction, optimization)
    (*b*) Control timing and logical sequencing of operations and experiments
    The latter types of operations are often combined with on-line record keeping (data logging) and data processing.

5. Real-time timing, switching, coding, and data storage in **communication systems,** especially in communications between digital computers and/or computer terminals.

Early digital computers were large, immovable, and costly.   This restricted them to efficient batch-processed "number-crunching"; digital hardware was too expensive to wait for real-time operations with real physical inputs and outputs (Fig. 1-1*b*).   Truly revolutionary hardware-cost reductions (medium- and large-scale integrated circuits) have changed this situation completely.   By far more (orders of magnitude more) digital computers now do real-time work than ever served for numerical calculations.

Referring to Fig. 1-2, the important point is that **a given set of computer hardware can serve a huge variety of different applications.   Different computer operations, or different dedicated computer systems, can be "designed" (and later changed) simply by writing different computer programs.**   Mass-produced small computers, programmed and reprogrammed for many different applications and conditions can, then, replace custom-designed hardware as *system components*.   Mass production, in turn, has made small digital computers so inexpensive that they often compete with time-shared large machines even in data-processing and numerical-problem-solving ("end-user") applications (see also Sec. 7-1).

1-2.   Minicomputers, Microprocessors, and Microcomputers.   Definitions classifying small digital computers are blurred.   Roughly a **minicomputer** is a digital machine suitable for general-purpose use (even though most are

Fig. 1-3a. Microprocessor on a chip. The 40-pin mN601 NMOS chip is a complete 16-bit central processor with microprogrammed multiplication and division instructions. (*Data General Corporation.*)

Fig. 1-3b. Microcomputer on a card. Intel SDK-80 has an 8-bit 8080A microprocessor; 2K bytes of erasable, programmable read-only memory; 256 bytes of random-access memory; a crystal clock; interface circuits; and a general-purpose wirewrap area for the user's own circuits. (*Intel Corporation.*)

not used that way) and costing between \$1,000 and \$25,000 for one processor, 4,000 words of memory, power supply, control panel, and some software. Short word length (Sec. 1-11) used to be taken for granted, but our classification now includes small 32-bit machines with floating-point instructions (Fig. 1-4 and Sec. 7-2).

NOTE: Practical *end-user* installations would require more memory, mass storage (disk, tape), and a keyboard/printer or other terminal costing together from \$6,000 to over \$30,000 (possibly more than the basic computer).

A **microprocessor** is, in general, *not* a complete computer, but a central processor unit (CPU, Fig. 1-2) implemented with, say, one to ten *large-scale-integrated-circuit chips*. We speak of large-scale integration (*LSI*) when a chip comprises 1,000 or more gates; many LSI chips hold over 6,000 gates *or a complete central processor* (Fig. 1-4).

The term **microcomputer** is even less well defined. This is a small stored-program computer comprising memory and input/output circuits together with a microprocessor CPU.* Microcomputers with less than 2,000 words of memory cost between \$25 and \$1,000 in quantities of 100. Practically all are special-purpose computers used as system components.

As we noted, the definitions are vague. Minicomputers come in software-compatible families, whose larger members are very powerful medium-sized machines (Sec. 7-1). And how large must a general-purpose microcomputer be to be called a minicomputer? Note, too, that all future minicomputers (and medium-sized computers as well) will be made with microprocessor chips (Sec. 7-12).

1-3. Hardware and Software. As we will see, small-computer hardware, although cleverly designed, is conceptually simple. It is also mass-produced and quite inexpensive. But the immense power transforming this bargain-priced hardware into a thousand ingenious and new special-purpose computers, controllers, simulators, and data loggers does not come built into our semiconductor chips. A computer is completely powerless and useless until we provide programs and programming systems (**software**) which make the dead general-purpose hardware do what we want. Providing the computer, plus some **interface circuits** appropriate to each application (Chap. 4), is only a start. Much of our engineering work remains to be done *but has been transformed into designing sequences of instructions for a computer program.* **Interface design and programming make the mass-produced microcomputer or minicomputer into a new special-purpose machine.**

Engineering by program-structure design can be more efficient than random-logic design, breadboarding, etc. Because of the wide range of

* A few manufacturers also refer to their smallest computers built from medium-sized-integrated (MSI) logic as microcomputers.

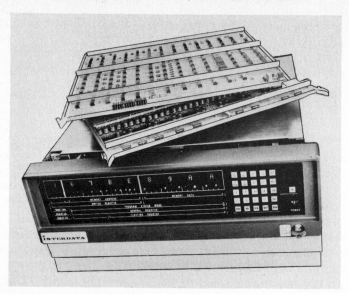

Fig. 1-4a. Minicomputer in a box, showing central-processor and memory cards. The 16-bit Interdata 6/32 uses bit-sliced microprocessor chips. (*Interdata.*)

possibilities, though, **programs can be much more complicated than the computer hardware, and programming costs will usually greatly exceed hardware costs** (see also Chaps. 3 and 6). In this connection, it can be vital to have *software designed to simplify computer programming* (translators for

Fig. 1-4b. This $40,000 minicomputer system includes 28K 16-bit words of memory, disk-cartridge and tape drives, a keyboard/printer, and a complete graphic display. (*GT-44 system based on PDP-11/40, Digital Equipment Corporation.*)

easy-to-use programming languages, program-editing and debugging systems, operating systems, Chap. 5). Such software is itself a set of very complicated programs, whose purchase cost must not be neglected in plans for computer projects.

DIGITAL-COMPUTER REPRESENTATION OF DATA AND TEXT

1-4. Binary and Digital Variables. While an **analog computer** represents problem variables by continuously variable physical quantities such as voltages or currents (Fig. 1-5a), a **digital computer** represents problem variables by physical quantities capable of taking only discrete and countable sets of values. Thus, the original "digital-computer user" long ago employed his fingers to count and add external objects, first up to five and then up to ten. The overwhelming majority of electronic digital computers, however, implements a **binary** representation in terms of basic variables which can take only **two** different states called (logical) 0 and 1. Most frequently, the state 1 is indicated by the presence of a voltage, usually 3 or 4 V, on a line associated with a variable, while logical 0 is indicated by the absence of that voltage (Fig. 1-5b). Many other pairs of voltage levels, such as -10 and 10 V or -1.75 and -0.5 V, are also employed to represent 0 and 1.

Such binary variables, which involve only the presence or absence of a signal, are especially easy to generate, transmit, and store reliably. We pay for this great convenience, however: most problem situations or variables admit a much greater variety of possible states than just two and must, therefore, be labeled (represented) in terms of ordered *combinations* of binary variables. We must, then, develop **binary codes** which associate problem states, messages, or numerical quantities with corresponding **digital words,** i.e., ordered sets of **binary variables.** Such codes may differ for different applications. The *reference manual* furnished with each digital computer will specify binary-word codes for numerical and alphanumeric data, as described in Secs. 1-5 to 1-11.

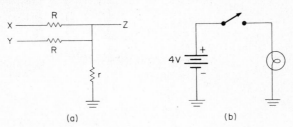

(a)　　　　　　　　　　　　　　(b)

Fig. 1-5a. Simple analog computation. The summing network produces the output voltage $Z = a(X + Y)$, where X and Y are input voltages and $a = (R/r + 2)^{-1}$.

Fig. 1-5b. Logic states represented by voltage levels in an elementary digital circuit.

It is, of course, especially important to represent **real numbers** in terms of binary variables. In general, a real integer m will require at least $\log_2 m$ binary units of information or **bits,** plus a **sign bit** to tell whether the integer is positive or negative (Sec. 1-5).

It is common practice to designate an entire set of binary variables (which may or may not represent a numerical quantity) as a single **digital variable.** The different bits of such a digital variable may appear on parallel bus lines **(parallel representation)** and may be stored in a *register* like that of the toggle switches in Fig. 1-6*a*. The different bits of a digital variable could also follow each other in time as consecutive samples of a voltage waveform which can take the values corresponding to 0 or 1 **(serial representation,** Fig. 1-6*b*). Parallel representation, which can transmit all the bits of a word at

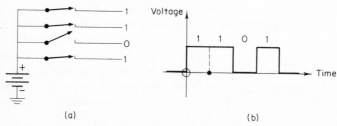

(a)   (b)

Fig. 1-6. Representation of the digital word 1101 by simultaneous levels on a *parallel* bus (*a*) and by a *serial* waveform (*b*).

the same time, is clearly faster and is most frequently employed in modern digital computers. Serial representation, on the other hand, simplifies long-distance data communication.

1-5. Fixed-Point Binary Numbers. (a) Nonnegative Integers. The n-bit binary word

$$
\begin{array}{|ll c|}
\hline
n-1 & & 0 \\
a_{n-1}\,a_{n-2} & & a_0 \\
\hline
\end{array}
\qquad (1\text{-}1)
$$

where a_k is either 0 or 1, can be interpreted as a one-to-one representation **(binary code)** for the nonnegative integers

$$ X = 2^{n-1}a_{n-1} + 2^{n-2}a_{n-2} + \cdots + a_0 \qquad (0 \le X \le 2^{n-1} - 1) \quad (1\text{-}2) $$

a_{n-1} is the **most significant bit (MSB),** and a_0 is the **least significant bit (LSB)** in our notation. Note that some computer manufacturers reverse the bit numbering, so that a_0 is the MSB and a_{n-1} is the LSB (Fig. 1-7).

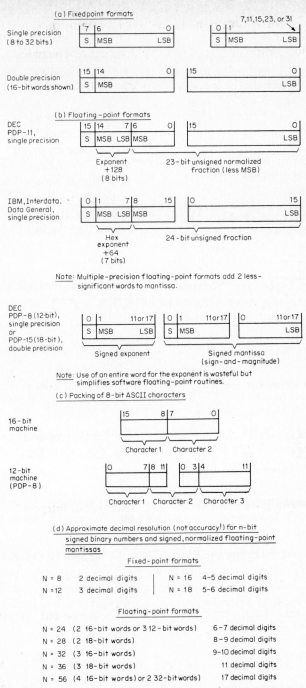

Fig. 1-7. Typical data formats for small digital computers. Most manufacturers employ the bit-numbering convention used in this book; i.e., less significant bits are *toward the right* and have *lower* numbers. But other conventions are used as well.

9

EXAMPLES: (a) $0101_2 = 0 + 4 + 0 + 1 = 5_{10}$
(b) The complete 3-bit code for the decimal integers (or octal integers, Sec. 1-6) from 0 to 7 is given by

DECIMAL	BINARY	DECIMAL	BINARY
0	000	4	100
1	001	5	101
2	010	6	110
3	011	7	111

The integers (2), in turn, constitute a *numerical code* for the *n*-bit binary words, whose original interpretation may not be numerical, e.g., a set of truth values.

Binary/decimal conversion is easiest with *decimal/octal tables* (Sec. 1-6 and Table A-3), or use the "doubling and dabbling" recursion (Ref. 4) $X = X_{n-1}$, where $X_0 = a_{n-1}$. $X_i = 2X_{i-1} + a_{m-1-i}$ and $i = 1, 2, \ldots, n - 1$; e.g.,

$$a_i \quad 1 \quad 0 \quad 1 \quad 1$$

$$X_i \quad 1 \quad 2 \quad 5 \quad 11 \qquad X = 11$$

(b) Binary Fractions. **Nonnegative fractions X between 0 and 1 are useful as scaled representations of physical variables** (Sec. 1-14). They are encoded into binary words (1) by the rule

$$X = \frac{1}{2} a_{n-1} + \frac{1}{2^2} a_{n-2} + \cdots + \frac{1}{2^{n-1}} a_0 \qquad (0 \le X \le 1 - 2^{1-n}) \quad (1\text{-}3)$$

EXAMPLES: (a) $0101_2 = \frac{1}{4} + \frac{1}{16} = \frac{5}{16} = 0.3125_{10}$

(b) 3-bit fraction code:

DECIMAL	BINARY	DECIMAL	BINARY
0.000	000	$\frac{4}{8} = 0.500$	000
$\frac{1}{8} = 0.125$	001	$\frac{5}{8} = 0.625$	101
$\frac{2}{8} = 0.250$	010	$\frac{6}{8} = 0.750$	110
$\frac{3}{8} = 0.375$	011	$\frac{7}{8} = 0.875$	111

(c) Signed Integers and Fractions. To encode signed numbers into *n*-bit binary words (1), we use a_{n-1} as the **sign bit** and employ one of the codes in Tables 1-1 and 1-2.

1-6. Shorthand Notation for Binary Data: Octal and Hexadecimal Numbers. Binary words are convenient for *machines* but not for people. To obtain a nice shorthand notation, we split a given binary word into *3-bit groups* (starting with a_0) and write the binary number corresponding to each group as an octal digit between 0 and 7:

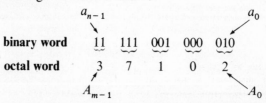

TABLE 1-1. Binary Codes for Signed Integers.

a_{n-1}	a_{n-2}	a_0
S	MSB	LSB

a_{n-1} is the **sign bit**, a_{n-2} the **most significant bit (MSB)**, and a_0 the **least significant bit (LSB)**.

1. 2s-Complement Code. Used in almost all small computers, this code simplifies arithmetic (Sec. 1-15) and counting. Signed integers X in the range

$$-2^{n-1} \leq X \leq 2^{n-1} - 1$$

are simply coded as the least significant n bits of the unsigned integers $2^n + X$, so that 1000 ... always denotes -2^{n-1}, and *there is a unique code 000 ... for zero:*

$$X = -2^{n-1}a_{n-1} + 2^{n-2}a_{n-2} + 2^{n-3}a_{n-3} + \cdots + a_0$$

The n-bit code for each nonnegative integer X is its $(n-1)$-bit unsigned-integer code preceded by the sign bit 0. *To obtain the code for $-X$, complement each bit and add 1 LSB;* or copy the least significant bits up to and including the first 1, then complement all the more significant bits.

EXAMPLE (4-bit code):

DECIMAL	2s-COMPLEMENT		DECIMAL	2s-COMPLEMENT	
-8	1	000	0	0	000
-7	1	001	$+1$	0	001
-6	1	010	$+2$	0	010
-5	1	011	$+3$	0	011
-4	1	100	$+4$	0	100
-3	1	101	$+5$	0	101
-2	1	110	$+6$	0	110
-1	1	111	$+7$	0	111

2. Offset-Binary Code. This is *the 2s-complement code with the sign bit reversed* and has the same range. Signed integers X code into unsigned integers $2^{n-1} + X$, so that 000 ... denotes -2^{n-1}, and *1000 ... is the unique code for zero.* This code is used for graphic displays and for indexing tables with negative arguments.

3. Sign-and-Magnitude Code. The n-bit code for each integer X in the range $1 - 2^{n-1} \leq X \leq 2^{n-1} - 1$ is the $(n-1)$-bit unsigned integer code for the absolute value $|X|$, preceded by a sign bit (0 if $X > 0$):

$$X = (-1)^{a_{n-1}}(2^{n-2}a_{n-2} + 2^{n-3}a_{n-3} + \cdots + a_0)$$

There are *two* binary codes for zero, 000 ... and 1000 .... This can cause complications, e.g., in statistical work. This code is used in some digital voltmeters. An analogous sign representation is used with BCD codes (Sec. 1-10).

EXAMPLE (4-bit code): $0101_2 = +5_{10}$ $1101_2 = -5_{10}$

4. 1s-Complement Code. n-bit codes for nonnegative integers $X \leq 2^{n-1} - 1$ are their unsigned-integer codes (i.e., sign bit = 0). Codes for the corresponding integers $-X \geq 1 - 2^{n-1}$ (negative or zero) are obtained simply *by complementing each bit* of the code for X, or

$$X = (1 - 2^{n-1})a_{n-1} + 2^{n-2}a_{n-2} + 2^{n-3}a_{n-3} + \cdots + a_0$$

There are *two* codes for zero, 000 ... and 111 ....

EXAMPLE (4-bit code): $0101_2 = +5_{10}$ $1010_2 = -5_{10}$

TABLE 1-2.   Binary Codes for Signed Fractions.

a_{n-1}	a_{n-2}	a_0
S	MSB	LSB

Scaled fractions between -1 and $+1$ are usually the best fixed-point representations of physical measurements (Sec. 1-14). a_{n-1} is the **sign bit**, a_{n-2} is the **most significant bit (MSB)**, and a_0 the **least significant bit (LSB)**.
CAUTION: Small-computer multiplication/division routines are usually designed for integers, not fractions (Sec. 1-15).

1. 2s-Complement Code.   Signed fractions X in the range

$$-1 \leq X \leq 1 - 2^{1-n}$$

are encoded by the rule

$$X = -a_{n-1} + \frac{1}{2}a_{n-2} + \frac{1}{2^2}a_{n-3} + \cdots + \frac{1}{2^{n-1}}a_0$$

1000 ... always denotes -1, and 000 ... is the unique code for zero.   The n-bit code for each nonnegative fraction X is its $(n-1)$-bit unsigned-fraction code (Sec. 1-5b) preceded by the sign bit 0.   *To obtain the code for $-X$, complement each bit and add 1 LSB;* or copy the least significant bits up to and including the first 1, then complement all the more significant bits.

EXAMPLE (4-bit code):

DECIMAL	2s-COMPLEMENT		DECIMAL	2s-COMPLEMENT	
-1	1	000	0	0	000
$-\frac{7}{8} = -0.875$	1	001	$+\frac{1}{8} = +0.125$	0	001
$-\frac{6}{8} = -0.750$	1	010	$+\frac{2}{8} = +0.250$	0	010
$-\frac{5}{8} = -0.625$	1	011	$+\frac{3}{8} = +0.375$	0	011
$-\frac{4}{8} = -0.500$	1	100	$+\frac{4}{8} = +0.500$	0	100
$-\frac{3}{8} = -0.375$	1	101	$+\frac{5}{8} = +0.625$	0	101
$-\frac{2}{8} = -0.250$	1	110	$+\frac{6}{8} = +0.750$	0	110
$-\frac{1}{8} = -0.125$	1	111	$+\frac{7}{8} = +0.875$	0	110

2. Offset-Binary Code.   This is *the 2s-complement code with the sign bit reversed* and has the same range.   000 ... denotes -1, and 1000 ... is the unique code for zero.   This code is used for graphic displays and for indexing tables with negative arguments (Sec. 3-11a).

3. Sign-and-Magnitude Code.   The n-bit code for each fraction X in the range $2^{n-1} - 1 \leq X \leq 1 - 2^{1-n}$ is the $(n-1)$-bit unsigned fraction code for the absolute value $|X|$, preceded by a sign bit (0 if $X < 0$):

$$X = (-1)^{a_{n-1}}\left(\frac{1}{2}a_{n-2} + \frac{1}{2^2}a_{n-3} + \cdots + \frac{1}{2^{n-1}}a_0\right)$$

There are *two* codes for zero, 000 ... and 1000 ....   This can cause complications, e.g., in statistical work.   This code is used in floating-point arithmetic (Sec. 1-7).

EXAMPLE (4-bit code): $0101_2 = +\frac{5}{8}$ $1101_2 = -\frac{5}{8}$

4. 1s-Complement Code. n-bit codes for nonnegative fractions $X \leq 1 - 2^{1-n}$ are their $(n-1)$-bit unsigned fraction codes preceded by the sign bit 0.   Codes for the corresponding fractions $-X \leq 2^{1-n} - 1$ (negative or zero) are obtained simply *by complementing each bit* of the code for X, or

$$X = (2^{1-n} - 1)a_{n-1} + \frac{1}{2}a_{n-2} + \frac{1}{2^2}a_{n-3} + \cdots + \frac{1}{2^{n-1}}a_0$$

There are *two* codes for zero, 000 ... and 111 ....

EXAMPLE (4-bit code): $0101_2 = +\frac{5}{8}$ $1010_2 = -\frac{5}{8}$

The resulting **octal word** $(A_{m-1}, A_{m-2}, \ldots, A_0)$ represents the integer in the form

$$X = 8^{m-1}A_{m-1} + 8^{m-2}A_{m-2} + \cdots + A_0 \left(0 \leq X \leq 2^{n-1} - 1; \, m < \frac{n}{3} + 1 \right)$$

$$(1\text{-}4)$$

The code we have just defined will describe every binary word as a *nonnegative octal integer* (4), even though the binary word may represent a negative number, a fraction, or a nonnumerical quantity such as a set of truth values or a text character.   There is little need to learn octal *complement codes* for negative numbers since minicomputer assembly languages (Sec. 3-3) which accept negative octal integers automatically translate ordinary sign-and-magnitude notation, e.g.,

$$-400_8 = -256_{10}$$

into binary code.   Computer *output* is usually in decimal form, except for some debugging and troubleshooting programs.   As an aid to binary-to-decimal conversion, it is useful to know the octal representation for *nonnegative pure fractions* encoded in the manner of Sec. 1-5b.   We again start 3-bit groups at the implied binary point, i.e., proceeding *to the right* from a_{n-1}:

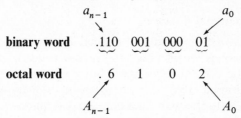

so that

$$X = \frac{1}{2}a_{n-1} + \frac{1}{2^2}a_{n-2} + \cdots + \frac{1}{2^n}a_0$$

$$= \frac{1}{8}A_{m-1} + \frac{1}{8^2}A_{m-2} + \cdots + \frac{1}{8^n}A_0 \quad \left(0 \leq X \leq 1 - \frac{1}{2^n}; \quad m \leq \frac{n}{3} \right) \quad (1\text{-}5)$$

Decimal-octal-decimal conversion is defined by Eqs. (1-4) and (1-5) but is usually done with the aid of *conversion tables* (Appendix).   Octal-number representations work perfectly well even if the given word length n is not divisible by 3.   Note, however, that the octal-*integer* code for nonnegative pure binary fractions is identical with the octal-*fraction* code if and only if the word size is divisible by 3.   For this reason, our Appendix presents an octal-fraction conversion table as well as an octal-integer conversion table.

TABLE 1-3.   Hexadecimal
Notation.

Hexadecimal	Binary	Decimal
0	0000	0
1	0001	1
2	0010	2
3	0011	3
4	0100	4
5	0101	5
6	0110	6
7	0111	7
8	1000	8
9	1001	9
A	1010	10
B	1011	11
C	1100	12
D	1101	13
E	1110	14
F	1111	15

Hexadecimal notation similarly divides each binary word into *4-bit groups* labeled with hexadecimal digits (Table 1-3):

$$a_0 \rightarrow 1\ 0\ 1\ 0\ 0\ 1\ 1\ 1\ 1\ 0\ 0\ 1\ 0\ 0\ 0\ 0\ 1\ 0$$

$$\underbrace{}_{2}\quad\underbrace{}_{9}\quad\underbrace{}_{E}\quad\underbrace{}_{4}\quad\underbrace{}_{2}\quad \text{(integer)}$$

Octal-integer arithmetic, useful for "manual" work with binary operations (design, programming, see also Sec. 4-2) is easy to learn for those used to decimal arithmetic.   We simply carry or borrow at 8 instead of 10 and learn a simple multiplication table.   Especially for occasional use, octal numbers are probably easier to live with than hexadecimal numbers.   But the latter are widely accepted in applications involving communications and/or IBM 360/370 computer systems, as well as with 4-bit and 8-bit micro-computers.   This is true because representation of the 8-bit words or partial words (**bytes**) used for alphanumeric characters (Sec. 1-9) requires *three* octal digits but only *two* hexadecimal digits:

$$10110010_2 = 262_8 = B2_{16}$$

Conversion and arithmetic tables for both systems will be found in the Appendix (Tables B-1 to B-6).

1-7.   Floating-Point Data Representation.   Binary **floating-point arithmetic** represents each real number X by *two* binary numbers, an N-bit signed fraction (**mantissa**) A and an M-bit signed integer (**exponent**) R so that

$$X = A \times 2^R \qquad (1\text{-}6)$$

This floating-point representation covers the range

$$-2^{2^{M-1}-1} < X < 2^{2^{M-1}-1} \tag{1-7}$$

This range is usually so very large $(2^{2^{M-1}-1} > 10^{38}$ for $M = 8)$ that *no scaling is necessary with most practical problems* (overflow is possible, but not likely, Sec. 1-16). This truly dramatic advantage over fixed-point computation is paid for with either extra computing time or more expensive hardware, and usually also with *reduced precision* per bit available to represent X (M bits are used for the exponent, which does not contribute "significant digits"). Roundoff errors can be multiplied by large factors 2^R in some parts of a computation. As in all computations, the *accuracy* of a floating-point result can be worse than the *resolution* corresponding to the N-bit mantissa. In particular, the two-word floating-point formats of 16-digit minicomputers (Fig. 1-7) may not do the job in calculations where many terms are added, as in numerical integration and averaging. In such cases, a double-precision floating-point format (Fig. 1-7) must be used.

Floating-point number representation is not unique since, for instance,

$$0.10100_2 \times 2^9 = 0.01010_2 \times 2^{10} = 0.00101_2 \times 2^{11}$$

The first form, where the most significant binary digit of the (nonnegative) mantissa is a 1, is often defined as the **normalized** form of the floating-point number. If we agree to store all floating-point numbers in normalized forms and use *sign-and-magnitude code* (Table 1-2) for the mantissa, then we can simply *omit* the mantissa-fraction MSB, which is always 1. The floating-point number is interpreted as zero whenever the normalized exponent turns out to be $< -2^{M-1}$ (*underflow;* for $M = 8$, X would have to be a fraction of 10^{-38}). The exponent can be a 2s-complement integer (Table 1-1); many floating-point number representations do not use the exponent R itself but employ instead a nonnegative **biased exponent** or **characteristic**

$$R' = R + B \tag{1-8}$$

where B is an agreed-on positive integer, typically 128 for $M = 8$.

Some computer manufacturers (e.g., IBM, Interdata, Data General) use a "hexadecimal" floating-point representation defined by

$$X = A \times 16^R \tag{1-9}$$

where A is a binary fraction and R is a binary integer. In this case, a properly normalized mantissa will have at least the magnitude $1/16$; i.e., at least *one of the four most significant bits* of the positive fraction is a 1.

Some typical small-computer floating-point formats are shown in Fig. 1-7. Fortunately, most minicomputer users meet *binary* floating-point formats only when troubleshooting. Input/output is almost always in *decimal* floating-point format, usually in the E format familiar to FORTRAN users:

$$0.2734E + 02 = 0.2734_{10} \times 10^2$$

1-8. Parity Checking. In the course of a digital program, thousands or millions of digital words are transferred between the processor, the computer memory, and external devices. To improve reliability at the expense of some extra circuits, we can augment each n-bit word with an extra (redundant) **parity bit** which is made to equal 1 if and only if the number of 1s in the n information bits is odd. We can then check for **even parity** (even number of 1s) over all $n + 1$ bits to detect errors in 1, 3, 5, . . . bits (including the parity bit) and stop or repeat the operation as needed. Errors in 2, 4, . . . bits will remain undetected but are much less likely than 1-bit errors. Related checking methods apply to transfers of long lists of words.

Parity checks for memory and interface transfers are recommended for critical applications, especially where a computer system is unattended. Note that simple parity checking does *not* check arithmetic or logic errors. Many end-user minicomputers operate satisfactorily without memory-transfer parity checks.

1-9. Alphanumeric-Character Codes. Computer input/output and digital data transmission, manipulation, and storage require binary coding of **alphanumeric-character strings** representing text, commands, numbers, and/or code groups. We use one binary word, or a byte, for each character. 4 bits ($2^4 = 16$) are enough to encode the 10 numerals 0 to 9 (*binary coding of decimal numbers*, Sec. 1-10). The 26 letters of the alphabet (uppercase only) and the 10 numerals, plus some mathematical and punctuation symbols, can be squeezed into a **6-bit code** ($2^6 = 64$) if resources are scarce; Table B-11 shows an example of such a code. Most applications employ **a 7-bit code with an added 8th bit for parity checking** (Sec. 1-8). Table B-9 shows the **ASCII code (American Standard Code for Information Interchange),** which admits uppercase and lowercase letters, numerals, standard symbols, and **control characters** for printers and communication links (tab, line feed, form feed, rubout, end-of-message, etc.), and still has room for extra agreed-on symbols and control characters ($2^7 = 128$). A similar 8-bit code is the EBCDIC code used by the IBM Corporation.

8- and 16-bit minicomputers neatly handle one or two ASCII-character bytes in a computer word. Perforated paper tape also has eight-hole columns fitting 8-bit bytes (Fig. 5-7*a*). 12- and 18-bit machines must pack successive 8-bit characters into multiple words through rather uncomfortable packing operations (Fig. 1-7); 6-bit character sets are more convenient for such machines but may not have enough characters.

Groups of alphanumeric characters (e.g., three-character or six-character symbols in programming languages) can be packed and stored more efficiently than single characters.   In particular, *three-character groups* taken from a 40-character alphabet (26 letters, 10 numerals, and 4 other symbols) pack into only 16 bits, since $40^3 = 64,000 < 2^{16}$.   The **Mod 40** (or **Rad 50$_8$) code** labels 40 characters with the octal integers 0 to 47_8 and encodes character groups C1, C2, C3 into octal numbers

$$50_8^2 C1 + 50_8 C2 + C3$$

which represent the desired 16-bit binary code (Sec. 1-6).

1-10.   Binary-Coded-Decimal (BCD) Numbers and Other Number Codes.

Table 1-4 shows some **binary-coded-decimal (BCD) codes** which express numerical data in terms of strings of 4-bit character codes corresponding to decimal digits.   As an example, the **8, 4, 2, 1 BCD code** encodes each decimal digit into the corresponding binary integer:

$$\begin{array}{cccccc} 9 & 2 & 1 & 7 & 8 & 3 \\ 1001 & 0010 & 0001 & 0111 & 1000 & 0011 \end{array}$$

The numbers 8, 4, 2, 1 are the "weights" assigned to the binary bits defining each decimal digit.   Some business-oriented computers employ BCD-coded arithmetic circuits, but this is not economical for general-purpose minicomputers (4 bits can specify 16 binary numbers, but only 10 BCD numbers).   Thus, BCD circuits serve mainly in numerical displays, printers, and counters used directly by 10-fingered bipeds.   BCD *arithmetic* will be discussed in Sec. 2-26.

A large number of other number codes, both with and without redundant check bits, have been used.   In particular, the *Gray code* (*reflected code*, Ref. 6) serves in some analog-to-digital converters (especially shaft encoders) where it is desirable to switch only 1 bit at a time during up or down counting operations.

TABLE 1-4.   Some BCD Codes.

(See Ref. 6 for special applications.)

Decimal	8, 4, 2, 1	Excess-3 (8, 4, 2, 1, code for $x + 3$)	2, 4, 2, 1
0	0000	0011	0000
1	0001	0100	0001
2	0010	0101	0010
3	0011	0110	0011
4	0100	0111	0100
5	0101	1000	1011
6	0110	1001	1100
7	0111	1010	1101
8	1000	1011	1110
9	1001	1100	1111

Conversions between different coding schemes are important computer operations and are implemented both by hard-wired logic and by computer programs. **Coding schemes for punched cards and for punched tapes are illustrated in Figs. 5-6 and 5-7.**

1-11. Word Length and Data Formats (see also Sec. 2-19). Intuitively, the number of bits quoted refers to the length of the most frequently used data word and thus to the number of bits in the main arithmetic registers. This interpretation has become somewhat blurred because software and/or micro-programming easily permits, say, an 8-bit computer to operate with composite 16-, 24-, or 32-bit words. Such an 8-bit machine may well have one or more 16-bit registers and can use single-word or multiple-word instructions. Again, modern 16-bit minicomputers can often address and fetch 8-bit half-words (bytes) as well as 16-bit words. We will speak of an *n*-bit computer if the *main data paths* (buses) connecting memory, processor circuits, and external devices are parallel *n*-bit paths (not counting extra bits used for parity checks and memory protection, Sec. 1-18). Advertising literature should be read somewhat critically in this respect.

Since computation with, say, a 4K memory can take 12 bits for addressing alone, most minicomputers with meaningful instruction sets require some double-word instructions, often implied or disguised by indirect or indexed addressing (Secs. 2-15 and 2-16). Depending on the application, longer word length may mean fewer double-word instructions and thus save memory and time. Clever design of short-word instruction sets is the central problem of minicomputer architecture and will be discussed in Chaps. 2 and 6. We now consider the choice of *data-word* length.

In minicomputers serving largely as *logic controllers* rather than as arithmetic processors, word length need not be determined by numerical precision. Where speed is not important, any number of, say, relay closures can be controlled and/or sensed through *successive* 8-bit words. But there are also applications where an 18-bit word length (rather than 8, 12, or 16 bits) is just the thing to simplify control interface, program, and memory requirements.

4-bit words neatly represent BCD numbers (Sec. 1-10); otherwise, they are usually concatenated into larger words. **8 bits** (resolution 1 in 256) also is rarely accurate enough for single-precision *arithmetic*, although 8 bits may be enough to *store and transfer data* from low-resolution instruments. Multiword instructions and operations, however, permit powerful 16- to 24- and even 32-bit computations (at reduced speed). Important applications involve manipulation, storage, recognition, and recoding of 8-bit alphanumeric characters (Sec. 1-9), and also of pairs of BCD digits.

12-bit words (resolution 1 in 4,096) accommodate the 0.1 percent of half-scale resolution of medium-accuracy instruments (e.g., 12-bit analog-to-digital converters). Note, however, that 12-bit accuracy in most arithmetic results requires a longer word length than 12 bits. For this reason, and because of the convenience of accommodating two 8-bit bytes, **16 bits is the predominant data-word length for minicomputers.** **24-bit** and **32-bit data formats** (also multiples of 8 bits) are also used. **Figure 1-7 illustrates the most important data formats for small digital computers.**

The extra resolution of an **18-bit word** (e.g., PDP-15, Sec. 7-2) is sometimes comforting, especially with floating-point operations (Sec. 1-7), but ASCII-character packing is clumsy (Fig. 1-7). Cathode-ray-tube or xy-recorder displays of fair resolution (512 by 512 points) can be very conveniently driven with 18-bit data words packed with 9-bit X and Y coordinate values; this arrangement halves both refresh memory and refresh time (Sec. 4-28).

NOTE: **16-bit signed binary numbers yield a half-scale resolution of about 0.003 percent, a little better than 4 decimal digits and sign.** With 18 bits, we get about 0.0008 percent, better than 5 decimal digits and sign.

DIGITAL OPERATIONS: LOGIC AND ARITHMETIC

1-12. Logic Operations. The reasons for the explosive success of computers with binary variable representation are not only the ease of binary-data storage and transmission but also the remarkable simplicity, reliability, and low cost of the basic *operations* on binary variables. Figure 1-8 shows a "black box" whose output Y is a **binary (Boolean) function** $F(X_1, X_2, \ldots, X_n)$ of n binary input variables X_1, X_2, ..., X_n. Since each input can take only two different values, *there are 2^{2^n} different Boolean functions of n inputs.* We can characterize each Boolean function by a simple table **(truth table)** showing the function values for all possible combinations of argument (input) values.

We would like to implement many different operations like that of Fig. 1-8 with electric circuits; inputs and outputs will be voltage levels corresponding to 0 and 1 (Sec. 1-4). Fortunately, *all Boolean functions can be obtained through combination of a few simple one- and two-input functions readily available in integrated-circuit form* **(logic inverters** and **gates).**

The elementary Boolean operations of **complementation (inversion), logical addition (union, ORing),** and **logical multiplication (intersection, ANDing)** combine according to the rules of **Boolean algebra** listed in Table 1-5a. The table also illustrates how these rules are used to obtain useful Boolean functions with simple gates. In particular, AND gates and

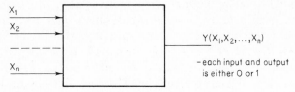

Fig. 1-8. Generation of a Boolean function Y of n inputs, $X_1, X_2, \ldots, X_n$.

TABLE 1-5a. Very Little Logic Goes a Long Way: Gate Circuits (Combinatorial Logic).

---

1. Basic Gates and Truth Tables. The basic *logic gates* implement simple functions of binary variables. Each gate function is defined explicitly by a *truth table* listing the gate output for all combinations of inputs.

NAND and NOR gates also serve as *logic inverters* complementing a single input (1 becomes 0, and vice versa).

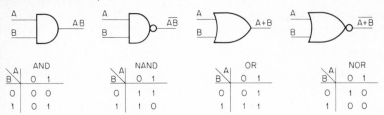

NOTE: In some types of logic, gate outputs can be ORed together.

2. Inverters. NAND and NOR gates also serve as **logic inverters** for **complementing** a single input. We use the following inverter symbols:

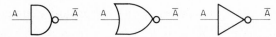

Some gates have *two complementary outputs*, and some logic modules provide gates with *inverting inputs*:

3. The Rules of Boolean Algebra. When we proceed to combine simple logic functions into more complicated functions of more variables, we find that the combinations satisfy the following *rules of Boolean algebra*. These rules are established by a simple combination of the basic truth tables. The rules may be applied to simplify logic circuits (logic optimization).

$$A + B = B + A$$
$$AB = BA$$
(COMMUTATIVE LAWS)

$$A + (B + C) = (A + B) + C$$
$$A(BC) = (AB)C$$
(ASSOCIATIVE LAWS)

$$A(B + C) = AB + AC$$
$$A + BC = (A + B)(A + C)$$
(DISTRIBUTIVE LAWS)

$$A + A = AA = A$$
(IDEMPOTENT PROPERTIES)

$$A + B = B \text{ if and only if } AB = A$$
(CONSISTENCY PROPERTY)

$$A + 0 = A \qquad AI = A$$
$$A0 = 0 \qquad A + I = I$$

$$A(A + B) \equiv A + AB \equiv A$$
(LAWS OF ABSORPTION)

$$(\overline{A + B}) \equiv \overline{A}\overline{B}$$
$$(\overline{AB}) \equiv \overline{A} + \overline{B}$$
(DUALITY OR DE MORGAN'S LAWS)

$$\overline{\overline{A}} \equiv A \qquad \overline{I} = 0 \qquad \overline{0} = I$$

$$A + \overline{A}B \equiv A + B \qquad AB + AC + B\overline{C} \equiv AC + B\overline{C}$$

Every Boolean function is either identical to 0 or can be expressed as a unique sum of **minimal polynomials (canonical minterms)** $Z_1 Z_2 \cdots Z_n$, *where* Z_i *is either* X_i *or* $\bar{X}_i$ (*canonical form of a Boolean function*).

In view of de Morgan's laws, *every Boolean function not identically 0 can also be expressed as a unique product of* **canonical maxterms** $Z_1' + Z_2' + \cdots + Z_n'$, *where* Z_i *is either* X_i *or* $\bar{X}_i$. There are altogether 2^n minterms and 2^n maxterms.

These canonical forms show that *every* Boolean function can, in principle, be implemented with *two levels* of logic gates (either ORing of AND-gate outputs or ANDing of OR-gate outputs). But the number of gates and/or connections needed might be reduced decisively if we admit some intermediate levels of logic at the expense of extra time delay.

4. Examples of Combinatorial Logic. *Combinatorial logic* involves only gates (including inverters), no memory or delays.

(*a*) **NAND/NOR and NOR/AND Conversion** (by de Morgan's theorem).

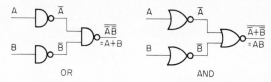

These conversion rules are useful when we have to work with specific commercially available components.

NOTE: *All* combinatorial logic *can* be implemented with NAND gates alone, or with NOR gates alone.

(*b*) **Single-Pole/Double-Throw Switches (Multiplexer Gates).**

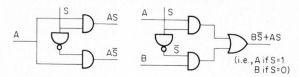

(*c*) **EXCLUSIVE OR (XOR, Modulo-2 Adder).**

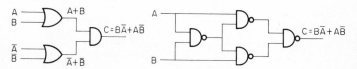

NOTE: $C = 0$ indicates that $A = B$ (coincidence detection).
      Many other implementations exist.

(*d*) **Recognition Gates (Decoding Gates)** for selecting devices identified by a binary address code, for presetting counters, etc.

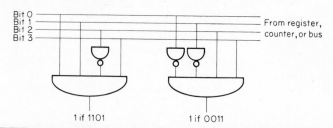

21

TABLE 1-5b.   Very Little Logic Goes a Long Way: Flip-Flop Circuits.

1. Flip-Flops. A **flip-flop,** like the familiar toggle switch, will stay in a given output state (0 or 1) even after inputs have been removed. Flip-flops thus implement *memory* for binary variables and permit *data storage* and *automatic sequential operations.* (That is, logic states can determine the sequence of future logic states, as in data transfers, counting, etc.) Although a somewhat bewildering variety of different flip-flops are sold, all are derived from a few simple types. Specifically, the basic **reset/set (RS) flip-flop** retains its output state through regenerative feedback until a new reversing input is applied. Other types of flip-flops add different input-gating circuits.

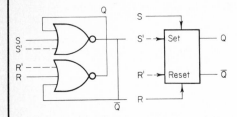

(a) Reset/set (RS) flip-flop. $R = 1$ (level or pulse) **resets (clears)** the flip-flop ($Q = 0$) until $S = 1$ **sets** the flip-flop ($Q = 1$). $R = S = 0$ leaves output *unchanged.* $R = S = 1$ is *illegal* (indefinite output), or $R = 1$ may *override* $S = 1$. Multiple set inputs or multiple reset inputs are ORed together.

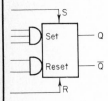

(b) General-purpose flip-flop with enabling gates. Many different types exist. Inputs may include inverting set and/or reset inputs, multiple gate inputs, etc. Frequently, the lower reset input is designed to override all other inputs.

In some general-purpose flip-flops (diode/transistor logic, DTL), gates have *ac-coupled inputs,* which set or reset the flip-flop when a voltage *step* (either up or down, depending on the type) is gated by a logic level.

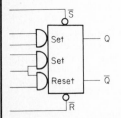

(c) Another type of general-purpose flip-flop. The two set-gate inputs are ORed together. The *inverted* set and reset inputs require $\bar{S} = 0$ to set and $\bar{R} = 0$ to reset.

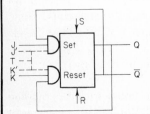

(d) General-purpose flip-flop connected as a *JK* flip-flop, which acts like an *RS* flip-flop except that $J = K = 1$ always reverses the output state. With J' and K' connected (dash lines), we have a **T(trigger) flip-flop:** For $J = K = 1$, output reverses whenever T goes to 1.

TABLE 1-5*b*.   Very Little Logic Goes a Long Way: Flip-flop Circuits (*Continued*).

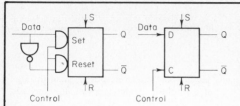

(*e*) **Data/control** (sometimes called **type D**) **flip-flop.** Output *Q* takes data-input value when control input goes to 1—it acts as a *binary sample-hold circuit*. It is important for jam transfer of data timed by control (strobe) pulses and in shift registers.

Dual-rank (master-slave) type D flip-flops are designed to establish a definite time interval between input and output steps.

Consult manufacturers' logic manuals for exact logic, fanout, logic-level tolerances, noise immunity, pulse duration, and step rise time required to trigger flip-flops, etc.

2. Important Flip-Flop Circuits.

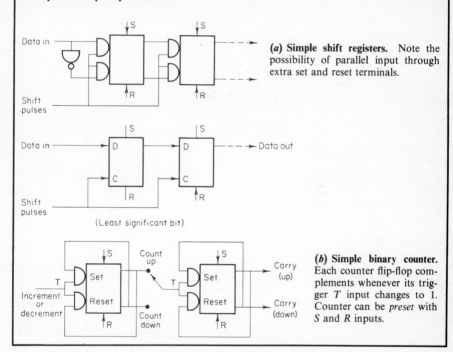

(*a*) **Simple shift registers.** Note the possibility of parallel input through extra set and reset terminals.

(*b*) **Simple binary counter.** Each counter flip-flop complements whenever its trigger *T* input changes to 1. Counter can be *preset* with *S* and *R* inputs.

inverters alone, NAND gates alone, or NOR gates alone can perform *all* Boolean operations. This is of great practical importance because some types of solid-state logic make it easier to implement NAND gates, while others lead to a preference for OR and NOR gates. Many commercially available logic systems also offer logic gates with more than two inputs, which are often convenient (Figs. 1-9*a–d*).

A **flip-flop** is a 1-*bit memory device* for storing a binary variable; **flip-flop registers** are ordered sets of flip-flops for storing digital words. Table 1-5*b*

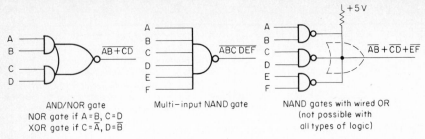

Fig. 1-9a. Some multi-input gates available as integrated circuits. Many other types exist.

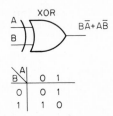

Fig. 1-9b. EXCLUSIVE OR(XOR) gate or modulo-2 adder and truth table. Note that (1) the XOR-gate output is 0 if and only if $A = B$ (*coincidence detection*) and (2) the XOR-gate output is A if $B = 0$ and $\bar{A}$ if $B = 1$ (*complementing operation switched by B*).

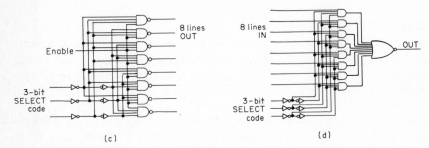

Fig. 1-9c, d. 3-line-to-8-line decoder (*c*), and 8-line selector (multiplexer) circuit.

defines each of the most useful flip-flop types by the method of data entry and shows two important applications (see also Fig. 1-10*a* and *b* and Sec. 1-13).

Digital-computer *arithmetic circuits* will be designed as logic circuits operating on the bits of binary-number inputs to produce desired binary output numbers, with inputs, outputs, and intermediate results stored in flip-flop registers (Sec. 1-15).

Techniques for simplifying logic circuits (i.e., minimizing the number of gates and flip-flops, gate inputs, interconnections, and/or crossovers) form the subject of **logic optimization** for digital-system design (Refs. 1 to 5). Optimization of a large digital system, such as a complete computer, is

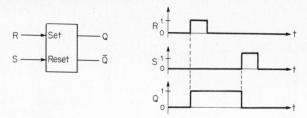

Fig. 1-10a. The output (state) Q of an RS flip-flop can depend on *past* values of the R and S inputs and thus implements *memory*.

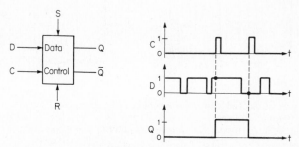

Fig. 1-10b. The output Q of a CD flip-flop *tracks* the D input when $C = 1$ and *holds* the last value when $C = 0$.   An initial state can be set and reset with the R and S inputs.

often itself done with the help of a digital computer.   On the other hand, a researcher or engineer who merely wants to use a small digital computer, and to interface it to some real-world instruments and controls, will seldom require formal logic optimization.   *All we usually require is the material in Table 1-5, some reasonable common sense, and a nice collection of tried logic circuits we can adapt and modify.*   Manufacturers' catalogs and application notes should be consulted for special tricks and precautions applicable to specific types of commercially available logic.   Digital-computer interface logic will be discussed in Chap. 4.

1-13.   Sequential Machines and Register-Transfer Operations.   If we agree to admit logic-state changes only at clocked time intervals 0, Δt, $2\Delta t$, ..., then *every* sequential machine can be built from N CD flip-flops (Table 1-5b and Fig. 1-10b) plus combinatorial logic (e.g., AND gates, OR gates, and inverters; or NAND gates; or NOR gates) as shown in Fig. 1-11.   The N flip-flop outputs

$$^{k}X_i = X_i(k\Delta t) \qquad (i = 1, 2, ..., N, K = 1, 2, ...)$$

are **Boolean state variables** defining the state of the system during the kth clock interval.   Each flip-flop output equals its input at the time of the last

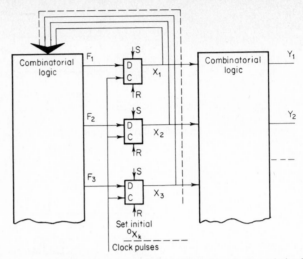

Fig. 1-11. A general clocked sequential machine. The given logic and the initial register contents ^0X determine all subsequent flip-flop states $^kX \equiv (^kX_1, {}^kX_2, ...)$ and outputs $^kY \equiv (^kY_1, {}^kY_2, ...) = Y(^kX, k)$ through the recursion relations

$$^{k+1}X = F(^kX, k) \qquad k = 0, 1, 2, ...$$

If N is the number of flip-flops, there are 2^N different states.

clock-pulse upswing. Given the N initial values $^0X_i = X_i(0)$, *all future states are determined by the N recursion relations* (**state equations**).

$$^{k+1}X_i = F_i(^kX_1, {}^kX_2, ..., {}^kX_N; k) \qquad (i = 1, 2, ..., N; k = 0, 1, 2, ...) \quad (1\text{-}10)$$

where each F_i is a Boolean function of the X_i. The M **output variables** $^kY_i = Y_i(k\Delta t)$ are Boolean functions of the state variables ^kX_i and may, like the F_i, depend explicitly on the time variable k (and thus on time-dependent **logic inputs**).

In a digital computer, the state-determining flip-flops are grouped into *processor registers* and *memory-word locations* (equivalent to flip-flop registers, Sec. 1-18) which contain numerical and control information. Figure 1-12 *a, b,* and *c* show specifically how suitably timed control pulses parallel-transfer binary words into flip-flop registers. Most computer operations are conveniently described at this **register-transfer level**. Figure 1-12*d* illustrates how the contents of two registers are added or subtracted by appropriate combinatorial logic circuits (*arithmetic/logic unit,* Fig. 1-15) in the course of a transfer operation.

1-14. Fixed-Point Arithmetic and Scaling. Registers in mini/microcomputers usually hold data words 4, 8, 12, 16, or 18 bits long. It is also possible to concatenate two or more such words for **double or higher precision** (Fig. 1-7). We have seen how binary words can represent integers or fractions

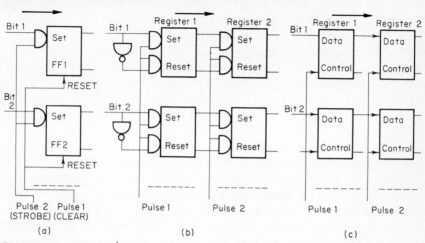

Fig. 1-12a, b, c. Clear-and-strobe transfer into a flip-flop register (*a*) and jam transfer between registers (*b*) and (*c*). If the dual transfers in (*b*) or (*c*) are to take place simultaneously, we can use dual-rank flip-flops to make sure that the old output of the first register is transferred before it is updated.

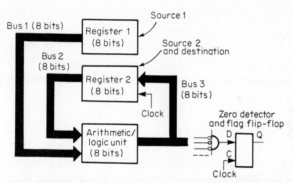

Fig. 1-12d. Register-transfer level description of a computer system deals with operations on entire *words*. Here an 8-bit microcomputer arithmetic/logic unit (ALU) adds (or subtracts, etc.) the 8-bit word in Register 1 (*Source* 1) to the 8-bit word in Register 2 (*Source* 2 and *Destination*). Transfers between registers and ALU are on 8-bit parallel *buses*. A clock pulse loads the result into Register 2 and also sets a *flag flip-flop* if a recognition gate on the ALU output bus detects a zero result.

(Tables 1-1 and 1-2). In principle, a binary computer word $(a_{n-1}, a_{n-2}, \ldots, a_0)$ could also represent, say, a nonnegative binary number of the more general form

$$X = 2^r \left(\frac{1}{2} a_{n-1} + \frac{1}{2^2} a_{n-2} + \cdots + \frac{1}{2^n} a_0 \right) \quad (0 \le X \le 2^r - 2^{r-n}) \quad (1\text{-}11)$$

with a *binary point* implied ahead of a_{n-r-1} (if $r < 0$, we imply 0 digits between a_{n-1} and the binary point, as in $X = 0.00101 = 0.101 \times 2^{-2}$. An analogous generalization applies to signed (positive or negative) numbers. With such representations, we must keep track of the exponent r determining the *binary-point location* throughout the computation; in particular, terms in a sum or difference must have the same r. **Floating-point arithmetic** programs or circuits (Secs. 1-16 and 2-27) employ some or all the bits in an extra register to specify the exponent r and compute exponents separately at each step of the computation at considerable expense in either computing time or special hardware.

With fixed-point arithmetic, it is best to consider all numerical quantities in computer registers and memory as either integers or pure fractions (Tables 1-1 and 1-2). **We propose to employ integers (which may be positive, negative, or zero) only to represent actual real integers used in counting, ordering, and addressing operations. All other real numerical quantities X in the computer will be regarded as signed or unsigned pure fractions (-1 machine unit $< X < +1$ machine unit) proportional to corresponding quantities x occurring in the given problem:**

$$X = [a_x \quad x] \tag{1-12}$$

Each bracketed quantity $[a_x \quad x]$ is a **scaled machine variable** representing the corresponding problem variable x in the computer. *It is convenient to restrict the scale factors a_x to integral powers of 2.*

For best accuracy in fixed-point computations, we try to pick each scale factor a_x as the largest (positive, negative, or zero) integral power of 2 which will still keep the machine variable $[a_x x]$ between -1 and $+1$:

$$a_x = \frac{1}{2^r} < \frac{1}{\max |x|} \tag{1-13}$$

Unfortunately, bounds for $\max |x|$ are not always known ahead of time, so that we may pick too small or too large scale factors. Too small scale factors waste computer precision. Too large scale factors cause **overflow** of the corresponding computer variables, **which makes the computation invalid** (Fig. 1-13). Digital computers have flip-flops (flags) which set to

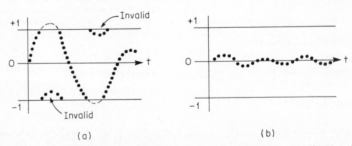

(a)   (b)

Fig. 1-13. Time histories of two digital variables representing, say, sensor outputs (voltages) by scaled 2s-complement fractions. In (*a*), the scale factor is too large, causing invalid results due to overflow. In (*b*), the small scale factor aggravates roundoff and other computing errors.

indicate overflow in arithmetic operations. *These flags will not stop the computation by themselves but must be tested by programmed instructions* (Secs. 2-7 and 2-22).

To scale mathematical relations for any given problem, we simply express each problem variable x in terms of the corresponding scaled machine variable $[a_x x]$:

$$x = \frac{1}{a_x} [a_x x] \tag{1-14}$$

Our scaling procedure is best exhibited through an example.

EXAMPLE: Scale

$$y = ax + bx^2$$

given

$$a = 10 \qquad b = 0.05 \qquad -7 \leq x \leq 19$$

Since multiplication consumes more computer time than fixed-point addition, we rewrite

$$y = x(a + bx) = xz$$

We must scale the intermediate result $z = a + bx$ as well as y; substitution yields $|z| < 11 < 16$ and $|y| < 256$.   Now we simply replace a, b, x, z, and y by

$$16 \left[\frac{a}{16} \right], \qquad \frac{1}{16} [16b], \qquad 32 \left[\frac{x}{32} \right], \qquad 16 \left[\frac{z}{16} \right], \qquad \text{and} \qquad 256 \left[\frac{y}{256} \right]$$

where the bracketed quantities are machine variables between -1 and $+1$.   We thus find the scaled machine equation

$$\left[\frac{y}{256} \right] = 2 \left[\frac{x}{32} \right] \left\{ \left[\frac{a}{16} \right] + \frac{1}{8} [16b] \left[\frac{x}{32} \right] \right\}$$

which is easily checked against the given problem equation through cancellation of scale factors. Note that *our computation involves only scaled machine variables and multiplying factors* 2^r $(r = 0, \pm 1, \pm 2, \dots)$ *corresponding to simple signed-shift operations* (Sec. 1-15b).

Our scaling procedure, as it were, keeps track of the correct exponents r in Eq. (1-6) outside of the computer.

Although fixed-point computation requires us to *program* with scaled variables, *we may not have to bother with the job of scaling reams of machine input and/or output data.* Entering and printing arabic numerals requires some computation (translation to and from binary numbers) in any case, and it is usually readily possible to incorporate scaling operations in such input/output programs.

1-15. Some Binary-Arithmetic Operations. (a) Addition, Subtraction, and Overflow. As discussed in Sec. 1-14, *we will consider all fixed-point binary numbers as signed or unsigned integers and pure fractions;* 2s-complement coding is most common.

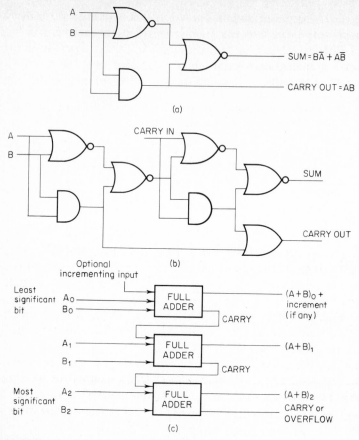

Fig. 1-14. Half-adder (*a*), full adder (*b*), and a 3-bit adder with ripple-through carry propagation (*c*).

The **half-adder (modulo-2 adder)** of Fig. 1-14*a* is a logic circuit for adding *one-digit* binary numbers and is seen to involve an XOR circuit. For *multidigit* addition, e.g.,

$$
\begin{array}{r r}
19 & 1\ \ 0\ \ 0\ \ 1\ \ 1 \\
09 & 0\ \ 1\ \ 0\ \ 0\ \ 1 \\
\hline
28 & 1\ \ 1\ \ 1\ \ 0\ \ 0 \\
\end{array}
$$
carries

each bit-by-bit addition can generate a carry bit, which must be added to the next-higher-order digit. This is accomplished by the **full-adder** scheme of Fig. 1-14*b*. Figure 1-14*c* shows a complete three-digit binary adder made up of three full-adders.

Such adders will produce correct results with **signed numbers** (2s- or 1s-complement code) if we follow these simple rules:

1. **With 2s-complement arithmetic, simply add as though words represented nonnegative numbers, and disregard sign-bit carries.**

2. *With 1s-complement arithmetic,* add the sign-bit carry (if any) to the least significant digit (*"end-around" carry*).

EXAMPLES:

DECIMAL (Integer)	2s-COMPLEMENT CODE	1s-COMPLEMENT CODE
6	0 | 1 1 0	0 | 1 1 0
−7	1 | 0 0 1	1 | 0 0 0
−1	1 | 1 1 1	1 | 1 1 0
6	0 | 1 1 0	0 | 1 1 0
−4	1 | 1 0 0	1 | 0 1 1
2	← 0 | 0 1 0	0 | 0 1 0

discarded carry   "end-around" carry

In simple adders like that of Fig. 1-14c, low-order carries must propagate ("ripple through") all the way to the highest-order bit before the sum output is complete.   To save time, one could, in principle, compute the result bit of each given order as a Boolean function of all summand bits of the same and lower orders within two gate-delay times.   Practical **carry-lookahead** circuits constitute various tradeoffs between circuit simplicity and speed (Refs. 1 and 3, and Fig. 1-15; see also Sec. 6-22).

Minicomputer adders usually add a number in a processor arithmetic register (**accumulator**) to a number taken from memory (or from another register) and place the result into the accumulator (hence its name).

Fixed-point addition of two numbers produces **arithmetic overflow** if and only if:

1. Both terms of the sum have identical signs but the computed sum has a different sign.

2. Or, equivalently, addition produces a carry out of the sign bit *or* out of the most significant bit but *not both* (that is, the EXCLUSIVE OR of these carries is 1).

EXAMPLES:

+6	0 | 110	+6	0 | 110	−6	1 | 010
−4	1 | 100	+6	0 | 110	−6	1 | 010
+2	0 | 010	(+12)	1 | 100	(−12)	0 | 100

no overload   overload   overload
(two carries)   (one carry)   (one carry)

The same reasoning applies to subtraction if we regard differences as sums of positive and/or negative numbers.   Logic circuits can test summand and sum signs and set an **overflow-flag flip-flop**.   Some small computers, however, do not have a true overflow flag but only a **carry flag (accumulator-**

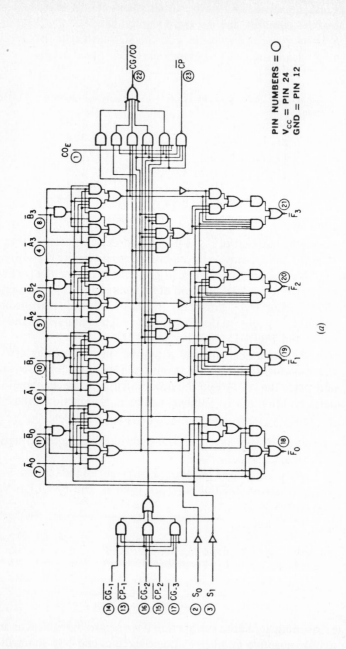

(a)

PIN NUMBERS = ○
V_{CC} = PIN 24
GND = PIN 12

32

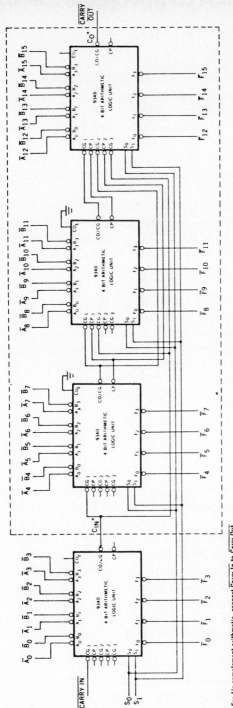

For 1's complement arithmetic, connect Carry In to Carry Out
For 2's complement arithmetic, connect Carry In to S_0

(b)

Fig. 1-15. Complete 4-bit TTL arithmetic/logic unit on a single integrated-circuit chip (a) and a 16-bit minicomputer arithmetic/logic unit with group carry lookahead using four such chips (b). A 12-bit arithmetic/logic unit is also shown in dash lines. Bits marked $\bar{A}_i$, $\bar{B}_i$ on two input buses are combined to form output-bus bits $\bar{F}_i$. Two function-control bits S_0, S_1 determine the function:

00	SUBTRACT	01	XOR
10	ADD	11	AND

Shifting would be done with register-gate circuits. (*Fairchild Semiconductor.*)

Maximum delay is 35 nsec for 4 bits, 49 nsec for 16 bits.

33

extension or **link flip-flop),** which is complemented by carries from the highest sum bit. Overflow tests for negative numbers then require several programmed instructions (Sec. 3-11c).

Binary **subtraction** can utilize modified adder circuits (*half-subtractors* and *full-subtractors* with *negative carries* or "*borrows,*" Ref. 1), or we may negate the subtrahend (Tables 1-1 and 1-2) and add.

Figure 1-15a illustrates the logic design of **a complete 4-bit arithmetic/logic unit,** which can implement the bit-by-bit **AND** or **XOR** functions as well as addition and subtraction. The entire circuit is a single integrated-circuit chip. Figure 1-15b shows how such circuits combine into 12-bit and 16-bit arithmetic/logic units.

(b) Shifting (see also Sec. 2-9). The definition of binary-number codes (Tables 1-1 and 1-2) implies that *shifting each digit of an unsigned 1s-complement or 2s-complement number 1 bit to the right will multiply the number by* $\frac{1}{2}$, *provided that the new leftmost bit equals the old sign bit or is 0 for unsigned numbers.* The old least significant bit is lost (chopped rather than rounded off).

Conversely, *each 1-bit shift to the left will multiply the original number by 2, provided that the new rightmost bit is made 0 for unsigned and 2s-complement numbers and equals the original sign bit for 1s-complement numbers.* Such multiplication by 2 will produce *overflow* if and only if the most significant bit of the given number was 1 for positive numbers and 0 for negative numbers.

EXAMPLES (4-bit 2s-complement code):

0110 represents +6 (or $+\frac{6}{8}$)	1010 represents -6 (or $-\frac{6}{8}$)
0011 represents +3 (or $+\frac{3}{8}$)	1101 represents -3 (or $-\frac{3}{8}$)

0110 and 1010 cannot be shifted left without overflow in this code (sign bit and most significant bit differ).

Digital computers employ shift operations for multiplication by integral powers of 2, and also to move partial words (bytes) in character-handling operations. Shifting could be accomplished with a shift register (Table 1-5b), but in most computers gate circuits like those in Fig. 1-16 move each bit of a word "sideways" during parallel register-to-register transfers.

(c) Binary Multiplication. One ordinarily computes the product of two n-bit binary numbers A and B as a *2n-bit number*, so that no information is lost. This works nicely for *unsigned* integers or fractions,

$$\left.\begin{array}{l} 3 \times 3 = 9 \\ \tfrac{3}{4} \times \tfrac{3}{4} = \tfrac{9}{16} \end{array}\right\} \text{ is represented by } 11 \times 11 = 1001$$

or

and also for *signed integers,* say in 2s-complement code:

$(-3) \times 3 = -9$ is represented by $101 \times 011 = 110111$
$(-4) \times (-4) = +16$ is represented by $100 \times 100 = 010000$

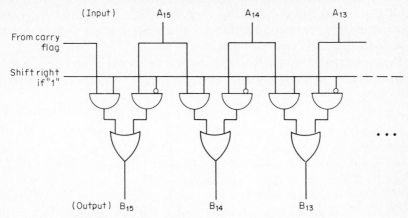

Fig. 1-16. A simple right-shift circuit using multiplexer gates.

A fast multiplier for short words can use logic or table lookup to form product digits, but this is too expensive for most small computers.   Instead, we proceed as in pencil-and-paper multiplication.   We multiply the multiplicand by each multiplier digit in turn to form *partial products;* these are then multiplied by successive powers of 2 (i.e., shifted) and added.

For simplicity, let us consider multiplication of unsigned integers.   Instead of shifting partial products, the computer adds the most significant partial product into a cleared $2n$-bit register (actually two n-bit registers), shifts the register contents to the left, adds the next partial product, etc.   With binary numbers, each multiplier bit is either 0 or 1, so that each partial product simply adds either 0 or the given multiplicand.   These operations are accomplished either through successive computer instructions (multiplication subroutine, software multiplication) or more quickly by hard-wired or microprogrammed logic (see also Secs. 2-25 and 3-11).

EXAMPLE ($3 \times 5 = 15$):

$$
\begin{array}{r}
011 \times 101 \\
\hline
011 \\
000 \\
011 \\
\hline
001111
\end{array}
$$

For signed multiplication, one employs *Booth's algorithm*, where partial products are either added or subtracted depending on the sequence of the multiplier bits (Ref. 6).

CAUTION: Most mini/microcomputer multipliers or multiplication routines are designed to multiply signed or unsigned *integers*.   If the inputs to such a multiplier are now interpreted as *unsigned fractions*, then the result will still be the correct unsigned-fraction code.   But if both inputs

A, B are interpreted as **signed fractions** (and this is important in data processing), then the multiplier output is the signed-fraction code for $\frac{1}{2}AB$ (**not** AB). Thus, in 2s-complement code:

$$101 \times 011 \to 110111 \text{ represents } \tfrac{1}{2}(-\tfrac{3}{4}) \times \tfrac{3}{4} = -\tfrac{9}{32}$$
$$100 \times 100 \to 010000 \text{ represents } \tfrac{1}{2}(-1) \times (-1) = +\tfrac{1}{2}$$

Multiplication of a signed fraction by a signed integer requires no extra division by 2.

If a $2n$-bit 2s-complement product fraction is reduced to an n-bit fraction by simple omission of the less significant n bits ("chopping" or truncation), the result is not properly rounded off: it will never be larger than the correct product. We can, if necessary, gain an extra half-bit of accuracy by shifting the least significant register left and adding the carry to the most significant register. **Fixed-point sums of many $2n$-bit fraction products (integrals, statistical averages) require double-precision accumulation for n-bit accuracy.** Otherwise, with N terms, as many as $\log_2 N$ of the least significant sum bits could be meaningless.

(d) Division. Division subroutines or hardware employ a *double-length dividend* and a *one-word divisor*. The result will be a *one-word quotient* plus a *one-word remainder*.

We again consider only unsigned integers or unsigned fractions. We begin by comparing the divisor with the high-order half of the dividend: the division *overflows* (and is stopped as unsuccessful) unless the divisor is larger. No quotient bit is entered at this point.

The entire two-word dividend is next shifted 1 bit to the left, and the contents of the most significant register are again compared with the divisor. If it is still larger, we enter 0 as the most significant quotient bit and shift again; if not, we enter 1 and subtract the divisor into the most significant dividend register and shift. We continue in this way (much as in pencil-and-paper division) until all quotient bits are computed. At this point, *the most significant dividend register will contain the remainder; the least significant dividend register contains the (integral part of the) quotient.*

NOTE: With a nonzero remainder, quotients are "chopped," not properly rounded.

EXAMPLE ($15 \div 7 = 2\frac{1}{7}$, 3-bit words):

(a) 0 0 1 1 1 1	(b) 0 1 1 1 1 0	(c) 1 1 1 1 0 0
1 1 1	1 1 1	1 1 1
no overflow, shift	shift	subtract and shift

Quotient: 0 1 0   Remainder: 0 0 1

For division of *signed numbers*, consult your computer manual as to the specific format used. Most frequently, the correctly signed quotient is left in the least significant dividend register, while the remainder, again in the most significant dividend register, is an unsigned number preceded by the sign of the *dividend*.

Note that such division cannot directly produce **fractional quotients** X/Y, where $|Y| > |X|$. To compute the N-bit **unsigned** fraction X/Y, where N and Y are N-bit **unsigned** integers or fractions, simply place X into the *most significant* dividend register and clear the least significant register. The desired fractional quotient will be correctly produced in the form 2^{-N} $(2^N X/Y)$.

To produce the **signed** fractional quotient X/Y of **two signed integers** or **two signed fractions** X, Y ($|X| < |Y|$), place X into the most significant dividend register, clear the least significant register, and *then shift the 2N-bit-dividend one bit to the right* (with the sign bit correctly extended) before dividing. Otherwise, the division scheme will try to produce the incorrect result $2X/Y$.

EXAMPLE: A 4-bit signed-integer division circuit interprets

$$0001 \quad 0000 \quad \div 0100 = 0100$$

as

$$(+16) \div (+4) = +4$$

But we can also interpret the same operation as

$$2 \times (+1) \div (+4) = \tfrac{1}{2}$$
$$2 \times (+\tfrac{1}{8}) \div (+\tfrac{1}{2}) = \tfrac{1}{2}$$

Division of a signed fraction by a signed integer requires no extra multiplication by 2.

In any case, **division will overflow** if the absolute value of the quotient (whether integer or fraction) is too large for the N-bit code used. Hardware division circuits will usually set an overflow flag.

1-16. Floating-Point Arithmetic.   *Addition* and *subtraction* of floating-point numbers (Sec. 1-7)

$$X = A \times 2^R$$

(where the exponent R may be represented in signed-integer, biased, or power-of-16 format, Sec. 1-7) require the computer to perform the following —fairly involved—operations:

Compare exponents
Shift mantissa of smaller term so that both terms have equal exponents
Add (or subtract) mantissas
Normalize result; check for overflow, return 0 on underflow

Floating-point overflow occurs (and sets a flag or starts an error routine) if the M-bit normalized exponent R exceeds its maximum admissible value $2^{M-1} - 1$. **Underflow** simply returns 0 when $R < -2^{M-1}$ for a normalized mantissa (Sec. 1-7).

With floating-point arithmetic, *multiplication* and *division* are rather simpler than addition and subtraction:

Enter with normalized data; multiply (or divide) mantissas—exit if 0
Add (or subtract) exponents; check for overflow, return 0 on underflow
Normalize result

All these operations must be implemented with software (subroutines), with a microprogram (Sec. 2-31) or with optional hardware **(floating-point arithmetic unit)**. *We must also provide for the additional operations of "floating" fixed-point numbers and "fixing" floating-point numbers.* Suitable assembly-language subroutines will be found in computer manufacturers' software listings; floating-point hardware is discussed in Refs. 3 and 11.

1-17. Integrated-Circuit Logic (Refs. 13–15, 18, 19). Figure 1-17 reviews the gate structures of the most important integrated-circuit logic families. Design information on power-supply requirements, fanout, wiring, noise immunity, and special precautions for each type of logic is best obtained from manufacturers' handbooks. In mini/microcomputer work, such information is needed mainly for interface design (Chap. 4). The purpose of this section is merely to review the logic-family properties bearing on their selection for microprocessors and solid-state memories (see also Sec. 1-21 and Chap. 6).

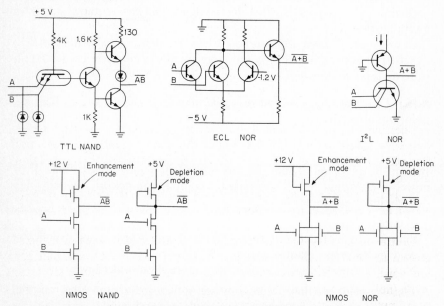

Fig. 1-17a. Static logic: inverting TTL, ECL, I²L, and NMOS gates. MOSFET Q1 serves as a load resistor and may be an *enhancement-mode* FET kept ON by a positive gate voltage or, in more modern circuits, a *depletion-mode* FET which is normally ON.

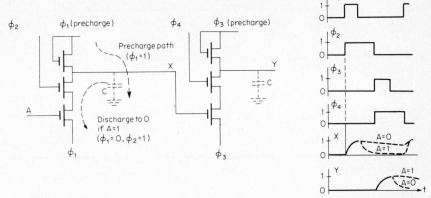

Fig. 1-17b. Four-phase dynamic logic. For simplicity, two cascaded simple inverters are shown. The gate capacitances C are *precharged* to read 1 and then discharged to 0 if the gate input is 1. The only power required is that to charge and discharge the small (1 pF) gate capacitances, so that power dissipation is very low. But alternate gates must be read during alternate time slots. The "pseudo-four-phase" clock signals shown are easily derived from a two-phase clock.

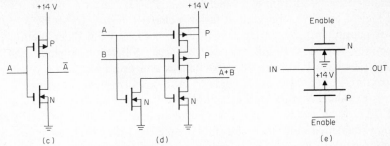

Fig. 1-17c, d, e. CMOS inverter (c), NOR gate (d), and transmission gate or series switch (e).

Referring to Fig. 1-17 and Table 1-6, most bipolar-transistor logic is **transistor-transistor logic (TTL)**; more and more newer machines use **Schottky-diode-clamped TTL,** which speeds gate turn-off by preventing transistor saturation. TTL-gate outputs cannot be wire-ORed together (Fig. 1-9a), but this is possible for TTL-compatible **tri-state bus drivers,** which are connected to common bus lines by special enabling signals (Sec. 4-1).

Emitter-coupled logic (ECL), also using unsaturated bipolar transistors, is even faster than Schottky-clamped TTL, permits wire-ORing, and has low-noise, low-impedance outputs. ECL's disadvantages include low logic levels (noise-sensitive, hard to interface to other types of logic), high power consumption, and the need for greater care in circuit wiring.

Current-injection logic (I²L) and related newer logic families employ no resistors at all. Very low power consumption and small circuit areas

TABLE 1-6. Integrated-Circuit Logic Families.

	Typical Gate Delay, nsec	Typical Clock Rate, MHz	Supply, V	Typical Power/Gate, mW*
TTL	12	15–30	+5	12
TTL (Schottky)	4–8	20–60	+5	20–40
ECL	1–4	50–400	−5.2	40–60
I²L	50–500	1–8	+5	0.01–0.1
PMOS (dynamic)	200–600	0.5–2	−13, −27	0.2–2
NMOS (dynamic)	100–300	1–4	+8, +15, or +5	0.1–1
CMOS	20–100	1–12	+5 to +16	0.01–2

* Dynamic-MOS, CMOS, and I²L power is proportional to clock rate.

combine with fair speed to make I²L very attractive for large-scale integrated circuits.

Metal-oxide-silicon field-effect-transistor (MOSFET) logic gates (Refs. 14, 15), switched by voltage rather than current, have low power consumption and simple gate structures favorable to large-scale integration. MOSFET logic has progressed from **p-channel devices** (PMOS, *negative* power supply and logic 1 level) to smaller and faster **n-channel devices** (NMOS, *positive* power supply and logic 1 level) and, in both cases, from older metal-gate structures to newer silicon-gate devices. **Silicon-on-sapphire (SOS) MOSFETs** have lower circuit capacitances and are, thus, faster, but their more complicated fabrication tends to raise costs by yield problems.

Low-threshold NMOS logic can employ ordinary 5-V TTL power supplies and TTL logic levels to simplify system design. Modern NMOS logic employs **depletion-mode** (normally ON) load FETs rather than enhancement-type (normally OFF) loads to reduce power dissipation and thus circuit size, and to increase logic speed (Fig. 1-17a). **High-threshold MOSFET logic** can use much larger logic-signal voltages and has replaced old-fashioned diode-transistor logic in applications requiring *high noise immunity*. MOSFETs are also more resistant to radiation than bipolar transistors, and are thus very suitable for airborne and military requirements. Although MOSFET circuits are not as fast as the fastest bipolar logic, respectable computing speeds can be obtained. The MOSFET gates in Fig. 1-17a represent **static logic**; i.e., gate-output levels are stable as long as this is true for the gate-input levels, as with most bipolar logic. To lower the power dissipation from the thousands of gates on an LSI chip, one resorts to **dynamic logic** (Fig. 1-17b). Here the power supply never drives direct current to ground as in Fig. 1-17a, but serves only to charge and discharge MOSFET substrate capacitances. Each gate output capacitance is always *precharged* during the first part of its clock cycle and then discharged or not, depending on its logic inputs. Each gate output, therefore, can be read only after the discharge portion of its clock cycle. It follows that alternate succeeding gates must have their precharge/conditional-discharge cycles spaced at alternate time intervals (*multiphase logic*).

The four clock voltages shown are easily derived from a two-phase clock. Several similar dynamic-logic schemes exist. All complicate gate interconnections and servicing (no static testing is possible). Dynamic logic is interfaced to static-logic circuits through appropriately clocked CD-flip-flop registers.

Complementary-MOS (CMOS) logic combines *p*-channel and *n*-channel devices into gate structures drawing only capacitance-charging currents without elaborate multiphase clocks (Fig. 1-17c). CMOS gate areas are somewhat larger than NMOS. CMOS logic combines very low power consumption with excellent noise immunity and respectable speed and power consumption and is a good choice for noisy industrial and auto-motive environments. Supply-voltage increases can trade power consumption for increased computing speed (see also Sec. 4-25). Silicon-on-sapphire CMOS is fastest.

MOSFET gate outputs can be wire-ORed, and simple series switches (Fig. 1-17c) neatly implement tri-state bus drivers. *Ordinary MOSFET gates, however, will need buffer amplifiers to drive more than a few high-impedance gates* (Secs. 4-30 and 6-7).

MEMORY AND COMPUTATION

1-18. Memory. A **computer memory** is needed to store *data* and *instruction sequences;* in addition, a finite instruction set makes it necessary to compute and store *intermediate results.* In effect, a computer memory consists of a large number of binary storage registers **(memory locations)** each capable of storing a complete computer word, plus circuits to address a program-selected memory location for reading or writing a word (Fig. 1-19).

To access a memory location, we place its number **(memory address)** in the **memory address register.** A "tree" of **decoding gates** (Table 1-5a) connected to the memory address register will then direct logic signals to read the selected memory word *into* the **memory data register (memory buffer register)** or write a word *from* the memory data register into the selected memory location. Modern 16-bit minicomputers can select 8-bit bytes as well as 16-bit words. Read and write **access time** is the time needed to select and read or write. A **memory cycle** is the minimum time required between successive accesses; read and write cycle times may or may not be the same.

The main memory (read/write memory, **random-access memory RAM)** of a small digital computer usually has between 1K and 64K words or bytes ($K = 1,024 = 2^{10}$) of semiconductor or core memory, with cycle times

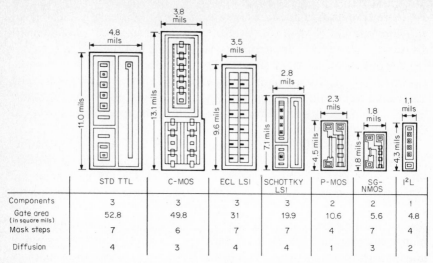

	STD TTL	C-MOS	ECL LSI	SCHOTTKY LSI	P-MOS	SG-NMOS	I²L
Components	3	3	3	3	2	2	1
Gate area (in square mils)	52.8	49.8	31	19.9	10.6	5.6	4.8
Mask steps	7	6	7	7	4	7	4
Diffusion	4	3	4	4	1	3	2

Fig. 1-18. Comparison of different integrated-circuit techniques. (*Adapted from Electronics, July 10, 1975, copyright McGraw-Hill, Inc., 1975.*)

between 300 and 3,000 nsec. The relatively inexpensive main memory may be supplemented by very fast (50 to 300 nsec) intermediate storage **(scratchpad memory)** in the form of extra processor registers or semiconductor memory. In addition, we often add slow but inexpensive **mass storage** in the form of magnetic disks, drums, and tape (Chap. 5). These

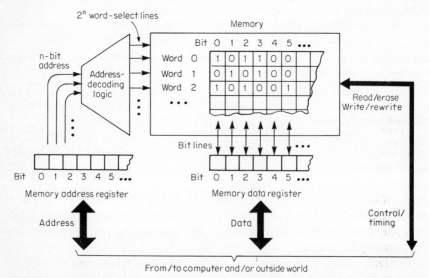

Fig. 1-19. A computer memory system. The memory address register may be located in the memory or in the processor, or it may be duplicated in both.

can store large programs and data blocks (up to millions of words) which are (one hopes) not immediately needed at all times, but which can be transferred to and from the main memory as need arises. We thus have a *hierarchy of storage systems* (Table 1-7).

TABLE 1-7. **Comparison of Typical Computer Memories.**

	Access Time, nsec	Cycle Time, nsec	Power (Operating) mW/bit*	Cost/bit (in 5,000), cents
Core	300–800	600–1,600		0.5
Plated-wire	200–500	400–1,000		5–10
Dynamic PMOS	150–400	250–800	0.2	0.1–0.2
Dynamic NMOS	100–300	200–600	0.1	0.1–0.2
Static NMOS	60–200	70–300	0.3–0.7	0.2–0.5
Static CMOS	100–150	150–800	0.15–0.3	0.5
Statis CMOS (SOS)	80–200	120–500	0.03–1	0.7–1
Bipolar	30–100	60–150	0.1 (I^2L)–2	0.2 (I^2L)–2
Masked ROM	35–1,000	70–1,500	0.1–0.5	0.1–1
PROM	50–500	80–800	0.1	0.5–2
EPROM	500	1,000	0.1	1.5–3

* Dynamic MOS, CMOS, and I^2L power is proportional to clock rate.

1-19. Memory Mapping, Cache, and Virtual Memory. A 16-bit address can access only 64K ($2^{16} = 65,536$) words or bytes, but optional **memory-mapping hardware** can compute larger addresses (and thus address more memory) under program control. The same hardware can also apportion memory among different programs and users and prevents mutual overwriting **(memory protection).** This memory-protection scheme often replaces the earlier method of *setting an extra bit* in each word to be protected (see also Secs. 2-30 and 5-22).

To speed up accesses to, say, an inexpensive 800-nsec-cycle core memory, *one can insert a fast scratchpad memory* **(cache)** *between main memory and processor;* one swaps words in and out of the scratchpad so that the computer "sees" only fast scratchpad accesses much of the time. Cache logic keeps track of the main-memory addresses of all items in the cache and swaps when a needed item is not found. The simplest schemes are "lookahead" registers holding a few successive words, since many memory accesses are to successive addresses. A "true" cache may use elaborate strategies to swap 1,000-word memory pages, or sections of pages. Cache systems can reduce the effective memory access time by 10 to 50 percent (depending on the program as well as hardware).

A **virtual-memory** system, somewhat analogous to a cache system, accesses a mass-storage disk with, say, 1M ($2^{20} = 1,048,576$) words as though it were addressing a 1M-word main memory; a hardware or software scheme swaps appropriate pages from the disk into an 8K to 64K core or semiconductor memory interfaced to the computer.

1-20. Core Memories. A **core memory** stores **(writes)** each bit by mag-netizing a toroidal ferrite core in the 1 or 0 direction (Fig. 1-20a, b). To **read** the information stored in such a core, one first pulses the core in the 0 magnetization direction; if a 1 had been stored in the core, the resulting flux reversal would cause an output current pulse in a sense wire threaded through the core (Fig. 1-20b). To select only the cores associated with a specific *word* in the memory, we implement the read and write currents through superposition of select and inhibit currents in two or three wires threading each core (*coincident-current selection,* Fig. 1-20*a* and *b*). Figure 1-20*c* illustrates a typical core-memory word-selection scheme *3D scheme,* and Fig. 1-20*d* shows the wiring of a typical bit plane; the sense wire is threaded through all cores in the plane in a pattern designed to cancel the effects of the half-select current pulses associated with unselected cores. At the expense of a little extra switching logic, *the same bit-plane wire can be used for both inhibiting and sensing,* so that only *three* wires need to be

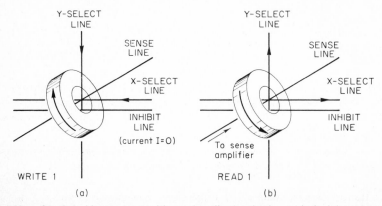

Fig. 1-20*a* and *b*. Coincident-current writing and reading/erasing in a typical minicomputer core memory. (*a*) WRITING: We start with all cores magnetized in the 0 direction. Writing a 1 into a given core (i.e., a given bit of a selected word) depends on *three* current pulses. Each of the two *select currents X, Y* must be one-half of the required magnetizing current (word selection), *and* the *inhibit current I* (which would oppose 1 magnetization) must be 0 (bit setting). The inhibit line, common to all *words,* belongs to a specific memory-data-register bit. (*b*) READING/ERASING: The *X* and *Y* select wires are both pulsed with current in the 0 magnetization direction. This produces no change if the core is already magnetized in the 0 direction. If a 1 was stored, it will be erased, and the flux reversal will cause a 1 pulse in the sense line. The latter, common to all *words,* sets a specific memory-data-register *bit* via a sense amplifier.

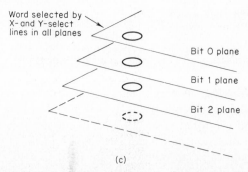

Fig. 1-20*c*. The cores belonging to a given *word* have the same *X, Y* position in each bit plane. Each plane has inhibit and sense lines associated with one memory-data-register *bit*.

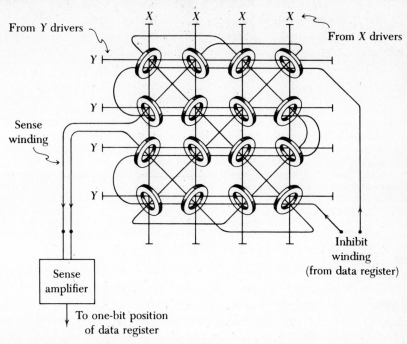

Fig. 1-20*d.* One bit plane of a 16-word 3D core-memory unit.   (*H. Hellerman, Digital Computer System Principles, McGraw-Hill, New York, 1971.*)

threaded through each core.   Reference 3 describes two different word/bit arrangements for core memories (2D and $2\frac{1}{2}$D).

The following properties of core memories bear on their applications in complete systems:

1. **Core storage is nonvolatile;** i.e., a core memory continues to store its contents even when computer power is off.
2. **Core-memory readout is destructive,** since reading clears the addressed memory location.   Ordinarily, the words thus read into the memory data register are rewritten into core during the second half of a READ memory cycle.
3. **Full-cycle times** (CLEAR/WRITE or READ/REWRITE) *are between* 600 and 2,000 nsec.   The access time (READ half-cycle time) is about one-half the cycle time.

Nonvolatility is an important advantage of core memories, which are somewhat more expensive than MOSFET memories (Table 1-6).   Cycle times, typically 800 nsec, are quite long compared to logic delays. *The half-cycle needed to rewrite an instruction fetched from memory can be used for computation, but not for addressing the same memory bank.*   Computers with *multiple memory banks*, however, can **overlap** rewriting and reading of successive words stored in different memory banks **(memory interleaving).** This reduces (typically roughly halves) the effective memory cycle (see also Sec. 2-5).

Core-magnetization retention at temperatures much above 85°F requires either high-temperature core material or an automatic decrease of core-driving currents with temperature. Typical minicomputer core memories can work at ambient temperatures up to 110 to 130°F; *you should check this specification carefully against your application requirements.*

1-21.   Plated-Wire Memories.   Plated-wire memories are magnetic memories which utilize small zones of magnetizable thin films plated onto wires, rather than magnetic cores, for bit storage.   Plated-wire memories permit **fast access** (access time as low as a few hundred nanoseconds) with **nondestructive readout,** are nonvolatile, and have been the subject of considerable hopes and expectations.   In fact, excellent plated-wire memories are commercially available.   But although batch-production methods have been developed, quality control is not simple.   As a result, plated-wire memories are not cheap (5 to 10 cents/bit) and have been applied mostly in higher-priced digital computers (especially in aerospace-vehicle computers).   MOSFET memories have overtaken plated-wire circuits in the low-cost computer field.

1-22.   Semiconductor Memories.   Semiconductor random-access memories **(RAMs)** can be cheaper and/or faster than core memories and are, therefore, replacing them in many applications.   Unlike core memories, typical semiconductor memories are **volatile;** i.e., they do not retain memory contents when power is lost.   Critical data storage, then, requires a **backup battery,** and possibly a power-failure interrupt program which saves memory contents on a disk or tape (see also Sec. 2-30*b*).   Semiconductor RAMs do not have destructive readout like core memories, but cycle times are still longer than access times.

Properties of different semiconductor memories (Table 1-7) parallel those of the corresponding logic families (Sec. 1-17).   **Bipolar memories,** really arrays of Schottky-clamped TTL, I^2L, or ECL flip-flops with appropriate addressing circuits, are the fastest commercially available RAMs.   Their relatively high cost still restricts their use to small scratchpads (Sec. 1-19), writable control stores (Sec. 2-33), and special applications requiring extra high speed.

Static MOSFET memories are also static flip-flop arrays (Fig. 1-21*a*). They are easy to use in small microcomputer systems (they do not require the refresh logic of dynamic MOSFET memories) and for expanding existing memories.   Static CMOS RAMs have quite low power consumption, especially while no reading or writing is done.   Again, silicon-on-sapphire CMOS is fastest.

The lowest-cost RAMs are **dynamic MOS memories,** mainly of the *n*-channel type, and available with as many as 16K bits on a single chip (Fig. 1-21*b*).   Here, each bit is stored in the output capacitance of a dynamic MOSFET inverter (see also Sec. 1-17).   Each bit charge, unfortunately,

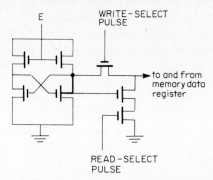

Fig. 1-21a. One-bit cell of a static MOSFET memory.

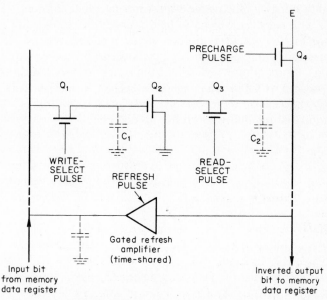

Fig. 1-21b. A dynamic MOSFET memory. Q_1, Q_2, and Q_3 form a 1-bit memory cell. PRE-CHARGE, WRITE-SELECT, READ-SELECT, and REFRESH pulses are associated with consecutive phases of a four-phase clock. Each pulse, if enabled by the cell-selecting logic, will transfer a bit from one parasitic capacitance to the next in a clockwise direction. PRE-CHARGE charges C_2 by turning Q_4 ON and OFF. WRITE-SELECT turns Q_1 ON and OFF; if a 1 is written, C_1 is charged. READ-SELECT turns Q_3 ON and OFF; if a 1 is stored, Q_2 turns ON and discharges C_2 so that the (inverted) output is 0. The gate refresh amplifier (essentially another similar memory cell) inverts the selected output bit and transfers it back to its cell input once every millisecond or so.

tends to leak off and **must be periodically refreshed** by a time-shared refresh amplifier (MOSFET inverter) on the chip, once every 150 to 2,000 μsec. This requires extra circuitry, wastes time, and risks errors. *Static memories simplify design, checkout, and maintenance.*

Figure 1-22 illustrates typical organizations of semiconductor-chip memories. In general, small memories are byte-oriented, while larger memories are bit-oriented. Each chip usually has **decoding circuitry** for its own addresses, plus an AND gate for decoding **chip-select inputs.**

Semiconductor memories as well as core memories often have an extra bit per word for *checking parity* (Sec. 1-8) on each data transfer to and from the memory (but not with refresh operations); errors interrupt computation to give an error indication. 16-bit RAMs with *five* check bits per word permit not only *multiple-bit error detection*, but also **correction** of single-bit errors. Such memories continue to function even when one bit per word is defective.

Serial memories (Ref. 14) are shift registers (Table 1-5e) which may be paralleled to store, say, successive 8-bit words in 8 shift registers. Dynamic MOSFET shift registers, which can be thousands of bits long, are especially inexpensive and are useful in display-refresh memories (Sec. 4-29), and for storing successive samples of fast voltage transients for subsequent computer processing. In the future, new solid-state serial memories such as **charge-coupled devices (CCDs) and magnetic-bubble memories** will become sufficiently inexpensive to replace at least small mass-storage disks with greatly improved reliability and faster access times.

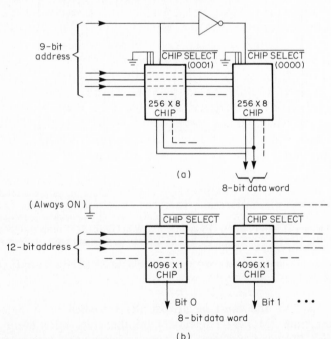

Fig. 1-22. Organization of a small (512 × 8-bit) solid-state memory (*a*), and of a larger (4,096 × 8-bit) memory (*b*).

1-23.   Read-Only Memories.   Read-only memories (ROMs), whose contents are usually checked out and written once and for all at the time of manufacture and then cannot be overwritten, are used for safe and inexpensive storage of frequently required program sequences and bit patterns:

1. *Complete special-purpose programs,* especially in industrial logic-sequence controllers replacing old-fashioned relay-ladder logic
2. *Important library subroutines* for special arithmetic sequences, control or emergency routines, scale or format transformations, etc.
3. *System programs* such as bootstrap loaders (Sec. 5-3), input/output subroutines (Sec. 5-10), and even simple compilers
4. Special *directories* and *function tables*
5. *Microprograms* (firmware) for implementing or emulating special instructions or instruction sequences (Secs. 2-31 and 6-21)
6. *Bit-pattern generators* such as *character generators* for displays and *test-signal generators*

Magnetic ROMs, based on a pattern of wires woven through U-shaped magnetic cores, are obsolete.   Most **semiconductor ROMs** are essentially *crossbar matrices* (Fig. 1-23a) whose crosspoint connections may be conductive links, diodes, transistors, or MOSFET inverters (Fig. 1-23b).   The storage pattern is established by selective erasure of crosspoint connections during manufacture (masking) or before use **(field-programmable ROMs, PROMS).**   Field programming is typically done with a keyboard- or tape-programmed fixture **(PROM programmer,** see also Sec. 5-28), which applies voltage pulses to an addressed word line and to the bit lines corresponding to the bits to be erased.   This may fuse a bit connection.   In a widely used type of **erasable PROM (EPROM, EROM)** the erasure pulses establish a static charge which turns a crosspoint MOSFET permanently OFF (and thus stores a 1 in Fig. 1-23b) unless the charge is made to leak off by irradiation with an ultraviolet light used for erasure.

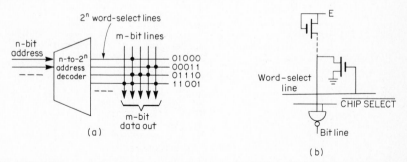

Fig. 1-23. (*a*) In a crossbar-matrix read-only memory (ROM), each crosspoint connection is made through a conductive link, diode, or transistor circuit.   Part (*b*) shows how a MOSFET inverter is used for the crosspoint connection.

Electrically alterable ROMs (EAROMs) can be erased and reloaded through application of suitable voltages to address and data-write lines; they may be regarded as slow-write/fast-read RAMs.   Reloading is relatively slow (takes milliseconds) but can be done without removing the chip from its circuit board.   EAROMs are convenient, but expensive ($10 to $12 for 256 bits) and usually require special power supplies for extra input voltages.

ROM access times vary between 35 and 1,500 nsec, with costs between 0.1 and 5 cents/bit; very fast ROMs, and erasable PROMs are, of course, the most expensive.   As many as 16K bits may be had on a chip, with memory organizations like those in Fig. 1-22.

1-24.   Logic-Function Implementation with ROMs.   Programmable Logic Arrays (Refs. 16, 17).   The m-bit data word produced by a ROM together with its address decoder (Fig. 1-23) is a *preprogrammed function* of the n-bit address input.   *Each output bit can be programmed to be any desired Boolean function of the n address bits.*   The mass-produced, general-purpose ROM thus substitutes for custom-designed gate logic at some sacrifice in speed.

The crossbar ROM is a special case of the **programmable logic array (PLA)** of Fig. 1-24, which substitutes another programmable crossbar matrix for the address decoder of Fig. 1-23.   While an n-bit address ROM has 2^n word lines energized *one at a time*, the more flexible PLA *can energize two or more word lines simultaneously but need not provide word lines for unused input-bit combinations.*   This permits economical generation of less than 2^n functions when n is larger than, say, 5.   Note that the output matrix ORs programmed combinations of minterms (Table 1-5a, 3) to produce the desired Boolean functions.

PLAs can be used in the scheme of Fig. 1-11 to produce completely general sequential machines from standard LSI logic (see also Sec. 6-21).

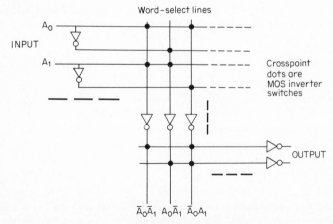

Fig. 1-24. A programmed-logic array (PLA).

REFERENCES AND BIBLIOGRAPHY

1. Sobel, H. S.: *Introduction to Digital-Computer Design*, Addison-Wesley, Reading, Mass., 1970.
2. Richards, R. K.: *Digital Design*, Wiley, New York, 1971.
3. Hellerman, H.: *Digital-Computer-System Principles*, 2d ed., McGraw-Hill, New York, 1971.
4. Baron, R. C., and A. T. Piccirilli: *Digital Logic and Computer Operations*, McGraw-Hill, New York, 1968.
5. Hill, F. J., and G. R. Peterson: *Introduction to Switching Theory and Logic Design*, Wiley, New York, 1968.
6. Huskey, H. D., and G. A. Korn: *Computer Handbook*, McGraw-Hill, New York, 1962.
7. Klerer, M., and G. A. Korn: *Digital Computer User's Handbook*, McGraw-Hill, New York, 1967.
8. Korn, G. A.: *Random-Process Simulation and Measurements*, McGraw-Hill, New York, 1966.
9. Korn, G. A., and T. M. Korn: *Mathematical Handbook for Scientists and Engineers*, 2d ed., McGraw-Hill, New York, 1968.
10. Korn, G. A., and T. M. Korn: *Electronic Analog and Hybrid Computers*, 2d ed., McGraw-Hill, New York, 1972.
11. Hill, F. J., and G. R. Peterson: *Digital Systems: Hardware Organization and Design*, Wiley, New York, 1973.
12. Soucek, B.: *Minicomputers in Data Processing and Simulation*, Wiley, New York, 1972.
13. Fink, D. G. (ed.): *Electronic Engineers' Handbook*, McGraw-Hill, New York, 1975.
14. Penney, W. M., et al.: *MOS Integrated Circuits*, Van Nostrand, New York, 1972.
15. Riley, W. B. (ed.): *Electronic Computer Memory Technology*, McGraw-Hill, New York, 1971.
16. Luecke, J., et al.: *Semiconductor Memory Design and Applications*, McGraw-Hill, New York, 1973.
17. Gorman, K.: The Programmable Logic Array, *EDN*, Nov. 20, 1973.
18. Hart, C. M., et al.: Bipolar LSI Takes on a New Direction with Integrated Injection Logic, *Electronics*, Oct. 3, 1974.
19. Horton, R. L., et al.: I^2L Takes Bipolar Integration a Significant Step Forward, *Electronics*, Feb. 6, 1975.
20. Meade, R. M.: Design Approaches for Cache-Memory Control, *Comput. Des.*, January 1971.
21. Brunner, D.: Designing Minicomputer Memory Systems with 4-Kilobit NMOS Memories, *Comput. Des.*, July 1975.
22. Frankenberg, R. J.: Designer's Guide to Semiconductor Memories, *EDN*, August–December 1975.
23. Greene, R., and D. House: Designing with Intel PROMs and ROMs, *Application Note AP-6*, Intel Corp., Santa Clara, Calif., 1975.
24. Barna, A., and D. J. Porat: *Integrated Circuits in Digital Electronics*. Wiley, New York, 1973.
25. Report on the 1975 Lake Arrowhead Workshop on Advances in Storage for Minis and Micros, *Computer*, March 1976 (includes papers on tape, floppy disks, CCDs, and bubble memories).
26. Sander, W. B., et al.: Dynamic I^2L Memory, *Electronics*, August 19, 1976.

CHAPTER 2

PROCESSORS AND INSTRUCTION SETS

INTRODUCTION AND SURVEY

This chapter describes the operation of typical mini/microcomputers, illustrating common features of many small machines. The principal components of such a system—memory, registers, buses, and arithmetic/logic unit—are introduced in Secs. 2-3 to 2-5. Sections 2-6 to 2-23 then describe *machine instructions* and *addressing methods*, discuss their implementation in terms of the system block diagram, and note the most important uses of various instructions; their applications in practical computer programs will be discussed in Chap. 3. Sections 2-24 to 2-30 list various useful options, and Secs. 2-31 to 2-33 describe *microprogram control of instruction execution*. Input/output will be dealt with in Chaps. 4 and 5. More advanced instruction sets and architectures for a new generation of mini/micro-computers will be described in Chap. 6.

THE BASIC SINGLE-ADDRESS MACHINE

2-1. Instructions and Stored Programs. From a very general point of view, *the essential objective of any digital computation is to obtain digital output words*

$$Y_1 = F_1(X_1, X_2, \ldots)$$
$$Y_2 = F_2(X_1, X_2, \ldots) \qquad (2\text{-}1)$$

. . . .

from input words X_1, X_2, ... Both input and output words will be ordered sets of 0s and 1s in suitably addressed computer registers and/or memory cells. Words may represent various types of numbers and alphanumeric-character strings or simply describe problem-logic states.

The desired relationships [Eq. (2-1)] may be numerous and enormously complicated. They must be broken down into elementary mathematical relations implemented by a (we hope small) set of **computer instructions.** It will, then, be necessary to supply additional registers or memory locations for storing *intermediate results* from elementary operations. The basic digital computer is, moreover, designed to perform all the various elementary arithmetic/logic operations *successively* with *the same* arithmetic/ logic system (unlike, for instance, a conventional analog computer, which has separate adders, multipliers, etc., for separate operations). The resulting sequence of elementary instructions designed to implement a desired computation is called a **program.**

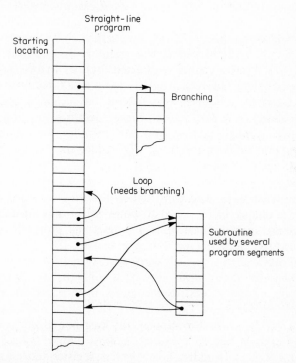

Fig. 2-1. The program counter addresses successive instructions to be executed and traces the program through the computer memory. For sophisticated programs, these program paths can be very complicated. Their design may be much more difficult (and expensive) than that of the computer hardware. A *flow diagram* (Sec. 3-8) is a map of the program paths through memory.

The maching will most often simply read instructions in sequence (**straight-line program**) but can also **branch** to a different program segment as a result of *decisions* made in the course of the computation (e.g., branch if the contents of a register are zero, or if an external device is ready to supply data). To save memory, *the program can traverse the same instruction sequence* (**loop, subroutine**) *again and again to repeat certain operations* (Fig. 2-1). The extraordinary power of the modern digital computer is due not simply to its speed and memory capacity, but also to the flexibility of the stored-program concept. Branching and looping, together with a variety of data-addressing schemes (Secs. 2-10 to 2-19), permit us to construct dramatically complicated programs from very simple instruction sets.

Instruction words stored in a computer memory are sets of 0s and 1s quite indistinguishable from data words. A program can, therefore, *modify instructions* stored in a random-access memory, i.e., replace them by other instructions. But this programming technique has been largely abandoned in favor of branching, since the original program must usually be saved for reuse in any case. ROM-stored programs, of course, cannot be modified.

2-2. Two-Address and Single-Address Instructions. A computer instruction might, say, add two numbers taken from memory by specifying **ADD WORD** (addressed by) **A AND WORD** (addressed by) **B; PLACE RESULT INTO MEMORY LOCATION** (addressed by) **C; TAKE NEXT INSTRUCTION FROM MEMORY LOCATION** (addressed by) **N**. Note that such an instruction would require *four* addresses **A, B, C**, and **N**. Since it requires $16 = \log_2 65{,}536$ bits to specify even a single address in a 64K memory, we would need very cumbersome multiword instructions. To reduce the number of addresses needed in an instruction,

1. We normally take the next-instruction address from a *program counter*, which is simply incremented to point to the next instruction. For branching, special instructions will reset the program counter to a specified new address (Sec. 2-22; see also Sec. 2-23).
2. *We always make the second source address and the destination address of binary operations identical* (e.g., **B ← A + B**, see also Fig. 1-12*d*). This will, of course, destroy the source operand, which may have to be saved elsewhere.
3. In practically all small computers, at least one of the remaining two addresses must be a *CPU-register address*. Since typical CPUs have only 1, 2, 4, 8, or 16 addressable registers, register-address specification requires at most 4 bits.

As a result, our *single* four-address instruction will be replaced by several simpler instructions.

LOAD INTO REGISTER 2 (the word addressed by) **A**
ADD INTO REGISTER 2 (the word addressed by) **B**
STORE REGISTER 2 (in memory location addressed by) **C**

Since the addition is done in a register (*accumulator*), both source operands are preserved. Since each instruction references (at most) a single memory location, we speak of a **single-address computer.**

Most mini/microcomputers are single-address machines and also do not permit addition (or subtraction, etc.) *into* a memory location. The Digital Equipment Corporation PDP-11 series is a notable exception (Sec. 7-6).

2-3. A "Basic" Mini/Microcomputer. Figure 2-2 shows the organization of a typical small digital computer. The machine has all the ingredients described in Secs. 1-12 to 1-22, viz.,

1. A core or semiconductor **memory,** which will store instructions and data
2. A set of **processor registers** (flip-flop registers), viz.,
    (*a*) **Memory buffer register (memory data register):** contains the instruction or data word currently leaving or entering the memory
    (*b*) **Memory address register:** contains the address of the currently addressed memory location
    (*c*) **Program counter:** contains the address of the instruction to be executed
    (*d*) **Instruction register:** contains the current instruction
    (*e*) **General-purpose register (accumulator, arithmetic/storage register) or registers**
    (*f*) **Address pointer or index register(s),** if any (Secs. 2-15 and 2-16)
    (*g*) **One-bit registers ("flags")** indicating **overflow, zero, sign, carry,** etc., in a current or past result
3. **An arithmetic/logic unit (ALU):** logic to combine register contents by addition, subtraction, bit-by-bit ANDing, etc.; and to complement, increment, and shift computer words
4. **Control logic:** decodes the 0s and 1s of the instruction currently in the instruction register to generate logic levels and time pulses, which
    (*a*) *Gate* (*steer*) *words between process registers*
    (*b*) *Determine the function of the arithmetic/logic circuits*

In Fig. 2-2, there are three **buses** for transfers between registers, always via the arithmetic/logic unit. This is a practical compromise: some extra register-to-register paths would permit more concurrent register transfers and speed computation, but we would pay for more complex interconnections and logic. Some small computers have only two processor buses, or even a single one (Secs. 6-5 and 7-1).

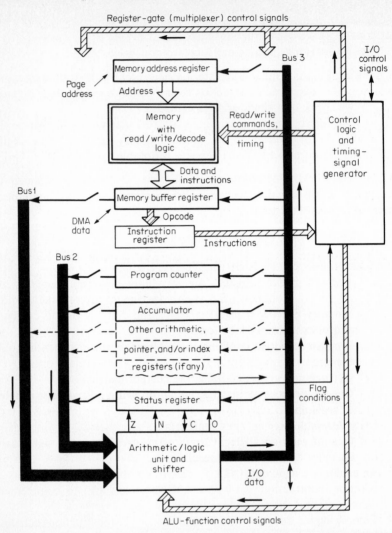

Fig. 2-2. A basic single-address computer permitting *concurrent data transfers on three buses during each microcycle.* Less elaborate *two-bus machines* time-share a single input bus to the arithmetic/logic unit, which must then have an input register to store (latch) one of two inputs (Figs. 6-12 and 7-1). *Single-bus computers* time-share a single processor bus for all register input and output (Sec. 6-5). Bus sharing necessarily reduces computing speed.

Finally, we must have **input/output connections** for external devices through processor buses or register gates.

2-4. Instruction Sets. The choice of an **instruction set** is a crucial feature of computer-system design. All conceivable digital-computer operations can be implemented with very primitive instruction sets, but more elaborate instruction sets can greatly reduce the number of instructions needed for a given task. This saves *program memory*, *programming effort*, and *execution time* at the expense of more logic.

Microprogrammed control (Sec. 2-31) permits inexpensive implementation of sophisticated instructions and will even let users create new instructions for special applications.

Most small computers have fewer than 60 types of instructions, which can be represented by 3 to 6 **operation-code bits.** More bits will be needed to *address registers and memory locations* (Secs. 2-10 to 2-19). To save fetch cycles, we would like to avoid multiword instructions as much as possible.

Instruction types can be classified in the manner of Table 2-1; *such a tabular arrangement is useful for comparing the instruction sets of different machines.*

2-5. Processor Operation and Microoperations. (a) Instruction Fetching. With a suitable program and data in memory, processor operation proceeds as a sequence of clock-timed steps (microoperations). We will consider the fetching and execution of a typical one-word instruction.

1. The **program counter,** which we assume to be preset to an instruction address (by control-panel switches as in Sec. 5-3, or by preceding computer operations), transfers this address to the **memory address register.**
2. The instruction word thus addressed is read into the **memory buffer register (memory data register,** Sec. 1-18) and from there into the **instruction register.**
3. The program counter is incremented to point to the next instruction address (this can also be done later in the instruction-execution sequence).

With a *core* memory, these instruction-fetch microoperations (which are common to all instructions) require one memory half-cycle (READ half-cycle, Sec. 1-20). The instruction word must be rewritten into core while its address is still in the memory address register (RESTORE half-cycle), so that one cannot access the same core-memory bank again during one full core-memory cycle (**FETCH cycle**). But even with a core memory, processor operations which do not involve the same memory bank can "overlap" the restoring operation. Hence most *non-memory-reference* instructions can be executed in a single core-memory cycle. *Memory reference instructions* requiring movement of data from or to memory will require at least one additional memory cycle.

Computers with multiple core-memory banks having separate address registers can fetch successive words from alternate memory banks in

TABLE 2-1. Common Instructions for Single-Address Computers.

	Non-memory-reference instructions (one memory cycle)	Memory-reference instructions (used with different addressing *modes*, Secs. 2-10 to 2-13; typically need two or more memory cycles)	Input/output instructions (to or from addressed device)
Move data (word or byte)	MOVE (register-to-register) EXCHANGE REGISTERS SWAP BYTES (in 16-bit register)	LOAD | STORE | (specified register) EXCHANGE (register and memory)	READ (device-to-register) WRITE (register-to-device)
Arithmetic/logic single operand (register or memory)	CLEAR COMPLEMENT NEGATE INCREMENT/DECREMENT TEST		Issue logic levels or timed pulses; clear flags; test register or flag; load status and control registers
two operands (register-to-register or memory-to-register)	ADD/SUBTRACT ADD/SUBTRACT CARRY (or with CARRY/BORROW) DECIMAL ADJUST MULTIPLY/DIVIDE		
bit-by-bit logic	AND/OR/XOR BIT SET/CLEAR		

	SHIFT/ROTATE MULTIPLE SHIFT	SHIFT/ROTATE	Shift register bits out/in
shift/rotate (one register or two)			
Program control unconditional branch	NO OPERATION HALT SKIP NEXT INSTRUCTION	EXECUTE BRANCH (JUMP) JUMP TO SUBROUTINE RETURN	
conditional branch (if result of past operation was = 0, ≠0, <0, >0, ≤0, ≥0, overflow, carry)	SKIP ON CONDITION	EXECUTE ON CONDITION BRANCH ON CONDITION JUMP TO SUBROUTINE ON CONDITION (rare) COMPARE WORD (BYTE) AND SKIP	SKIP ON FLAG (sense line)
loop indexing	INCREMENT/DECREMENT REGISTER, SKIP IF ZERO DECREMENT REGISTER, BRANCH IF NOT ZERO	INCREMENT/DECREMENT, SKIP IF ZERO	

successive half-cycles (**memory interleaving**), and semiconductor memories do not .need any rewriting.   It is also possible to store instructions and data words likely to be used next in **lookahead registers** or **cache memories** for faster access (Sec. 1-19).   Note that such techniques must be matched by faster processor logic (see also Sec. 6-22).

(b) **Instruction Execution.**   As soon as the instruction code is in the instruction register, its 0s and 1s are decoded to control successive micro-operations needed for the execution of a specific instruction.   Figure 2-3 shows how **hard-wired control logic** can produce sets of control bits (**control words**) which determine the operation of register gates, ALU, memory, and I/O functions during successive **microcycles** (typically 4 to 12 per memory cycle).   Most small digital computers use **microprogrammed control**; i.e., successive control words are fetched from a special control memory (Secs. 2-31 to 2-33).

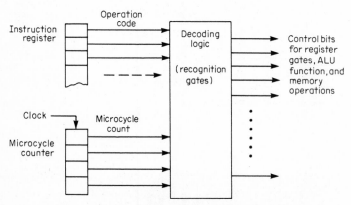

Fig. 2-3. A hard-wired control unit decodes instruction-register operation-code bits and microcycle-counter bits together to produce appropriate data-gating, ALU-function, and memory-operation control bits during successive microcycles.

Multiword instructions (Sec. 2-19) will require extra memory accesses. When an instruction is completed, the program counter will have been suitably incremented to point to the next instruction in a straight-line program, or a new branch address has been supplied (Sec. 2-22). The machine (unless halted) then proceeds with a new FETCH phase.

REGISTER OPERATIONS

2-6.   Simple Register Operations.   Programmable processor registers (Fig. 2-2) provide *simply addressable fast-access storage for data* before and after arithmetic/logic and input/output operations and are also used for *memory* *addressing* (pointer and index registers, Secs. 2-15 and 2-16). The simplest computer instructions modify the contents of *one* specified register:

CLEAR (set all 0s)	**INCREMENT**
COMPLEMENT (each bit)	**DECREMENT**
NEGATE (multiply by -1)	

Two registers (**source** and **destination**) must be specified for

MOVE (contents of) **REGISTER 1 TO REGISTER 2**

ADD REGISTER 1 INTO REGISTER 2

SUBTRACT REGISTER 1 INTO REGISTER 2

and for the **bit-by-bit-logic instructions**

AND REGISTER 1 INTO REGISTER 2

OR REGISTER 1 INTO REGISTER 2

XOR REGISTER 1 INTO REGISTER 2

If the source and destination registers contain

01110101

and

11110000

then

AND produces the destination contents	**01110000**
OR produces the destination contents	**11110101**
XOR produces the destination contents	**10000101**

OR is also called BIT SET, since each 1 in the source sets the corresponding destination bit. Some machines have a BIT CLEAR instruction, which combines COMPLEMENT SOURCE with AND to clear destination bits corresponding to 1s in the source.

Small digital computers rarely have more than 16 addressable processor registers, so that at most 4 bits would be required to specify a register. Thus, register instructions usually require only one instruction word or byte. To save instruction bits (and gates), many small computers restrict the destination of **ADD, SUBTRACT, AND, OR,** and **XOR** instructions to one or two of the registers. These registers are then called **accumulators.**

Note also that each instruction listed so far replaces an operand with the result, so that *the operand is destroyed* (unless it is previously saved in another location). The nondestructive instruction

EXCHANGE (the contents of) **REGISTERS 1 AND 2**

is useful if registers 1 and 2 have different properties (e.g., if one is an accumulator and one an index register).

2-7. Processor Flags and Test/Compare Operations. The **Z, N, O, and C processor flags** in modern computers are flip-flops whose states determine **conditional program branching** (Secs. 2-1 and 2-21). The Z, N, and O flags are, respectively, set when the result (output) of an ALU operation is **zero, negative,** or causes **arithmetic overflow** (2s-complement overflow). Otherwise, these flags are reset after each ALU operation.

Operation of the carry (C) flag differs in different machines (check your manual carefully). Typically, the C flag sets when addition causes a **carry** from the sign bit (MSB of an unsigned result) and when subtraction causes a sign-bit "borrow." This is used in multiple-precision arithmetic (Sec. 2-24) and for comparing unsigned numbers (Sec. 2-21). In most modern computers (e.g., PDP-11, Motorola 6800), incrementing/decrementing can cause overflow, but no carry; the C flag is *unaffected* by **MOVE (LOAD, STORE), AND, OR,** and **XOR** instructions and thus "remembers" the last carry. The C flag is unaffected by non-ALU operations.

NOTE: As far as the processor flags are concerned, "ALU operations" include rotate/shift operations (Sec. 2-9) and multiplication/division, both of which may use hardware separate from the main ALU in some machines.

Most computers have instructions which set, clear, or complement individual processor flags. In modern machines, the flags constitute part of a **processor status register,** whose contents (**processor status word**) may be stored, if desired, to postpone a branching decision (Secs. 3-11 and 4-8). More primitive machines (e.g., PDP-8-type computers, Sec. 6-15) have only one flag, viz., a carry flag or *link* (accumulator extension) which is *complemented* (not set) by accumulator carries and may require resetting before critical operations (see Fig. 3-8a for an *overflow test* using such a flag).

The instruction

TEST REGISTER 3

passes the register contents through the ALU, sets Z, N, and/or O appropriately, and clears C, all without modifying the register contents. The instruction

COMPARE REGISTERS 1 AND 2

sets the Z, N, O, and C flags as determined by the difference of the register contents but **does not destroy the contents of either register by depositing the difference itself.** *Be sure to check your computer manual as to whether the difference tested subtracts the contents of register 1 or register 2,* and check Sec. 2-21 carefully. The nondestructive **COMPARE** instruction can be very useful.

A few machines also have nondestructive **ADD, XOR**, and **AND** instructions used for various tests. In particular, the nondestructive **AND** or **BIT TEST** instruction sets the Z flag unless the destination has at least one 1 bit corresponding to a 1 bit in the source. The N flag is set if and only if the leftmost bits of both source and destination are 1s.

Machines with decimal-arithmetic instructions also have **half-carry flags** used by the **DECIMAL ADJUST** instruction to effect BCD addition and subtraction (Sec. 2-26).

2-8. Microoperation Sequence. Each register instruction fetched into the processor instruction register (Sec. 2-5a and Fig. 2-2) is decoded by the control unit (Sec. 2-5b) into control bits which

1. Gate the contents of the specified register or registers into the ALU via bus 1 and/or 2.
2. Cause the ALU to perform the desired operation and to set appropriate flags.
3. Gate the result into the destination register via bus 3.

(see also Fig. 1-12d).   For **TEST/COMPARE** instructions (Sec. 2-7), *the last microoperation is omitted;* i.e., we set appropriate processor flags but do not overwrite any register contents.

Most register instructions can be executed while the instruction word is rewritten into a core memory, so that instruction fetching and execution requires a single memory cycle (see also Sec. 2-5).

2-9. Rotate/Shift Operations. One-cycle instructions like

ROTATE ACCUMULATOR LEFT

ROTATE REGISTER NO. 3 RIGHT

rotate (circulate) the contents of the specified register **and the carry-flag bit** by 1 bit, as shown in Fig. 2-4a,b,c. Some machines also have 2-bit one-cycle rotate instructions.

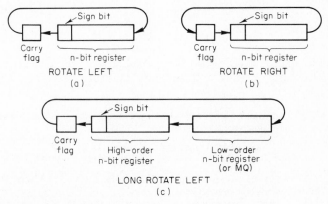

ROTATE LEFT
(a)

ROTATE RIGHT
(b)

LONG ROTATE LEFT
(c)

Fig. 2-4a, b, c. ROTATE/SHIFT operations.   The carry-flag flip-flop can be set, reset, or equated to the sign bit before each 1-bit rotation.

Physically, the register bits go to the ALU via bus 1 or 2 in Fig. 2-2, are "shifted sideways" by multiplexer gates (Fig. 1-16), set or reset processor flags, and return to the register via bus 3.

Rotation has **three** important applications:

1. **Individual bits of a register word** (which might represent, say, logical states in an external device, Sec. 4-7) **can be rotated into the sign-bit and/or carry-bit positions for bit tests and branching** (Sec. 2-22).
2. **Partial words or bytes can be moved, packed, and unpacked** in connection with input/output operations (see, e.g., Fig. 3-8d).
3. **With the carry bit appropriately cleared or set, rotations act as arithmetic shifts implementing multiplication or division by 2** (Sec. 1-9b).

Specifically, *an unsigned binary number (no sign bit) is multiplied or divided by 2 if we first clear the carry flag and then rotate, respectively, left or right.* Such an operation is called an **unsigned shift** or "logical" shift. After multiplication by 2, a 1 in the carry flag signifies *overflow*.

Signed 2s-complement numbers are also multiplied by 2 through an *unsigned* left shift. Overflow is indicated by a sign-bit change (result sign bit XOR carry flag = 1). To *divide* by 2, *we first copy the sign bit into the carry flag and then rotate left* (**signed** shift). Most computers have explicit **LEFT/RIGHT ARITHMETIC SHIFT** instructions for multiplication and division by 2, as well as **ROTATE** and/or **UNSIGNED SHIFT** instructions.

Note that multiplication by 2 is equivalent to *addition back into the same register*, so that an explicit opcode and logic for left arithmetic shifts may be omitted. Note also that *1s-complement arithmetic* (Tables 1-1 and 1-2) requires signed shifts for multiplication as well as for division.

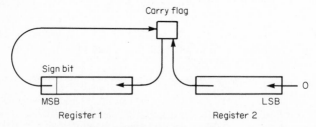

Fig. 2-4d. A one-bit **ARITHMETIC SHIFT COMBINED, LEFT** of registers 1 and 2 can be implemented through two successive single-register operations

ARITHMETIC SHIFT LEFT	**REGISTER 2**
ROTATE LEFT	**REGISTER 1**

which correctly transfers the carry from register 2 to register 1. A one-bit **ARITHMETIC SHIFT COMBINED, RIGHT** is similarly obtained with

ARITHMETIC SHIFT RIGHT	**REGISTER 1**
ROTATE RIGHT	**REGISTER 2**

Multiple-arithmetic-shift instructions, implementing multiplication and division by powers of 2, are not usually single-cycle instructions. The **shift count** n is entered into a processor register (general-purpose register or special **step counter**), which is decremented after each one-bit shift. Such instructions usually save time only if $n > 2$. **Combined ("long")** **arithmetic shifts** similarly shift two concatenated processor registers for double-precision multiplication and division (Fig. 2-4d and Sec. 2-24).

NOTE: Each division by 2 will "chop" rather than round the result, i.e., the result is always less than or equal to the correct result (Sec. 1-15).

MEMORY-ADDRESSING MODES

2-10. Memory-Reference Instructions. The most common **memory-reference instructions** produce operations similar to the register operations described in Secs. 2-6 and 2-7, *but with an operand and/or result in the computer memory, e.g.,*

LOAD ACCUMULATOR 1 (with the contents of)	**MEMORY LOCATION**
ADD INTO REGISTER 3 (the contents of)	**MEMORY LOCATION**
STORE (contents of) **REGISTER 2** (in)	**MEMORY LOCATION**
INCREMENT (the contents of)	**MEMORY LOCATION**
TEST (the contents of)	**MEMORY LOCATION**

Single-address instructions (Sec. 2-2) reference only one memory location, and the result of a two-operand instruction (**ADD**, **SUBTRACT**, etc.) is practically always in a register, not in memory. Some computers can exchange register and memory words. A few machines can rotate/shift (the contents of) a specified memory location.

2-11. Direct Addressing. **Direct addressing** of even a single operand or result in memory is complicated by short mini/microcomputer word lengths. If we allow 8 bits for the opcode, *8-bit microprocessors will need 3-byte memory-reference instructions,* and *16-bit machines require two-word instructions* for direct addressing of more than $256 = 2^8$ memory locations (Fig. 2-5a). Typical micro/minicomputer memories must address between 1K and 64K word or byte locations.

Even a one-word memory-reference instruction requires *two* memory accesses, and thus usually two memory cycles, for instruction fetching and execution. An *additional* memory access, and additional time, is required for each extra word of a multiword instruction (see also Sec. 2-20).

2-12. Program/Data Structures and Effective-Address Computation. Direct addressing can waste program memory and computer time, because few memory-reference instructions will address new "random" locations in memory; the referenced locations tend to "cluster" in local program and data structures. In particular, *many instructions reference words in arrays or tables shorter than 256 words*, and many program-branching and looping operations reference only locations less than 128 words away (Sec. 2-22). It is, therefore, economical to have some one- or two-word instructions whose second byte or word represents not an absolute address but a positive or negative *offset* from a previously established reference address.   The **effective address** defined by such an instruction must, then, be *computed* before the actual memory reference is made.   The specific type of address computation or **addressing mode** is identified by special opcode bits (**addressing-mode field** of the instruction).   **The choice of addressing modes is a vital computer design feature which critically affects execution speed, memory requirements, and programming convenience.**   Sections 2-13 to 2-18 list the most important addressing modes.

2-13. Paged Addressing.   The instruction-address byte or word is interpreted as the (positive) offset from a **page origin.**   Memory is divided into successive **pages** of, say, 256 words or bytes for an 8-bit instruction-address byte.   Locations 0–255 are then page 0, 256–511 are page 1, etc.

Minicomputers also use 7-bit, 9-bit, 12-bit, and 13-bit page-address bytes (128, 512, 4K, and 8K words/page, see also Chaps. 6 and 7.

Either the **page number** is the **current page** (the same page as the current instruction), or (preferably) the page number is set into a special **page register** by an earlier instruction.   Note that a current-page reference cannot cross a page boundary.   An address-mode bit may also switch page addressing to **page 0,** where one frequently keeps special tables or service programs.

Page registers permit one to address very large memories, and separate page registers for different users or tasks can protect critical areas in memory (memory mapping and protection, Sec. 2-30).   It is possible to add "outboard" page registers for homemade memory extensions.[13]

2-14. Relative Addressing.   The instruction-address byte or word is interpreted as *a positive or negative offset from the location of the current instruction*, e.g.,

STORE ACCUMULATOR   . + 4

stores the accumulator contents 4 words (or bytes) ahead of (the end of) the current instruction.

Relative addressing with an 8-bit address byte is especially useful for branching instructions (Sec. 2-22).   Relative addressing with a full 16-bit address is sometimes used to replace direct addressing because programs containing only relative-address information are easy to *relocate* in the computer memory (Secs. 3-18, 5-5, and 7-7).

2-15. Register-Deferred and Indirect Addressing.   Automatic Incrementing and Decrementing.   In **register-deferred** (or **register-indirect**) **addressing,** the

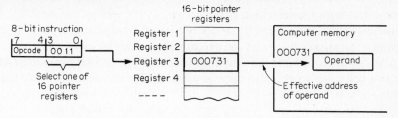

Fig. 2-5a. Register-deferred addressing. A short (8-bit) microprocessor instruction specifies one of 16 pointer registers, where the effective operand address is found. Incrementing the pointer register steps the effective address through an array or table in memory.

instruction needs only 3 to 5 bits to specify one of 8 to 32 **pointer registers,** which has been previously loaded with the effective operand address, e.g.,

ADD INTO ACCUMULATOR (the contents of the

location addressed) **VIA REGISTER 3**

(Fig. 2-5a). *This short instruction format is especially effective in applications where the pointer register is incremented (or decremented) to step through an array or table of memory locations.* Note that the pointer register needs to be loaded only once with the initial table location. The pointer register is then incremented (or decremented) with short-format register instructions. Some machines have a special **autoincrement** addressing mode which increments the pointer register automatically after the address has been read. Automatic decrementing is also possible (Sec. 2-17).

Indirect addressing places the effective operand address into a *memory location* (pointer location), which can be specified by any other addressing mode (direct, paged, relative, register-deferred, etc.), e.g.,

STORE ACCUMULATOR, INDIRECT VIA 007

(Fig. 2-5b). Every memory location can thus be used as a pointer register, but **indirect addressing requires an extra memory cycle** for the extra memory access.

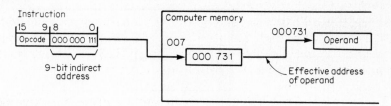

Fig. 2-5b. Indirect addressing.

One may again **autoincrement** the contents of a pointer location, either through a special instruction bit or, more commonly, by designating 10 to 20 memory locations on page 0 as **autoincrement locations.** Hardware automatically increments the contents of such a location after every indirect-address reference to it. *Autodecrementing* is also possible (see also Secs. 6-15, 7-3, and 7-7).

A few minicomputers have **multilevel indirect addressing;** i.e., the word in a pointer location is again interpreted as an *indirect* address if a mode bit, usually the MSB, in that word is set. The indirect-addressing range of a 16-bit address word is necessarily reduced to $2^{15} = 32K$ words or bytes. The process can be repeated.

NOTE: Indirect addressing, like register-deferred addressing, permits the program to compute and modify operand addresses (and thus the program itself) in response to intermediate results.

2-16. Index Registers and Base Registers. An **indexed** memory-reference instruction has an address byte or word whose (positive or negative) contents are added to the contents of a specified **index register** to form the effective operand address, e.g.,

LOAD ACCUMULATOR, INDEXED BY REGISTER 2   000007

(Fig. 2-5c). The index register is, typically, a 16-bit processor register. Most 16-bit minicomputers have *two-word* indexed instructions, so that the address word specifies a 16-bit offset. But some minicomputers and micro-computers also have indexed instructions with an 8-bit or 9-bit offset specified within a "short" (16-bit or two-byte) instruction format.

A typical application is *to access an operand from a table in memory,* where

$$\text{operand address} = \text{table-origin address} + \text{offset}$$

With a 16-bit word, we can place the *offset* (*table index*) in the index register and the *table address* in the address word of the instruction. A single register can then index analogous items in two or more tables or arrays, as for

$$A_i = B_i + C_i$$

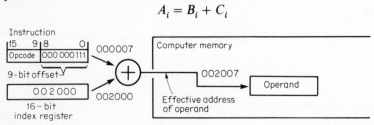

Fig. 2-5c. Indexed addressing with a 9-bit address offset in the instruction and a 16-bit index register.

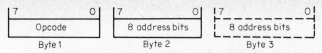

Fig. 2-6a. Direct addressing with one or two address bytes in an 8-bit machine.

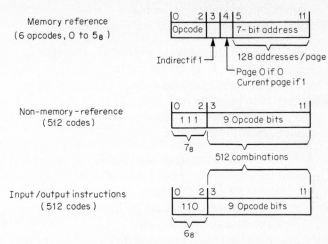

Fig. 2-6b. Instruction formats for a widely used class of simple 12-bit machines (PDP-8-type minicomputers, Intersil 6100 microprocessors, see also Sec. 6-15). To save memory-reference opcodes, the single accumulator is loaded through successive CLEAR ACCUMULATOR and ADD INTO ACCUMULATOR instructions. Indirect addressing is used for crossing page boundaries.

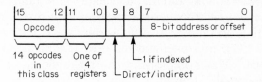

Fig. 2-6c. A 16-bit instruction format with an 8-bit address byte.

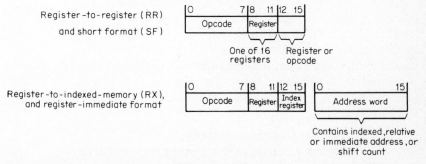

Fig. 2-6d. Instruction formats for 16-bit Interdata minicomputers are similar to IBM formats. With 16 general-purpose registers, it takes 4 bits to specify a source/destination register and 4 bits to specify an index register, so that memory-reference instructions use two 16-bit words. Interdata computers do not use indirect addressing. Interdata 7/32 and 8/32 also have *three*-word instructions which can address up to a million bytes, admit double indexing (Sec. 3-10), and can handle 32-bit immediate operands (see also Sec. 6-2).

We can also increment or decrement the index register to *step through a table, or through corresponding items in two or more tables.* The index register can, moreover, maintain a *count* of such stepping operations. Section 3-9 shows a programming example.

Indirect addressing can be combined with indexing:

1. **Preindexing:** The instruction-word address bits, interpreted as a signed or unsigned integer, are added to the contents of a specified index register to determine the indirect address (pointer address).
2. **Postindexing:** The contents of a specified index register are added *to the indirect address* to form the effective operand address. The pointer stays in memory without change.

Section 3-26 shows an interesting application of preindexing. Postindexing is useful for accessing a set of tables selected by the index value.

In some computer systems, the contents of a specified **base register** may be added to effective addresses obtained by direct, indirect, indexed, etc., addressing. Base registers are usually employed to relocate entire program segments or data areas in the computer memory (see also Secs. 2-30, 7-2, and 7-12).

2-17. Stack Operations in Memory. Besides array indexing, the newer digital computers exploit another fortunate opportunity to use short (one-word) memory-reference instructions. Intermediate results in arithmetic and sorting operations, as well as subroutine and interrupt return addresses (Sec. 2-23), are stored and retrieved in a natural **last-in–first-out (LIFO) sequence.** This is implemented through addition and removal of words or bytes at the top of a **stack** of locations in the computer memory.

Figure 2-7 shows how such a stack is built and accessed with instructions referencing a pointer register called a **stack pointer.** The stack begins with location 216 and builds *downward;* i.e., memory addresses get *lower* toward the top of the stack (this is customary but not necessary). The stack pointer is originally loaded with the address 217; either 216 or 217 = 216 + 1 is referred to as the **stack base.** To **push** the first item onto the stack (i.e., into location 216), say from accumulator 3, we need the instruction sequence

> **DECREMENT STACK POINTER**
> **DEPOSIT ACCUMULATOR 3 VIA STACK POINTER**

Modern computers combine these instructions into a *single one-word memory-reference instruction*

> **PUSH ACCUMULATOR 3**

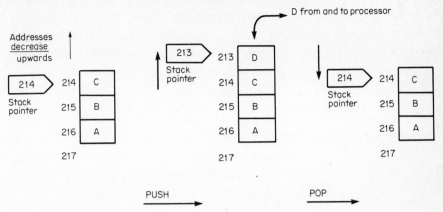

Fig. 2-7. PUSH and POP operations in a simple pushdown stack in memory.

which automatically *predecrements* the stack pointer before using the effective address stored there.

We can now push more items, as needed; the stack pointer is always left pointing at the current top item. To **pop** the top item off the stack, say into accumulator 1, we use

LOAD ACCUMULATOR 1 VIA STACK POINTER
INCREMENT STACK POINTER

which may be combined into the convenient one-word instruction

POP INTO ACCUMULATOR 1

which *postincrements* the stack pointer, so that it again points at the current top item.

NOTE: In some processors (e.g., Motorola 6800, Sec. 6-6), the stack pointer does not point at the current top item in the stack, but at the next available stack location (i.e., at the next lower address). In this case, PUSH involves *post*-decrementing, and POP involves *pre*-incrementing the stack pointer.

Sections 3-15, 3-16, and 4-9 illustrate stack applications. *It will be necessary to reserve enough memory to accommodate the largest possible number of stack items.* Unfortunately, this is not always precisely known, so that we may have to allow extra locations. To make sure that a stack will not *overflow* (and thus overwrite other data or program items), one may compare the stack pointer with a predetermined lower *stack limit* before every **PUSH** operation. This can be done with conditional-branching instructions or by automatic interrupt hardware.

Some computers permit not only data-moving but also arithmetic and logic operations with stack items, with short-form memory-reference instructions like

POP AND ADD

This pops the top item, adds it to the second item, and leaves the stack pointer pointing to the resulting sum at the new top of the stack. Such stack instructions permit efficient computation of expressions like

$$D = A*(B + C)$$

with short-form memory-reference instructions. With A, B, C stacked, bottom to top, in "reverse Polish order," the instruction sequence

POP AND ADD
POP AND MULTIPLY

leaves the result D at the new top of the stack.

A program may use more than a single stack in memory, in which case each stack instruction must reference the pointer register to be used as a stack pointer. Many microprocessors have small *hardware stacks* comprising 4 to 16 processor registers and a stack-pointer register for fast storage and retrieval of subroutine and interrupt return addresses (Sec. 2-23). On the other hand, stack operations are so useful (Secs. 3-15, 4-9, and 4-12) that they are employed even in machines without special stack pointers or short-format stack instructions. If there is no pointer register or index register, one can still use a pointer in memory (indirect addressing, see also Secs. 2-15 and 3-15).

2-18. Immediate Addressing (see also Sec. 3-4). **Immediate-address** instructions are not really memory-reference instructions, although instruction formats are similar. Immediate-address instruction like

LOAD ACCUMULATOR, IMMEDIATE   (integer)
ADD INTO ACCUMULATOR NO. 2, IMMEDIATE   (integer)

are one-word ("short-format") instructions with a 4- to 13-bit address byte, or two-word (or three-byte) instructions (see also Fig. 2-6). Either way, the address bits are interpreted as a signed or unsigned integer **operand.** Immediate-address instructions are handy for setting up pointer addresses, index registers, and counters, and for operations with fixed parameters or bit patterns (bit tests, Sec. 2-7).

> *NOTE:* The *indirect/immediate* addressing mode found in some minicomputers uses the immediate-operand word or byte as pointer address. This is equivalent to direct addressing and may be the only way to force *direct addressing* in some machines which generally employ relative addressing or base-register addressing for easier program relocation.

2-19. Instruction Formats. Micro/minicomputer **instruction formats** are much constrained by short word length, since multiword-instruction fetching uses additional time. Nevertheless, the trend is to more sophisticated instruction sets, which require longer opcodes and more bits to specify extra pointer/index registers, more address modes, and a larger address space. Figure 2-6b shows the complete set of instruction formats for a simple 12-bit machine without index registers; much addressing is done indirectly, and with autoincrement locations in memory. Figure 2-6c shows a *one-word* memory-reference format for a minicomputer with a single index register. This short format is useful, but even with a 16-bit index register, the 8-bit offset in the address byte limits addressing possibilities, so that such instructions have to be supplemented with at least a few two-word instructions. By contrast, Interdata computers (Fig. 2-6d) have *no* one-word memory-reference instructions and no indirect addressing; but an indexing instruction can select one of 15 different index registers. Indirect addressing is replaced by two-instruction sequences which place the indirect address in an index register.

2-20. Microoperations for Memory-Reference Instructions. As noted earlier, opcode bits in memory-reference instruction words select the addressing mode (Fig. 2-6c,d). Referring to Fig. 2-2, a *direct-address* instruction transfers its address bits from the memory buffer register to the memory data register during the EXECUTE phase of an instruction-fetch cycle by way of bus 1, the arithmetic/logic unit, and bus 3. For *paged addressing*, program-counter bits (*current page*) or page-register bits can be transferred at the same time.

Relative-address and indexed instructions can employ the arithmetic/logic unit to add program-counter or index-register bits to the address bits via bus 2. Such address addition usually fits into the rewrite half-cycle of a core memory. More elaborate computers may speed microprogram execution by providing a separate adder for addresses.

Two-word and *indirect-address* instructions use an extra memory cycle to transfer the operand address from memory into the memory buffer register and then into the memory address register. *Memory-autoincrementing* or *postindexing* operations can take place in the course of this transfer via the ALU and bus 3.

With the effective address in the memory address register, we can now perform four types of operations:

1. *Clear* the addressed memory location.
2. Read the addressed memory word into the memory buffer register and *increment* or *decrement* it in the ALU before *rewriting* it into memory.
3. Read the memory word and *move, add*, etc., it from the memory buffer register into another processor register (using buses and ALU as in Sec. 2-6).
4. *Store the contents of a processor register* by moving the register word to the memory buffer register and then *write* it into the addressed memory location.

As noted in Sec. 2-11, *a memory-reference instruction requires one memory cycle to fetch each instruction word, plus one memory cycle for the memory-reference operation,* typically 2 or 3 cycles.   Computers with multiple inter-leaved memory banks can save time by overlapping multiple-instruction word fetches (Sec. 1-20).

In 4-bit microcomputers, address-register loading and memory-reference operations may be implemented through *two* successive instructions (Sec. 6-5).

INSTRUCTIONS CONTROLLING PROGRAM EXECUTION, BRANCHING, AND SUBROUTINES

2-21.   NO OPERATION and HALT.   The instruction **NO OPERATION** does nothing but increment the program counter.   This intentionally wastes an instruction-fetch cycle and an instruction location to produce a time delay (e.g., to let an external device settle), or to reserve an instruction location for later program modification.   The instruction **HALT** stops program execution until the operator checks computer operation, services a device, etc., and presses a control-panel switch or key to continue execution.

In static-logic machines, **HALT** can simply stop the processor clock; with dynamic MOSFET logic (Sec. 1-17), **HALT** can produce recurring jumps to the current location.

2-22.   Unconditional and Conditional Branching.   The instruction

JUMP (BRANCH) TO   (effective address)

places the effective address (which may be direct, relative, indirect, indexed, etc.) into the *program counter,* so that the next instruction is taken from the new location, and *the program branches unconditionally* (Fig. 2-1).   The instructions

SKIP ON CONDITION
BRANCH ON CONDITION TO   (effective address)

modify the next-instruction address in the program counter *subject to a condition specified by the opcode bits,* typically if the latest data-move or arithmetic/logic operation produced

a result <0, >0, ≤ 0, ≥ 0, or $\neq 0$
a carry (from the leftmost bit), or *no carry*
arithmetic overflow, or *no overflow*

or various combinations of these conditions.   **Conditional branching instructions give digital computers their essential capability to make decisions** based on earlier results, as determined by the status of the **Z, N, C, and O** processor flags (Sec. 2-7).

It is **not** in general sufficient to test only the sign bit (N flag) if you want to compare two numbers with a **SUBTRACT** or **COMPARE** operation (Sec. 2-7).

1. If the subtraction of two signal numbers produces 2s-complement *overflow*, the sign bit reverses: you must test $N \: XOR \: O$, not N.
2. If the two numbers are *unsigned* (e.g., counts and especially *addresses*), then the *carry flag* rather than the sign flag indicates that the difference is negative.

Some modern processors (PDP-11, Motorola 6800) have complete sets of separate branching instructions governing all such conditions. Thus, instructions like **BRANCH IF LESS (LESS OR EQUAL, GREATER OR EQUAL, GREATER)** compare signed numbers correctly regardless of overflow.

NOTE: In most modern computers, the flag status is determined *anew* with each data-move or arithmetic/logic instruction; i.e., each such instruction initially resets the flags, except possibly for the carry flag, which may require a reset instruction before critical operations (see also Fig. 3-8a). Check your computer manual carefully (see also Sec. 2-7).

Many computers can *combine conditional branching with a preceding arithmetic/logic operation.* In particular, one may *terminate a preset counting operation* with

INCREMENT/DECREMENT (register or memory location) **AND SKIP IF ZERO**
DECREMENT REGISTER AND BRANCH IF NOT ZERO (effective address)

Section 3-9 shows typical applications (program loops). Another type of instruction,

     SKIP IF REGISTER DIFFERS FROM   (effective address)

is useful for quick detection of command words or bytes.

The most useful conditional-branching instruction format has an 8-bit address byte for *relative addressing* (Sec. 2-14) of up to 128 bytes before and 127 bytes after the current instruction. This fits a 16-bit word (or two bytes) and accommodates most programs; longer jumps branch to an unconditional jump instruction. Conditional **SKIP** instructions use even fewer bits, but generally require an extra unconditional jump instruction, e.g.,

     SKIP ON CONDITION   / Condition true?
     JUMP TO (effective address) / No, go to branch 2
     (next instruction)   / Yes, continue on branch 1

(see also Sec. 3-8).

2-23. Subroutine Jump and Return. Nested Subroutines. A **subroutine** is a program section (e.g., a square-root-computation routine) which can be entered (**called**) repeatedly by other program sections (Fig. 2-1; see also Sec. 3-12). The instructions

JUMP TO SUBROUTINE   SUBR

or

JUMP AND SAVE   SUBR

may use any available memory-addressing mode (direct, indirect, indexed, etc.) to cause a jump to the effective address of the subroutine **entry point SUBR** (or **SUBR** + 1 word, see below). The presumed **return address** (incremented program-counter contents) is automatically **saved** in one of the following ways:

1. **In memory,** at the effective address **SUBR**; the true entry point of the subroutine is then taken to be **SUBR** + 1 word. Return now simply requires an *indirect jump* via **SUBR**.
2. **In a specified pointer register (linkage register).** Return is effected by a *jump via the same register.*
3. **On a stack in memory (software stack)** addressed by a specified stack pointer (Sec. 2-17). Return jump is via this stack pointer, which is then incremented (i.e., the used-up return address is popped off the stack).
4. **On a hardware stack** made up of 4 to 16 special processor registers addressed by a special stack-pointer register (Fig. 2-8).

With either a software or hardware stack, the return jump is facilitated by a special instruction

RETURN FROM SUBROUTINE

which causes a jump via the stack pointer and then automatically increments the stack pointer. **Such stack methods automate storage and retrieval of the successive return addresses needed for nested subroutines** (subroutines calling other subroutines, Fig. 2-8). *Programming methods will be discussed in Secs. 3-12 to 3-16.*

Subroutines can save much memory and programming effort, so that efficient operation is very important. Hardware return-address storage (linkage register or hardware stack) saves one memory access per jump (two per subroutine). But *the software-stack method permits essentially unlimited nesting and also facilitates subroutine data transfer and intermediate storage* (Secs. 3-15 and 3-16). Some machines *combine* methods 2 and 4, or 3 and 4 (Secs. 6-16 and 7-8).

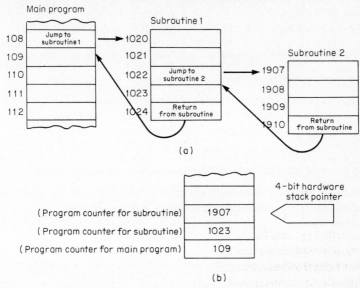

Fig. 2-8. Nested subroutines (*a*), and a hardware stack for saving subroutine return addresses (*b*), shown at the time subroutine 2 is called. The hardware stack is made up of hardware registers; the register pointed at by the hardware stack pointer is used as the current program counter.

Some computers have the instruction

          EXECUTE   (effective address)

which causes execution of one instruction stored at the effectively addressed location (one-instruction subroutine). A few machines also have *conditional* subroutine jumps and/or EXECUTE operations.

EXTENDED ARITHMETIC AND OTHER OPTIONS

2-24. Multiple-Precision Arithmetic. Multiple-precision fixed-point data formats, which are often needed with short-word-length computers, "concatenate" two or more *n*-bit registers or memory locations to represent 2*n*-bit or longer integers or fractions (Fig. 1-7*a*). For **multiple-precision addition or subtraction,** we first add or subtract the least-significant parts and then *add or subtract the contents of the carry flag* before computing the sum or difference of the next-more-significant parts. *Figure 3-8b shows a typical addition program.* Multiple-precision operations are simplified by special instructions like

ADD (SUBTRACT) CARRY INTO   (register)
ADD (SUBTRACT) WITH CARRY (BORROW) INTO ACCUMULATOR
                        from (register or memory location)

A few minicomputers have explicit **DOUBLE MOVE** and **DOUBLE ADD** instructions operating on pairs of registers and/or memory locations.

To *transform a single-precision integer to double-precision format*, we must *extend its sign* into the new most significant register or memory locations. To transform a 2s-complement *fraction*, we simply *clear* the new least significant register or memory location.

Multiple-precision arithmetic shifts can be implemented through successive single-register **ARITHMETIC SHIFT** and **ROTATE** instructions (Rig. 2-4d). Computers with multiplication/division hardware or microprograms usually also have "long" shift instructions for a pair of concatenated registers, like

ARITHMETIC SHIFT COMBINED, n BITS   (register pair)

A right or left shift may be specified, or negative values of the shift count n may signify a right shift (multiplication by a negative power n of 2).

The shift count n may be part of the instruction code, or it may be loaded into a specified register or memory location.

NOTE: As in the case of single-register shifts (Sec. 2-9), multiple-bit shift instructions are rarely faster than combinations of single-register **ARITHMETIC SHIFT** and **ROTATE** instructions (Fig. 2-4d) unless $n > 2$.

2-25. Multiplication and Division (see also Sec. 1-15). Computation of a product $A * B = C$, whether implemented by a hardware/microprogrammed instruction or by a subroutine (Fig. 3-8e), typically starts with the *n-bit multiplicand A* in memory and the *n-bit multiplier B* in a processor register. The *2n-bit (double-precision) result C* is produced in a pair of registers. Similarly, computation of a quotient $C/A = B$ starts with a *2n-bit dividend A* in a register pair and the *n-bit divisor B* in memory; the resulting *n-bit quotient C* and an *n-bit remainder* then appear in the processor registers.

Typical hardware or firmware multiply/divide instruction times are between 4 and 30 memory cycles. This compares with between 25 and 150 cycles required for typical subroutines.

Most mini/microcomputers with "extended arithmetic" implement *signed* 2s-complement *integer* multiplication and division with instructions like

MULTIPLY INTO REGISTER 2   (effective address)
DIVIDE REGISTERS 2, 3 BY   (effective address)

For each particular machine (and also for each multiplication or division subroutine!) you must consult your computer manual to find out precisely

whether multiplication and division are signed or unsigned
how to deal with binary fractions
which registers and/or memory locations contain the various terms and, in particular, the most significant and least significant word of the two-word product or dividend
how overflow, if any, is indicated

These points are discussed in Secs. 1-15c and d.

2-26. Decimal (BCD) Arithmetic. Multidigit **decimal numbers** can be represented by 4-bit BCD groups (half-bytes or "nibbles") for each decimal digit in successive computer words (Sec. 1-10). Most 8-bit microprocessors facilitate decimal addition and subtraction in the 8, 4, 2, 1 BCD code (Table 1-4) by a **half-carry flag** set on carries from the least significant 4-bit BCD group. *One adds multidigit BCD numbers with ordinary binary* **ADD, ADD CARRY,** *and/or* **ADD WITH CARRY** *instructions* (Sec. 2-24) *each followed by a special* **DECIMAL ADJUST ACCUMULATOR** instruction. **DECIMAL ADJUST** corrects each BCD group, starting with the least significant half-byte, by adding $0110_2 = 6_{10}$ to it if the uncorrected binary addition produced a 4-bit number >9 or a carry or half-carry. Note that this will produce correct decimal carries. Figure 3-15d shows a typical microprocessor program.

Negative BCD numbers X are represented by the BCD code for $10^n - X$, where n is the number of decimal digits (**10s-complement code,** see also Sec. 1-5c). This requires an extra BCD-digit group which (just like a 2s-complement sign bit) will be 0 for nonnegative X. To obtain the BCD code for a negative number X as an array of 4-bit BCD, groups, set the least significant group to $1010_2 = 10_{10}$ and all others to $1001_2 = 9_{10}$. Then subtract the BCD representation of $-X$ by ordinary multiprecision 2s-complement binary subtraction (no decimal adjustment will be needed).

This negation procedure also produces the correct BCD code for $-X$ if X is negative. *Subtraction* of a positive or negative BCD number X simply requires BCD addition of $-X$, using multiprecision 2s-complement addition and decimal adjustment, as above. Figure 3-15e shows a typical program.

EXAMPLE: The 10s complement of

$$25 \qquad 0010 \qquad 0101$$

is $100 - 25 = 75$. We obtain this by subtracting the BCD code for 25 from 100 represented in the form

	9×10	+	10
100	1001		1010
-25	-0010		0101
75	0111		0101

We can now add, say, 99 to obtain $99 - 25 = 74$:

$+99$	$+1001$	1001
binary sum:	0000	1110
DECIMAL ADJUST	(carry)	(>9)
$+66$	$+0110$	0110
74	0111	0100

2-27. Floating-Point Operations. Many small digital computers implement floating-point arithmetic operations, such as those needed for FORTRAN or BASIC, with manufacturer-supplied *subroutines*. Other subroutines generate square roots and transcendental functions such as sine and cosine. More elaborate minicomputers and microcomputers have **extended microprogrammed instruction sets** which include the most important floating-point operations, typically only register-to-register floating-point addition, subtraction, multiplication, and division, with single-precision (32-bit, Fig. 1-7*b*) floating-point operands and results moving between two sets of processor registers. More elaborate minicomputers have an optional separate **floating-point processor (FPP)** connected to the main CPU through a special bus. Such floating-point processors have their own multiple registers and arithmetic/logic circuits for 32-bit and 64-bit (double-precision) floating-point operations. FPPs can implement memory-reference operations with various addressing modes. They also have additional instructions, such as FIX, FLOAT, NORMALIZE (Sec. 1-16), FLOATING-POINT COMPARE, and can do double-precision operations.

Accessory FPPs are sold by minicomputer manufacturers and also by other suppliers such as Floating Point Systems, Inc. (Portland, Ore.). In either case, the instruction set intended for a specific minicomputer must be designed to work efficiently with its software, and specifically with its FORTRAN compiler. Preferably, a compiler modification supplied with the FPP will replace floating-point *subroutines* with FPP *instructions*, so that timesaving straight-line code is generated. This is preferable to mere modification of FORTRAN-library subroutines. Since the better FORTRAN compilers cause FORTRAN-expression operands and intermediate results to be stored on a stack in memory, a good FPP ought to provide for stack addressing (Sec. 2-17).

Table 2-2 lists *execution times for floating-point operations* implemented by subroutines, microprogrammed instructions, and floating-point processors. When judging advertised floating-point execution times, you should check whether register-to-register or memory-to-register operations are specified, since storing and retrieving the multiple words needed for floating-point operations can take substantial extra time (2 to 4 memory cycles per operand). Execution of FORTRAN statements like C = A + B can take even longer, since data words are usually moved to and from a software stack where the floating-point subroutine or instruction deals with them.

In general, FORTRAN execution involves many operations other than floating-point arithmetic, so that a $10:1$ reduction in floating-point-arithmetic times will not reduce the total execution time by nearly as much. A more efficient FORTRAN compiler may speed execution more than floating-point hardware. All this depends critically on the specific problem solved.

Since an FPP is a separate processor, the main minicomputer CPU can, at least in principle, execute other instructions (usually I/O instructions) while floating-point operations are in progress.

2-28. 8-Bit Operations with 16-Bit Computers: Byte Manipulation and Byte Addressing. Word-processing and communications applications, as well as translators and other system programs, deal largely with 8-bit bytes

TABLE 2-2. **Examples of Floating-Point Execution Times** (*memory/register* times in microseconds).

A two-word floating-point format is assumed for single-precision operations, except as stated.

	Add	Multiply	Divide
SUBROUTINE			
Varian 620/f	168	177	245
Varian V75 (MOS memory)	125	171	
DEC PDP-11/20	160	204	205
Data General NOVA 3	32	48	59
MICROPROGRAMMED INSTRUCTIONS			
DEC PDP-11/03 (LSI)	97 avg.	90 avg.	151 avg.
DEC PDP-11/40	25 avg.	32 avg.	51 avg.
Interdata 7/32	6–9	13	13–14
Interdata 80	12	19	35
HP 21MX	23–60	33–41	52–56
Varian V75 (MOS memory)	19	39	
FLOATING-POINT PROCESSOR			
DEC PDP-8/FPP-12 (3 words)	31 max	37 max	38 max
DEC PDP-15/FPP-15	19–24	24–29	27–30
DEC PDP-11T55 (core memory)*	6.6 avg.	8.2 avg.	9.2 avg.
DEC PDP-11T55 (bipolar memory)*	5 avg.	6.6 avg.	7.6 avg.
Data General NOVA 3 (MOS memory)†	8.61 avg.	11.7 avg.	14.9 avg.
Data General ECLIPSE†	4 avg.	5.8 avg.	6.7 avg.
Varian V75 (bipolar memory)	3	5	6

* Add 0.2 μsec for memory mapping.

† Add 0.8 μsec if CPU and FPP operations cannot be overlapped.

(ASCII character and parity, Sec. 1-9). Modern 16-bit computers, therefore, have special instructions for clearing, masking, and exchanging 8-bit bytes in processor registers; they may also have a complete set of **ADD, SUBTRACT, COMPARE, AND, XOR**, etc., instructions for *bytes* as well as for 16-bit words. For this reason, all memory addresses in most new 16-bit machines are **byte addresses,** just as in 8-bit computers. *Memory-reference instructions operating on full 16-bit words must usually have even addresses*, while byte instructions can reference odd or even locations.

CAUTION: In some computers, the *most significant* byte of each 16-bit word in memory has the high address, while in other machines the *least significant* byte has the high address; and either the high or the low address could be the word address. *Consult your computer manual.*

Byte addressing can save memory but is not an unmixed blessing (remember that memory is cheap). *Address space is halved* (e.g., 16 bits address 64K bytes rather than 64K *words*); and programs and hardware must increment addresses by two to access successive 16-bit words.

2-29. Input/Output-Related Instructions. Some mini/microcomputers reserve a respectable number of instruction codes for **input/output instructions** intended to select and operate external devices (Fig. 2-6*b* and Chap. 4). Other machines address external devices as though they were memory locations (Secs. 4-5 and 7-1). In addition, each machine has some instructions for controlling its interrupt system, such as **INTERRUPT ON** and **DISABLE INTERRUPT** (Chap. 4).

2-30. Memory-Management Hardware and Other Optional Features. (a) Memory Protection and Mapping. **Memory-protection circuits** prevent user programs (and loader programs, Secs. 5-3 and 5-5) from writing into specified memory locations occupied by system programs, valuable data tables, or other users' programs. The protection system may compare each write address with the contents of "fence registers" loaded with addresses bounding a protected area, or an extra bit in each memory word is set to denote a protected location. The protection circuit prevents writing and interrupts the processor.

More advanced minicomputers obtain memory protection as part of a **memory-mapping system,** which uses status-register bits to associate each program segment or data table with one of, say, 32 **mapping registers.** Mapping registers are either *page registers* (Sec. 2-13) or *base registers* (Sec. 2-16) which modify the normal instruction addresses so as to "map" program segments or data tables into specified **memory partitions.** Programs or data mapped into separate memory partitions will be naturally protected. What is more, the memory addresses defined by the combinations of instruction addresses and page or base addresses can have more than 16 bits, so that, say, *four users of a 16-bit minicomputer would each address separate 32K-word partitions of a 128K-word memory with their 16-bit instruction addresses.*

In a typical memory-mapping system, only the system manager may assign partitions (through "privileged" instructions loading mapping registers and assigning status-register bits to different users). Available minicomputer software will not usually permit user *programs* to cross partition boundaries or to exceed the 32K words (64K bytes) accessible to normal 16-bit instruction addresses. Users may, however, be permitted to access *data* in COMMON areas outside their own partitions (see also Sec. 5-22).

Address modification by the page or base registers of a memory-mapping system does not interfere with normal relative, indexed, indirect, etc., addressing. Base-register mapping permits more flexible partitioning than page-register mapping. But, since the memory-mapping system is usually an optional accessory added to the basic computer, base-address addition typically adds about 100 nsec to each memory-access time, a serious penalty (see also Secs. 7-2 and 7-10).

(b) Other Special Features.   Parity-check interrupt on all word or byte transfers to and from memory requires an extra bit per memory word, plus parity logic (Sec. 1-8).   Solid-state memories (especially dynamic memories) may have additional check bits which permit *single-error correction* as well as *multiple-error detection* (Sec. 1-22).

Power-failure protection/restart circuits cause an interrupt if a power-supply voltage is low.   With *core memories*, power-supply capacitors hold the supply voltage long enough for an interrupt-service routine (Sec. 4-8) to store the contents of all processor registers in memory, so that a *restart routine* can restore the processor status and resume computation when power is again available.   With semiconductor memories, a trickle-charged battery keeps the computer working; if necessary, memory as well as register contents must be saved on a disk or magnetic tape.

MICROPROGRAMMED CONTROL

2-31.   "Horizontal" Microprogramming and Next-Address Logic. A **microprogrammed control unit** (Fig. 2-9*a*) generates the sequence of micro-operations (Secs. 2-8 and 2-20) implementing each computer instruction by fetching successive **microinstructions (control words)** from a fast **control memory.**   The control memory is, typically, a 50- to 250-nsec-cycle *read-only memory.*   Each control word is made up of the explicit control bits

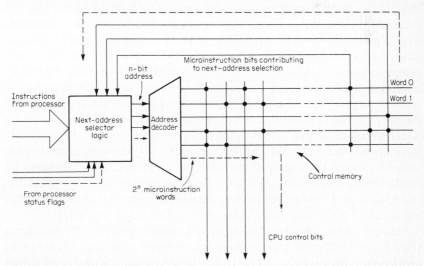

Fig. 2-9*a*. True ("horizontal") microprogrammed control.   The next-address logic selects successive microinstruction words, as determined by the instruction-bit input, processor-flag status, and the microprogram itself.

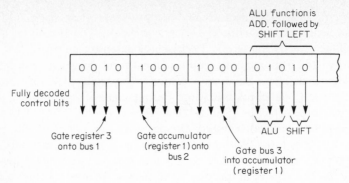

Fig. 2-9b. Microinstruction word for a horizontally microprogrammed three-bus machine (Fig. 2-2). Fully decoded bits in each microinstruction word determine the functions of register gates (multiplexers), ALU/shifter, memory, and I/O during one microcycle. The microinstruction may also specify a literal constant (immediate operand). There may or may not be a field specifying the address of the next microinstruction.

needed to set up register gates, ALU function, and memory or input/output function during one microoperation cycle. To save logic circuits and gate delays, one employs fairly long control-memory words (24 to 80 bits) with fully decoded fields (Fig. 2-9b).

Each user-level computer instruction in the instruction register (Fig. 2-2) is decoded into a *microprogram starting address*, which locates the first microinstruction word of a microprogram in control memory. Each control word can contain a field indicating the address of the next microinstruction (Fig. 2-9a). More frequently, one obtains the next control-word address simply by incrementing a **microprogram counter,** and the special next-address field is used only for *branching* in the control memory. The next-address logic can, in particular, provide for *conditional branching* of the microprogram, say on various processor-flag conditions. Since, moreover, many microprograms contain similar segments, one saves the relatively expensive control memory by employing *subroutine jumps and returns* in control memory. Micro-subroutine return addresses are best saved in a small hardware stack, so that micro-subroutines can be *nested* just like ordinary subroutines (Sec. 2-23). Figure 2-10 illustrates the functions of a complete **next-address logic system** with a microprogram counter and provisions for unconditional or conditional branching and nested subroutines. The last microinstruction of each microprogram returns control to the computer instruction register and resets the microprogram counter (if any).

Control bits which remain the same throughout most of a microprogram (e.g., register-selection bits in register-to-register addition) need not be repeated in successive control words but can be obtained from the processor instruction register, or they may be initially loaded into special "static" control registers (*residual control*).

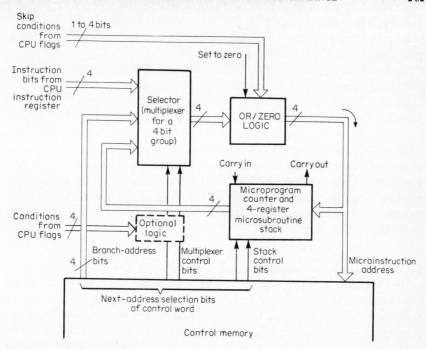

Fig. 2-10. One 4-bit slice of the next-address logic for a microprogram controller (Advanced Micro Devices Am 2909). Each 4-bit address slice can originate from the computer instruction register, from a microprogram counter, from a stacked micro-subroutine return address, or from a microinstruction field (branch address).

2-32. Microprogrammed-Computer Performance. "Vertical" Microprogramming (Refs. 3, 6, 7). **Practically all new small computers employ microprogramming, which replaces much random control logic with inexpensive LSI read-only memory and easily implements large and sophisticated instruction sets.** Instruction-set modifications, moreover, require only reprogramming rather than hardware changes. Microprogramming, in fact, permits a computer to *emulate the entire instruction set of another machine* and thus utilize its software.

On the other hand, the need to access even a fast control memory 4 to 15 times for typical computer instructions makes their execution on a "horizontally" microprogrammed computer *slower* than on an equivalent machine with hard-wired control. Instruction microprograms of inexpensive computers all too often will not fit into even a 1-μsec main-memory cycle. Faster computers, besides using faster logic (Schottky-TTL or ECL), must be designed to reduce the number of microinstructions by doing more *concurrent operations* during each microcycle. This means use of multiple CPU buses (no single ALU-input bus as in Figs. 6-12 and 7-1) and possibly a separate adder for index-register arithmetic (Sec. 6-22). Fast microprogrammed machines can also fetch the next control word while each microoperation is still executing (Sec. 6-22).

To speed up instruction execution, one can combine microprogramming with hard-wired control by letting each microinstruction word generate *a control-bit sequence for not one but several microoperation cycles* in the manner of Fig. 2-3. While more complicated and expensive, this replaces control-memory accesses with faster flip-flop and gate operations. Such **"vertically" microprogrammed computers** usually encode their multicycle microinstructions much like computer instructions for a small "inner" computer which executes the "outer" computer's instructions as control-memory routines. The Interdata Model 80 and 85 minicomputers, for instance, can implement a complete register-to-register multiplication as one microinstruction.

2-33. Extended Instruction Sets and User Microprogramming. The computing speed of a microprogrammed computer can often be substantially improved if there is enough control memory to microprogram not just simple computer instructions but frequently used utility subroutines, such as floating-point arithmetic, trigonometric functions, I/O routines, or even integration routines, Fourier analysis, etc. This is so because efficient microprogram sequences fetched from the relatively fast control memory replace instruction fetches from main memory. ROM-stored microprograms are often referred to as **firmware** (part hardware and part software).

For the best possible utilization of a microprogrammed computer in special user programs, one employs **writable control memory (writable control store, WCS)** which users can load with their own microprograms, usually from a disk or tape. A writable control store is, mainly, a multibit-word, random-access memory with a fast read cycle (70 to 250 nsec) and is therefore not inexpensive ($5,000 to $8,000 for 1,000 32-bit words). With judicious use of micro-subroutines, though, 1,000 WCS words can go a long way.

User microprogramming involves much attention to the details of CPU data transfers, particularly with "horizontal" microprogramming. To simplify user microprogramming, manufacturers typically supply software in the form of a **microassembler** which translates a set of microinstruction mnemonics into a sequence of binary microinstruction words, much as an assembler translates assembly language (Chap. 3).

EXAMPLE: Estimated execution times for computation of sin x by table-lookup and linear interpolation (fixed-point accuracy ± 1 LSB in 16 or 18 bits) by the technique of Fig. 3-7:

DEC PDP-15 assembly-language program	36–38 μsec
DEC PDP-11/40 assembly-language program	30–40 μsec
Varian 73 (horizontal, 64-bit) microprogram	7–8 μsec
Interdata 85 (vertical, 32-bit) microprogram	7 μsec

These execution times should be compared with the FORTRAN single-precision execution times in Table 2-2b; all are faster than CDC-6400 FORTRAN execution!

REFERENCES AND BIBLIOGRAPHY

Instruction sets and instruction timing for the various minicomputers and microcomputers are given in their manufacturers' reference manuals; see also the bibliography for Chap. 1.

General

1. *An Introduction to Microcomputers*, Adam Osborne and Associates, Inc., Berkeley, Calif., 1976.

Microprogrammed Control for Small Computers

2. Design of Microprogrammable Systems, *Application Note* SMS 0052, Signetics Memory Systems, Sunnyvale, Calif., 1970.
3. Ramamoorty, C. V., and M. Tsuchya: A Study of User-Microprogrammable Computers, *Proc. SJCC*, 1970.
4. Dollhoff, T. L.: Microprogrammed Control for Small Computers, *Comput. Des.*, May 1973.
5. Gorman, K.: The Programmable Logic Array: a New Approach to Microprogramming, *EDN*, November 1973.
6. Schultz, G. W.: Optimized Microprogrammed Control Sections for Microprocessors, *Comput. Des.*, April 1974.
7. Johnson, R., and R. E. Merwin: A Comparison of Microprogramming Minicomputer Control Words, *Proc. COMPCON (IEEE)*, Washington, D.C., 1974.
8. Conley, S. W.: A Comparison of Block-Diagram-Language Routines Microprogrammed on Four Different Minicomputers, *CSRL Report* 259, The University of Arizona, 1974.
9. Agrawala, A. K., and T. G. Rauscher: Microprogramming: Perspective and Status, *IEEETC*, August 1974.
10. Weissberger, A. J.: User Microprogram Development for an LSI Processor, *EDN*, December 1974.
11. Mery, H.: Microprogrammable Logic, *Report*, Kitt Peak National Observatory, Tucson, Ariz., 1975.
12. Casaglia, G. F.: Nanoprogramming vs. Microprogramming, *Computer*, January 1976.
13. Raphael, H.: How to Expand a Microcomputer's Memory, *Electronics*, December 23, 1976.

CHAPTER 3

PROGRAMMING WITH ASSEMBLERS AND MACROASSEMBLERS

INTRODUCTION AND SURVEY

Assembly-language programming enables us to obtain the greatest possible efficiency from a given minicomputer or microcomputer, i.e., to optimize computing speed and/or memory requirements. **Sequences of assembly-language statements correspond directly to actual hardware instructions and data-word structures in the memory of a specific machine and thus permit us to exploit its features cleverly.** Such programming detail is avoided by convenient programming languages like FORTRAN, BASIC, and PL/M (Chap. 5 and Appendix A; one FORTRAN statement can replace 10 to 50 assembly-language instructions); but FORTRAN compilers designed to run in the smaller minicomputer memories (4K to 8K) cannot produce very efficient code. Even the improved compilers furnished for larger mini-computers cannot possibly match assembly-language execution speed (see also Sec. 5-27).

Modern symbolic assemblers not only *translate instruction mnemonics into machine code* but also permit *symbolic memory references* by assigning binary location numbers to symbols (Sec. 3-2). The better symbolic assemblers can also *compute addresses by evaluating symbolic expressions* (Sec. 3-3), can *reserve blocks of storage locations* (as well as single storage locations) for data or instructions, and can arrange for storage and formatting of decimal, double-precision, and floating-point data (Sec. 3-5). Good general-purpose assemblers further free the programmer from assigning program pages and work with a companion linking-loader program to facilitate *relocation and linkage of multiple program segments* (Sec. 3-17; see also Sec. 5-5). Finally, *macroassemblers* can generate useful multi-instruction sequences from one-line commands (Sec. 3-21) and, together with *conditional assembly* (Sec. 3-23), can combine some of the programming simplicity of a compiler language with assembly-language efficiency.

With a suitable operating system, assembly-language program segments can be neatly combined with FORTRAN programs (Sec. 3-20) so that even a little knowledge of assembly language can be used to improve important or frequently used routines.

Sections 3-8 to 3-15 illustrate **programming techniques** with examples which can be actually used and modified in practical applications. Sections 3-25 and 3-26 present **programming techniques specifically useful for 4-bit and 8-bit microcomputers.** Input/output programming will be discussed in Chap. 4.

ASSEMBLY LANGUAGES, ASSEMBLERS, AND SOME OF THEIR FEATURES

3-1. Machine Language and Primitive Assembly Language. A typical program sequence for a 12-bit microcomputer, say

2	5	
3	. . .	
4	LOAD INTO ACCUMULATOR (the contents of)	2
5	INVERT ACCUMULATOR	
6	STORE ACCUMULATOR IN	3

specifies the contents of successive memory locations 2, 3, 4, 5, *and* 6. Location 2 contains a *data word* (5) given by our program, but location 3 is only *reserved* for an as yet unspecified data word to be stored there by the program. The program proper (i.e., the first instruction) starts at location 4 (**entry point**). *The program counter will be initially set to* 4 and will step to 5, 6, and on to 7 as each instruction is executed.

Such a program is actually entered into the computer in **binary machine language,** viz.,

```
000   000   000   010        000   000   000   101
000   000   000   011        . . .   . . .   . . .   . . .
000   000   000   100        001   000   000   010
000   000   000   101        111   000   100   001
000   000   000   110        011   000   000   011
```

perhaps from a binary paper tape or from front-panel toggle switches. The first 12-bit word on each line is the memory address of the second word.

The first line again locates the data word **(5)**. The second line reserves location **3** for a data word which is not supplied by the program, but will be stored there at run time by our last instruction; some assemblers would deposit 0 in such a location for the time being.

The first word of the third line is, again, the address of the second word. This time, this stored-program word represents an *instruction code* and, since this is a memory-reference instruction, some address bits needed to determine an effective memory address. In our simple example, the five leading instruction-code bits **001 00** signify **LOAD INTO ACCUMULATOR** with the "page 0" direct-addressing mode (Sec. 2-11). In this case, the remaining seven address bits **0 000 010** directly represent the binary address. The remaining two instructions are similarly translated.

To work with long programs in this machine-language form would be decidedly uncomfortable even if we make the program easier to read and write by using *octal code* or *hexadecimal code* (Sec. 1-6),

(OCTAL)		(HEXADECIMAL)	
0002	0005	002	005
0003	. . . .	003	. . .
0004	1002	004	202
0005	7041	005	E21
0006	3003	006	603

which the machine could decode quite readily from typed input. Short microcomputer routines are quite often written directly in hexadecimal machine language. But practically all computers have **assembler programs** designed to **translate** source programs (see also Sec. 5-4) written in terms of **mnemonic instruction codes**, e.g.,

0002	0005	
0003	. . . .	
0004	LDA	002
0005	NEG	
0006	STO	003

Mnemonics like **LDA**, **NEG**, and **STO** approximate English words; the assembler program translates mnemonics into binary code by table lookup. We have supplied addresses and address bits in octal form, just as in octal machine language.

To improve our primitive assembly language, it would be convenient if we could specify the actual 12-bit *effective address* of each memory-reference instruction, say

0006	STO	0003

Note that now the assembler must not only translate **STO** by table lookup, but it must also *compute* the correct address bits determined by the addressing mode (implicit in **STO** without extra character codes) together with the effective address. If the desired address cannot be reached by direct current-page or relative addressing, the assembler will either stop and print an error message, or (preferably) it will automatically substitute multiword addressing, or possibly indirect addressing (Secs. 2-11 and 2-15). Such simple one-pass assemblers are used with primitive microcomputer development systems (Sec. 5-28) and some small minicomputers. They generate **absolute code;** i.e., program word locations and addresses are fixed by the assembler; the binary program produced by the assembler *must* be loaded starting at the location specified in the source program (see also Sec. 3-17).

3-2. Symbolic Assembly Language. Most practical assemblers are **symbolic assemblers, which permit the user to refer to instruction and operand addresses in terms of symbols.** In a **symbolic assembly language,** the sample program segment of Sec. 3-1 might look like Fig. 3-1. **Each symbol (a string of up to 5 or 6 alphanumeric characters) represents a location (symbolic memory address).** The word in the **location-tag field (label field)** of a line represents the location of the corresponding instruction or data word. *Unless the contrary is specified,* consecutive lines still represent consecutive program words. Therefore, if **INPUT** represents location **2**, **RESLT** *must* represent location **3**, **START** *must* represent location **4**, and the last two instruction words *must* go into locations **5** and **6**, *although we omitted their location tags in Fig. 3-1.*

The first pass of a symbolic assembler scans the user's source program and creates a **symbol table** which lists all user symbols defined as location tags together with their location numbers relative to a starting address. Symbolic instruction addresses as well as mnemonic instruction codes can then be translated by table-lookup operations. Taking due account of each addressing mode used, the assembler still has to compute the address bits

INPUT	0005		/ Data
RESLT	...		/ Reserved for result
START	LDA	INPUT	/ Get data word
	NEG		/ Invert it
	STO	RESLT	/ Deposit result
Location-tag field (label field)	Instruction code (if any)	Instruction address (if any)	Comment field
	Instruction or data word (2 fields)		

Fig. 3-1. The program segment of Sec. 3-1 written in symbolic assembly language. Note that each line **(assembly-language statement)** has four **fields,** all but one of which could be empty. When such statements are typed or punched (one to a teletypewriter line or punched card), the fields must be separated by spaces, teletypewriter tabs, or other *field delimiters* (colons, slashes, etc.) so that the assembler can recognize the end of each field.

PROGRAMMER					DATE		PAGE	
PROGRAM							CHARGE	
LOCATION ⊕	OPERATION ⊕	ADDRESS, X			⊕ COMMENTS			⊕ₑ
1 4	6 10	12			30			72 7
S T R T	L D A	C∅NS			L∅AD C∅NSTANT			

Fig. 3-2. Some people like to use *coding forms* similar to the one shown for assembly-language programming. The column numbers indicated on the form are for punched cards. In teletypewriter-prepared programs, the fields are delimited by tabs, colons, slashes, etc. (*Honeywell Information Systems.*)

for each memory-reference instruction. Most symbolic assemblers will automatically introduce indirect or two-word addressing when a symbolic address is not within reach of one-word paged or relative addressing (Secs. 2-13 and 2-14).

Multiply defined symbols will stop the assembly process and/or produce an error printout (Fig. 3-3). Some assemblers also indicate an error if a symbolic address has no location-tag counterpart (*undefined symbol*). A few assemblers, though, may automatically supply each undefined symbolic address with a corresponding storage location at the end of the program so that the programmer is relieved of this task. You can see that a good symbolic assembler is a fairly complex system program.

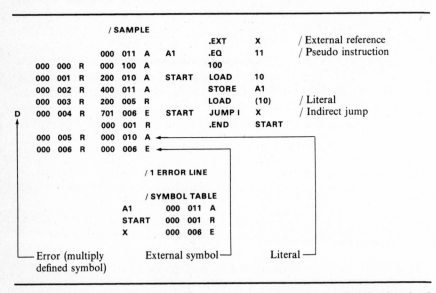

Fig. 3-3. Listing produced by a symbolic assembler. The assembler has started at location 0 and has marked each location and address as absolute *A*, relocatable *R*, or external *E* for the linking loader (Sec. 3-18). Words which do not contain addresses are marked absolute (their *locations* may be relocatable). An *error line* has been found and marked with an error code by the assembler.

NOTE: Precisely, **A** represents the assembler-determined **address** of the memory location whose **contents (A)** at run time will be the **value** of a constant *A* or **values** of a variable *A*.

If requested by a front-panel switch setting or typed command, the assembler will print an **assembly listing** in an extra pass. The listing shows *the user's symbolic source program and the resulting octal machine code side by side* with some extra annotations (Fig. 3-3; see also Sec. 3-4). The assembler can also produce a **symbol-table printout** for reference (either in alphabetical or numerical order). You should consult your minicomputer manual for the *maximum number of symbols* and the *maximum number of program lines* which can be handled with a given computer memory.

3-3. Symbolic Expressions and Current-Location References. Since correct addressing requires computations at assembly time in any case, many symbolic assemblers improve programming convenience further by permitting **symbolic expressions** in address fields. For example,

03	ADD INTO ACCUMULATOR	SYM	/ Adds 000 173
	STORE ACCUMULATOR IN	LEAP − HOP + 2	/ Address is **06**
HOP	JUMP TO	SYM + 2	/ Address is 11_8
	000 000		
SYM	000 173		
	101 201		
LEAP	JUMP IF ACCUMULATOR NEGATIVE SYM − 4		/ Address is **03**

Note carefully that each expression involves **addresses** and **not** data. Integers will be interpreted as *octal* unless the contrary is stated (Sec. 3-5c). Such more elaborate assemblers usually make *two* passes through the source program, plus an optional listing pass.

Some assemblers also admit *multiplication and division* in address expressions, but these operations may not have the customary precedence, and no parentheses may be allowed. Thus, **A + B*C** *may* be interpreted as **(A + B)*C** in an address expression; *consult your assembler manual.* Some assemblers also permit bit-by-bit **AND, OR,** and **XOR** operations with symbolic-address words.

NOTE: Numerical values of symbols and expressions are necessarily fixed at *assembly time.* The program can only change the *contents* of symbolically addressed locations at run time.

As a further convenience, it is usually possible to **reference the location of the current instruction,** say as **.,** so that

03	LOAD ACCUMULATOR	. + 3	/ Address is **06**
BOUND	JUMP IF ACCUMULATOR ZERO	. − 1	/ Address is **03**
	JUMP	. + A − 1	/ Address is **A + 4**

NOTE: For the sake of clarity, *we have treated every source program instruction as one location (word) in memory* throughout this book, unless the contrary is specifically stated. Practically all microcomputer assemblers and many minicomputer assemblers count memory locations in *bytes*, and a two-byte, three-byte, etc., instruction counts as 2, 3, etc., locations in determining expressions like **SYM – 4** or **.+7**. *Be sure to check your assembler manual on the manner used to count locations.*

3-4.   Immediate Addressing and Literals.   Most computers permit you to specify the *operand* (rather than the address) of a memory-reference instruction through *immediate addressing* (Sec. 2-18), e.g.,

LOAD ACCUMULATOR, IMMEDIATE   010 711

where **010 711**$_8$ is the actual number loaded, *not* an address. Similarly, **LOAD ACCUMULATOR, IMMEDIATE SYMBL + 2** loads the *numerical value* of the symbolic address **SYMBL + 2**, *not* its contents.

For computers without true hardware immediate addressing, a symbolic assembler may implement memory-reference operations on **literals** like **(010 711)** or **(SYMBL + 2)**, which are defined as follows:

(010 711) is a symbolic memory location *which contains* **010 711**.
(SYMBL + 2) is a symbolic memory location *which contains the numerical value of* **SYMBL + 2**.

The assembler automatically assembles memory locations containing each literal value at the end of the program (Fig. 3-3). It follows that

LOAD ACCUMULATOR   (010 711)

actually loads **010 711**. Note also that

LOAD ACCUMULATOR, INDIRECT VIA   (010 711)

produces the same result in the accumulator as

LOAD ACCUMULATOR   010 711

3-5.   Pseudo Instructions.   (a) Introduction.   The assembler can perform still more operations to improve programming convenience. To request **operations to be done at assembly time,** we enter **pseudo instructions (assembler directives)** into the source program. To distinguish pseudo instructions from true instructions (which directly correspond to operations at *run time*), we will write a word in each pseudo instruction with a preceding dot (**.**). The remainder of this section will help you to interpret advertised lists of assembler features.

(b) Pseudo Instructions for Defining and Redefining Symbols.   As we have seen, one can *define* a symbol (i.e., give it a numerical value) by using it as a location tag (label). Another way to define a symbol is through a pseudo instruction (assignment statement) like

SYMBL1   .EQ   SYMBL2 + SYMBL3 – 1

which assigns the value of the expression on the right to **SYMBL1** in the *following* program statements. Such assignment can be used to define or redefine a symbol before or after it is used as a label or address. Note, however, that with the usual two-pass assembler

```
SYMBL1    .EQ    7
SYMBL2    .EQ    SYMBL1-2
```

is legal, but

```
SYMBL2    .EQ    SYMBL1-2
SYMBL1    .EQ    7
```

will cause an error message ("UNDEFINED SYMBOL") unless **SYMBL1** was defined (as a label, or by another assignment statement) earlier in the program.

    (c) Pseudo Instructions for Defining Data Types. Many assemblers normally interpret integers in source-program addresses, expressions, or data as **single-precision octal integers,** so a statement like

```
ALFA    017002
```

reserves *one* memory location. Especially when both bytes and two-byte words are used, **word** and **byte** locations would be respectively reserved by statements like

```
ALFA    .WORD    017002
CHAR    .BYTE    00012
```

Similarly,

```
BETA    .DOUBLE    7173514
```

could reserve space for a **double-precision number** (two words) in locations **BETA, BETA + 1**, or four bytes. If we enter no specific integer, e.g.,

```
C4    .BYTE
```

most assemblers will enter zeros, which are then replaced by data words during computation.

    As we noted, most assemblers interpret integers as octal (or possibly hexadecimal; check the manual) unless told otherwise. More elaborate assemblers (including microcomputer cross assemblers Sec. 5-29) permit the user to specify (and change) the integer radix to be used by statements such as **.DECIMAL, .HEX**, etc. Some assemblers also let you label individual integers with a desired radix, e.g., **10011H** $= 10011_{16}$ (as in PL/M, Appendix A). Some minicomputer assemblers can also recognize, and reserve, locations for *floating-point data.*

The pseudo instruction **.ASCII** followed by alphanumeric text (usually delimited by quotation marks) causes ASCII characters to be packed into successive computer words, where they can be accessed, for example, by output routines for printing error messages, say

.ASCII   'BOOBOO IN LINE 12'

(d) Pseudo Instructions for Reserving Storage Blocks. A pseudo instruction like

SYMBL   .BLOCK   N

where N is a positive integer, **reserves N storage locations, starting with the location SYMBL,** for data or instruction words. **N** can be a symbol or, in fact, an expression; the block size is, in any case, given its numerical value at assembly time. The statement

START   .BLKB   M

would similarly save M *byte* locations.

Some assemblers automatically reset all reserved locations to 0 if their contents are not specified. Some assemblers can also reserve blocks *ending* at a specified location.

NOTE: Locations reserved for noninstruction words *must be situated at the beginning of a program, at its end, or immediately following an unconditional-jump instruction.* Otherwise, the machine might execute a noninstruction as the program counter advances, with regrettable results!

(e) Pseudo Instructions for Controlling the Assembly Process. The pseudo instruction

.ORIGIN   (address)

causes the subsequent program to start (or continue) from the specified address (which can be relocatable, Sec. 3-18).

Every assembly-language source program *must* terminate with the pseudo instruction

.END

to tell the assembler that no more program statements follow. If the program segment to be assembled is a *main program* (not a subroutine to be entered from another program, Sec. 3-12), we append the starting address **(entry point)** to the **.END** statement, e.g.,

.END   START

so that a loader program (Sec. 3-19) can insert a jump to the starting address and a **HALT** for convenient restarting. With simpler operating systems, absolute starting addresses are set up with front-panel switches (Sec. 5-3).

NOTE: The *pseudo instruction* .END signifies the end of *assembly.* *Program* execution may end with the *instruction* HALT or with a jump to an executive program.

(f) Other Pseudo Instructions. Additional types of pseudo instructions are used to *link programs* (Secs. 3-17 and 3-19) and to define *macros* (Sec. 3-21) and *conditional assembly* (Sec. 3-23). Some assemblers also have pseudo instructions *to control or format listings.*

3-6. The .REPEAT Pseudo Instruction. The pseudo instruction .REPEAT is a program-writing convenience. The statement

.REPEAT   m,n

where the **count** m is a positive integer and the **increment** n is a signed integer (positive, negative, or zero), causes the immediately following program word (instruction or data word) to be repeated m times with $0, n, 2n, \ldots, (m-1)n$ added to successive words. For example,

```
.REPEAT    3,2
0001
.REPEAT    2,-1
0002
```

generates

```
0001
0003
0005
0002
0001
```

Note that addresses as well as data can be incremented. Some assemblers have more elaborate .REPEAT pseudo operations capable of repeating *groups* of words.

INTRODUCTION TO PROGRAMMING

3-7. Program Documentation: Use of Comments. Unless you intersperse your program statements with plenty of explanatory comments, not even you yourself (and surely no one else) will be able to understand your program one month later. This is true for FORTRAN programs and any other programs as well as for assembly-language programs.

Comments are not restricted to the comments fields of assembly-language statements; the assembler will recognize any line preceded by / (or similar delimiters such as : , *, etc.) as a comment line, say

/ THIS IS A COMMENT LINE

Such comment lines can also be used for *program titles.* Comments will not cause any program words to be assembled, but comments will be reproduced in the assembler listing for future reference.

Another useful trick is to *indent* the second line and all following lines of multiline comments. Also, in assembly-language programs involving fixed-point fractions (Sec. 1-5), it helps to utilize the FORTRAN convention reserving symbols beginning with I, J, K, L, M, N addresses of *integers.*

3-8. Branching and Flow Charts. Many minicomputers do not have conditional-jump instructions but combine unconditional jumps with conditional skips (which fit better into short instruction words):

```
/ THE FOLLOWING COMPARISON OF THE CONTENTS OF
/ LOCATIONS A AND B IS AN EXAMPLE OF A
/ THREE-WAY DECISION USING CONDITIONAL SKIPS
TEST    LOAD ACCUMULATOR                A
        SUBTRACT INTO ACCUMULATOR      B / A − B in  accumulator
        SKIP IF ACCUMULATOR POSITIVE     / A > B?
        SKIP                             / No, test for A = B
        JUMP TO                       POS / Yes, branch to POS
        SKIP IF ACCUMULATOR ZERO         / A = B?
        JUMP TO                       NEG / No, branch to NEG
ZERO    (program continues)              / Yes, go on
```

JUMP is likely to be a two-word (or three-byte) instruction which can address all of memory.   More modern microcomputers and minicomputers have one-word (or two-byte) short-branch instructions (Sec. 2-22); if the locations **POS** and **NEG** are within $-128 + 127$ bytes of the branch instruction, our program would simplify to

```
        LOAD ACCUMULATOR                A
        SUBTRACT INTO ACCUMULATOR       B
        BRANCH IF ACCUMULATOR POSITIVE  POS
        BRANCH IF ACCUMULATOR NEGATIVE  NEG
ZERO    (program continues)
```

which is shorter and also easier to understand.   For longer jumps, we conditionally short-branch to a nearby location containing a **JUMP** instruction.

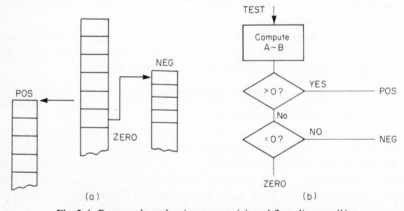

Fig. 3-4. Program branches in memory (*a*), and flow diagram (*b*).

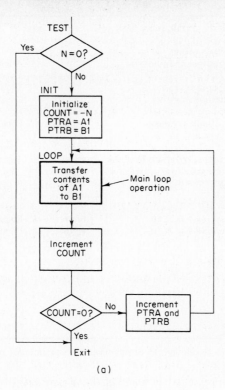

(a)

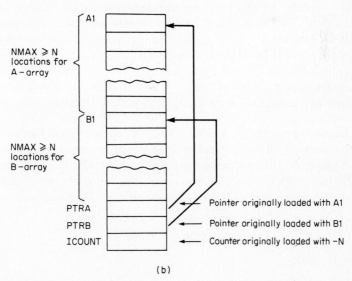

(b)

Fig. 3-5a, b. Flow chart for a simple program loop (a) and relationship of arrays and pointers in memory for the program of Fig. 3-5c in (b).

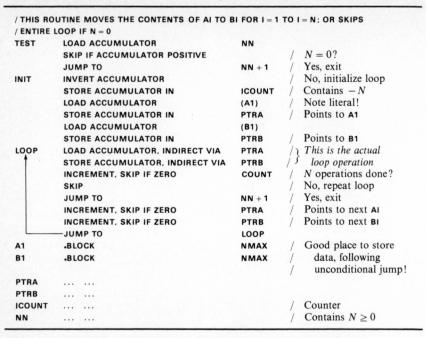

```
/ THIS ROUTINE MOVES THE CONTENTS OF AI TO BI FOR I = 1 TO I = N; OR SKIPS
/ ENTIRE LOOP IF N = 0
TEST    LOAD ACCUMULATOR                      NN
        SKIP IF ACCUMULATOR POSITIVE                    /   N = 0?
        JUMP TO                               NN + 1    /   Yes, exit
INIT    INVERT ACCUMULATOR                              /   No, initialize loop
        STORE ACCUMULATOR IN                  ICOUNT    /   Contains − N
        LOAD ACCUMULATOR                      (A1)      /   Note literal!
        STORE ACCUMULATOR IN                  PTRA      /   Points to A1
        LOAD ACCUMULATOR                      (B1)
        STORE ACCUMULATOR IN                  PTRB      /   Points to B1
LOOP    LOAD ACCUMULATOR, INDIRECT VIA        PTRA      /⎫  This is the actual
        STORE ACCUMULATOR, INDIRECT VIA       PTRB      /⎭    loop operation
        INCREMENT, SKIP IF ZERO               COUNT     /   N operations done?
        SKIP                                            /   No, repeat loop
        JUMP TO                               NN + 1    /   Yes, exit
        INCREMENT, SKIP IF ZERO               PTRA      /   Points to next AI
        INCREMENT, SKIP IF ZERO               PTRB      /   Points to next BI
        JUMP TO                               LOOP
A1      .BLOCK                                NMAX      /   Good place to store
B1      .BLOCK                                NMAX      /      data, following
                                                        /      unconditional jump!
PTRA    ... ...
PTRB    ... ...
ICOUNT  ... ...                                         /   Counter
NN      ... ...                                         /   Contains N ≥ 0
```

Fig. 3-5c. A simple loop programmed *without* an index register.

A *flow chart is a topological model of the actual paths traced through the computer memory*, as the program executes instructions along different branches (Fig. 3-4); flow charts can be helpful with programs involving multiple decisions and loops (Sec. 3-9 and Fig. 3-5a).   The source program itself, on the other hand, is a *one-dimensional* rendering of each path in turn, together with listings of memory locations reserved for data and addresses (these do *not* appear on flow charts).   It can be helpful to supplement your flow chart with a **memory map** listing data-storage locations (Fig. 3-5b).

3-9. Simple Arrays, Loops, and Iteration.   A **one-dimensional array** of, say, 1,000 variables $A1, A2, \ldots, A1000$ will be stored in the computer memory as an example of a **data structure** arranged to simplify access to the data during common operations with this type of data.   For our one-dimensional array, we simply reserve 1,000 consecutive memory locations with

```
              .DECIMAL
        A1    .BLOCK      1000
```

or (in octal code)

```
        N .EQ 1750   / Permits N to
    A1    .BLOCK   N/   be changed at assembly
```

(Sec. 3-5). You should always check carefully whether the starting value of the array **index** I in AI is $I = 1$ or $I = 0$. This is a frequent source of errors.

Programs for typical array operations, e.g., moving the contents of **AI** to **BI**, or

$$CI = AI + BI \qquad I = 1, 2, \ldots, N$$

$$S = \sum_{I=1}^{N} (AI)(BI)$$

require execution of a number of instructions proportional to N. Since memory capacity is limited, it is not just convenient but quite necessary to use **program loops,** which repeat the same instructions with successively incremented addresses **AI**, **BI**, and/or **CI**; a *counting operation* will be set up to advise us when the loop has run N times (Fig. 3-5).

Figure 3-5c shows how a simple loop can be programmed for a primitive minicomputer *without index registers.* Some minicomputers (PDP-8 series) would simplify the incrementation of **PTRA** and **PTRB** by *autoindexing* (Sec. 2-15); the **ISZ** instruction would still be needed to increment **COUNT** since it is necessary to sense when N operations have been completed. But *by far more efficient loop operations are possible with an index register.* Figure 3-6 shows how *a single index register is used to step two data addresses as well as the loop count.* Many computers, though, will require separate instructions for stepping an index register and testing it for 0 (see also Sec. 2-1b).

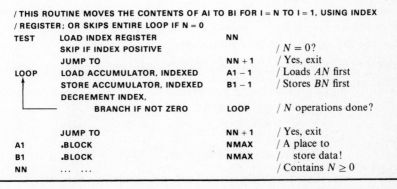

```
/ THIS ROUTINE MOVES THE CONTENTS OF AI TO BI FOR I = N TO I = 1, USING INDEX
/ REGISTER; OR SKIPS ENTIRE LOOP IF N = 0
TEST     LOAD INDEX REGISTER           NN
         SKIP IF INDEX POSITIVE                   / N = 0?
         JUMP TO                       NN + 1     / Yes, exit
LOOP     LOAD ACCUMULATOR, INDEXED     A1 – 1     / Loads AN first
         STORE ACCUMULATOR, INDEXED    B1 – 1     / Stores BN first
         DECREMENT INDEX,
             BRANCH IF NOT ZERO        LOOP       / N operations done?

         JUMP TO                       NN + 1     / Yes, exit
A1       .BLOCK                        NMAX       / A place to
B1       .BLOCK                        NMAX       /    store data!
NN       ...  ...                                 / Contains N ≥ 0
```

Fig. 3-6. This program uses an index register to deal with the same simple loop, starting at the *bottom* of each array. Indexed load and store instructions will each require *two* 16-bit words. Note the use of the **DECREMENT INDEX, BRANCH IF NOT ZERO** instruction.

We have stepped the loop index *after* each actual loop operation. We could do this *before* the loop operation instead. Note also:

1. The loop index (or **COUNT**, **PTRA**, and **PTRB** in Fig. 3-5*a*) must be *initialized* before the actual loop processing begins. While assembly-language statements like

COUNT   000   000

would initialize the loop before it runs *for the first time* after assembly, subsequent runs would *not* be initialized!
2. Since a loop may be traversed many times, *it is uneconomical to include unnecessary operations in the loop.* For instance, in the computation of

$$\sum_{i=1}^{n} ab_i = a \sum_{i=1}^{n} b_i$$

the multiplication by a is common to all terms and should *not* be included in the loop. The same is, of course, true in FORTRAN, BASIC, and PL/M programming.

An array may well contain two-word or multiword items, such as multiple-precision or floating-point data. In such situations, index-register incrementing becomes only a little more complicated. To access, say, every fourth word of an array *without index registers*, however, is a more cumbersome (but still straightforward) operation.

Every loop must contain a test to branch out of the loop when a desired condition is met. In our simple example, this condition was the completion of exactly N elementary operations, but a loop could be terminated by other conditions, e.g., when a sum exceeds a specified value or when an error becomes small enough.

In fact, *the loop technique is in no way restricted to operations* with elements of stored arrays; array elements could be *generated* by the loop. This is the case for *iterative-approximation operations.*

3-10. More Data Structures.   (a) Two-Dimensional Arrays. Two-dimensional arrays, like

A11	A12	...	A1N
A21	A22	...	A2N
...	...	...	...
AM1	AM2	...	AMN

($M \times N$ array), are usually stored in the computer memory as one-dimensional arrays, say *by rows,* as

A1, A2, ..., A(MN)

where the single subscript J in AJ is related to the subscripts I and K of AIK by

$$J = (K - 1)N + I \qquad I = 1, 2, \ldots, N; \; K = 1, 2, \ldots, M \qquad (3\text{-}1)$$

To access the location **AIK** of the array element AIK, the computer will have to add $J - 1$ to the address **A11** (starting address), i.e.,

$$\textbf{AIK} = \textbf{A11} + (K - 1)N + I - 1 \quad I = 1, 2, \ldots, N; \; K = 1, 2, \ldots, M \qquad (3\text{-}2)$$

Larger digital computers permit computation of such addresses by *double indexing* (adding contents of two index registers), but this is *not* possible with most minicomputers even if two index registers are available. Accessing of the individual array elements AIK (as in matrix computations) will, therefore, be somewhat cumbersome unless *postindexing* (Sec. 2-16) is available (as in the Honeywell 316/516 and the Varian Data Systems 620/f and 73/4). In that case, $(K - 1)N$ can be generated in the index register by successive additions of N, while $A11 + I - 1$ will appear in an indirectly addressed memory location which is incremented to advance I.

NOTE: As with one-dimensional arrays, you should make sure that row and column subscripts of given arrays really start with 1 and not with 0.

(b) Stacks (Pushdown Lists). A practically important class of data structures are **stacks,** i.e., arrays permitting words or subarrays **(items)** to be adjoined, removed, or accessed from the top of the stack *on a last-in–first-out basis.* Such stacks are also known as **pushdown lists** or **LIFO (last-in–first-out) lists.** Stacks are especially useful for orderly intermediate-result storage and for various systems-programming applications (Secs. 2-17, 3-16, 4-9, and 4-12).

(c) Other Data Structures (see Refs. 1 to 4). Structures of multiple (and possibly variable-length) subarrays which can be *created* and *deleted* in the course of computation are often organized as various types of **(linked) lists,** rather than as multidimensional arrays, which might waste permanently assigned storage space. A **(linked) list** or **chain** is an ordered set of word arrays **(items),** *each comprising a pointer to the next item in the list or to a directory array of item starting addresses.* Individual-item arrays can be located *wherever memory space is available.* One usually keeps a separate **list of available space;** an item is deleted from this available-space list whenever an item is added to another list, and vice versa.

List structures are used to store and access program lines (character strings) in editing programs, catalog and inventory items, bibliographical references, graphic-display items (Sec. 4-29), and rows or columns of sparse matrices (i.e., matrices with many 0 elements—this would make simple two-dimensional-array storage uneconomical). List items can also contain *backward pointers* to preceding items, pointers to subitems, and/or counters indicating sizes of item arrays. Reference 4 is a good introduction to your study of list processing, which has opened up many interesting new programming techniques.

3-11.   Miscellaneous Programming Techniques.   (a) Table-Lookup Operations.   Section 3-8 illustrates a *triple* branch implemented with conditional skip-jump instructions.   When a decision has more than a few possible outcomes, though, it may be best to store the jump-destination addresses in an array **(jump table)** addressed in the manner of Sec. 3-9.   The result of each decision will correspond to the value of an **array index** I placed in an index register or address pointer to access an address in the array.   If the decision depends on more than one factor, we can use a multidimensional-table array with an index computation like the one in Sec. 3-10a.

Such table-lookup operations are, of course, precisely those needed to look up values of tabulated numerical functions.   To reduce the size of the function table needed to compute a continuously differentiable function with suitable accuracy, we can *combine table lookup and interpolation.*

Figure 3-7 illustrates a high-speed method for **fixed-point table-lookup/interpolation approximation** of a function $Y = F(X)$ in the form

$$Y \approx (Y_{i+1} - Y_i) \frac{X - X_i}{X_{i+1} - X_i} + Y_i \tag{3-3}$$

where scaled function values $Y_i = F(X_i)$ are tabulated for $2^N + 1$ uniformly spaced breakpoint abscissas

$$X_i = 2^{1-N} i - 1 \qquad i = 0, 1, 2, \ldots, 2^N \tag{3-4}$$

between $X_0 = -1$ and $X_{2^N} = 1$ (Fig. 3-7a).   The program of Fig. 3-7b begins with the n-bit 2s-complement fraction

$$X = X_i + (X - X_i)$$

in the form

Sign	$(N-1)$ bits	$(n-N)$ bits

represents X_i represents $X - X_i$

Note that the right-hand $(n - N)$ bits represent the nonnegative difference $X - X_i$ needed for interpolation; *we shift them into a second accumulator* (combined shift, Sec. 2-9) and save them for multiplication.   The sign bit of X_i is complemented to form the breakpoint index i, which is added to the table origin **YO** (location of Y_0) to produce a pointer to Y_i. With typical minicomputers, the entire operation requires under 40 memory cycles (typically less than 35 μsec).   The program can be generalized for non-uniform breakpoint spacing and functions of two or more variables (Ref. 19).

(b) Program Flags.   A **program flag (program switch)** stores the result of a binary or multiple branching decision to implement the actual branching

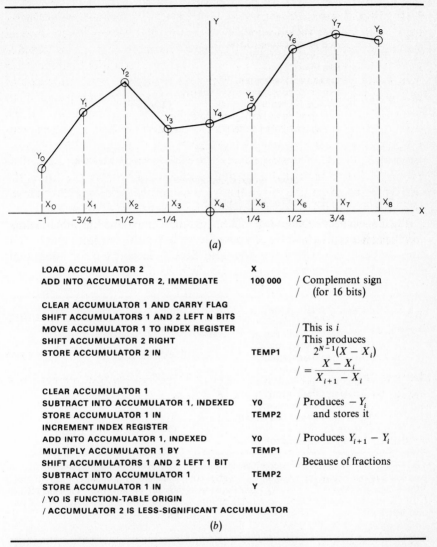

(a)

LOAD ACCUMULATOR 2	X	
ADD INTO ACCUMULATOR 2, IMMEDIATE	100 000	/ Complement sign
		/ (for 16 bits)
CLEAR ACCUMULATOR 1 AND CARRY FLAG		
SHIFT ACCUMULATORS 1 AND 2 LEFT N BITS		
MOVE ACCUMULATOR 1 TO INDEX REGISTER		/ This is i
SHIFT ACCUMULATOR 2 RIGHT		/ This produces
STORE ACCUMULATOR 2 IN	TEMP1	/ $2^{N-1}(X - X_i)$
		/ $= \dfrac{X - X_i}{X_{i+1} - X_i}$
CLEAR ACCUMULATOR 1		
SUBTRACT INTO ACCUMULATOR 1, INDEXED	Y0	/ Produces $-Y_i$
STORE ACCUMULATOR 1 IN	TEMP2	/ and stores it
INCREMENT INDEX REGISTER		
ADD INTO ACCUMULATOR 1, INDEXED	Y0	/ Produces $Y_{i+1} - Y_i$
MULTIPLY ACCUMULATOR 1 BY	TEMP1	
SHIFT ACCUMULATORS 1 AND 2 LEFT 1 BIT		/ Because of fractions
SUBTRACT INTO ACCUMULATOR 1	TEMP2	
STORE ACCUMULATOR 1 IN	Y	
/ Y0 IS FUNCTION-TABLE ORIGIN		
/ ACCUMULATOR 2 IS LESS-SIGNIFICANT ACCUMULATOR		

(b)

Fig. 3-7. Table-lookup/interpolation approximation of a function $Y = F(X)$ with 2^N equal breakpoint intervals (Sec. 3-11b). To make this useful routine reentrant (Sec. 3-16), replace the temporary-storage locations TEMP1 and TEMP2 with processor registers, or use a stack in memory.

later on in another part or parts of the program. An example is precomputation and storage of decisions for use inside loops (Ref. 3) to free the latter of repeated decision making. The decision result can be stored in a memory location, in a processor flag (if it is not otherwise in use) or, if possible, in an index register.

EXAMPLE:

```
LOAD ACCUMULATOR              A1
ADD INTO ACCUMULATOR          A2
ADD INTO ACCUMULATOR          A3
SUBTRACT                      B
CLEAR INDEX REGISTER
SKIP IF ACCUMULATOR NOT POSITIVE
INCREMENT INDEX REGISTER        / Positive
SKIP IF ACCUMULATOR NEGATIVE
INCREMENT INDEX REGISTER        / Positive or zero
```

The index register now reads 0, 1, or 2 if A1 + A2 + A3 − B was negative, zero, or positive, respectively. The desired three-way branch can be obtained now or later with

JUMP, INDEXED, INDIRECT VIA   PTR

The program will jump via PTR, PTR + 1, or PTR + 2.

(c) Miscellaneous Examples. The program segments of Fig. 3-8 illustrate useful programming techniques possible with typical microcomputer and minicomputer instruction sets (see also Secs. 3-25 and 6-5 for additional examples illustrating programs for specific machines).

```
LOAD ACCUMULATOR              A
SHIFT LEFT, UNSIGNED
STORE ACCUMULATOR IN          TEMP
LOAD ACCUMULATOR              B
SHIFT LEFT, UNSIGNED
CLEAR CARRY FLAG
ADD INTO ACCUMULATOR          TEMP
LOAD ACCUMULATOR              A
ADD INTO ACCUMULATOR          B
SKIP ON CARRY FLAG CLEAR
JUMP TO                       OFLO    / Overflow-error routine
STORE ACCUMULATOR IN          C
```

Fig. 3-8a. Overflow check for 2s-complement addition $(A + B = C)$ on a machine having no overflow flag but only a carry flag (link) which is complemented by accumulator carries (e.g., PDP-8; see also Sec. 2-7). Carries from the most significant bit and from the sign bit are both allowed to complement the carry flag in turn, so that they are effectively XORed (see also Sec. 1-15b).

```
CLEAR CARRY FLAG
LOAD ACCUMULATOR              A2
ADD INTO ACCUMULATOR          B2
STORE ACCUMULATOR IN          A2
LOAD ACCUMULATOR              A1
SKIP IF NO CARRY                / If available, use ADD WITH CARRY
INCREMENT ACCUMULATOR          /   or ADD CARRY instruction
ADD INTO ACCUMULATOR          B1
STORE ACCUMULATOR IN          A1
```

Fig. 3-8b. Double-precision addition on a minicomputer without DOUBLE ADD or ADD CARRY instructions. A double-precision number is added from B1, B2 into A1, A2. A1 and B1 hold signs and most significant bits. No overflow check is included.

```
/ ONE-ACCUMULATOR MACHINE          / TWO-ACCUMULATOR MACHINE
/ NEEDS 12 CYCLES                  / NEEDS 8 CYCLES
    LOAD ACCUMULATOR        A          LOAD ACCUMULATOR 1        A
    STORE ACCUMULATOR IN    TEMP       LOAD ACCUMULATOR 2        B
    LOAD ACCUMULATOR        B          STORE ACCUMULATOR 1 IN    B
    STORE ACCUMULATOR IN    A          STORE ACCUMULATOR 2 IN    A
    LOAD ACCUMULATOR        TEMP
    STORE ACCUMULATOR IN    B
```

Fig. 3-8c. Multiple accumulators can often save time-consuming memory references by serving as quickly accessible temporary-storage locations. As an example, the Data General NOVA/ SUPERNOVA manual compares routines for interchanging the contents of two memory locations A, B (e.g., in sorting operations).

```
    LOAD ACCUMULATOR, IMMEDIATE    777000    / Load mask
    AND INTO ACCUMULATOR           Y         / Mask 9 low-order bits
    STORE ACCUMULATOR IN           TEMP      / Save result
    LOAD ACCUMULATOR               X
    SHIFT RIGHT 9 BITS, UNSIGNED             / Shift right
    ADD INTO ACCUMULATOR           TEMP      / Combine with Y
```

(Store in array, or output and display packed word)

Fig. 3-8d. This routine truncates two 18-bit numbers X, Y to 9 bits and packs the truncated words into one 18-bit word for a cathode-ray-tube display. Y is truncated by masking, and X is truncated by shifting.

```
/ N-BIT UNSIGNED-INTEGER MULTIPLICATION; RESULT
/    IN R1 (HIGH) AND R2.  USES REGISTER-
/    TO-REGISTER ADDITION FOR SPEED.
         LOAD REGISTER 3              M1      / Multiplicand
         LOAD REGISTER 4, IMMEDIATE   N       / Loop counter
         CLEAR                        R2
         LOAD REGISTER 1              M2      / Multiplier
LOOP     ARITHMETIC SHIFT LEFT        R2      / Test multiplier bit,
         ROTATE LEFT                  R1      /    shift sum
         BRANCH IF CARRY CLEAR        BITO    / Multiplier bit = 0?
         ADD INTO REGISTER 2          R3      / No, add multiplicand
         ADD CARRY                    R1      / Double-precision
BITO     DECREMENT                    R4      / Decrement bit count
         BRANCH IF NOT ZERO           LOOP    / Done?
```

Fig. 3-8e. A program for multiplication of unsigned N-bit binary integers stored in memory locations M1 and M2. The 32-bit result will be in the concatenated processor registers R1 and R2, with the least-significant part in R2 (see also Sec. 1-15c).

SUBROUTINES AND
DATA-TRANSFER TECHNIQUES

3-12. Introduction. Return-Address Storage and Nested Subroutines (see also Sec. 2-23). In many applications, a reasonably involved program section is used over and over again in the course of a computation. We may then save a great deal of memory if we store such a **subroutine** only

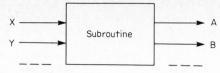

Fig. 3-9. Block-diagram representation of a subroutine operation with inputs (arguments, parameters) *X*, *Y* and outputs (results) *A*, *B*.

once, jump to its tagged starting location whenever the subroutine is needed, and make a return jump to the calling program when the subroutine is finished. Besides saving memory, the use of subroutines can give our programs a more easily understood "modular" structure. A subroutine can represent a complete easily interpreted operation (e.g., extracting a square root, moving an array of data) which produces output data or **results** from input data or **arguments** (Fig. 3-9; see also Sec. 3-14). **Frequently used subroutines can be assembled (translated into binary code) once and for all** and can be linked to other programs by a linking loader (Sec. 3-17). Subroutines will *not* save time compared to straight-line programming; they will (at the least) add extra jump instructions as "overhead."

We recall from Sec. 3-2 that each subroutine-jump instruction must save the presumed return address (incremented program-counter contents) in memory (Fig. 3-10), in an index register (linkage register), or on a software

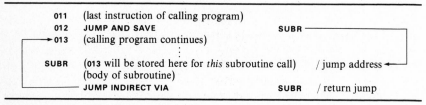

Fig. 3-10. Simple subroutine call and return with the return address saved in memory. No provisions to transfer arguments and results are included.

or hardware stack. Most modern machines utilize a stack method, which automates the saving and disposal of successive return address and data for **nested subroutines** (subroutines calling other subroutines, Fig. 2-8; see also Sec. 3-16).

NOTE: Contents of processor registers (accumulators, index registers, processor flags, page register, interrupt mask) needed later by the calling program may have to be saved in memory before we call a subroutine which uses these registers.

3-13. Subroutines without Direct Data Transfer. COMMON Areas. The simplest subroutines do *not* process data passed to them directly by the various subroutine-calling sections of the main program. A good example is a subroutine which, at several points of a data-processing program, transfers the words of the same buffer area in memory to a line printer, perhaps doing some reformatting and checking on the way. This can be a rather long subroutine (100 or more instructions, see also Sec. 5-14). It will be a real relief to store it only once in memory and to have to write it only once in our program. Calling this particular subroutine is simple, for *the calling program need not tell the subroutine what data to process:* the subroutine always operates on the same buffer (just like a COMMON area in a FORTRAN program).

NOTE: COMMON areas specified in separately assembled relocatable program sections must have absolute addresses, or the assembly language must specify relocatable **labeled** COMMON areas in each program segment (as in FORTRAN). The load-module generator will then correctly superimpose COMMON areas named in two or more program sections.

3-14.   Argument and Result Transfer through Processor Registers. Many subroutines will process **arguments (parameters)** passed to them *by each program section which calls the subroutine.* Arguments can be data words but may also be symbolic addresses. Subroutines will also have to return **results** to calling programs. Quite often, only one argument and/or result or only a few arguments and/or results must be passed, as in a function-generating subroutine (e.g., square root, table-lookup function). Note that while the code for the subroutine remains the same for each call, argument(s) and/or result(s) will differ. A simple way to pass one data word is to place it into an accumulator or index register during the subroutine jump or return jump; several words can be passed if several registers are available.

3-15.   Argument and Result Transfers through Arrays, Calling Sequences, and Stacks. Quite often, we must pass more subroutine arguments and/or results than we have processor registers. We can then place arguments and/or results for each call into an array in memory; we need only pass the array starting address to the subroutine, which can now access the data through indirect or indexed addressing.

A traditional **subroutine calling sequence** has such a data-passing array immediately following the subroutine call in the calling program, say

```
JUMP AND SAVE    SUBR
X
Y
A
B
```

The return-address location (memory location or index register, Sec. 2-23) can then be incremented to serve as a pointer to successive calling-sequence data words (Fig. 3-11a, b).

In the examples of Fig. 3-11a, b, **X**, **Y**, **A**, **B** are data words, *not* addresses. But with the linkage-register technique of Fig. 3-11b we can also pass

011	(last instruction of calling program)	
012	JUMP AND SAVE	SUBR
	x (X stored in 013 by calling program)	
	y (Y stored in 014 by calling program)	
	A (A will be stored in 015 by subroutine)	
	B (B will be stored in 016 by subroutine)	
017	(calling program continues)	
SUBR	(013 will be initially stored here for this call)	/ jump address
	(subroutine starts)	
	LOAD ACCUMULATOR, INDIRECT VIA	SUBR / transfer X
	(subroutine continues)	
	INCREMENT MEMORY	SUBR
	LOAD ACCUMULATOR, INDIRECT VIA	SUBR / transfer Y
	(subroutine continues, places A in accumulator)	
	INCREMENT MEMORY	SUBR
	STORE ACCUMULATOR, INDIRECT VIA	SUBR / return A
	(subroutine continues, places B in accumulator)	
	INCREMENT MEMORY	SUBR
	STORE ACCUMULATOR, INDIRECT VIA	SUBR / return B
	(subroutine ends)	
	INCREMENT MEMORY	SUBR
	JUMP INDIRECT VIA	SUBR / return jump

3-11a. A calling-sequence method for passing two arguments X, Y and returning two results A, B. A computer permitting autoincrementing or postindexing of the indirect-address pointer SUBR would make this program simpler and faster.

	.OCTAL	
011	(last instruction of calling program)	
012	JUMP AND SAVE IN INDEX	SUBR
013	JUMP TO	.+5 / Jump around argu-
		/ ments and results
014	X	
015	Y	
016	A	
017	B	
020	(calling program continues)	
SUBR	(subroutine starts)	/ Jump address
	LOAD ACCUMULATOR, INDEXED	1 / Transfer X
	(subroutine continues)	
	LOAD ACCUMULATOR, INDEXED	2 / Transfer Y
	(subroutine continues, places A in accumulator)	
	STORE ACCUMULATOR, INDEXED	3 / Return A
	(subroutine continues, places B in accumulator)	
	STORE ACCUMULATOR, INDEXED	4 / Return B
	(subroutine ends)	
	JUMP, INDEXED	0 / Return jump

3-11b. Subroutine and calling sequence employing the JUMP AND SAVE IN INDEX instruction. Note that arguments and results could be just as easily accessed in any other order. The return jump was made to location 013 (immediately following the subroutine jump) with an extra jump around the calling-sequence items. This is a convention expected of subroutines called by system programs in some computer systems. Otherwise, a return jump through JUMP, INDEXED 5 would be simpler and faster. Such calling sequences can also transfer *addresses* of arguments and results (see also Sec. 3-20).

addresses of data words and data arrays by using preindexed indirect addressing to fetch and store data (see also Sec. 3-20). This may save moving data into different calling sequences.

With the more primitive subroutine-jump instruction of Fig. 3-11a, address passing is more complicated, unless two-level indirect addressing is available (see also Sec. 3-25).

Much existing software employs the traditional calling sequence. But with modern computers having convenient stack **PUSH** and **POP** instructions (Sec. 2-17), it is preferable to transfer subroutine arguments and results (or their addresses) through a *software stack*, like other intermediate-result data (Fig. 3-12). This can save time (shorter instructions) and memory. Calling programs and subroutines then can become pure procedures, which do not mix data with instructions (reentrant code, Sec. 3-16).

NOTE: Stacked data can be reached with **PUSH** and **POP** instructions alone only if data-word accesses can be arranged in special ordered sequences (e.g., reverse-Polish order produced by a compiler). Otherwise, we need indexed addressing, as in Fig. 3-12a. We must make sure that each program segment pops its used-up data off the stack (*stack cleanup*); some machines have special stack-cleanup instructions. Stack operations like

---

```
        ....
        (calling program produces X in accumulator)
        PUSH ACCUMULATOR                              / Push argument X
        (calling program produces Y in accumulator)
        PUSH ACCUMULATOR                              / Push argument Y
        JUMP TO SUBROUTINE                  SUBR      / Push return address
        (return here with A and B on the stack, A on top)
        .......

        .......
SUBR    (subroutine starts, needs X)
        MOVE STACK POINTER TO INDEX REGISTER
        LOAD ACCUMULATOR, INDEXED           2         / Get X
        (subroutine continues, needs Y)
        LOAD ACCUMULATOR, INDEXED           1         / Get Y
        (subroutine continues, produces a temporary-
            storage word in accumulator)
        PUSH ACCUMULATOR                              / Push temporary
        (subroutine continues, produces A)            /    item
        STORE ACCUMULATOR, INDEXED          1         / Result A in stack
        (subroutine continues, needs temporary item)
        POP INTO ACCUMULATOR                          / Get temporary item
        (subroutine produces B)
        STORE ACCUMULATOR, INDEXED          2         / Result B in stack
        (subroutine ends)
        RETURN FROM SUBROUTINE                        / Return, pop
                                                      /    return address
```

Fig. 3-12a. Use of a software stack for all intermediate-result storage permits reentrant subroutine programming. The stack stores return addresses, data passed to and from the subroutine, and intermediate results within the subroutine. Subroutine nesting is possible, and no intermediate data will be overwritten if the subroutine is interrupted and called again from an interrupt-service program.

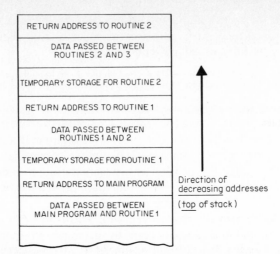

Fig. 3-12b. Contents of a processor stack after the jump to the third of three nested subroutines. Intermediate results stored for each routine can include register contents saved until the return from a subroutine.

those in Fig. 3-12b become simpler if one uses separate stacks for return addresses and data (e.g., a hardware stack and a software stack).

Refer to Sec. 7-14 for the novel and different data-passing techniques used in the Texas Instruments 990-family computers.

3-16. Interrupt-Service Routines and Reentrant Subroutines. An **interrupt-service routine** is a subroutine called into action by a signal **(interrupt request)** from outside the computer or because of an alarm condition in the computer (power-supply failure, violation of memory protection), rather than by a computer-program call. Interrupt-system hardware and programming will be discussed in some detail in Chap. 4.

A special problem arises when a subroutine (say a library routine for computing the square root) is interrupted, and the interrupt-service program calls *the same* subroutine. The original subroutine call may cause intermediate-result storage in temporary storage locations, say TEMP1 and TEMP2. Unless special precautions are taken, intermediate results from the second subroutine call can *overwrite* TEMP1 and TEMP2 so that the program will fail upon return from interrupt. *The library subroutines of many FORTRAN systems fail in this manner.*

Subroutines designed to work properly when they are interrupted and reentered for interrupt service are called **reentrant.** Since "real-time" computations involving many interrupt-driven program segments are important minicomputer applications, reentrant programming is often desirable. A good way to obtain reentrant subroutines, as well as assured saving of return addresses, register contents, etc., is *to store all temporary-*

storage and saved items in a stack. The stack pointer is advanced and retracted as the subroutine is called and completed (Fig. 3-12; see also Secs. 4-12 and 6-6). *In modern computers having one-word* **PUSH** *and* **POP** *instructions* (Sec. 2-17), *this technique also saves memory and time.*

A reentrant subroutine can call itself (**recursive** subroutine call); there must be a conditional jump out of the recursive sequence, say when some iterative computation has become sufficiently accurate.

RELOCATION AND LINKING OF PROGRAMS

3-17. Problem Statement (see also Sec. 5-5). Microcomputers and minicomputers which run mainly single special-purpose programs or interpreter programs (such as BASIC, Sec. 5-25) will not require program **relocation.** For general-purpose computation, though, *one will want to combine different program segments and library subroutines;* so it must be possible to *relocate programs* anywhere in the computer memory. Program segments will, moreover, want to call other program segments as subroutines, and it will be necessary to pass arguments and results between programs. This requires techniques for **program linkage,** i.e., for associating the proper relocated addresses with symbolic names of **external references.** Programming systems permitting relocation and linkage will require:

1. An assembler (or compiler) *specifically designed* to permit relocation and linkage
2. A **relocating/linking loader program,** which supplies the correct addresses and cross references at load time

More powerful minicomputer systems separate relocation/linkage and loading. The linking loader is replaced by a **load-module generator (linkage editor, linker)** which links program sections into a **load-module file** in mass storage. A load module can be loaded by a simple absolute loader (starting at a fixed location) in response to an operating-system RUN command (Sec. 5-15).

With a memory-mapping system (Sec. 2-30), load modules can themselves be relocated through addition of base-register addresses. This is simplified if programs are written in **position-independent code** based on extensive use of relative addressing (Sec. 2-14). Different load modules, loaded into different memory partitions, can be called to execute in turn by the operating system (Sec. 5-22). Different load modules are not linked and can, thus, not communicate directly, but they can communicate through absolute COMMON locations.

3-18. Relocation. An assembler (or compiler) designed to produce relocatable code creates a preliminary version of the object program, with addresses and program-counter readings normally referred to location **0** as a fictitious origin. The assembler (or compiler) will, moreover, **mark** every word, address, and symbol to be relocated with a **relocation bit, byte, or word** so that the load-module generator will know which words and addresses to modify. These words and addresses usually appear marked with an **R** in the assembler listing (Fig. 3-3) and include:

1. Most of the normal *instruction and data words* of the program, with the exception of data in some COMMON areas
2. Symbolic and numerical *addresses* in the program, again with the exception of references to absolute pointers, tables, and COMMON areas, e.g., those associated with special system programs (often on memory page 0)

The nonrelocatable addresses are known as **absolute addresses** (see also Fig. 3-3).

The load-module generator will complete the assembly (or compilation) process to produce the actual executive object program. The load-module generator determines the true relative origin (relocation base) for each program segment, normally the first free location following the instructions and data of a preceding program. **This relocation base is then added to each address marked as relocatable by the assembler** (Fig. 3-13).

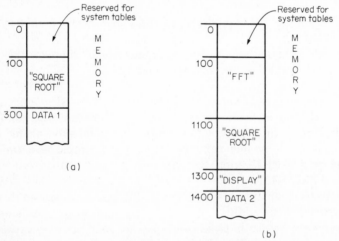

(a)

(b)

Fig. 3-13. Relocation of a 200-word program "SQUARE ROOT" in memory. In (*a*), the program is used by itself to process DATA 1. In (*b*), the same program has been *relocated* and *linked* as a subroutine with the main program "FFT" and the subroutine "DISPLAY" to process DATA 2. This requires recomputation of all *relocatable memory addresses* and insertion of cross-reference addresses (*external references*) linking the different program sections.

Special problems may arise with the relocation of addresses specified as *symbolic expressions* (Sec. 3-3). While an expression like A + 2 will be relocated correctly if we simply add the relocation base to A, A + B + 3 will cause trouble if *both* A *and* B are relocatable addresses; the assembler may mark the line containing A + B + 3 as a "possible relocation error." The expression A − B, on the other hand, defines an *absolute* address if both A and B are relocatable.

3-19. Linking External References. Libraries. Assemblers intended for use with a linking loader usually require the user *to list all external references* (and frequently all symbols to be used as external references by other program segments) somewhere in the program, thus,

.EXT   A1, ARG, SYMB

Note that these "global" symbols must be uniquely defined, while symbols not used as external references can be used with different meanings in different program segments without causing any trouble.

A load-module generator or **linkage editor** operates much like another assembler. It creates a **load-module symbol table** which includes the global symbols identified in each program segment, and then supplies the correct addresses relative to the relocation base of each segment. The new symbol table is then used much like an assembler symbol table for the load-module generator's "reassembly" job.

An entire set of frequently used named binary program segments (e.g., arithmetic or I/O routines) or data arrays can be combined into a **library.** The entire library is linked to user programs with a single special external symbol. The load-module generator will automatically search all libraries for unresolved symbol references and links/loads only those library items which were actually requested by other programs (see also Sec. 5-15).

A (binary) library is a named file consisting of named binary-object-program segments (e.g., arithmetic or I/O routines) or data tables, with a **library directory** listing these contents. *Library files are identified by special names or extensions* (Sec. 5-13, e.g. **.LIB**), *which are recognized by the load-module generator.* To access any item in a library, the user program needs only a single external reference to the library, which will then be automatically searched by the load-module generator for any unresolved symbol references.

Special utility programs **(library-maintenance programs)** permit users to create named library files, to insert or delete library items, and to list library directories in response to typed commands.

NOTE: Insertion rather than just addition of items in subroutine libraries is required, since the usual library-search procedure requires nested subroutines (Sec. 3-12) to occur in the relative order in which they will be called. Also, frequently called library items should precede those rarely called, in order to save load-module-generator search time.

3-20. Combination of Assembly-Language Programs and FORTRAN Programs. Combinations of assembly-language and FORTRAN program segments are of substantial practical importance because:

1. FORTRAN **READ, WRITE,** and **FORMAT** statements are often the most convenient way to call the complicated formatting and I/O routines required to deal with numerical data on standard peripherals such as card readers and line printers. This is true even for minicomputers with relatively convenient input/output macros (see also Secs. 5-11 to 5-14).
2. Frequently used or special-purpose program segments may be written in assembly language for efficient execution and called as subroutines or functions by FORTRAN programs. Again, input/output routines, this time for nonstandard peripherals, are good examples.

In general, the FORTRAN compiler for a given minicomputer will expand a call to an assembly-language subroutine, say

CALL   SUBR (I,K)

into code corresponding to a standardized assembly-language calling sequence specified in the computer reference manual, e.g.,

.EXT	**SUBR** / External reference
JUMP AND SAVE INDIRECT VIA	**SUBR** / Subroutine jump
JUMP	**.+3** / Jump around arguments
	/ after return
I	/ *Addresses*
K	/ of data

and the assembly-language subroutine must access **I** and **K** accordingly (Sec. 3-14). The FORTRAN compiler will expect a similar calling sequence when an assembly-language program calls a FORTRAN subroutine **SUBR (I,K)**. Refer to your minicomputer manual for the specific conventions used to access floating-point or double-precision data.

MACROS AND CONDITIONAL ASSEMBLY

3-21. Macros. (a) Macro Definitions and Macro Calls. A **macroassembler** allows the user to define an entire sequence of assembly-language statements as a **macro instruction (macro)** called by a symbolic name. Each macro is created by a *macro definition*, e.g.,

```
.MACRO     SUM     Z,X,Y
LOAD ACCUMULATOR          X
ADD INTO ACCUMULATOR      Y
STORE ACCUMULATOR IN      Z
.ENDMACRO
```

The pseudo-instruction words **.MACRO** and **.ENDMACRO** delimit the macro definition; **SUM** is the **macro name,** and **Z, X, Y** are **dummy arguments.** Once the macro is defined (which could be anywhere in a program), the user can employ a one-line **macro call** to generate the entire code sequence with new arguments as often as desired. Thus, the user-program sequence

```
START    SUM    A,A1,A2
         SUM    B,B1,B2
```

will produce code (and, if desired, a listing) corresponding to

```
START    LOAD ACCUMULATOR         A1    Expansion
         ADD INTO ACCUMULATOR     A2    of
         STORE ACCUMULATOR IN     A     SUM A,A1,A2
         LOAD ACCUMULATOR         B1    Expansion
         ADD INTO ACCUMULATOR     B2    of
         STORE ACCUMULATOR IN     B     SUM B,B1,B2
```

Note that the label **START** was not part of the macro-call expansion.

A macro may or may not have arguments. Arguments can be symbols, expressions, numbers, or literal constants and can appear as location tags as well as addresses. The better macroassemblers permit calls to other macros within a macro definition (see Sec. 3-22b for an example).

Calls to *the same* macro (**recursive** macro calls) lead to complications but can produce interesting program sequences when used in conjunction with conditional assembly (Sec. 3-23; see also Ref. 9).

Beware of unintentionally using symbols other than arguments in macro definitions; they will stay the same in different macro-call expansions and may cause overwriting. Thus, if a sequence like

```
TEST    SKIP IF ACCUMULATOR POSITIVE
        JUMP TO                   ACT
        JUMP TO                   ACT +2
ACT     INVERT ACCUMULATOR
```

appears in a macro definition, *it should be replaced with*

```
        SKIP IF ACCUMULATOR POSITIVE
        JUMP TO                   .+2
        JUMP TO                   .+3
        INVERT ACCUMULATOR
```

Some macroassemblers have the facility of automatically "creating" new symbolic labels in such situations when the macro is called more than once, but the necessary procedures rather complicate programming.

(b) Importance of Macros. Macros are not simply a programming convenience or shorthand notation: their power in enlarging the scope of assembly-language programming can hardly be overemphasized. A macro-assembler permits you to create and use entire classes of new computer operations, which can *simplify programming* and/or *help with applications-related modeling.*

(c) Macros and Subroutines. As we saw in Sec. 3-14, functional program modules can also be called as *subroutines*, with arguments and results in appropriate calling sequences. It is important to distinguish between subroutines and macros. Each macro call will generate *new in-line code* so that long macros will *not* save memory like long subroutines. Short macros can be more economical than short subroutines because of the overhead associated with subroutine jumps, calling sequence, and data transfers; in any case, macros will execute more quickly.

Macro calls with multiple arguments are more "natural" for most programmers than subroutine calling sequences. Hence it is convenient to define the complete data-transfer and calling sequences of frequently used subroutines as **subroutine-calling macros.** This technique is used, in particular, to define *system macros calling input/output subroutines* (Sec. 5-14).

3-22. Two Interesting Applications. (a) Computer Emulation. To emulate the operation (instruction set) of a different digital computer on an existing "host" computer, we can write a macro for each computer instruction to be simulated. If we can take care of input/output, our "host" computer should then be able to run any assembly-language program written for the emulated "target" computer.

EXAMPLE: Emulation of indexed addition on a single-accumulator minicomputer. The memory location INDEX simulates a single index register in the "target" computer.

```
.MACRO     ADDX    A
STORE ACCUMULATOR IN     SAVAC / Save accumulator
LOAD ACCUMULATOR         (A)   / Compute
ADD INTO ACCUMULATOR     INDEX /      indexed
STORE ACCUMULATOR IN     ADDR  /      address
LOAD ACCUMULATOR         SAVAC / Restore accumulator
ADD INDIRECT VIA         ADDR  / Perform addition
.ENDMACRO
```

Note that in this example the temporary-storage symbols SAVAC and ADDR will *not* cause trouble in later macro calls.

See also Sec. 2-31 for other computer-emulation techniques (micro-programming).

(b) Writing Simple Procedural Languages. Macros make it possible to write application programs solely in terms of operations directly related to the user's application. Once the macros have been written (perhaps by a professional programmer), the lucky user will be able to write application

TABLE 3-1. Macros for a Simple Block-Diagram Language.

Extra blocks, such as function-generator blocks (sine, cosine, table-lookup functions) can be added at will. X, Y, and Z are scaled fractions.

.MACRO SUM Z, X, Y		$/ Z = X + Y$
LOAD ACCUMULATOR	X	
ADD INTO ACCUMULATOR	Y	
OTEST	Z	/ Overflow-test macro, see below
STORE ACCUMULATOR IN	Z	
.ENDMACRO		
.MACRO NEGATE Z, X		$/ Z = -X$
LOAD ACCUMULATOR	X	
INVERT ACCUMULATOR		
STORE ACCUMULATOR IN	Z	
.ENDMACRO		
.MACRO SCALE Z, X, M		$/ Z = 2^M X$, where M is a positive integer
LOAD ACCUMULATOR	X	
LONG SIGNED SHIFT LEFT, M BITS		
OTEST	Z	
STORE ACCUMULATOR IN	Z	
.ENDMACRO		
.MACRO MULT Z, X, Y		$/ Z = XY$
LOAD ACCUMULATOR	X	
MULTIPLY BY	Y	$/ XY/2$ in accumulator (Sec. 1-15)
LONG SIGNED SHIFT LEFT, 1 BIT		$/ XY$ in accumulator
STORE ACCUMULATOR IN	Z	
.ENDMACRO		
.MACRO DIV Z, X, Y		$/ Z = X/Y$
LOAD ACCUMULATOR	X	
CLEAR ACCUMULATOR 2		/ Accumulator extension for division
LONG SIGNED SHIFT RIGHT, 1 BIT		/ Divide by 2 (fraction division)
DIVIDE BY	Y	
OTEST	Z	
STORE ACCUMULATOR IN	Z	
.ENDMACRO		
.MACRO OTEST	Z	/ Test for overflow of fraction
SKIP ON OVERFLOW FLAG		/ Overflow?
JUMP TO	.+3	/ No, go on
LOAD ACCUMULATOR, IMMEDIATE	Z	/ Identifies guilty variable for error-message routine
JUMP TO	ERROR	/ Error-message routine
.ENDMACRO		

programs using only a few simple rules (syntax) *without knowing any assembly language at all.* As a generally applicable example, we shall develop a block-diagram language suitable for doing any sort of arithmetic and/or function generation with fixed-point numbers (integers and scaled fractions, Sec. 1-5). The user need not know assembly language; the block-diagram language will actually be a simple substitute for a compiler language and will generate remarkably efficient code (see also Sec. 3-26).

Scaled-fraction *inputs* $X1$, $X2$, ... and *outputs* $Y1$, $Y2$, ... will be referred to as symbolic locations, whose contents can be accessed by input/output routines (which can also be called in macro form) as needed. We now define a set of macros for *algebraic-operation blocks* (Table 3-1), plus extra blocks for function generation (sine, cosine, table-lookup functions) if we need them. *We can now combine such blocks to compute any reasonable scaled expression*, say

$$RESLT = A1^2(BETA + GAMMA) + ALFA$$

in terms of a corresponding *block diagram*, much like an analog-computer block diagram (Fig. 3-14). We can then write an assembly-language routine producing the desired expression by simply listing the block macros with their input and output variables:

```
START    MULT    B, A1, A1
         SUM     C, BETA, GAMMA
         MULT    A, B, C
         SUM     RESLT, A, ALFA
```

As in any procedural language, *we have taken care to write any intermediate result* **A, B, C**, *as well as the result* **RESLT** *only if it has been computed (as a block output) in a preceding line*. Such a program is most easily written when we start with the *last* block: Our simple scheme is, in fact, simulating the reverse Polish string generated by an algebraic compiler! After some practice, we may not even have to draw the block diagram.

Our simple block-diagram language generates quite efficient code (probably better than most minicomputer FORTRAN). It includes an error-message routine (not shown in Table 3-1) which will print out the symbol-table number of any block-output variable that overflows because of faulty scaling. A similar set of blocks could readily be written for floating-point arithmetic.

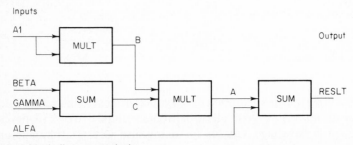

Fig. 3-14. A block diagram producing

$$RESLT = A1^2 (BETA + GAMMA) + ALFA$$

Expansion of our macro blocks shows that almost all block macros end with **STORE ACCUMULATOR IN Q**, which is often followed by **LOAD ACCUMULATOR Q** in the next macro.   Such store/fetch pairs are redundant; each wastes 4 to 6 memory cycles.   Our block-diagram language program can be modified (or reprocessed) to cancel redundant store/fetch pairs (Refs. 10 and 16); the resulting code can be as efficient as that written by a good assembly-language programmer (see also Sec. 3-25).

3-23. Conditional Assembly.   Conditional assembly directs the assembler *to suppress specified sections of code unless stated conditions are met by the program at assembly time.*   Conditional assembly is available with some ordinary assemblers but is most useful with macroassemblers. One can, in particular, modify the definitions of user-defined or system macros if named symbols do or do not appear in the program or if certain symbolic variables are zero, positive, or negative at *assembly time.*

Specifically, all statements (instructions and/or data) between the pseudo instructions **.IFDEF X** and **.ENDCOND** will be assembled if and only if the named symbol **X** is defined anywhere in the program.   Other conditions are similarly employed by the pseudo instructions **.IFUNDEF, .IFZERO, .IFNONZR, .IFPOS, .IFNEG**.   Note that the condition expressed by

.IFZERO   A − B

means that the symbols A and B reference the same variable or memory location.

As a very simple example, consider a multi-input summer block for the simple algebraic block-diagram language of Sec. 3-22b.   We will write a macro to add a maximum of four inputs, $X1$, $X2$, $X3$, and $X4$, to produce an output Z:

```
.MACRO     SUMR              Z, X1, X2, X3, X4
   LOAD ACCUMULATOR          X1
   CLEAR OVERFLOW FLAG
   ADD INTO ACCUMULATOR      X2
.IFDEF                        X3
   ADD INTO ACCUMULATOR      X3
.ENDCOND
.IFDEF                        X4
   ADD INTO ACCUMULATOR      X4
.ENDCOND
   OTEST
   STORE ACCUMULATOR IN      Z
.ENDMACRO
```

We now see the beauty of the conditional-assembly feature.   If our four-input summer is given only *three* inputs, say **X1, X2,** and **X4,** with **X3** undefined in our program, then the assembler will omit the unneeded **ADD INTO ACCUMULATOR X3**; this saves memory and execution time.   We could similarly omit **X4** or both **X3** and **X4**.

3-24. Nested Macro Definitions.   We mentioned in Sec. 3-21 that macro definitions may contain macro *calls* (see also Table 3-1).   A macro definition which contains another macro *definition*, as in

```
.MACRO     MAC1              Z, X
   LOAD ACCUMULATOR          X
   STORE ACCUMULATOR IN      Z
.MACRO     MAC2              U, V
   XOR INTO ACCUMULATOR      V
   STORE ACCUMULATOR IN      U
.ENDMACRO
   ROTATE ACCUMULATOR LEFT
.ENDMACRO
```

(nested definitions), is a different situation. The assembler regards MAC2 as *undefined* in the part of our program preceding the first call for MAC1, say

MAC1   P, Q

This results in the expansion

LOAD ACCUMULATOR   Q
STORE ACCUMULATOR IN   P
ROTATE ACCUMULATOR LEFT

Note that *no code due to* MAC2 *is generated this time*, but MAC2 is now defined and can be called either alone or through the next call to MAC1.   Multiple nesting of definitions is possible. We have here another means of turning assembly of a section of code off and on.

SOME SPECIAL PROGRAMS
FOR MICROCOMPUTERS

3-25.   Programmed-Logic and Counting Operations with Small Processors. Microcomputers used to replace hard-wired logic must often perform **logic operations with individual bits in registers;** these bits might represent contact or valve closures, objects detected, etc., in the real world.   The more sophisticated microprocessors do have **AND** and/or **XOR** instructions (Sec. 2-6), but the simpler 8-bit and most 4-bit machines must rotate each bit into the carry flag and then implement AND and OR operations (and their complements) by **sequences of conditional jumps** (Fig. 3-15a) (Ref. 13). XOR can be implemented as $A\bar{B} + \bar{A}B$, or one may test (each bit of) $A - B$ for zero.   One can then simulate *sequential machines* (Sec. 1-13) simply by implementing their state equations (recursion relations) (1-17).

Counting operations are of special interest.   A microprocessor can emulate any type of counter, and mix counting with arbitrary logic operations. **Preset counters** set up to permit exactly N loop operations were discussed in Sec. 3-9 (Fig. 3-15b).   To accommodate counts larger than 2^4 or 2^8 in 4-bit and 8-bit microprocessors, we can *concatenate counter locations* (Fig. 3-15c).

	LOAD ACCUMULATOR	A	
	ROTATE ACCUMULATOR LEFT		
	BRANCH ON CARRY CLEAR	AND0	/ Bit = 0?
	LOAD ACCUMULATOR	B	/ No, go on
	ROTATE ACCUMULATOR LEFT		
	ROTATE ACCUMULATOR LEFT		
	BRANCH ON CARRY CLEAR	AND0	/ Bit = 0?
AND1	(here if result of AND is 1)		

Fig. 3-15a. This routine tests the most significant bit in location A and the second most significant bit in location B.   The program branches to AND0 or goes on to AND1 if the logical AND of the two bits is 0 or 1, respectively.   A and B are processor register-file locations.

LOOP	LOAD REGISTER 0, IMMEDIATE	– N	/ Preset the counter
	(perform some operation)		
	INCREMENT REGISTER 0, BRANCH IF NOT ZERO	LOOP	/ Done?
	(b)		

LOOP	LOAD REGISTER 0, IMMEDIATE	– N0	/ Preset counter
LOOP 1	LOAD REGISTER 1, IMMEDIATE	– N1	
LOOP 2	LOAD REGISTER 2, IMMEDIATE	– N2	
	(perform some operation)		
	INCREMENT REGISTER 2, BRANCH IF NOT ZERO	LOOP 2	
	INCREMENT REGISTER 1, BRANCH IF NOT ZERO	LOOP 1	
	INCREMENT REGISTER 0, BRANCH IF NOT ZERO	LOOP	
	(c)		

Fig. 3-15b, c. A simple counting loop (b), and multiple-precision counting in a short-word-length microcomputer (c). The count values – N, – N0, – N1, – N2 could also be loaded from register-file or random-access-memory locations.

Counting loops will inexpensively implement **programmable time delays** synchronized with the processor clock. The designer must know the clock rate and the number of cycles required to execute each instruction (Ref. 13).

Programmed logic, counting, and timing operations permit very inexpensive 4-bit microcomputers to replace hard-wired logic, relays, and electromechanical timers controlling traffic lights, production machinery, vending machines, etc. **Arithmetic operations with small processors** require *multiple-precision operations*. A multiprecision addition program was shown in Fig. 3-8b; subtraction is quite similar. References 13 to 15 present routines for multiple-precision multiplication and division. Reference 13 also shows a *square-root routine* for 4-bit machines.

	LOAD POINTER REGISTERS 4,5, IMMEDIATE	A	/ Set up
	LOAD POINTER REGISTERS 6,7, IMMEDIATE	B	/ address pointers
	LOAD REGISTER 8, IMMEDIATE	– N	/ Number of digits
	CLEAR CARRY FLAG		
LOOP	USE 4,5 AS POINTER		/ Load accumulator
	LOAD ACCUMULATOR		/ with A-digit
	USE 6,7 AS POINTER		/ Add
	ADD WITH CARRY INTO ACCUMULATOR		/ B-digit
	DECIMAL ADJUST ACCUMULATOR		
	STORE ACCUMULATOR		/ Still via 6,7, i.e.,
			/ in B-array
	INCREMENT REGISTER PAIR	4,5	/ Next digit,
	INCREMENT REGISTER PAIR	6,7	/ unless we are
	INCREMENT REGISTER 8, BRANCH		
	IF NOT ZERO	LOOP	/ done?

Fig. 3-15d. Intel 4040 routine for N-digit decimal addition. BCD-coded units, tens, hundreds, ..., digits of two decimal integers are stored in 4-bit memory locations A, A + 1, A + 2, ... and B, B + 1, B + 2, ..., respectively addressed by the 8-bit pointer registers (pairs of 4-bit registers, Sec. 6-5), 4,5 and 6,7. The sum is left in B, B + 1, B + 2, ...; no overflow check is shown. 4-bit register 8 is the digit counter. Note that memory-reference operations require *two* 8-bit instructions.

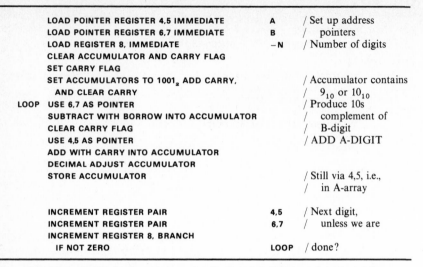

	LOAD POINTER REGISTER 4,5 IMMEDIATE	A	/ Set up address
	LOAD POINTER REGISTER 6,7 IMMEDIATE	B	/ pointers
	LOAD REGISTER 8, IMMEDIATE	– N	/ Number of digits
	CLEAR ACCUMULATOR AND CARRY FLAG		
	SET CARRY FLAG		
	SET ACCUMULATORS TO 1001$_2$ ADD CARRY,		/ Accumulator contains
	AND CLEAR CARRY		/ 9_{10} or 10_{10}
LOOP	USE 6,7 AS POINTER		/ Produce 10s
	SUBTRACT WITH BORROW INTO ACCUMULATOR		/ complement of
	CLEAR CARRY FLAG		/ B-digit
	USE 4,5 AS POINTER		/ ADD A-DIGIT
	ADD WITH CARRY INTO ACCUMULATOR		
	DECIMAL ADJUST ACCUMULATOR		
	STORE ACCUMULATOR		/ Still via 4,5, i.e.,
			/ in A-array
	INCREMENT REGISTER PAIR	4,5	/ Next digit,
	INCREMENT REGISTER PAIR	6,7	/ unless we are
	INCREMENT REGISTER 8, BRANCH		
	IF NOT ZERO	LOOP	/ done?

Fig. 3-15e. Decimal subtraction routine for the Intel 4040 (see also Sec. 2-26).

4- and 8-bit microcomputers often implement **decimal-arithmetic operations** for displays, printers, and calculators; each decimal digit is represented by a BCD-coded 4-bit "nibble" (see also Secs. 1-10 and 2-26). Figure 3-15*d* and *e* shows Intel 4040 routines for *N-digit decimal addition and subtraction*.

Reference 20 is a useful guide to National Semiconductor PACE microcomputer programs designed to replace a wide variety of hard-wired logic functions.

3-26. A Threaded-Code Block-Diagram Language (Ref. 12).

As we saw in Sec. 3-22*b*, block-diagram languages permit applications programmers to generate efficient code without having to learn assembly language. This technique has been exceptionally successful for minicomputer instrumentation and continuous-system simulation; in fact, fixed-point block-diagram computation with a PDP-15 or PDP-11/40 can beat the FORTRAN execution speed of a CDC 6400 (Refs. 10, 11). What is even more important is that **block-diagram operations can do input/output operations** (e.g., read analog-to-digital converters) as well as mathematical operations.

The in-line macros of Table 3-1 are suitable for end-user minicomputers, where extra memory use may be traded for execution speed and program simplicity. But *designers of quantity-produced microcomputer systems must minimize the number of memory chips in the interest of cost.* We will, therefore, implement each block-diagram operator as a *pure-procedure, reentrant subroutine* (no directly associated data storage, Secs. 3-15 and 3-16) *written once and for all into read-only memory.* Each routine can then be reused wherever the block-diagram program calls for it.

The block-diagram programmer must sequence the block-operator routines in procedural order and also arrange for data passing between the block-operator routines. This is neatly done by the following **threaded-code technique.**[1]

Using the block-diagram example of Fig. 3-14, we define memory addresses **A1, BETA, GAMMA, B, C, A, ALFA, RESULT,** in any order, for all block inputs and outputs. With the block operators in procedural order (i.e., no intermediate input occurs before it has been computed), *the entire block-diagram program reduces to an initial indexed jump and an address table,*

```
              LOAD INDEX REGISTER, IMMEDIATE    START
              JUMP PRE-INDEXED, INDIRECT           0
    START     MULT
              A1
              A1
              B
              SUM
              BETA
              GAMMA
              C
              MULT
              B
              C
              A
              SUM
              A
              ALFA
              RESLT
```

if the **MULT** routine takes the form

```
    MULT    INCREMENT INDEX REGISTER
            LOAD ACCUMULATOR, PRE-INDEXED, INDIRECT      0
            INCREMENT INDEX REGISTER
            MULTIPLY, PRE-INDEXED, INDIRECT              0
            INCREMENT INDEX REGISTER
            STORE ACCUMULATOR, PRE-INDEXED, INDIRECT     0
            INCREMENT INDEX REGISTER
            JUMP, PRE-INDEXED, INDIRECT                  0
```

[1] Data passing by the traditional calling-sequence method (Sec. 3-15) would be cumbersome, because intermediate results (e.g., c in Fig. 3-14) would have to be available in more than one calling sequence. In the simple example of Fig. 3-14, data could be passed through a software stack (Sec. 3-15; this is the reverse-Polish-stack method used in some calculators), but this also becomes complicated as soon as an intermediate result like c must be stored and recovered for use as more than one block-operator input.

with a completely analogous **SUM** routine.   We see that *each block-operator routine keeps incrementing the index register to access successive data addresses in the address list and then jumps to the next routine in the address list.*   A refinement of this technique provides each subroutine with alternate entry points to eliminate redundant store/fetch pairs (Sec. 3-22*b*), so that remarkably efficient code is generated (Refs. 16, 17).

Some processors (PDP-11, LSI-11) combine the preindexed, indirect operations and index incrementing into *single instructions.*   On the other hand, many 4-bit and 8-bit microprocessors *do not have indirect addressing,* so that it is necessary to load a pointer register with each item fetched by indexed direct addressing from the data list.   *By far the best way to implement the threaded-code subroutines is to make them into microprograms in control memory.*

TABLE 3-2.   Microprocessor Generation of Miscellaneous Control Signals.

These signals can be triggered by the computer program, by a sense/wait loop, or by an interrupt.

---

1. **Control Steps and Levels.** Load output port with an appropriate bit pattern. Increment/decrement an output/port register to switch one line quickly.
2. **Control Pulses** (replaces monostable multivibrator). Load output port with an appropriate bit pattern while a time-delay loop runs.
3. **Control Pulse** (fast strobe pulse for setting/resetting flip-flops, stepping counters or step motors). Use address-line decoder output *without* any data lines.
4. **Scan 4, 8, or 16 logic lines** by rotating a 1 through an output-port register (e.g., keyboard scan, data-acquisition-multiplexer scan).
5. **Sweep Waveform.** Increment a processor register or output-port register; reset to obtain recurrent sweeps.
6. **Arbitrary Waveform.** Increment the address of a function table in memory (ROM or RAM), with or without interpolation.

REFERENCES AND BIBLIOGRAPHY

1. Donovan, J. J.: *Systems Programming,* McGraw-Hill, New York, 1972.
2. Stone, H. S., and D. P. Siewiorek: *Computer Organization and Data Structures,* McGraw-Hill, New York, 1975.
3. Gear, C. W.: *Computer Organization and Programming,* 2d. ed, McGraw-Hill, New York, 1973.
4. Maurer, W. D.: *Programming: An Introduction to Computer Languages and Techniques,* Academic Press, New York, 1969.
5. *Introduction to Programming,* PDP-8 Handbook Series, Digital Equipment Corporation, Maynard, Mass. (current edition).
6. *Programming Languages,* PDP-8 Handbook Series, Digital Equipment Corporation, Maynard, Mass. (current edition).
7. *MACRO-11 Manual,* Digital Equipment Corporation, Maynard, Mass. (current edition).
8. *DAP/15 Mod 2 Assembler Manual,* Honeywell Information Systems, Framingham, Mass. (current edition).
9. McIlroy, M. D.: Macro-Instruction Extensions of Compiler Languages, *Comm. ACM,* April 1960.

10. Liebert, T. A.: "The DARE II Simulation System," Ph.D. thesis, The University of Arizona, 1970.
11. Korn, G. A.: Ultra-Fast Mini-Computation with a Simple Microprogrammed Block-Diagram Language, *Trans. ASEE/COED*, March 1974.
12. Korn, G. A.: Simplified Microcomputer Programming, *Proc. WESCON*, 1975.
13. *The Designer's Guide to Programmed Logic*, Prolog Corp., Monterey, Calif. (current edition).
14. *6800 Microprocessor Programming Manual*, Motorola Semiconductor Products, Inc., Phoenix, Ariz. (current edition).
15. *MCS-40 User's Manual for Logic Designers*, Intel Corp., Santa Clara, Calif. (current edition).
16. Korn, G. A.: A Proposed Method for Simplified Microcomputer Programming, *Computer*, October 1975.
17. ———: Optimal Block-Diagram Translation for High-Speed Mini/Microcomputation, *CSRL Report* 290, Electrical Engineering Department, The University of Arizona, 1975.
18. Conley, S., and T. Williams: A Portable Macro Language for Microprocessors, *CSRL Report* 300, The University of Arizona, 1976.
19. Korn, G. A., and H. M. Aus: Table-Lookup/Interpolation Function Generation, *IEEETC*, August 1969.
20. *Logic Designer's Guide to Programmed-Logic Equivalents of TTL Functions*, National Semiconductor Corp., Santa Clara, Calif., 1976.

CHAPTER 4

INTERFACING MICROPROCESSORS AND MINICOMPUTERS WITH REAL-WORLD DEVICES

INTRODUCTION AND SURVEY

The exceptional power of the small digital computer is substantially based on its ready interaction with real-world devices—analog-to-digital converters (ADCs), digital-to-analog converters (DACs), transducers, displays, logic controllers, alarm systems—in addition to the usual terminals, displays, printers, and tape drives. To the outside world, the computer presents a relatively small number (12 to 80) of bus-line terminations. These lines transmit and receive digital data words together with a few command pulses and control levels, which select devices and functions or alert the computer, in turn, to new real-world situations.

This chapter introduces the basic logic and programming principles for such interfaces. With inexpensive, off-the-shelf digital and analog system components widely and readily available, a little knowledge of interfacing principles can produce dramatically effective new systems and also surprising cost savings. A handful of integrated circuits, cards, and connectors, which you can wirewrap yourself for a total cost of $300, quite easily gets to be a $3,000 subsystem if you purchase it from an instrument manufacturer. The cost of programming the system must always be kept in mind (Sec. 6-1); sometimes, extra interface hardware can be traded for programming complexity.

Sections 4-1 through 4-7 deal with *program-controlled input/output and sensing operations.* Sections 4-8 to 4-15 describe *interrupt systems,* the basic means for time sharing a computer between different time-critical tasks. We next treat *direct memory access and automatic block transfers* (Secs. 4-16 to 4-23), which can save much computer time and greatly simplify programming. The remainder of the chapter discusses *complete interface systems,* including serial-data interfaces, data conversion, CAMAC and IEC module systems, and graphic displays, plus a little hardware know-how. *Input/output software* will be treated in Chap. 5.

PROGRAMMED INPUT/OUTPUT OPERATIONS

4-1. Input/Output Buses. Small digital computers usually transmit and receive data words or bytes on **parallel 4- to 18-bit buses;** i.e., data bits are transmitted simultaneously in the interest of operating speed. Serial data

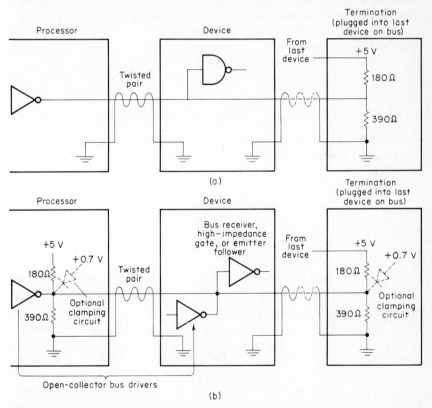

Fig. 4-1a, b. A *unidirectional processor-to-device bus* (a) and a *bidirectional bus* (b) both using inverting open-collector drivers. *Unidirectional device-to-processor* bus lines would also be terminated at both ends as in Fig. 4-1b.

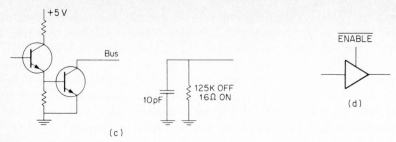

Fig. 4-1c, d. Output stages of an inverting *open-collector TTL bus driver* and equivalent-source circuit (*b*), and a noninverting *tri-state buffer* usable for either receiving or transmitting (*d*). The tri-state buffer is active when the ENABLE line is at ground potential and otherwise presents a high impedance at both its input and output.

transmission is usually reserved for communication over distances longer than a few hundred feet, and for slow printers and keyboards (Sec. 4-26). **Data-bus lines** connect to processor buses (Fig. 2-2) via buffer amplifiers (**bus drivers** and **bus receivers** for each data bit) and thus to processor registers. The data lines can be **bidirectional,** or we may have **separate input and output buses** (this takes less logic but more interconnections, Fig. 4-1*b*). A computer servicing only a few external devices could select

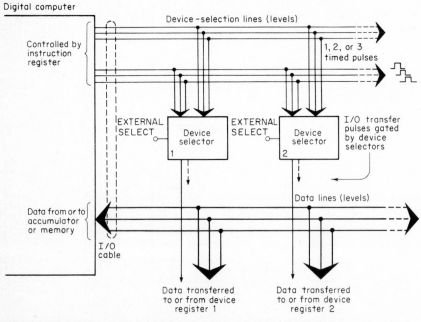

Fig. 4-2. Programmed control of multiple devices by a minicomputer with a party-line I/O bus. An I/O instruction addressed to a specific device is recognized by a device selector, which gates data-transfer or command pulses to the device in question (*based on Ref.* 15).

individual data buses through multiplexing gates (Fig. 1-9c, d). But a single small computer may communicate with a substantial number of devices, one at a time. Multiplexer circuits for over 4 (and perhaps as many as 1,000) data buses could compromise the processor design. Thus, most interface systems employ a **party-line I/O bus** of the general type illustrated in Fig. 4-2. Here, *all* devices (printers, displays, ADCs, DACs, etc.) intended to receive or transmit data words are wired to a parallel I/O data bus connected to a processor register via suitable logic. Additional party-line wires carry control-logic signals for selecting a specific device and its function (e.g., transmission or reception) and synchronize data transfers with the digital-computer operating cycle.

Signals originating from different sources (e.g., device data, various control signals) can each in turn use the same bus lines if we use **tri-state bus drivers** (Sec. 1-17, and Fig. 4-1d). **With TTL bus drivers, such signals are inverted on the bus,** so that the inverted signals are wire-ORed through open-collector driver circuits (Fig. 4-1c).

The simplest interfaces work with programmed digital-computer instructions (**input/output instructions, I/O instructions;** refer to Sec. 4-16 for direct memory access).

4-2. Synchronous-Bus Device Selection and I/O Operations. The simple interface scheme of Fig. 4-3 will move I/O data to or from a processor register (accumulator) in response to a programmed I/O instruction which

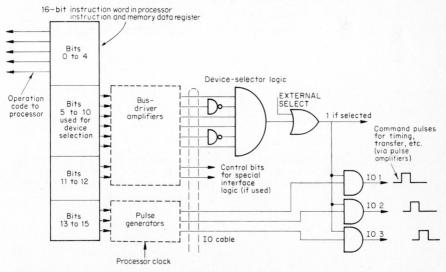

Fig. 4-3. Program-controlled selection (decoding) of device addresses and device functions. Note that (1) the I/O instruction word contains the device-address code, and (2) the IO pulses used for data-transfer operations are synchronized with the processor clock cycle.

contains the 6-bit **address code** for the selected device as part of the 16-bit instruction word.   **Individual instruction-word bits determine device-selection and control-line signals on a party-line I/O bus:**

1. Bits 0 to 4 tell the processor that an I/O instruction is wanted.   One of these bits can select a READ or WRITE operation, or this decision may be left to a logic input from the device.
2. Bits 5 to 10 (**device-address bits**) place logic levels (0 or 1) on **device-selection lines** parallel-connected to all devices on the I/O bus.   When these lines carry the **device-selection code** assigned to a specific device, its **device selector** (decoding AND gate) accepts (and regenerates) a set of one, two, or three successive command pulses (IO pulses) used to effect data transfers and other operations in the selected device as determined by instruction bits 13 to 15.
3. Bits 11 and 12 (**control bits, select bits,** or **subdevice bits**) determine levels on two control lines.   These can be used to select additional devices or different functions to be performed by a given device (see also Fig. 4-17).
4. Bits 13, 14, and 15, respectively, produce successive timed **command pulses** IO1, IO2, and IO3 on three separate control lines.   A pulse occurs if the corresponding bit is 1.

With the arrangement of Fig. 4-3, a 16-bit I/O instruction can select one of $2^{11} = 2,048$ possible devices and/or device functions through different combinations of device-address bits, control bits, and command pulses. This particular system requires four complete digital-computer memory cycles for each I/O operation, one to fetch the instruction, and one for each

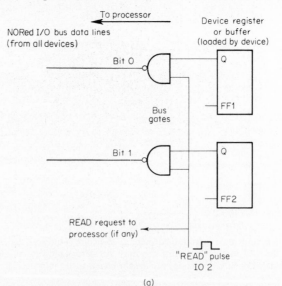

(a)

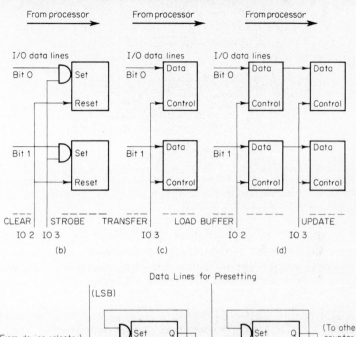

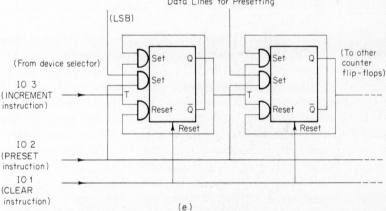

Fig. 4-4a–e. Programmed parallel data transfers using IO strobe pulses (or steps). In (a), the processor *reads a device register* through data bus lines common to all devices, (b) shows *clear-and-strobe transfer* of data into a device register, (c) shows a *jam transfer*, and (d) illustrates *transfer through a device buffer register*, as in a double-buffered digital-to-analog converter (see text). (e) is *a binary counter* which may be cleared, parallel-loaded (preset), or incremented through programmed I/O instructions using different IO pulses.

IO pulse. Many modifications of our basic programmed-I/O scheme are possible, e.g.,

1. Different numbers of processor-code bits, device-selection bits, control bits, and IO pulses may be used.
2. IO pulses can be simultaneous (on different lines), rather than successive, to save execution time (Fig. 4-17b).

More incisive modifications will be described in Secs. 4-3 and 4-4.

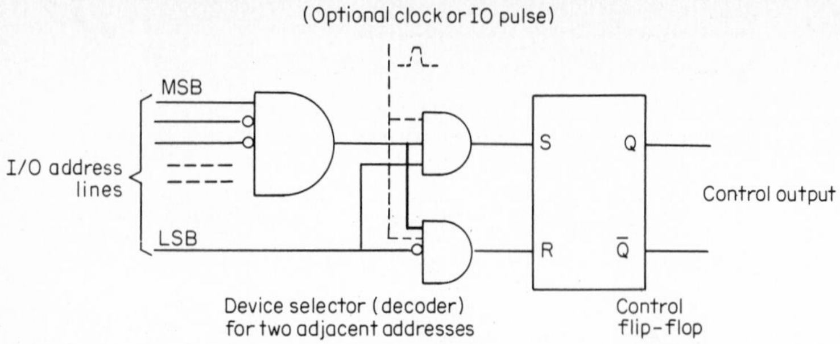

Fig. 4-4f. In this simple *one-bit interface*, the I/O-bus address signals, with or without an IO or clock pulse, switch a control flip-flop. No I/O-bus data lines need be connected to this interface, which is used for microcomputer control of relays, valves, solenoids, motors, counters, and simple serial communication links.

The most common application of the device-selector-gated command pulses is **data transfer to and from the processor.** In our basic programmed-I/O scheme, the IO pulses are synchronized with the processor operation cycle, and thus with the computer's ability to accept or transmit data.

In Fig. 4-4a, the correctly timed IO2 pulse gates data **from an external device** (e.g., an ADC) **into a processor register (accumulator)** via the I/O-bus data lines.

Figure 4-4b illustrates **clear-and-strobe data transfer** from the I/O data lines into the flip-flops of a device register. Each flip-flop is first cleared by IO2; then IO3 strobes the 1s on the data bus into the flip-flop register. Figure 4-4c shows **jam transfer** of bus data into a device register (see also Sec. 1-13). Jam transfers require only a single transfer pulse and must be employed whenever clearing and strobing operations would disturb device functions. This is true, for instance, with DACs required to switch through successive voltage levels without returning to 0 in between.

Figure 4-4d illustrates a **double-buffered-register data transfer.** Data are first transferred into the buffer register and then into the device register proper. In an analog/hybrid computer or display system, for instance, one can load a set of DAC buffer registers in turn and then "update" all DAC registers simultaneously with another I/O instruction or with a clock pulse.

Command pulses can also **set, reset, or complement special flip-flops and increment or decrement counters** in device interfaces (Fig. 4-4e and f).

Computer-read digital counters can also accumulate external **incremental data** (variables proportional to pulse rates) into parallel digital words. Incremental data representation is employed in control and navigation systems based on *digital-differential-analyzer (DDA) integrators.*

Synchronous-bus data transfers require that any external device accept or transmit data levels within a specific time interval after the start of an I/O instruction. More specifically, **timing diagrams** like Fig. 4-5, supplied in

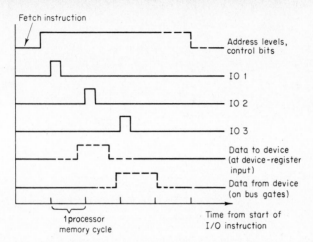

Fig. 4-5. Typical timing for processor-synchronized programmed data transfers. Data levels must be ready for the bus when transfer pulses occur.

every minicomputer interface manual, show (perhaps obviously) that *a set of data-bit levels must be established when the processor issues the data-transfer command pulse (IO pulse)*.

We assume here that our device (say an ADC) is already *prepared* to transfer data in the sense that an ADC conversion has been completed; we can, and should, make sure of this through a sense instruction (Sec. 4-7) or interrupt operation (Sec. 4-9).   What we *are* concerned with here is that data levels may not be established *soon enough* or *long enough* to complete a data transfer, allowing for cable-transmission and logic delays and rise times. Cable delays are, at best, about 1.5 nsec/ft; programmed-I/O instruction timing usually allows for at most 50 ft of I/O-bus cable.   These close timing requirements are a disadvantage of synchronous-bus systems (Sec. 4-5).

4-3.   Time-Multiplexed Device Addresses and Data.   To save interconnections at the expense of time and interface hardware, some computer I/O systems transmit the device address over the *data lines*.   After the address levels are on the bus, an ADDRESS control level or pulse from the processor sets an ADDRESS ACTIVE flip-flop in the addressed device and resets all other ADDRESS ACTIVE flip-flops (Fig. 4-6).   The output of the ADDRESS ACTIVE flip-flop substitutes for the simple device-selector output of Fig. 4-3; it can activate non-data-transfer operations immediately, or *it can gate data transfers from and to the bus after the address has been removed from the data lines.*

Instead of transferring device address and data automatically to the bus in the course of a single instruction (e.g., in Varian 620-series minicomputers), some microprocessors have *separate addressing and data-transfer instructions;* note that one addressing operation may do for several data transfers from and/or to the same device (see also Sec. 6-7).

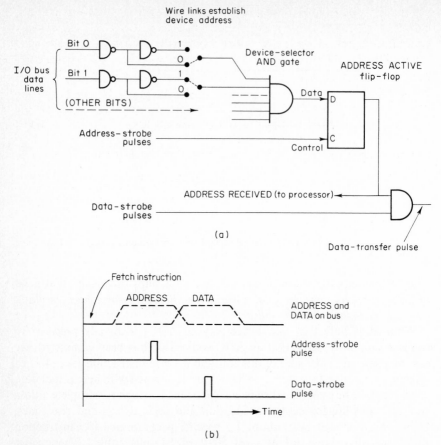

Fig. 4-6. A synchronous-bus system which transmits device addresses as well as I/O data on the data lines. THE ADDRESS ACTIVE flip-flop stores the device-selector output when the address is no longer on the bus and is cleared after the data are transmitted or received. Strobe pulses are timed so as to allow address and data to settle.

4-4. Asynchronous-Bus Systems and Cycle Stretching. For a synchronous-bus data transfer, the address and an IO pulse must reach a device, and data must be made available and transmitted over the length of the bus, *all within the fixed time interval allowed for one I/O instruction.* This constrains the time allowed for data-transfer operations in a selected device and also limits I/O bus length to about 30 to 50 ft (unless one resorts to a slower processor clock).

An **asynchronous-bus system** eliminates these constraints. Instead of rigid clock-synchronized timing, IO pulse transmission and termination of the I/O instruction are timed by "handshaking" signals returned from the device so as to ensure completion of each data transfer. The resulting slight time delay (50 to 150 nsec) is less damaging than slowing a synchronous-system clock.   Asynchronous-bus interfaces are also a little more complicated, but **asynchronous buses can simultaneously handle devices of widely differing speeds, including different memories** (Sec. 4-5).   Asynchronous buses can also be *extended* with the aid of buffer amplifiers (**bus extenders**).   The extra bus delays can slow operation, but they will not cause timing problems.

Figure 4-7*a* shows a basic interface.   The processor sends the device address and, after a 100- to 150-nsec delay to permit address and device-selector output to settle, an IO pulse called $\overline{\text{MSYN}}$ (actually, the inverted

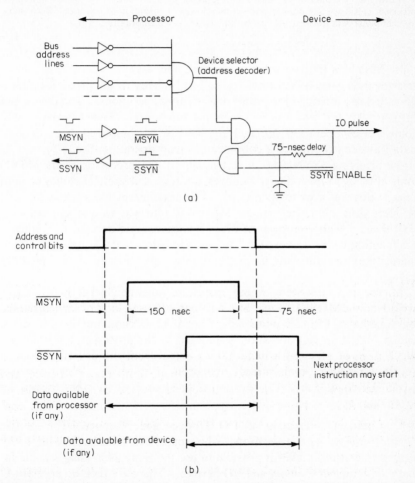

Fig. 4-7a, b. Asynchronous-bus interface (*a*), and timing at the processor end of the bus (*b*). $\overline{\text{MSYN}}$ can be used for data strobing, or $\overline{\text{MSYN}}$ may generate delayed strobe pulses in a device. Bus signals are inverted (Sec. 4-1).

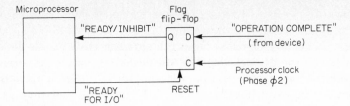

Fig. 4-7c. Quasi-asynchronous I/O operation of a MOSFET microprocessor (cycle stretching). The microprocessor signals the start of an I/O instruction cycle by resetting the flag flip-flop, whose output then halts the processor. The processor now waits until the device takes processor output data "frozen" on the I/O bus, or until device data are ready. Then the "OPERATION COMPLETE" handshaking signal from the device, synchronized with the processor clock, sets the flip-flop and permits processor operation to continue. Such quasi-asynchronous data transfers also permit the use of slow memories (Ref. 54).

pulse MSYN is transmitted over the bus, Sec. 4-1). The activated device selector then gates $\overline{SSYN}$ (inverted to SSYN) back to the processor after a 75-nsec delay intended for simple data-writing operations. The device can further delay the return of $\overline{SSYN}$ by placing a 0 on $\overline{SSYN}$ ENABLE until some device operation initiated by $\overline{MSYN}$ is completed (e.g., delayed data-transfer strobing, or a core-memory read operation, Sec. 4-5).

On receiving SSYN ($=0$, inverted signal), the processor clears $\overline{MSYN}$ and, after a 75-nsec delay, removes address and control voltages (and data, if this was a write operation). The next instruction cycle is allowed to start only after the cleared $\overline{MSYN}$ is returned to the processor as SSYN $= 1$. If the return of SSYN $= 0$ is excessively delayed (say when a malfunctioning or nonexistent device was addressed) a timeout circuit warns the user through an internal interrupt. Figure 4-7*b* illustrates asynchronous-bus timing.

Microcomputer systems whose operations must be clocked (e.g., systems with dynamic MOSFET logic, Sec. 1-17) can still use a kind of asynchronous-bus operation with all pulse delays equal to integral numbers of clock cycles. After an I/O operation is initiated by the processor, the processor clock is gated off until a handshaking signal from the device is received (**cycle stretching, cycle-extend** operation, Fig. 4-7*c*). With dynamic MOSFET logic (Sec. 1-17), the processor clock must not be stopped for more than a few clock cycles.

4-5. Common Addressing of I/O Devices and Memory. The flexible timing possible with asynchronous-bus machines (and even with cycle-extend operation) makes it possible **to use the same addressing scheme for both the computer memory and I/O devices.** There are then no special I/O instructions. An instruction like

STORE REGISTER 4 IN   ADDRS

may store the contents of register 4 in a device register or in a memory location; device registers will have *absolute* addresses (Sec. 3-18). Again, **memories with completely different cycle times (core, MOS, bipolar, RAM and/or ROM) can be connected to the asynchronous bus as computer peripherals.** The control, address, and data lines of such a **universal bus** will serve for asynchronous memory and I/O *data transfers*, but also for *interrupt-address transfers* (Secs. 4-12 and 4-14) and for *direct memory access* (Sec. 4-16). It is also possible to multiplex data and addresses, as in Sec. 4-3.

NOTE: Universal-bus systems may have a memory address register (**bus address register,** serving both memory and I/O) in the central processor and/or in the individual memory banks or chips. Some memory chips and I/O devices may also require external address registers (**address latches**) to hold the address during data transfers, especially if data and addresses are multiplexed.

4-6. Device Control Registers. Many peripheral devices have more different functions or operating modes than we can control with a few control bits or IO-pulse bits in a single I/O instruction. Such devices can be designed to accept, store, and execute multibit "device instructions" loaded into a **device control register** or registers via the I/O-bus data lines (just like into a data register). In general, control registers will require jam transfers or double-buffered transfers (Fig. 4-4b and c). An important example of a control register is the multiplexer control register for selecting different multiplexer input channels for an ADC. Control registers may permit incrementation; i.e., the control register can be a counter set to a given initial count by an I/O instruction and then incremented by I/O pulses as needed; the variety of possible arrangements is endless. Control registers of many old-fashioned process controllers simply operate *electromechanical relays.*

Control registers make interfaces and device functions programmable through processor instructions (**programmable I/O port,** Sec. 6-7). Device interfaces may have a single control-register bit (processor-controlled interrupt masking, Sec. 4-13), or they may need several 16-bit control registers. Examples of devices programmed through computer-loaded registers are automatic data channels (Sec. 4-18), cathode-ray-tube displays (Sec. 4-28), analog/hybrid computers, and other digital computers (Sec. 4-26).

4-7. Device Status Registers, Flags, and Sense Lines. Programmed I/O operations occur at times determined by the digital-computer program. *But the addressed device may not be ready* (e.g., a printer may be out of paper, an analog-to-digital converter may not have completed a conversion). If we can represent the device status by 0s and 1s in a **device status register,**

the processor can read or test the status register with a programmed instruction and branch conditionally before an actual data-transfer instruction is executed, e.g.,

TEST   READ ADC STATUS REGISTER INTO ACCUMULATOR
               COMPLEMENT ACCUMULATOR
               BRANCH IF NOT ZERO   TEST
               READ ADC DATA REGISTER AND CLEAR STATUS REGISTER

In this case, the status register can have as few as one bit; all must be set to 1 if the data transfer is to take place (e.g., signal source ON, ADC conversion completed). Otherwise, the processor loops until the status test is successful.

The status word can be used for *jump-table addressing* (Sec. 3-11a) of routines designed to service different status-bit combinations:

READ DEVICE STATUS INTO REGISTER 3
JUMP, INDEXED BY REGISTER 3   TABLE / TABLE is the
                                  /   jump-table
                                  /   starting address

Note that status flip-flops from *different* devices can be combined into a status register, so that several devices can be checked together (see also Sec. 4-11).

Many synchronous-bus minicomputers (e.g., NOVA, ECLIPSE, PDP-8, PDP-15, Hewlett-Packard) use the **sense/skip method** for testing single device-status flags. An ordinary I/O instruction addressed to, say, the ADC device selector gates one of the command pulses (IO1 in Fig. 4-8) into the **sense gate,** and, if the flag level (sense line) is up, onto the **skip line** common to all devices on the I/O bus. *The pulse on the skip line then*

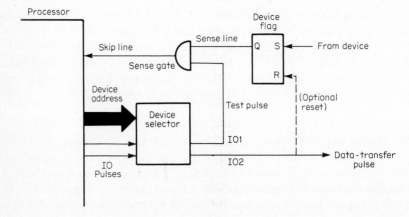

Fig. 4-8. Sense-line operation using a device selector, sensing gate, and common skip bus.

increments the processor program counter to produce a conditional skip (program branch).   An example would be:

```
TEST              SKIP IF ADC FLAG IS UP                    / I/O instruction
  └──────────── JUMP TO                        TEST / Try again!
                  READ ADC (AND CLEAR FLAG)                 / If flag is up
```

The program will cycle until the device flag is up, at which time the program continues, usually with a data-transfer instruction.   The ADC flag must be *reset* by the **READ ADC** instruction and/or by the **START CONVERSION** instruction or timing pulse.

Other sense-line systems exist.   Many computers do away with device-selector addressing of sense gates by simply accepting flag levels on **multiple sense lines,** which are interrogated with processor instructions like **SKIP IF SENSE LINE 5 IS UP.**

Flag logic levels controlled by manually operated **sense switches** permit a human operator to control program branching during computation.

Status sensing is inexpensive, but even small digital computers can rarely afford the time for "idle" sense/skip loops such as the simple ADC example shown above.   Sensing is, therefore, used mainly for decisions between device-dependent program branches which do *not* cause idling.   Otherwise we require *program interrupts.*

INTERRUPT SYSTEMS

4-8.   Simple Interrupt-System Requirements.   In an interrupt system a device-flag level (INTERRUPT-SERVICE REQUEST) **interrupts the computer program on completion of the current instruction.**   The interrupt line is tested during the current instruction by the microprogram (or hardware). **If the interrupt system is enabled, a service request causes an automatic subroutine jump to an interrupt-service routine,** as soon as the current instruction is executed.   The service-routine address **(trap location)** is placed by the programmer into a special pointer location associated with the interrupt system (usually on page 0 of memory).   Interrupt-service routines, which are often general-purpose I/O routines called when some device is ready, can be *relocatable* (Sec. 3-18).

On completion of an interrupt-service routine, **the processor must return to the interrupted program,** as after any subroutine (Sec. 2-23).   But unlike for ordinary subroutine calls, the program cannot know when an interrupt will "strike" (at best, we can *disable* interrupts during critical program phases, Sec. 4-13).   Therefore, an interrupt-service routine can transfer data to and from other program sections only through COMMON storage areas (Sec. 3-13).   Moreover, besides storing the **return address** (incremented program-counter contents), **it will be necessary to save and later restore every aspect of the processor status which bears on the execution of**

the interrupted program and which could be disturbed by the interrupt-service routine. This includes:

> Contents of any **processor register** used by the interrupt-service routine
> Status of the **processor flags** (Zero, Minus, Carry, Overflow)

but also

> **Base-register-selection status in memory-mapping systems** (Sec. 2-30)
> Contents of any **I/O control registers** (Sec. 4-6) modified by the interrupt-service routine, including *interrupt-mask flip-flops* in multiple-interrupt systems (Sec. 4-13).

Modern computers combine the processor status flags with additional status bits representing the memory-mapping base register in use, the interrupt/enable/disable status, and other information in a **processor status register,** whose contents (**processor status word**) can be saved or modified with simple instructions.

Saving and restoring operations can be *programmed* into each interrupt-service routine. Their execution takes time; in particular, status-saving instructions delay the actual useful interrupt service. For this reason, *modern micro/minicomputers implement some status-saving/restoring operations automatically (microprogram or hardware) and/or speed them up with special instructions.*

Interrupt-system hardware can automatically disable an interrupt which has been recognized, so that it cannot reinterrupt the beginning of its own service routine (status saving, data transfers). The state of any interrupt requesting service but not yet recognized or completely serviced is usually stored by its device flag, which is eventually cleared by the service routine. The interrupt can then be reenabled.

> *NOTE:* Interrupts do not work when the computer is HALTed; so *we cannot test interrupts when stepping a program manually.*

4-9. Interrupt-System Operation. A number of minicomputers, (e.g., Data General NOVA) have a single interrupt input which produces an indirect subroutine jump. *Hardware saves the return address at location 0 and resets the program counter to the relocatable service-routine address stored by the programmer at location 1.* All status saving/restoring must be done by the service routine. The *return jump* is an ordinary indirect jump (like the subroutine return for such machines, Sec. 2-23).

In the following program, the service routine reads an ADC after its CONVERSION-COMPLETE interrupt (see also Secs. 4-7 and 4-10).

```
          (main program)
   ⋮         ⋮
1713      (current instruction)              / Interrupt occurs here

0000      1714                               / Incremented program
                                             /    counter (1714) will be
                                             /    stored here by hardware
0001      SRVICE                             / This location contains
                                             /    address of relocatable
                                             /    service routine

          . . . . . . . . . . . . . . . . . . . . . .

SRVICE    STORE ACCUMULATOR IN  SAVAC / Save accumulator
          READ ADC AND CLEAR FLAG      / Read ADC into
                                       /    accumulator and
                                       /    clear ADC flag
          STORE ACCUMULATOR IN  X      / Store ADC reading
          LOAD ACCUMULATOR      SAVAC  / Restore accumulator
          INTERRUPT ON                 / Turn interrupt back on
          JUMP INDIRECT VIA     0000   / Return jump to 1714;
                                       / Interrupted program
                                       /    continues
```

Note (1) that there was no need to save processor flags, since the service routine did not use them, and (2) in such simple machines, the action of the **INTERRUPT ON** instruction is automatically delayed until the following instruction (return jump) is completed.

The single interrupt inputs of Digital Equipment Corporation PDP-8 series processors, and of machines emulating this series, produce a *direct* subroutine jump (Sec. 2-23). Hardware stores the return address in memory location 0 and resets the program counter to execute at location 1, where the programmer must insert an *instruction*, typically an indirect jump to a relocatable service routine.

More modern computers employ either a hardware stack or a software stack which automatically stores the return addresses for interrupts as well as for subroutines (Sec. 2-23 and 3-12). Some mini/microcomputers also automatically stack the processor status word (Sec. 4-12). In that case, we need not only the instruction **RETURN FROM SUBROUTINE** (pop and restore program counter, Sec. 2-23), but a new instruction, **RETURN FROM INTERRUPT**, which pops and restores both the return address and the processor status word.

Automatic stacking greatly simplifies nesting of subroutines and interrupts, including multiple interrupts (Secs. 3-12 and 3-10). As noted in Secs. 2-23 and 3-15, hardware stacks are faster but are size-limited.

Software stacks permit convenient register saving/restoring and inter-mediate-data storage (Sec. 3-15) and can still serve these purposes even if return addresses go on a hardware stack. Some computers have special instructions for pushing and popping multiple registers; note, though, that saving/restoring of registers not actually disturbed by an interrupt-service routine may waste time.

Altogether, interrupt-service action with a modern mini-microcomputer is *simpler and faster:*

$$\text{(main program)}$$
$$\vdots \qquad\qquad \vdots$$

1713   (current instruction) / interrupt occurs
/   here

(Return address 1714 and processor status word are automatically pushed into a software stack. Program counter and processor status are automatically reset to values prestored in specific memory locations)

0000   SRVICE   / Address of relocatable
/   service routine

0001   (status word to be used
for service routine, disables interrupt)

. . . .

SRVICE   PUSH ACCUMULATOR   / Save accumulator
/   on stack
                READ ADC AND CLEAR FLAG   / Read ADC and clear flag
                STORE ACCUMULATOR IN   X / Store ADC reading
                POP ACCUMULATOR   / Restore accumulator
                RETURN FROM INTERRUPT   / Return jump to 1714

(Processor status is restored, interrupt reenabled; interrupted program continues).

For the fastest possible interrupt service, several mini/microcomputers simply duplicate all processor registers (including program counter and status register) for use by an interrupt-service routine (context-switching or multiple-environment system).

4-10. Multiple Interrupts. Interrupt-system operation would be simple if there were only one possible source of interrupts, but this is practically never true. Even a stand-alone digital computer usually has several interrupts corresponding to peripheral malfunctions (tape unit out of tape, printer out of paper), and flight simulators, space-vehicle controllers, and process-control systems may have *hundreds* of different interrupts.

TABLE 4-1.   Data-Reconstruction Errors for Sinusoidal Signal Components $\sin 2\pi ft$.

Each table entry is the number $1/f\ \Delta t$ of sine-wave samples per period needed for a specified percentage error. Δt is the sampling period.*

	10%	1%	0.1%	0.01%
Zero-order hold	62.8	628	6,280	62,800
Zero-order hold with prediction	31.4	314	3,140	31,400
First-order hold	20	63	200	628
Polygonal hold	7	22	70	220

* Based on Korn, G. A., and T. M. Korn, *Electronic Analog and Hybrid Computers*, 2d ed., McGraw-Hill, New York, 1972.

A practical **multiple-interrupt system** will have to:

1. **"Trap" the program to different memory locations** corresponding to specific individual interrupts
2. Assign **priorities** to simultaneous or successive interrupts
3. **Service lower-priority interrupt requests** after higher-priority routines are completed
4. **Permit higher-priority interrupts to interrupt lower-priority service routines** as soon as the return address and any automatically saved registers are safely stored

"Nesting" of successive interrupts (reinterrupting lower-priority service routines) requires that programs and/or hardware carefully save successive levels of return addresses, processor status, and register contents, to be restored as needed.   This is neatly done with hardware and/or software last-in/first-out stacks, exactly as shown for nested subroutines in Sec. 3-15. The same stack can nest both interrupts and ordinary subroutines.

Although context-switching interrupt systems (Sec. 4-9) with as many as eight sets of registers exist, they must still be supplemented with stack-saving/restoring techniques if there are many interrupts.   Most multiple-environment systems have only one duplicate set of registers, which is reserved for use by system programs (supervisor state, Sec. 5-23).

4-11. Programmed Identification of Multiple Interrupts. Simple mini/microcomputers having only a single interrupt-request input can use various combinations of hardware and software to identify multiple interrupts. The most primitive system simply ORs all interrupt flags together; the interrupt-service routine then tests ("polls") successive device flags, in order of descending priority, with programmed instructions (Sec. 4-6). The first active device flag causes the program to branch to its associated service routine.

EXAMPLE: The following polling routine ("skip-chain" routine) uses sense-skip instructions (Sec. 4-6) to test interrupt flags indicating computer power-supply failure (Sec. 2-30), completion of an ADC conversion, and a fire alarm (note that the volatile ADC reading was considered to be more time-critical than the fire alarm!).

```
SRVICE   SKIP IF POWER FLAG LOW        / Power-supply
                                       /   trouble?
         JUMP TO LOWPWR                / Yes, go to service
                                       /   routine
         SKIP IF ADC DONE FLAG LOW     / No; ADC service
                                       /   request?
         JUMP TO ADC                   / Yes, service it
         SKIP IF FIRE-ALARM FLAG LOW   / No; fire alarm?
         JUMP TO FIRE                  / Yes, go to service
                                       /   routine
         JUMP TO ERROR                 / No; spurious
                                       /   interrupt—print
                                       /   error message (or return)
......................................................................
ADC      STORE ACCUMULATOR IN  SAVAC   / ADC service routine
         READ ACC AND CLEAR
            FLAG
         STORE ACCUMULATOR IN  X
         LOAD ACCUMULATOR      SAVAC   / Restore accumulator
         INTERRUPT ON                  / Turn interrupts back
                                       /   on
         JUMP INDIRECT VIA     0000    / Return jump
```

The example was written for a computer without automatic return-address stacking, and the interrupt was disabled throughout the service routine. It is, however, possible to reinterrupt a polling routine, provided that either the hardware or the program saves successive return addresses, processor status, etc.

Interrupt identification by polling requires a minimum of hardware and is used even with multi-input interrupt systems to service less time-critical peripherals.

An alternative low-cost technique collects up to 8 or 16 interrupt flags into a status register, which is read with a single processor instruction. The flag word is rotated and tested bit by bit (Sec. 3-25), or it can be used to index a jump table as in Sec. 4-7.

4-12. Hardware Priority-Interrupt Systems. The multilevel priority-interrupt circuit of Fig. 4-9a can be built into a processor, or a card or LSI chip may be added to a single-input interrupt system. The processor strobes the REQUEST flip-flops for all interrupts once per instruction. *This samples all enabled SERVICE REQUEST lines at the same processor-determined time to compare their priorities.* REQUEST flip-flops with active inputs will be set, and the **priority-arbitration gates** transmit a single 1 on the line corresponding to the highest priority level. The **priority-encoding logic** transforms this 1-out-of-2^n code into an n-bit code, which determines one of 2^n service-routine addresses ($n = 2$ for the four-level system of Fig. 4-9a).

If at least one REQUEST flip-flop sets, the resulting INTERRUPT REQUEST step causes the processor to store the return address at the end of the current instruction. The processor must then read the interrupt-level code with an ACKNOWLEDGE pulse and use this code to branch to the correct service routine.

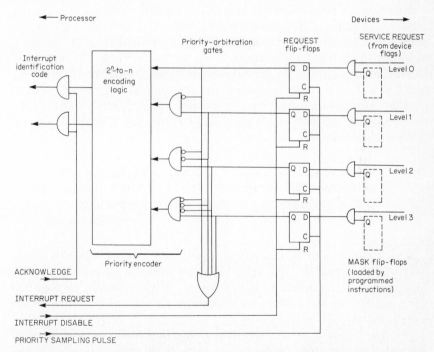

Fig. 4-9a. A simple priority-interrupt system. Service-request priorities are compared at the time of the priority-sampling pulse, usually once per processor instruction. The priority-arbitration gates transmit only the highest-level request, whose number is encoded to identify the corresponding interrupt-service address. Mask flip-flops can enable or disable individual request lines. A MASTER CLEAR bus line (not shown) resets all flip-flops on power-up and at the start of most programs.

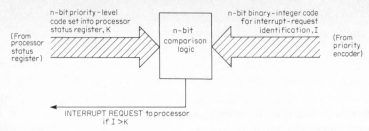

Fig. 4-9*b***.** Instead of masking 2^n individual request lines, the n-bit request-identification code is compared with a priority-level code set into n bits of the processor status register. Interrupts below level 0, 1, 2, ... can thus be inhibited.

NOTE: If the return address is saved in a memory location (e.g., location 0, as in the PDP-8 and NOVA minicomputers) or in a register, rather than in a stack, then the interrupt-system hardware must *disable the interrupt system* until the program can stack the return address for nesting.

The simplest interrupt-identification schemes, often used with add-on priority encoders, still employ programmed instructions. The interrupt-level code is placed on the I/0-bus data lines. INTERRUPT REQUEST causes a processor trap (say via location 1, as in Sec. 4-9) to the interrupt-identification program. In the following program, **ACKNOWLEDGE INTER-RUPT** is an I/O instruction which issues the ACKNOWLEDGE pulse to read the interrupt-level code into a processor index register. **TABLE** is the origin-address of a jump table (Sec. 3-11*a*) listing the relocatable service-routine addresses.

```
SRVICE   PUSH INDEX REGISTER                      / Save register first
         ACKNOWLEDGE INTERRUPT                     / Code in index register
         JUMP PREINDEXED, INDIRECT   TABLE / Jump to individual
                                          /    service routine
```

Such a routine can be microprogrammed into a single **ACKNOWLEDGE INTERRUPT** instruction. No index register is needed if the priority encoder itself produces the absolute addresses (**vector addresses,** usually on page 0 of the computer memory) where the relocatable service-routine addresses are stored (see also Sec. 6-15).

In a true automatic priority-interrupt system (**automatic vectored interrupt system),** *a microprogram* (*or hardware*) *activates the read-address-code/jump-direct sequence automatically after each interrupt is recognized, as soon as the current instruction terminates.* Absolute vector addresses can be read directly into the memory address register, either over the I/O-bus data lines or over special vector-address lines (e.g., PDP-15).

Many microprocessors (e.g., Motorola 6800, Sec. 6-6) have a fixed number of interrupt-request inputs each associated with an interrupt-vector location.   To expand the number of vector locations, one intercepts the memory address bus and modifies the memory address as a function of a priority-encoder output when a simple recognition gate detects a vector address (Fig. 6-6d).

The better priority-interrupt systems locate the prestored new *processor status word* for each individual service routine (Sec. 4-8) immediately following its vector-address location. *The interrupt sequence then automatically stacks the old processor status word as well as the return address and loads the processor status register with the new status word. The process is reversed on return from interrupt.*   Service-routine address and status word are said to form the **interrupt vector** for a given interrupt.

4-13.   Interrupt Masking, Priority Changes, and Software Interrupts.   In the priority-interrupt system of Fig. 4-9a, the entire system can be enabled or disabled by processor instructions.   In addition, *individual* interrupt-request inputs can be enabled or disabled by *mask flip-flops*.   Mask flip-flops are usually provided by the user as control-register bits in the device interfaces (Sec. 4-24) so that the interrupts associated with specific devices can be enabled or disabled by programmed instructions.

It is also possible to address the set of all mask flip-flops together as an *interrupt mask register*.   A processor instruction for loading this register with different mask words permits the user to change interrupt priorities by enabling or disabling any combination of interrupts.   While the relative priority of two enabled interrupts cannot be changed by masking, it is possible to prevent reinterruption of any service routine by any specified interrupt or interrupts.

The interrupt mask in force for any interrupted program segment or service routine is, then, a vital part of the processor status, which must be saved and later restored (Secs. 4-8 and 4-12).   The new service routine, in turn, may require a new interrupt mask corresponding to different priorities.

But it is impossible to fit many individual mask bits into an 8-bit or 16-bit processor status word.   Most computers, therefore, determine interrupt status by the method of Fig. 4-9b.   A priority encoder (Fig. 4-9a) produces an n-bit integer code $I = 0, 1, 2, \ldots$ corresponding to 2^n interrupts of increasing priority.   This code is compared with an n-bit interrupt-level code K stored in the processor status register; INTERRUPT REQUEST is passed on to processor if and only if $I > K$. *We thus control 2^n interrupts with only n status bits, but can no longer disable individual interrupts. We can disable all interrupts below level 1, level 2, etc.* Programmed individual interrupt masking is, however, still possible in the device control registers.

Typical processors use $n = 3$ status-register bits to protect program segments from interrupts below $2^n = 8$ different priority levels.   Priorities associated with different program sections can be programmed by instructions loading the processor status register **(dynamic priority allocation)**. Interrupt-vector status words set the initial protection level of the associated interrupt-service routines.

Internal interrupts respond to processor malfunctions (power-supply failure, parity errors in memory data transfers, Secs. 1-8 and 2-30) and to programming errors (illegal addresses, stack overflow, etc.).   Internal interrupts usually have higher priorities than I/O interrupts (in some processors, internal interrupts may be **unmaskable)**.

NOTE: Active direct-memory-access service requests (Sec. 4-16) always have priority over interrupt-service requests.

Software interrupts are *programmed instructions* which emulate an interrupt with a specified interrupt vector (service-routine address and new status word).   They can replace subroutine jumps when it is convenient to change the processor status word, and later restore it with a **RETURN FROM INTERRUPT** instruction.   The main application is for jumps to routines located in different memory partitions of memory-mapped computers (Sec. 5-22).   Software interrupts have their own assigned priority levels.

4-14. Chain-Priority Systems. (a) Synchronous-Bus Systems. Computer systems may require large numbers of interrupts.   While it is possible to cascade priority-encoder circuits to provide additional levels, the most common technique for interrupt-system expansion employs **chain-wired interrupt controllers** each capable of transmitting a unique vector address when its priority has been recognized.

Figure 4-10a shows a typical chain-wired interrupt controller for a synchronous-bus computer system (Sec. 4-2).   Figure 4-10b indicates how the PRIORITY IN/OUT connections of different controllers are chained along the I/O bus in order of decreasing priority.

Referring again to Fig. 4-10a, a (mask-enabled) SERVICE REQUEST will set the REQUEST flip-flop on a processor-timed clock pulse, unless a higher-priority controller has already set its own REQUEST flip-flop, thus inhibiting lower-priority controllers with a 0 on their PRIORITY IN inputs.   With simultaneous service requests, the controller closer to the processor wins, because it receives the clock pulse first.

Besides locking out lower-priority interrupts, the REQUEST flip-flop, when set, transmits a timed interrupt request to the processor and also pre-enables the ACTIVE flip-flop.   If the interrupt system is on (and no direct-memory-access is pending, Sec. 4-16) the processor answers with an ACKNOWLEDGE pulse just before the current instruction terminates (Fig. 4-10c).   This sets the pre-enabled ACTIVE flip-flop, which gates the

◄──────── Processor   Device ──────►

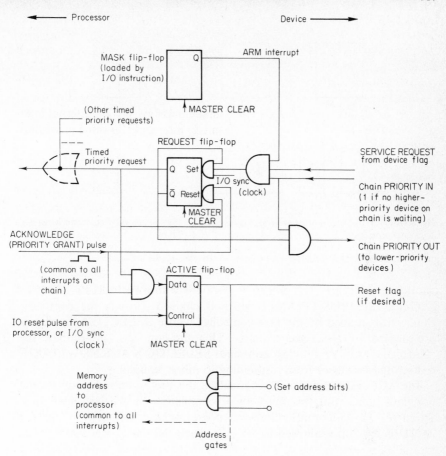

Fig. 4-10a. Synchronous-bus chain-priority logic for one device. The **PRIORITY GRANT** line is common to all interrupt controllers on the chain. Flip-flops are timed by processor-supplied pulses. MASTER CLEAR, issued by the processor when it is turned on or through a console pushbutton, resets flip-flops initially. Wire-ORed signals (timed priority request and address code) are actually inverted on the bus (Sec. 4-1); the inverted signals are not shown for the sake of clarity. Many different versions of this circuit exist. Similar logic is used to arbitrate direct-memory-access requests.

vector-address code to the processor (via I/O bus data lines or special address lines). REQUEST flip-flop and device flag are also reset.

(b) Asynchronous-Bus System. Chain-interrupt controllers for asynchronous-bus machines employ a complicated sequence of "handshaking" signals to free themselves of bus-delay effects (Fig. 4-11). A (mask-enabled) SERVICE REQUEST sets the REQUEST flip-flop, which pre-enables the SELECTED flip-flop and sends the request on to the processor without

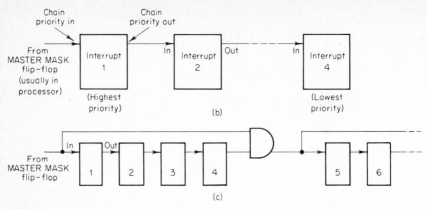

Fig. 4-10b, c. Wired-chain priority-propagation circuits. Since each subsystem and its wiring delays the propagated REQUEST-flip-flop steps (Fig. 4-10a) by 10 to 30 nsec, the simple chain of Fig. 4-10b should not have more than four to six links. The circuit of Fig. 4-10c bypasses priority-inhibiting steps for faster propagation. (*Hewlett-Packard Corp.*)

priority arbitration. The processor responds with a PRIORITY SAMPL-ING PULSE (BUS GRANT), which is chained through the controller chain until stopped by the first controller whose SELECTED flip-flop is pre-enabled by a service request. This flip-flop sets, pre-enables the controller's ACTIVE flip-flop, and sends SELECTION ACKNOWLEDGE to keep the processor from responding to other requests.

The ACTIVE flip-flop will set to place the vector-address code on the bus data lines. But this must await completion of the last bus trans-action (e.g., a data transfer between processor and memory). Thus the ACTIVE flip-flop is allowed to set only when the bus SSYN signal resets

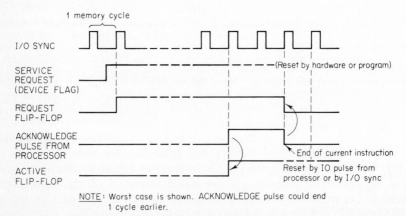

Fig. 4-10d. Timing diagram for the priority-interrupt logic of Fig. 4-10a. The ACKNOW-LEDGE pulse remains ON until the trap address is transferred.

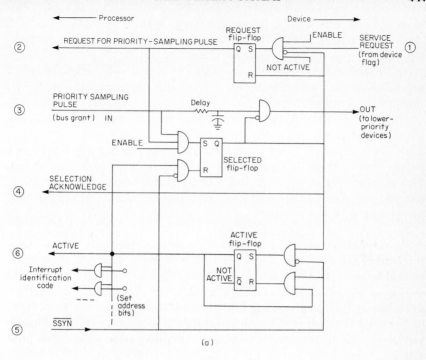

(a)

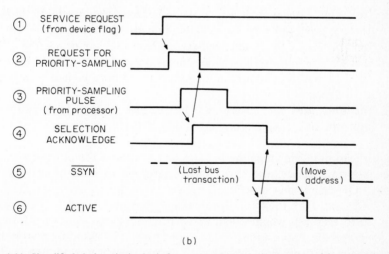

(b)

Fig. 4-11. Simplified chain-priority logic for an asynchronous-bus machine (*a*), and timing (*b*). The bus signals REQUEST FOR PRIORITY-SAMPLING PULSE, SELECTION AC-KNOWLEDGE, SSYN, ACTIVE, and INTERRUPT IDENTIFICATION CODE are actually inverted and wire-ORed on the bus; the inverted signals are not shown for the sake of clarity. Many modifications of this circuit, which is also used for direct memory access, exist.

to signal the end of the transaction (Sec. 4-4). The ACTIVE signal interrupts the processor and also evokes a new SSYN from the processor's bus controller as the vector address is transmitted.

(c) Multiple-Chain Systems. In Figs. 4-10 and 4-11, each interrupt controller can be disabled by an individual mask flip-flop (Fig. 4-10a). To permit a degree of level masking with a few processor status bits (Sec. 4-13), the complete interrupt system can comprise four to eight chains, with the chain priority levels arbitrated by the scheme of Fig. 4-9a and b. Then, priorities within each chain are determined as before, but any device in a higher-priority chain has priority over all devices in lower-priority chains. The processor status word can lock out all chains below chain 1, chain 2, etc. Vector addresses are read from the controller whose priority has been recognized.

4-15. Discussion of Interrupt-System Features. Interrupts are the basic mechanism for sharing a digital computer between different, often time-critical tasks. The effectiveness of an interrupt system depends on **the time needed to service possibly critical situations,** on **the number of interrupts available,** and on **programming flexibility and convenience.**

The total time between an interrupt-service request and the first **useful** service-routine instruction is composed of **three parts** which you must **add up:**

1. The "raw" **latency time,** i.e., the time needed to complete the longest possible processor instruction (including any indirect addressing).
2. **The time needed by the interrupt-system hardware and/or microprogram to reach the first service-routine instruction.** This, typically between 2 and 20 μsec, is often all that manufacturers quote as their "interrupt-service time."
3. **The time used for "overhead" instructions** needed to identify the interrupt and to save processor status, registers, etc.

Overhead time, including the time needed to restore the processor status after interrupt service, also slows system response to lower-priority interrupts. Overhead time is reduced by the hardware features described in Secs. 4-9 and 4-12 to 4-14. You should, however, take a hard-nosed attitude to establish whether you really need advanced hardware features in your specific application. Many interrupts are associated with I/O routines for relatively slow devices such as teletypewriters and tape reader/punches, and thousands of minicomputers service these happily with simple skip-chain systems. Things become more critical in instrumentation and control systems, which must not miss real-time-clock interrupts intended to log time, to read instruments, or to perform control operations. Time-critical jobs require *fast responses*. If there are many time-critical operations or any time-sharing computations, *the computing time wasted in overhead operations* becomes interesting. Some real-time systems may have periods of peak loads when it becomes actually impossible to service *all* interrupt requests. At this point, the designer must decide whether to buy an improved system or which interrupt requests are at least temporarily expendable. It is in the latter connection that *dynamic priority allocation* becomes useful: it may, for instance, be expedient *to mask certain interrupts during peak-load periods*. In other situations we might, instead, *lower the relative priority of the main computer program by unmasking additional interrupts during peak real-time loads*.

If two or more interrupt-service routines employ the same library subroutine, we are faced, as shown in Sec. 3-16, with the problem of *reentrant programming*. Temporary-storage locations used by the common subroutine may be wiped out unless we either duplicate the subroutine program in memory for each interrupt or unless we provide true reentrant subroutines.

It is fair to say that the most effective applications of interrupts initiate computer operations more complicated than simple data transfers. The best method for time-critical reading and writing as such is not through interrupt-service routines with their awkward programming overhead but with a *direct-memory-access system*, which has no such problems at all.

DIRECT MEMORY ACCESS AND AUTOMATIC BLOCK TRANSFERS

4-16. Cycle Stealing. Step-by-step program-controlled data transfers limit data-transmission rates and use valuable processor time for alternate instruction fetches and execution; programming is also tedious. It is often preferable to use additional hardware for interfacing a parallel data bus directly with the digital-computer memory data register and to request and grant 1-cycle pauses in processor operation for **direct transfer of data to or from memory (interlace** or **cycle-stealing** operation). In larger digital machines, and optionally in a few minicomputers (PDP-15), a data bus can even access one memory bank without stopping processor interaction with other memory banks at all.

Note that **cycle stealing in no way disturbs the program sequence.** Even though smaller digital computers must stop computation during memory transfers, the program simply skips a cycle at the end of the current memory cycle (no need to complete the current *instruction*) and later resumes just where it left off. One does not have to save register contents or other information, as with program interrupts.

4-17. DMA Interface Logic. To make **direct memory access (DMA)** practical, the interface must be able to:

1. **Address desired locations in memory**
2. Synchronize cycle stealing with processor operation
3. **Initiate transfers** by device requests (this includes clock-timed transfers) or by the computer program
4. Deal with **priorities** and queuing of service requests if two or more devices request data transfers

DMA priority logic typically employs chain-wired controllers like those described in Sec. 4-14. The same controller cards often serve interrupts and DMA. **DMA service requests always have priority over concurrent interrupt requests.**

A **synchronous-bus DMA system** employs a controller like that in Fig. 4-10 to produce a timed **cycle-steal request** unless a higher-priority DMA request is pending. The processor answers with an ACKNOWLEDGE (PRIORITY GRANTED) pulse. This sets a pre-enabled ACTIVE flip-flop, which gates the appropriate memory address into the memory address register and then causes memory and device logic to gate data from or to the DMA data lines (Fig. 4-12). These data lines may or may not be identical with the programmed-transfer data lines. It is also possible to multiplex addresses and data.

Asynchronous-bus DMA systems employ controllers like that of Fig. 4-11 to obtain control over the asynchronous bus and to transmit the desired memory address over the bus address lines. Additional device-interface circuits (not shown) are needed to generate the handshaking signal MSYN and to produce an asynchronous data transfer between device and memory in the manner of Sec. 4-4 (Ref. 20). The processor plays no part in this transfer. With universal-bus systems (Sec. 4-4), such direct **nonprocessor data transfers** can also link *two devices*, rather than a device and a memory (see also Sec. 7-9).

Cycle-stealing direct memory access is especially easy with microcomputer three-state memory address and data buses. One simply stops the processor clock while a device controller places a memory address on the bus and cycles the memory.

In most post-1970 computer systems, the DMA data lines are identical with the programmed-transfer data lines. This simplifies interconnections at the expense of processor hardware. In other systems, the DMA data lines are also used to transmit the DMA address to the processor before data are transferred. This further reduces the number of bus lines, but complicates hardware and timing.

4-18. Automatic Block Transfers. As we described it, the DMA data transfer is *device*-initiated. A *program-dependent* decision to transfer data,

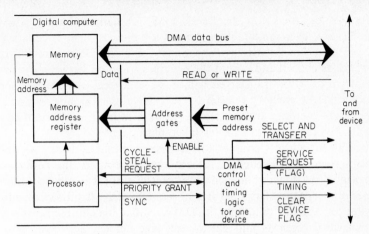

Fig. 4-12. A direct-memory-access (DMA) interface.

even directly from or to memory, still requires a programmed instruction to cause a DMA service request. This is hardly worth the trouble for a *single-word* transfer. Most DMA transfers, whether device or program initiated, involve not single words but **blocks** of tens, hundreds, or even thousands of data words.

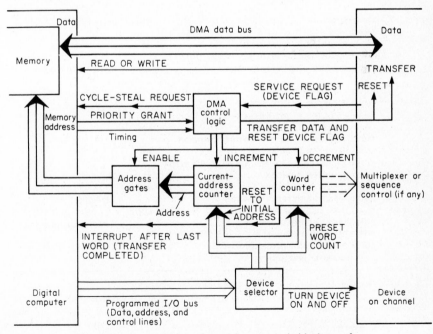

Fig. 4-13a. A simple data channel for automatic block transfers.

Figure 4-13*a* shows how the simple DMA system of Fig. 4-12 may be expanded into an **automatic data channel** for block transfers. Data for a block can arrive or depart asymchronously, and the DMA controller will steal cycles as needed and permit the program to go on between cycles. A block of words to be transferred will, in general, occupy a corresponding block of adjacent memory registers. Successive memory addresses can be gated into the memory address registered by a counter, the **current-address counter.** Before any data transfer takes place, a programmed instruction sets the current-address counter to the desired initial address; the desired number of words **(block length)** is set into a second counter, the **word counter,** which will count down with each data transfer until 0 is reached after the desired number of transfers. As service requests arrive from, say, an analog-to-digital converter or data link, the DMA control logic implements successive cycle-steal requests and gates successive current addresses into the memory address register as the current-address counter counts up (see also Fig. 4-5*a*).

The word counter is similarly decremented once per data word. When a block transfer is completed, the word counter can stop the device from

```
            / Initialization
A1          .BLOCK                              NMAX / A-buffer
B1          .BLOCK                              NMAX / B-buffer
NN          ... ...                                  / Contains block size N
                                                     /   ≤ NMAX
INIT        LOAD REGISTER 1                     NN   / Set up DMA
            MOVE REGISTER 1 to DMA WORD COUNTER
            LOAD REGISTER 2, IMMEDIATE          A1
            MOVE REGISTER 2 to DMA ADDRESS COUNTER
            TURN ON ADC AND INTERRUPT                / Set control register
                    ...         ...          ...
            / Interrupt-service routine
SRVCE       PUSH REGISTER 1 ONTO STACK               / Save registers
            PUSH REGISTER 2 ONTO STACK
            LOAD REGISTER 1                     NN
            MOVE REGISTER 1 TO DMA WORD COUNTER      / Reset DMA
            LOAD REGISTER 2, IMMEDIATE          A1
            MOVE REGISTER 2 TO DMA ADDRESS COUNTER
LOOP        LOAD REGISTER 2, INDEX 1            A1-1 / Move data from
            STORE REGISTER 2, INDEX 1          B1-1  /   A-buffer to
            DECREMENT REGISTER 1, BRANCH             /   B-buffer
                            IF NOT ZERO        LOOP
            POP STACK INTO REGISTER 2                / Restore registers
            POP STACK INTO REGISTER 1
            TURN ON ADC AND INTERRUPT                / Reset control register
            RETURN FROM INTERRUPT
```

Fig. 4-13*b*. This simple program sets up a DMA block-transfer channel to read N words from an analog-to-digital converter (*initialization routine*) and then responds to each completed block with an *interrupt-service routine*, which resets the DMA channel and transfers the data to a new buffer (see also Fig. 3-6).

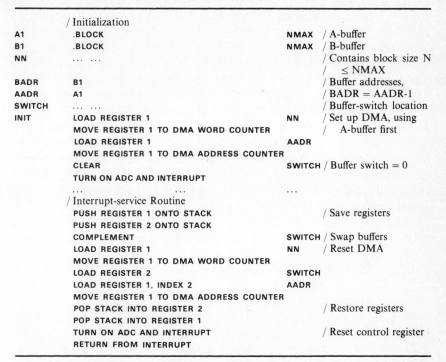

```
            / Initialization
A1          .BLOCK                                    NMAX   / A-buffer
B1          .BLOCK                                    NMAX   / B-buffer
NN          ... ...                                          / Contains block size N
                                                             /   ≤ NMAX
BADR        B1                                               / Buffer addresses,
AADR        A1                                               / BADR = AADR-1
SWITCH      ... ...                                          / Buffer-switch location
INIT        LOAD REGISTER 1                           NN     / Set up DMA, using
            MOVE REGISTER 1 TO DMA WORD COUNTER              /   A-buffer first
            LOAD REGISTER 1                           AADR
            MOVE REGISTER 1 TO DMA ADDRESS COUNTER
            CLEAR                                     SWITCH / Buffer switch = 0
            TURN ON ADC AND INTERRUPT
            ...              ...                      ...
            / Interrupt-service Routine
            PUSH REGISTER 1 ONTO STACK                       / Save registers
            PUSH REGISTER 2 ONTO STACK
            COMPLEMENT                                SWITCH / Swap buffers
            LOAD REGISTER 1                           NN     / Reset DMA
            MOVE REGISTER 1 TO DMA WORD COUNTER
            LOAD REGISTER 2                           SWITCH
            LOAD REGISTER 1, INDEX 2                  AADR
            MOVE REGISTER 1 TO DMA ADDRESS COUNTER
            POP STACK INTO REGISTER 2                        / Restore registers
            POP STACK INTO REGISTER 1
            TURN ON ADC AND INTERRUPT                        / Reset control register
            RETURN FROM INTERRUPT
```

Fig. 4-13c. This DMA service program swaps DMA and user buffers each time the DMA channel has filled the buffer (*swinging buffers*). The user program is no longer part of the interrupt-service routine, so that DMA operation can resume much more quickly. User-program operations on each buffer can start when a sign change in SWITCH is sensed. Operations on each buffer must complete by the time the DMA channel is ready to reload that buffer.

requesting further data transfers. The word-counter carry pulse can also cause an *interrupt* so that a new block of data can be processed. The word counter may, if desired, also serve for sequencing device functions (e.g., for selecting successive ADC multiplexer addresses). Figures 4-13b and c show typical programs.

Some computers replace the word counter with a program-loaded **final-address register,** whose contents are compared with the current-address counter to determine the end of the block.

A DMA system often involves several data channels, each with a DMA control, address gates, a current-address counter, and a word counter, with different priorities assigned to different channels. For efficient handling of randomly timed requests from multiple devices (and to prevent loss of data words), data-channel systems may incorporate buffer registers in the interface or in devices such as ADCs or DACs.

4-19. Advantages of DMA Systems. Direct-memory-access systems can transfer data blocks at very high rates (10^6 words/sec is readily possible) without elaborate I/O programming. The processor essentially deals mainly with buffer areas in its own memory, and only a few I/O instructions are needed to initialize or reinitialize transfers.

Automatic data channels are especially suitable for servicing peripherals with high data rates, such as disks, drums, and fast ADCs and DACs. But data transfer with minimal program overhead is extremely valuable in many other applications, especially if there are many devices to be serviced. To indicate the remarkable efficiency of cycle-stealing direct memory access with multiple block-transfer data channels, consider the operation of a training-type digital flight simulator, which solves aircraft and engine equations and services an elaborate cockpit mock-up with many controls and instrument displays. During each 160-msec time increment, the interface not only performs 174 analog-to-digital conversions requiring a total conversion time of 7.7 msec but also 430 digital-to-analog conversions, and handles 540 eight-bit bytes of discrete control information. The actual time required to transfer all this information in and out of the data channels is 143 msec per time increment, but because of the fast direct memory transfers, cycle-stealing subtracts only 3.2 msec for each 160 msec of processor time (Ref. 52).

NOTE: A microprocessor memory (or part of the memory) faster ·than needed by, say, a MOSFET microprocessor can support DMA operations which are much faster than processor operations.

With the advent of inexpensive LSI DMA controller chips (Sec. 4-24), DMA operations can be used even for slow data transfers simply in order to simplify I/O programming. Note, though, that *the CPU program must usually be informed when a DMA data transfer has been completed, so that the program can branch to use or replace the transferred data.* This is typically achieved with an end-of-block interrupt (Sec. 4-18). The program can, instead, test an interface status flag or a special memory location (software flag) cleared as the last transaction of the DMA operation (see also Sec. 5-14b).

4-20. Memory-Increment Technique for Amplitude-Distribution Measurements. In many minicomputers, a special pulse input will *increment* the contents of a memory location addressed by the DMA address lines; an interrupt can be generated when one of the memory cells is full. When ADC outputs representing successive samples of a random voltage are applied to the DMA address lines, the **memory-increment feature will effectively generate a model of the input-voltage amplitude distribution in the computer memory:** Each memory address corresponds to a voltage class interval, and the contents of the memory register represent the number of samples falling into that class interval. Data taking is terminated after a preset number of samples or when the first memory register overloads (Fig. 4-14a). The empirical amplitude distribution thus created in memory may be displayed or plotted by a display routine (Fig. 4-14b), and statistics such as

$$\overline{X} = \frac{1}{n} \sum_{k=1}^{n} X_k \qquad \overline{X^2} = \frac{1}{n} \sum_{k=1}^{n} X_k^2 \cdots$$

are readily computed after the distribution is complete. This technique has been extensively applied to the analysis of pulse-energy spectra from nuclear-physics experiments.

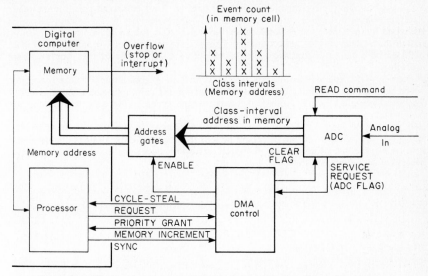

Fig. 4-14a. Memory-increment technique of measuring amplitude distributions.

Joint distributions of two random variables X, Y can be similarly compiled. It is only necessary to apply, say, a 12-bit word X, Y composed of two 6-bit bytes corresponding to two ADC outputs X and Y to the memory address register. Now each addressed memory location will correspond to the region $X_i \leq X < X_{i+1}$, $Y_k \leq Y < Y_{k+1}$ in XY space.

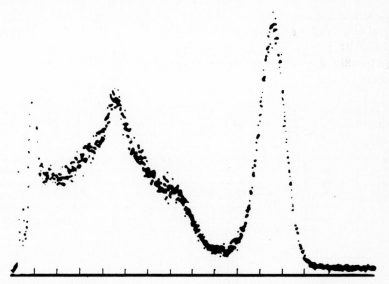

Fig. 4-14b. An amplitude-distribution display obtained by the method of Fig. 4-14a. (*Digital Equipment Corp.*)

4-21. Add-to-Memory Technique of Signal Averaging. Another command-pulse input to some DMA interfaces will *add* a data word on the I/O-bus data lines to the memory location addressed by the DMA address lines without ever bothering the digital-computer arithmetic unit or the program. This "add-to-memory" feature permits useful linear operations on data obtained from various instruments; the only application well known at this time is in **data averaging.**

Figures 4-15a and b illustrate an especially interesting application of data averaging, which has been very fruitful in biological-data reduction (e.g., electroencephalogram analysis). Periodically applied stimuli produce the same system response after each stimulus so that one obtains an analog waveform periodic with the period T of the applied stimuli. To pull the desired function $X(t)$ out of additive zero-mean random noise, one adds $X(t)$, $X(t + T)$, $X(t + 2T)$, ... during successive periods to enhance the signal, while the noise will tend to average out. Figure 4-15c shows the extraction of a signal from additive noise in successive data-averaging runs.

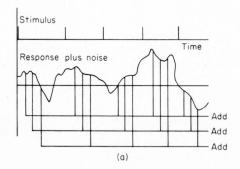

(a)

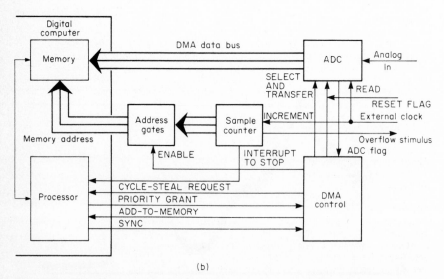

(b)

Fig. 4-15a, b. Signal enhancement by periodic averaging (a), and add-to-memory technique for signal averaging (b).

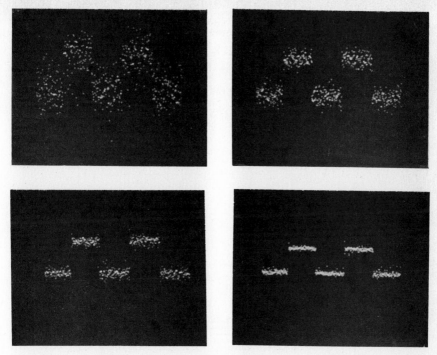

Fig. 4-15c. A periodically retriggered waveform extracted from additive noise through successive signal-averaging runs. The display is self-scaling; i.e., ordinate words are shifted right by 1 bit after 2, 4, 8, ... repetitions to divide accumulated sums by the number of repetitions. (*University of Arizona; PDP-9 data taken by H. M. Aus.*)

4-22. Implementing Current-Address and Word Counters in the Processor Memory. Some minicomputers (in particular, PDP-9, PDP-15, and the PDP-8 series) have, in addition to their regular DMA facilities, a set of fixed core-memory locations to be used as data-channel address and word counters. Ordinary processor instructions (not I/O instructions) load these locations, respectively, with the block starting address and with minus the block count. The data-channel interface card (Fig. 4-16) supplies the address of one of the four to eight address-counter locations available in the processor; the word counter is the location following the address counter. Now, successive service requests steal not one but three or four cycles since the processor must increment the two counter locations, and they then transfer data to or from successive memory cells indirectly addressed via the address counter. When the word counter reaches 0 (from its negative initial setting), the processor issues a special signal which is used to stop further service requests and usually to interrupt the processor (Fig. 4-16).

Some memory-implemented data channels will also permit add-to-memory operation (PDP-9, PDP-15). The Honeywell 316/516 machines implement a final-address register in memory rather than a word counter (Sec. 4-18) and permit automatic alternation of data transfers to or from two blocks of memory locations (*swinging buffers*).

Memory-implemented data channels permit automatic block transfers with a minimum of interface hardware since they eliminate the two external counter/registers plus the circuits needed to preset them. On the other hand, **true DMA circuits are becoming more and more inexpensive, and true data channels steal only one-third to one-fourth as much processor time as memory-implemented channels.**

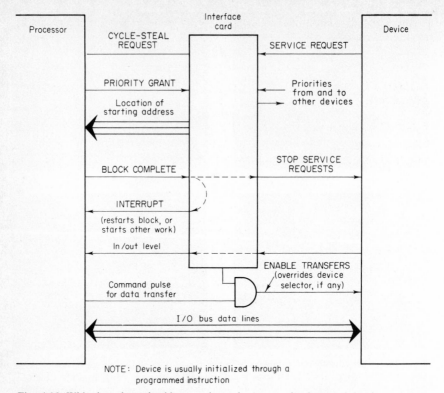

Fig. 4-16. With data-channel address and word counters implemented in the processor memory, data-channel operation requires only a simple interface card containing priority/ queuing and address logic like that in Fig. 4-10, but each data transfer steals three or four processor cycles, not just one cycle.

4-23. Pseudo-DMA Block-Transfer Techniques. A complete minicomputer DMA interface steals one memory cycle per word and costs the end user between $400 and $1,200 in small quantities. Memory-implemented block-transfer counters (Sec. 4-22) reduce the interface to a pair of interrupt controllers (one for the DMA and one for the end-of-block interrupt) at the expense of two or three extra memory cycles per word. Modern computers capable of programmed I/O data transfers *to and from memory* can do block transfers even more simply by interrupt-service routines which, like DMA, *do not require register-saving operations:*

MOVE I/O DATA WORD, INDIRECT VIA	POINTER
INCREMENT	POINTER
INCREMENT	COUNTER
BRANCH IF ZERO	DONE
RETURN FROM INTERRUPT	

It is possible to implement such a sequence with a single microprogrammed instruction (a good idea for user-microprogrammable machines!).   Such a **pseudo-DMA** data transfer will take on the order of 10 memory cycles, but only a simple interrupt controller is needed.

COMPLETE INTERFACES, SERIAL-DATA CONVERSION, AND GRAPHIC DISPLAYS

4-24.   Complete Interfaces.   Logic Cards and LSI Chips.
A complete interface for programmed device operations (Fig. 4-17*a*) comprises a *device selector* together with *data*, *control*, and/or *status registers* (Secs. 4-2, 4-4,

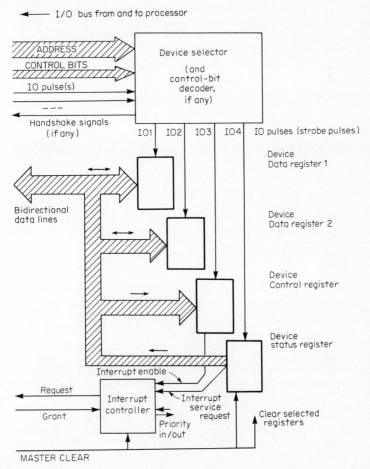

Fig. 4-17a. A complete interface for program-controlled device operations.   Four different IO pulses are either generated by the processor itself (Fig. 4-3) or they are obtained by gating a single pulse with different control-bit combinations (Fig. 4-17*b*).   The two device data registers can have separate jobs, or they may contain high and low 8-bit bytes of a 16-bit word.

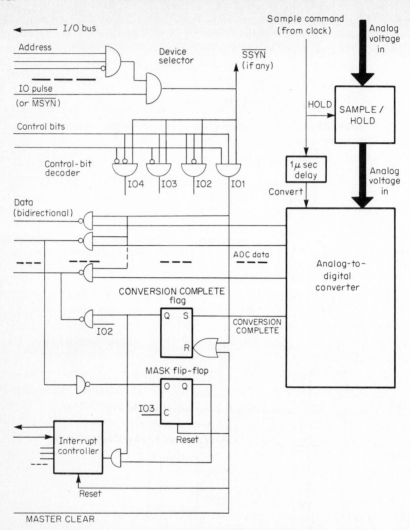

Fig. 4-17b. Complete interface for an analog-to-digital converter (ADC). With the proper interrupt controller (Sec. 4-14), this interface works with either a synchronous or an asynchronous bus. Control-bit decoding gates the single IO pulse (or $\overline{MSYN}$, Sec. 4-14) to read the *ADC data register* (IO1), to read the one-bit *status register* (IO2), or to write into the one-bit *control register* (IO3). The spare IO4 pulse can be used to write a multiplexer-channel number into an *analog-multiplexer control register*. MASTER CLEAR resets all interface flip-flops on power-up, or through a special I/O instruction. The same type of interface is used to read device registers in counters, paper-tape readers, and many other devices.

4-6, and 4-7). An *interrupt controller* is usually added to speed operations which depend on device status (Secs. 4-11 to 4-15). Strobe pulses for the different operations associated with the same device address are either generated by the processor itself (Fig. 4-3), or a single pulse is gated with different combinations of control bits (subdevice bits) associated with different I/O instructions (Fig. 4-17b).   Different device data registers may have separate jobs (Sec. 4-28), or they may contain high and low 8-bit bytes of a 16-bit word.

One can similarly expand the number of control bits and/or address bits by loading extra control registers.

To reset device interfaces to some desired *initial state*, most computer I/O buses provide an **I/O RESET line,** which is energized by a special I/O RESET instruction, and usually also whenever power is turned on.   The I/O reset line is wired to set or reset control and status flip-flops in each device interface, as needed.

Reference 13 describes the design of *data buffers* for interfaces which must deal with bursts of data at higher data rates than a programmed or DMA interface can ordinarily handle.

Computer manufacturers and component houses supply both complete interface cards and smaller cards (device selectors, registers, bus gates, interrupt controllers) which can be conveniently interconnected by backplane wirewrapping.   Such interface cards plug either into slots in the computer cabinet or into a device chassis (Fig. 4-19).

Interface cards made from MSI logic are relatively expensive ($40 to $85 for registers and device selectors, $110 for two interrupt controllers, or $400 for a complete interface quickly runs up to more than the CPU cost in a multidevice system).   To reduce interface costs, *try to utilize LSI interface chips made for microcomputers*.   Some of these chips are quite suitable for general-purpose use.   A single LSI chip (Fig. 4-19c) can comprise

Device-selector logic (decoding gates)
8 to 16 gated bus-driver amplifiers
Two 8-bit data registers, plus control and status flip-flops
Shift registers and control logic for serial/parallel interfacing (Sec. 4-27)
A complete interrupt controller
A complete *multichannel* 8-bit DMA controller
A real-time clock (interval timer)
Floppy-disk and CRT-terminal controllers

For experimental interfaces and microcomputer systems, use *wirewrapping* (with a simple battery-driven wirewrap gun) rather than soldering for convenient and reliable connections, except for fast emitter-coupled logic (ECL) and radio-frequency circuits.   Mount integrated circuits in sockets unless your system is in quantity production with incoming-IC inspection, because desoldering ICs is lots of trouble.

4-25. Data Conversion and Real-Time Clocks. (a) Digital-to-Analog Converters. The most commonly used **digital-to-analog converters (DACs)** are resistance networks whose output voltage or current is determined by an analog input **(reference voltage)** and a digital number set into the DAC flip-flop register. Each register bit controls one of the electronic switches **(bit switches),** which together determine the correct output. As a typical example, the **ladder-network DAC** of Fig. 4-18a is designed to convert 2s-complement-coded binary numbers (Tables 1-1 and 1-2) into positive and negative analog output. Converters for many other codes (e.g., BCD, Table 1-4) exist (Ref. 14).

If two or more DACs must be updated simultaneously (as in cathode-ray-tube displays, Sec 4-28 or analog/hybrid computers), the **double-buffering** scheme of Fig. 4-4d permits individual loading of DAC buffer registers. All DACs can then be updated simultaneously through a programmed instruction producing a common transfer pulse. If one must service more

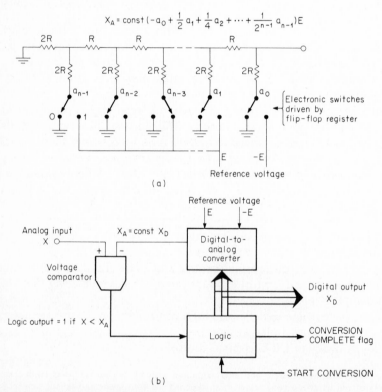

(a)

(b)

Fig. 4-18. Ladder-network digital-to-analog converter for converting 2s-complement binary numbers (a), and a feedback-type analog-to-digital converter (b). (*Based on G. A. Korn and T. M. Korn, Electronic Analog and Hybrid Computers, 2d ed., McGraw-Hill, New York, 1972.*)

DACs than there are readily available I/O addresses, DAC addresses can be entered as data words into a control register **(DAC address register).**

(b) Analog-to-Digital Converters. Analog-to-digital converters **(ADCs)** are treated in detail in Refs. 14 to 17. There are two principal types. Many digital voltmeters employ **analog-to-time conversion;** i.e., the START CONVERSION command causes a binary or decimal counter to count clock pulses while an analog sweep voltage varies between a reference voltage level and a voltage level proportional to the unknown input (or, in the more accurate **integrating converters,** to a time average of the input). See Ref. 18. The count then terminates, and the CONVERSION COMPLETE flag level goes up; the counter can now be read by the digital computer. 8- to 14-bit precision is possible, with conversion times between 0.5 and 500 msec.

Faster binary ADCs employ the **feedback principle** illustrated in Fig. 4-18b. After the START CONVERSION signal, *digital logic tries to set a DAC register so that the DAC output approximates the unknown analog input as closely as possible.* A *voltage comparator* (basically a high-gain amplifier) produces logic 1 output if the comparison DAC output is too large, and 0 otherwise.

Fig. 4-19. Interface cards either plug directly into a minicomputer backplane section, or they can be mounted on a peripheral-device chassis. (*Digital Equipment Corporation.*)

The most commonly used ADC feedback logic successively tries the sign bit (with all other DAC bits at 0), then the most significant bit, etc. (*successive-approximation ADC*).   This requires n voltage comparisons for n bits.   The CONVERSION COMPLETE flag goes up, and the ADC output can be read from the DAC register when the comparison voltage equals the unknown input within one-half of the voltage step determined by the least significant bit.   Up to 15-bit precision is possible, but that may require 30 to 50 μsec; 1 to 20 μsec is typical for 8- to 12-bit precision.

The ADC flag is reset (cleared) by the **READ ADC** instruction and/or by the **START CONVERSION** instruction or timing pulse.

An ADC often serves multiple analog channels through an analog-switching scheme (relay or electronic **analog multiplexer**).   The multiplexer address is determined by a control register (*multiplexer address register*), which may be set by the digital computer or can be incremented to scan successive input channels.

Because of the finite ADC conversion time, accurately timed sampling of time-variable analog signals may require an analog **sample-hold circuit,** which holds the desired analog voltage sample long enough for conversion (Ref. 14).   The combination of ADC, sample/hold, and analog multiplexer is a **data-acquisition system.**

(c) **Real-Time Clocks.   Timing pulses** needed to relate computer operations to real time are derived either from the 60-Hz line frequency (50 Hz in Europe) or from a 10-Hz to 1-MHz crystal oscillator **(clock oscillator);** counter flip-flops yield submultiples of the clock frequency, as desired. Timing pulses can be started by an external gate signal or by a programmed instruction setting a control-register bit (Sec. 4-6), or the clock may run free.

Timing pulses are counted by a **clock counter.**   If the clock counter is initially reset to 0 by a programmed I/O instruction, the count will be proportional to **elapsed time** and can be read by the computer program when desired.   **To mark a preset time interval,** we preset the clock-counter recognition gate (NAND gate, see also Table 1-5a), which detects when the counter reaches 0 after N clock pulses.   The gate output then interrupts the processor **(clock interrupt).**   The ensuing interrupt-service routine performs whatever timed operation is wanted and can reset the clock counter to *repeat periodic cycles.*

In many minicomputers, the clock counter is not a flip-flop register but an *incrementable memory location.*

4-26.   Serial-Data Interfaces, Modems, and Data Communication (Refs. 19 to 25, 55).   Digital communication systems, teletypewriter keyboard/printers, most alphanumeric CRT-display terminals, and disk or drum storage systems employ bit-by-bit **serial data representation** (Sec. 1-4), while computer-bus data appear as *parallel* words or bytes.   For data communication over more than a few hundred feet, **serial bits modulate a carrier** on a communication line or wireless data link.   Amplitude, phase, frequency-shift, or combination amplitude and phase modulation is used.   Communication links specially designed for digital data transmission may employ radio-frequency carriers, but audio frequencies are used on telephone lines (which are not primarily designed for data transmission).   At each end of any carrier link, one requires a **modulator/demodulator (modem).**

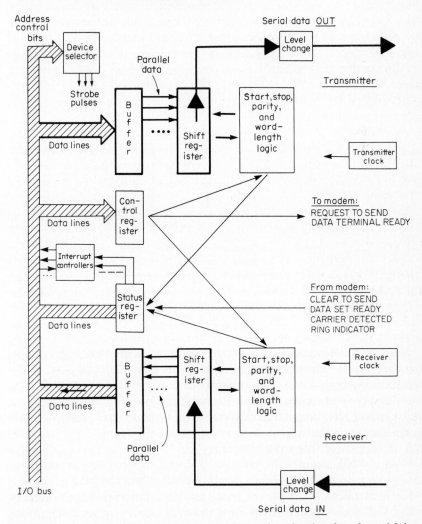

Fig. 4-20a. A data-set interface, combining transmitter and receiver interfaces for serial data. Without the device selector, clock, interrupt controllers, and level shifters, the entire interface fits a single integrated-circuit chip.   The same interface can also link a modem to a teletypewriter or alphanumerical CRT terminal.

Parallel-to-serial and **serial-to-parallel conversion** can be done by bit-shifting processor instructions, but this is slow, and almost all computer systems employ **shift-register interfaces.** In Fig. 4-20a, serial data words (usually 8-bit bytes) are shifted into or out of a **shift register** (Table 1-5b) which is parallel-interfaced with the computer I/O bus through an interface data register. The computer can communicate with this **buffer register** while the next byte is shifted into or out of the shift register. The shift pulses needed to transmit or receive a complete byte are counted by a **control counter.** To mark the start of a new byte for the receiver, an **asynchronous** data-transmission system "frames" each byte with **start and stop bits,** which can be recognized in the receiver to start and reset its control counter (Fig. 4-20b).

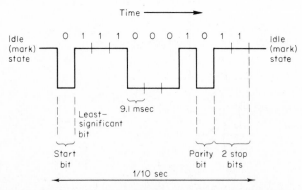

Fig. 4-20b. Serial representation for an ASCII 7-bit-and-parity character. Start and stop bits "frame" the serial character representation for asynchronous transmission. Timing is for an ASR-33 teletypewriter operating at 110 baud (bits/sec) or 10 characters/sec.

Most low-cost serial-data systems employ asynchronous transmission, but the 2 or 3 start/stop bits per 8-bit byte waste 2/10 or 3/11 of our transmission time. Fast long-distance data communication justifies the extra cost of **synchronous** transmission, which employs a continuous stream of true data bits; accurate receiver and transmitter clock oscillators are synchronized at the start of a message through an extra communication link or carrier (or subcarrier) frequency.

Figure 4-20a includes the logic for a complete 8-bit **data-set interface,** really two independent interfaces for transmitting and receiving at possibly different bit rates. The interface permits **simplex transmission** (one direction only); **half-duplex transmission** (both directions, but only one at a time); and **full-duplex transmission** (simultaneous transmission and reception, e.g., on two two-wire lines). As usually, we have output and input **data registers,** a **control register,** and a **status register** capable of requesting interrupts.

Status bits monitoring asynchronous transmission and reception of successive data bytes are

TRANSMITTER REGISTER EMPTY—transmitter buffer contents have been transferred into shift register; *ok to write a new byte*
RECEIVER REGISTER FULL—a complete byte has been shifted in and then transferred into the receiver buffer register, *ready to be read*
OVERRUN ERROR—*last byte was not read*
FRAMING ERROR—*no stop bit received*
PARITY ERROR
BREAK DETECTED—*all 0s received*

Further status and control bits correspond to **handshaking signals** used by interface and modem (or terminal) to indicate their readiness for communication:

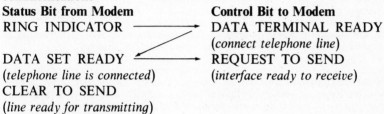

Status Bit from Modem	Control Bit to Modem
RING INDICATOR	DATA TERMINAL READY
	(*connect telephone line*)
DATA SET READY	REQUEST TO SEND
(*telephone line is connected*)	(*interface ready to receive*)
CLEAR TO SEND	
(*line ready for transmitting*)	
CARRIER DETECTED	

Additional control bits (usually wire-link selected) constitute a code to determine

Word length (8 bits, or 7 bits and parity)
Even or odd parity
1 or 2 stop bits
Receiver and transmitter bit rates
Enable receiver and/or transmitter interrupts

There may be extra programmed telephone functions, in particular *automatic dialing*. Some interfaces include hardware to check not only byte parity but also blocks of characters through check bytes computed from each block before and after transmission (**cyclic redundancy check, CRC**).

Computer programs and terminal operators must establish a **communications protocol,** i.e., a definite response sequence of special characters (breaks, start-of-message, end-of-message, check characters) at the beginning and end of each message. A complete computer program will be found in Ref. 6.

Without the device selector, interrupt controllers, clocks, and level shifters, *the entire serial/parallel interface of Fig. 4-20a fits a single IC chip costing of the order of $10* (Ref. 20). For asynchronous systems, these chips

are referred to as **UARTs (Universal Asynchronous Receiver/Transmitters).**
Some serial-interface ICs can handle *synchronous* as well as asynchronous
data systems. Modems, too, are available in IC form. The level shifters
shown in Fig. 4-20*a* interface TTL logic either to the 0, − 12-V levels specified by the *data-set standard EIA RS-232C of the Electronic Industries
Association*, or to an optically isolated *teleprinter 20-mA current loop.*

Serial data links for computer terminals operate at 110 to 330 bits/sec (*bps, bauds*) for
teletypewriters, or up to 9,600 bits/sec for alphanumeric CRT terminals, using the 11-bit
character format of Fig. 4-20*b*. *Dial-up telephone lines*, which involve telephone-exchange
switching, can have data rates up to 2,400 bits/sec, but special line conditioning is needed
to get more than 1,800 bits/sec. *High-quality private lines*, line conditioning, and special
modems permit rates above 40,000 bits/sec, and direct memory access becomes useful.

Since many data streams—say, to and from teletypewriters—are slower than a line will
admit, several data streams may share the line bandwidth (**frequency multiplexing**); or we can
interleave bits or (preferably) characters in time (**time-division multiplexing**). Multiplexer
interfaces are used in **data concentrators/deconcentrators** with a **buffer memory** which
transfers parallel bytes to and from a digital computer as needed, while it attempts to transmit
and receive serial data streams over different communication links at their optimal bit rates.
This saves line charges; it is also possible to store messages on a disk for forwarding at
nighttime telephone rates, or during line failures (**store-and-forward system**).

A small digital computer with special communication interfaces and special microprogrammed I/O and error-checking instructions can neatly implement data multiplexing,
writing, and concentration/deconcentration, using its memory for buffering. Such a **communications processor** can perform additional useful functions, such as error correction,
checking for spurious echoes, formatting and code conversion, automatic dialing, and
computation of traffic statistics and charges.

4-27. Interface-Module Systems. (a) Simple Serial-Data Systems. Asyn-
chronous serial-data transmission, with inexpensive, mass-produced UARTs
(Sec. 4-26), requires only simple twisted-pair or coaxial-cable interconnections and does not even need modems over distances of several hundred
feet. *Such a system becomes an attractive substitute for multiwire parallel
I/O buses when data rates do not exceed a few kbytes/sec.* This is especially
true if data, status, and control information is encoded into ASCII or BCD
characters, which can be transmitted, as well as typed and printed, with
ordinary FORTRAN or BASIC READ, WRITE, and PRINT statements—
the computer thinks it is addressing another teleprinter or keyboard
terminal (Fig. 4-21).

The Analog Devices, Inc., SERDEX modules are low-speed (<20,000 bit/sec) interfaces
designed to fit computer teletypewriter ports. They can also interface, say, an analog-to-
digital converter directly to a teletypewriter or CRT terminal. As an example, if the interface in Fig. 4-21 is designed to wait for an ADC conversion and to transmit the result when
it decodes the ASCII character " ? " then the teletypewriter or computer command.

WHAT IS THE VOLTAGE?

will return a three-digit voltage in decimal-integer form as three successive ASCII
characters. References 12 and 31 describe more sophisticated serial-data systems, with pro-
tocols for exchanging status, control, and data information.

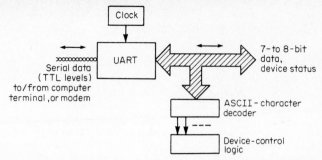

Fig. 4-21. A serial-data device interface designed to operate by ordinary FORTRAN or BASIC READ, WRITE, and PRINT statements. The ASCII decoder recognizes specified characters to make the device-control logic read or write a byte or multiple bytes, set a sub-device address (e.g., to read one of four registers), or implement other device functions. Device-status information is also encoded in terms of ASCII characters.

(b) The CAMAC System (Refs. 28 to 35). The CAMAC system provides standards[1] for the physical configuration, logic functions, and electrical signals of instrumentation modules. Single- and multiple-width modules fit standard **crates** (Fig. 4-22a, b). Modules plug into a crate backplane bus (**dataway,** Fig. 4-22c) to communicate with one another and with a **crate controller** interposed between any digital computer and the individual modules.

Figure 4-22d illustrates the dataway organization (Ref. 28). Module addresses are decoded by device-selector logic in the crate controller, which can address up to 24 module slots through individual select lines (*N lines*). The dataway also provides

24-bit unidirectional *read (R)* and *write (W) lines*
4 subdevice (subaddress)-bit lines (*A lines*)

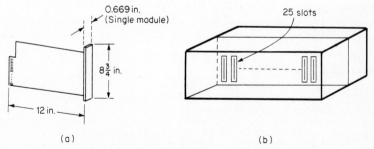

(a)   (b)

Fig. 4-22a, b. CAMAC module (a), and crate (b).

[1] CAMAC (Computer Aided Measurement and Control) standards are supervised by the European Standard on Nuclear Electronics (ESONE) Committee and are compatible with the former U.S. Atomic Energy Commission's Nuclear Instrument Modules (NIM) standards (Refs. 28 to 33) and IEEE Standard 583 (1975).

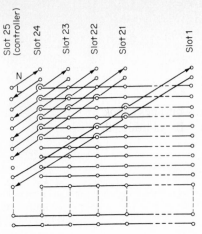

Fig. 4-22c. CAMAC dataway. The *N* signal to each module slot is a decoded select signal, and the *L* (LOOK AT ME, LAM) signal from each slot is a status signal.

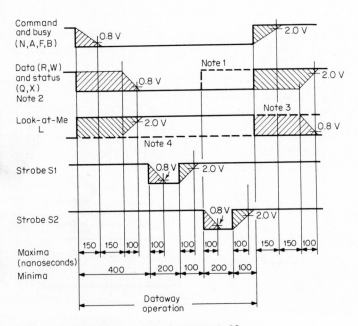

Note 1: Data and status may change in response to S2.

Note 2: During some operations Q may change at any time.

Note 3: LAM status may be reset during operation.

Note 4: L signal may be maintained during operation.

Fig. 4-22d. Standards for CAMAC dataway command-operation signals.   (*From Ref. 28.*)

5 function (control)-bit lines (*F lines*), with code standards for various read, write, bit-set, and register-clearing operations

2 strobe (IO-pulse) lines (*S lines*)

3 extra control-bit lines available to *initialize* (*Z*), *clear* (*C*), and *inhibit* (*I*) selected module functions

plus individual status-bit lines (*Look At Me, LAM lines*) for each of the up to 24 module slots. In addition, there are three status-bit lines, *X* (*command accepted*), *B* (*busy*), and *Q* (*spare response bit*), which can be set by any module on the dataway. Power-supply and ground lines are also included.

A crate controller designed for computer interfacing typically contains device-selection and control-signal-decoding logic, data, control, and status registers, and interrupt logic. CAMAC crate controllers capable of interfacing a variety of instrument modules can be complicated; future designs are likely to be programmable microcomputers. The maximum data rate is one 24-bit word per 1μsec CAMAC cycle (Fig. 4-22*d*) if the controller implements direct memory transfers; faster instruments would require buffering in the modules. Larger CAMAC systems employ multiple crates interfaced to a computer via another system of bus lines and interface controllers (**branch highways** and **branch drivers,** Fig. 4-22*e*). Standards exist for *serial* branch highways capable of communicating over longer distances as well as for bit-parallel branch highways (Refs. 29 to 32).

The CAMAC approach relieves instrument users and manufacturers of the need to develop interfaces for many different computers. A fair number of CAMAC-compatible instrumentation and process-control modules are

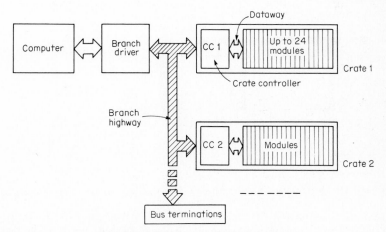

Fig. 4-22e. A multicrate CAMAC system.

commercially available (see the bibliography). But computer manufacturers have rarely responded by providing CAMAC controllers, which present a smaller market and are more difficult to standardize than modules. This situation might be improved by the advent of programmable microprocessors. Still, *CAMAC hardware, with its double or triple interfaces and its many, often unneeded, bus lines and connections, tends to be far more costly than a straight 16-bit minicomputer interface.* CAMAC applications, therefore, favor expensive instrumentation systems, as in nuclear-physics laboratories.

(c) The IEC System (Refs. 36 to 38). The IEC[1] interface bus system (Fig. 4-23) involves only 16 TTL-level bus signals:

8 *bidirectional data lines*, which are also used for addressing selected devices. Multiple data and address bytes can be used. A 7-bit address byte comprises 5 address bits and a 2-bit code telling selected devices to talk, listen, receive additional address bits, etc.

3 *handshake-signal lines* for controlling asynchronous data- and address-byte transfers.
DAV—data valid
NRFO—not ready for data
NDAC—data not accepted

5 *status/control lines*
IFC—interface clear
ATN—attention
SRQ—service request
REN—remote enable
EDI—end or identify

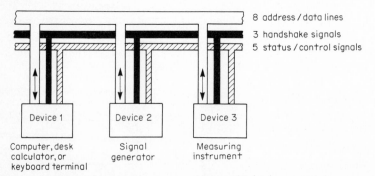

8 address / data lines
3 handshake signals
5 status / control signals

Device 1   Device 2   Device 3

Computer, desk   Signal   Measuring
calculator, or   generator   instrument
keyboard terminal

Fig. 4-23. The IEC/Hewlett-Packard instrument-interface-bus system. (*Based on Ref. 36.*)

---

[1] Standards supervised by the International Electrotechnical Commission (IEC). The system is essentially similar to that designed originally for Hewlett-Packard Corporation instruments and to IEEE Standard 488 (1975). Note that the U.S. ASCII code is compatible with the International Standard (ISO) 7-bit code.

Devices on the bus can receive (*listen*) and/or transmit (*talk*). Bus operations can be controlled by computers, desk calculators, or keyboard terminals, but an IEC system need not involve such devices; any suitably interfaced instrument could control simple operations such as data transfers to a printer or remote indicator. Up to 15 devices can be interconnected with stackable connectors and up to 20 meters of total cable length. Larger systems require booster amplifiers. The highest feasible data-transfer rate is 10^6 8-bit bytes per second, but many applications involve ASCII- or BCD-coded decimal-data transfers from relatively slow instruments. Remote instruments or controllers can communicate through serial interfaces and modems.

IEC-interface design is described in Refs. 36 to 38. IEC systems permit especially simple interconnections, but IEC interfaces are more complicated (and slower) than simple minicomputer interfaces.

4-28. Simple Graphic Displays and Servo Plotters. A **cathode-ray graphic display** positions and brightens a CRT beam to plot a sequence of points (and/or brightens the beam *between* points to draw line segments or "vectors"). Small displays (up to 11-in-diameter) employ *electrostatic deflection* in the X and Y directions and can plot up to 10^6 distinct points/ sec. Larger displays use *electromagnetic deflection* for better focusing and resolution, but such displays are slower (up to 100,000 points/sec). High-quality electromagnetic-deflection displays may add fast electrostatic deflection for small beam displacements (e.g., to display characters labeling a picture).

Figure 4-24 shows how the X and Y deflection amplifiers of a CRT display are driven by **X and Y digital-to-analog converters** (DACs). A digitally controlled **brightening voltage (Z-axis voltage)** is also indicated.

The minimum satisfactory resolution for X and Y is 512 steps (9 bits); 8-bit displays tend to look ragged. Most displays have 10-bit DACS, but 12-bit DACs cost little more and, with 16-bit computer words available, make for smoother lines.

Very elaborate displays can use full 16-bit resolution to specify points in a picture much larger than actually displayed on the CRT screen. 10-bit portions of the 16-bit X- and Y-coordinate words are then shifted into position to display small or large portions of the overall picture at different scales (*scissoring*).

Displayed pictures range from simple 256-point graphs with coordinate axes to elaborate design drawings with several thousands of points, plus alphanumeric characters. A *storage-tube CRT display* permits you to view the displayed points after they have been written only once—the display remains visible until a manually controlled or computer-controlled voltage pulse is applied to an erasing electrode in the storage tube. Storage CRTs have excellent resolution and greatly simplify display operation. But they

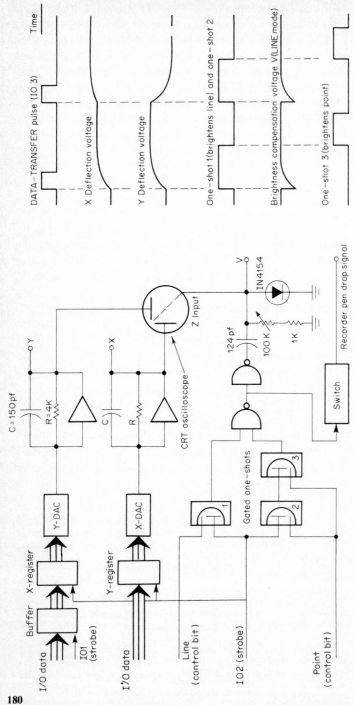

Fig. 4-24. A simple digital CRT display suitable for Dertouzos-type line-segment display as well as for point display (*a*), and waveforms (*b*). The low-pass-filter capacitors C establish equal X and Y time constants RC and also reduce transients ("glitches") due to switching spikes and different DAC bit-switching times. The line-brightness-compensation-voltage waveform also has the time constant RC to brighten the beam most when it moves most quickly. But perfect compensation is not possible (Fig. 4-25*a*). The X and Y display outputs can operate at a slow rate with an XY servo recorder, in which case the brightening logic drops the recorder pen on the paper.

cannot display *moving* pictures and require complete erasure and rewriting for *display editing*. Most digital displays, therefore, use short-persistence cathode-ray tubes (P7 phosphor) and must **rewrite (refresh) the entire display periodically** 30 to 60 times/sec. This requires not only many fast writing operations but a **display-refreshing memory** capable of storing coordinate and brightness information for 1,000 to 6,000 points and/or vectors. *Alphanumeric characters* are generated and refreshed as sets of points or vectors (strokes) usually stored in special read-only memories (**character generators**) and called out by special character-code display-instruction words.

Each display point will require 18 to 20 bits of refresher storage for X and Y plus, possibly, some extra bits to specify brightness or special display operations. Some CRT displays, especially the more elaborate displays used with larger digital computers, have their own 16- to 24-bit refresher memories, perhaps 4K to 16K words. With a simple direct-memory-access interface, *a graphic display can conveniently share the minicomputer memory*. This simplifies computer operations on display words and makes the extra memory available to the computer when the display is not used. The display-refreshing operations will, of course, slow concurrent computations. With a 1-μsec memory cycle, transferring X and Y words for a 1,000-point display 60 times per second takes $60 \times 1,000 \times 2 = 120,000$ μsec/sec, or 12 percent of our computing time.

To display a point, we can successively transfer the coordinates X and Y into X- and Y-DAC registers and then brighten the point by triggering a monostable multivibrator with the Y transfer pulse. In Fig. 4-24, we have double-buffered the X-DAC (see also Sec. 4-2), so that the X- and Y-DACs can be updated simultaneously with the IO2 strobe pulse, which also brightens the beam. **Beam intensity** could be program-controlled with control-register bits modifying the intensity-pulse duration or amplitude.

The double-buffered display interface also permits a primitive form of **line-segment** (**"vector"**) **generation** due to Dertouzos.

The X and Y DACs shown drive operational-amplifier low-pass filters with equal time constants RC, so that the beam will move from point to point along a straight line after the X and Y DACs have been loaded simultaneously (Fig. 4-25b).

This line is brightened if a control bit gates the DAC transfer pulse into monostable multivibrator 1. Unfortunately, the beam speed varies exponentially along each line segment; so the beam becomes progressively brighter. This is partially compensated in Fig. 4-24 by a differentiating network in the brightness control circuit, but beam defocusing makes perfect compensation impossible (Fig. 4-25a). *The simple Dertouzos line-segment generation technique is, however, excellent for producing hard copy with a simple servo plotter.* Figure 4-25b shows a drawing produced by feeding the X and Y inputs of a servo recorder with the display circuit of Fig. 4-24; the brightness voltage lowers the pen to plot line segments. The transfer rate was about 10 points/sec, and the monostable-multivibrator time constant was appropriately longer (Ref. 27).

Some improved line-segment generators employ operational-amplifier integrators for *straight-line* interpolation between successive coordinate voltages so that line brightness will remain constant between successive display points. If the time interval between successive

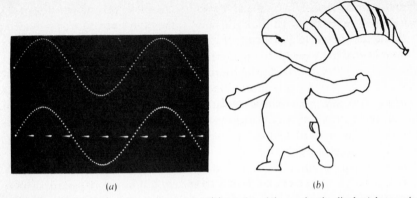

(a)   (b)

Fig. 4-25. CRT displays (a), and servo plot (b) produced by a simple display/plotter circuit similar to Fig. 4-24. Both POINT and LINE modes are used in Fig. 4-25a; note the effect of adjusting the line-brightness-compensation time constant. Perfect compensation for the exponential change in the writing rate was not possible, because the compensation voltage tends to defocus the beam. (*University of Arizona.*)

display points remains constant, though, short line segments will necessarily be brighter than long ones. For this reason, elaborate displays employ *digital interpolation* (hardware or software similar to numerical-control methods) to place extra display points between widely separated points; analog interpolation may still be used. Electromagnetically deflected CRT beams can, in general, follow short displacements more quickly than long ones.

4-29. More Elaborate Display Systems. (a) From Display Control Registers to Display Processors.

The simplest graphic displays have only a simple point mode with a single brightness level. Such a display can be operated with only *two* I/O instructions, viz., **TRANSFER X** and **TRANSFER Y AND BRIGHTEN**. If we use packed 18-bit X, Y words, a *single* I/O instruction will do (**TRANSFER AND BRIGHTEN**).

As we noted, though, it is *by far* more efficient to fetch alternate X- and Y-coordinate words, or packed X, Y words, *by direct memory access*. To display a picture, we create a **display file** comprising the corresponding sequence of display instructions and load its starting location **PICT** and its size (number of words) into two pointer locations in memory. The program then enables interrupts from a real-time clock in the display or processor to refresh the display 30 to 60 times/sec through the following interrupt-service routine:

1. Programmed I/O instructions preset a *current-address counter* and a *word counter* to **PICT** and to **N**, respectively.
2. Another programmed instruction enables a **DMA request-pulse oscillator** in the display to produce successive cycle-stealing coordinate-data transfers and to display successive points.
3. The word counter counts down from N with each DMA transfer and *stops the request oscillator* when the count reaches 0, presumably before the next clock interrupt repeats the process.

More complicated display programs will display multiple blocks of points, corresponding to different portions of an overall picture.

A **display control register** controlling, for instance, the beam brightness can be loaded with control bits packed with the display-file data words (a 16-bit word might contain 19 Y-coordinate bits and 6 control bits). More often, the display hardware is designed to recognize display-file words starting with, say, 1 as **control words,** so that the DMA interface can load the display control register instead of a DAC register. We can insert such control words at will into a display file to set and change display "modes," such as different beam intensities, blinking, line-segment generation, and character generation.

In particular, **increment-mode operation** can save many display-file words in pictures containing continuous curves or small detail at the expense of extra display-logic hardware. For example, the 10-bit X and Y coordinates of a single point require *two* 16-bit words. But a *single* 16-bit word can represent two 7-bit *increments* ΔX and ΔY, plus a 2-bit code to specify (or partly specify) the display mode. *Subpictures* represented in terms of such increments can be displayed *in different positions determined by that of a preceding absolute point* (Ref. 26).

Many displays also have a **graphplot mode** such that data words specify a 10-bit Y coordinate and "constant ΔX increment" for Y-versus-X graph plotting.

With elaborate control logic, our DMA graphic-display interface becomes a peripheral processor (**display processor**), which shares the computer memory to accept programmed display instructions and can respond with interrupts. The display processor has *data and I/O registers, arithmetic circuits* for increment-mode operations, an *instruction register* (the display control register), and a *program counter* (the DMA current-address counter). Special display instructions can reset this program counter to branch to a different picture or subpicture file in memory (display jump) or to execute, and return from, a *display subroutine* corresponding to a subpicture which may be used more than once (Ref. 26). It will be expedient to structure display files for more complicated pictures as *linked lists* (Sec. 3-10c): each item in the list is a subpicture file ending with a pointer to the start of the next subpicture file and its block size. Display requests can then fetch each subpicture in turn, and it will still be possible to perform operations such as erasure, scaling, or rotation only on selected subpictures.

Suitable header or label words can further structure subpictures into hierarchies of sub-subpictures; so operations can be performed on sets of sub-subpictures which in some sense "belong together." Display-structuring and display-modifying operations can be called as assembly-language subroutines or macros and as FORTRAN subroutines, with symbolic names for display files and subpictures.

(b) Operator/Display Interaction.   Joy sticks, various **tablet-stylus combinations,** and the
"mouse" rolling on a table surface all contain dual analog-to-digital conversion devices
which enter X and Y coordinates into a computer display file so that the operator can
"draw" points and lines on the CRT screen.

A **light pen** contains a photocell, which is held against a CRT display screen and which
responds to the flash of a display point with an interrupt or senseline response.   The computer
can then mark the X and Y coordinates of the point in question to *erase* or further brighten
the point.   The computer can generate a dimly lighted raster or random-scan pattern and
brighten points touched by the light pen (which contains a button switch to disable this
action, if desired), so the operator can draw pictures on the CRT screen.   The computer can
also generate a *tracking pattern* with a program designed to move this pattern in order to
center it on the light pen; this can also be used for drawing on the screen and for moving
subpictures (e.g., circuit or block-diagram symbols) into desired screen positions with the light
pen.

Finally, the computer may display a "menu" of possible decisions or commands on the
CRT screen, each with a "light-button" pattern which is touched by the light pen to
implement the command.

**4-30.   Some Interface-Hardware Considerations.   (a) IC Fanout and I/O-
Bus Signals.**   Figure 4-1 shows some typical bus circuits; if you have a
choice, tri-state buses are best (Sec. 4-1).   **Be sure to check all integrated-
circuit fanout specifications.**   Many so-called "single-chip" microprocessors
are not really complete without external bus-driver amplifiers, and most
microprocessor outputs will drive only a few devices.   On the device side,
off-the-shelf ICs not specifically designed as line drivers may require testing
for voltage levels and rise times.   Never use flip-flops as line drivers; they
may be triggered by line noise.   IC gates used as line receivers may also
have to be tested for safe logic-level thresholds.

Transmission-line time delays (at least 1.5 nsec/ft) can be critical with
synchronous-bus systems (Sec. 4-2).   **Transmission-line reflections** are mini-
mized by parallel termination at the ends of buses (Fig. 4-1), or by series
termination (Fig. 4-26).   **If the power to each device on a daisy-chained bus
can be turned off separately, the interface designer must make sure that this
will not affect proper operation of other devices** (see also Figs. 4-1 and 4-27).

Use lines whose characteristic impedance Z_0 is at least 90 Ω (93-Ω coax
or 100-Ω No. 26 or 28 twisted pair, about 30 turns/ft), with ground return.
Flat cable, with signal conductors separated by ground returns, and possibly with a shielding backplane, is very convenient, especially for short
(below 1 to 3 ft) cable runs.   A diode or Schottky-diode reverse termination
at the output end will limit negative overshoot (Fig. 4-1b).

**You must consult the interface manual for your specific computer in every
case to check on:**

The specific interface-logic scheme employed and details of its operation
and timing

Special I/O instructions used

Tolerances on logic levels, rise times, pulse-timing permissible circuit loads
(fanout), total bus length, etc.

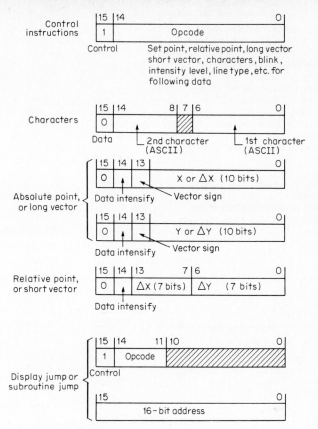

Fig. 4-26. Display-processor instruction formats.

Integrated-circuit modules recommended for interfacing
Whether the power to individual devices can be turned off without
   affecting the rest of the system

(b) Noise, Interconnections, and Ground Systems. Digital-computer
interfaces are very often connected to sensitive and accurate analog
instrumentation and computing circuits. **Digital-system noise,** especially
high-frequency spikes and pulse ringing, can cause very objectionable noise
in analog circuits via ground currents and radiation. This can be true even
though the digital circuits themselves work well within their noise-immunity
limits. Transistor/transistor logic (TTL) and diode/transistor logic (DTL),
with their harsh ground-current transients and relatively high output impedances, are bad offenders in this respect. Emitter-coupled logic (ECL) has
near-constant ground current, low logic levels, and low output impedances,
and it is a good choice for critical wide-band analog/digital circuits, but may

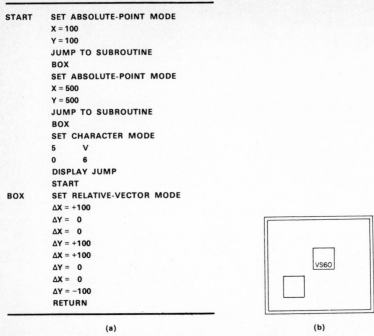

```
START    SET ABSOLUTE-POINT MODE
         X = 100
         Y = 100
         JUMP TO SUBROUTINE
         BOX
         SET ABSOLUTE-POINT MODE
         X = 500
         Y = 500
         JUMP TO SUBROUTINE
         BOX
         SET CHARACTER MODE
         5      V
         0      6
         DISPLAY JUMP
         START
BOX      SET RELATIVE-VECTOR MODE
         ΔX = +100
         ΔY =  0
         ΔX =  0
         ΔY = +100
         ΔX = +100
         ΔY =  0
         ΔX =  0
         ΔY = −100
         RETURN
```

(a)   (b)

Fig. 4-27. Display file (*a*) for a simple picture (*b*) with a repeated subpicture (**BOX**) and some alphanumeric characters. Each line describes one display-processor instruction word (*not* a central-processor instruction) for the Digital Equipment Corporation VS60 display system.

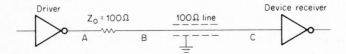

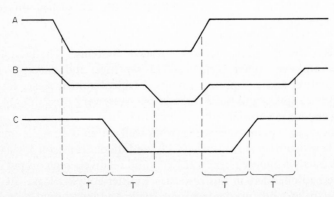

Fig. 4-28. A series-terminated transmission line. The effect on the driving circuit does not change when the receiver power supply is turned off. T is the line-propagation delay.

itself be vulnerable to other noise because ECL logic levels are low.   High-threshold MOSFET logic, especially CMOS, has good noise immunity. Low-speed logic circuits can be shunted with small capacitors to reduce their sensitivity to high-frequency noise from motors, contact closures, etc.

Ground-system noise and common ground impedances can cause serious problems.   A good earth ground is not always easy to come by, and the power-line "industrial" ground should be used for ac return only.   To minimize common ground impedances within a cabinet or subsystem, it is best to select a single **common ground point** and to return all signal, power, and chassis grounds separately to this point, which is also connected to earth ground.

Unfortunately, this simple technique may not work when we must ground widely separated subsystems interconnected by signal lines (e.g., digital computer and an analog subsystem 40 ft away).   We will then give each subsystem a common ground point and try to keep all power-supply loops within each subsystem.   But if each subsystem has an earth ground (often required for electrical safety), then we have a **ground loop** enclosed by the ground connections and each signal wire.   Such inductive loops will pick up and/or radiate noise (Fig. 4-29).   The best way to fix this is to use differential (push-pull) signal transmission or at least **differential signal receivers,** which will cancel ground-loop noise and other disturbances common to both differential inputs (Fig. 4-29; see also Table 4-2).

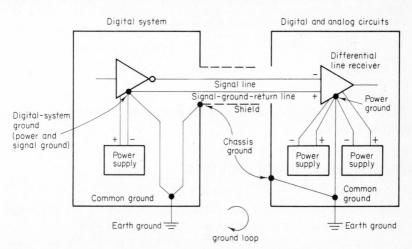

Fig. 4-29. Interconnection and grounding of two typical subsystems.   Differential line receivers cancel common-mode ground-loop and other disturbances.   An even better method is to use push-pull line receivers and line drivers without any ground return between subsystems. Radiation from digital circuits is still a problem (see also Table 4-2).   Earth-ground connections, required for electrical safety, may need shielding.   Power-supply ac inputs may need radio-frequency filters, and power transformers may need electrostatic shields.

Optical isolators (light-emitting diode/phototransistor) may also be used to break the conductive path of a signal-line ground loop.

If electrical safety is no problem, we may omit one earth ground and interconnect the subsystem grounds through a ground return line in the signal cable. Signal-cable shields must *never* carry ground currents; they ordinarily connect to chassis ground at the source end. Even so, we may still have a gound loop formed through leakage resistances and capacitances.

TABLE 4-2. Check List for Minimizing Digital-Noise Effects in Combined Analog/Digital Systems (based on Refs. 15 and 41).

1. *To reduce the digital noise at its source,* avoid long lines which are not carefully terminated and/or clamped to prevent ringing. Consult the applications manual for the type of logic circuits used. Wires from each circuit should fan out, not continue from point to point.
2. *It is important to keep as much of the digital noise as possible within the digital-circuit cards and out of power-supply and ground circuits, and to keep the remainder out of the analog circuits as best possible.* For this reason, every digital and analog circuit card should have a *decoupling circuit* on each power-supply line. A *ground plane* ought to be used on each card, not so much for electrostatic shielding as to reduce the areas of inductive loops. *Laminated power-supply buses* also help with decoupling.
3. Digital ground returns (which act as transmitting antennas!) should be kept separate and well away from analog ground leads. It is, in fact, a good idea to keep digital and analog circuits in separate shielded enclosures and to operate their power supplies from different phases of the three-phase line, with RF filters in each ac lead.
4. *Where a digital computer is connected to a linkage or analog subsystem, we must avoid returning any digital signals through the common ground.* It is best to use *push-pull line drivers* with twisted and shielded lines into *differential line receivers,* or at least differential line receivers fed with the digital signal and digital ground-return lines. Balun transformers have also been successfully used to replace actual differential lines. Slow logic signals (below 20 to 100 kHz) can be isolated by light-coupled semiconductor switches.
5. Finally, make sure that all operational amplifiers and other analog feedback circuits are equalized so as to avoid high-frequency peaks (which cause ringing when excited by digital noise).
   With all these precautions, it is possible to keep digital noise on analog circuits below 5 to 10 mV peak to peak.

Table 4-2 summarizes **general rules for minimizing digital-circuit noise in analog subsystems.**

REFERENCES AND BIBLIOGRAPHY

Manuals

For detailed interface-design information, refer to computer manufacturers' *interface manuals* and to integrated-circuit manufacturers' *applications manuals.* Among the more useful publications of this type are the current editions of

1. *Logic Handbook*
2. *Logic-System Design Handbook*
3. *Small-Computer Handbook*
4. *PDP-11 Peripherals Handbook*

5. *A Pocket Guide to Interfacing HP Computers*, Hewlett-Packard Corp., Cupertino, Calif.
6. *M6800 Microprocessor Applications Manual*, Motorola Semiconductor Products, Inc., Phoenix, Ariz.
7. *Intel 3212 Multi-Mode Latch Buffer*
8. *Intel 3214 Interrupt Control Unit*
9. *Intel MCS-40 User's Manual for Logic Designers*

References 1 through 4 are available from Digital Equipment Corp., Maynard, Mass., and Refs. 7 through 10 from Intel Corp., Santa Clara, Calif.

General

10. Wilkins, J.: The PDP-9/LOCUST Interface, *M.S. Thesis*, The University of Arizona, 1969.
11. *SERDEX Application Notes* (current edition), Analog Devices, Norwood, Mass.
12. Meng, J. D.: A Serial Input/Output Scheme for Small Computers, *Comput. Des.*, March 1970.
13. Bounds, P.: Buffering High-Speed Data for Minicomputer Input, *Comput. Des.*, July 1973.

Data Conversion

14. Wait, J. V., L. Huelsman, and G. A. Korn: *Operational Amplifiers, Theory and Application*, McGraw-Hill, New York, 1975.
15. Korn, G. A., and T. M. Korn: *Electronic Analog and Hybrid Computers*, 2d ed., McGraw-Hill, New York, 1972.
16. Schmid, H.: *Electronic Analog/Digital Conversions*, Van Nostrand Reinhold, New York, 1970.
17. *Analog-Digital Conversion Handbook*, Analog Devices, Inc., Norwood, Mass., 1972.

Data Communications

(See also Ref. 6 and the communications-products catalogs of various minicomputer firms)

18. Stimler, S.: *Real-Time Processing Systems*, McGraw-Hill, New York, 1969.
19. *Data Sets 201A and 201B*, Bell System Data Communications, New York, N.Y. (current edition).
20. *The Communications Handbook*, Microdata Corp., Irvine, Calif. (current edition).
21. Jones, W. S.: System Aspects of Data Modems, *Electron. Prod.*, February 1971.
22. Cushman, R. H.: Communication Circuits: Putting Data on the Telephone Network, *EDN*, June 1973.
23. Davis, S.: Modems: Their Operating Principles and Applications, *Comput. Des.*, September 1973.
24. Stelmach, E. V.: *Introduction to Minicomputer Networks*, Digital Equipment Corp., Maynard, Mass., 1974.
25. Nash, G.: Build Compact Modems into Digital Equipment, *Electron. Des.*, January 1975.

Graphic Displays

26. Newman, W. M., and R. F. Sproull: *Principles of Interactive Computer Graphics*, McGraw-Hill, New York, 1973.
27. Korn, G. A., et al.: A New Graphic Display/Plotter for Small Digital Computers, *Proc. SJCC*, 1969.

CAMAC Systems

CAMAC information is documented in EUR reports 4100e, 4600e, 5100e, in the periodical *CAMAC Bulletin*, and in the yearly CAMAC Conference Proceedings, all published by the Office for Official Publications of the

European Communities, P.O. Box 1003, Luxembourg. The *CAMAC Bulletin* also has articles, bibliographies, and updated lists of commercially available equipment. CAMAC specifications are also available in the following reports of the U.S. Energy Research and Development Administration (formerly Atomic Energy Commission), Washington, D.C. 20545:

28. TID-25875, July 1972 (general specifications)
29. TID-25876, March 1972 (multicrate systems)
30. TID-25877, December 1972 (supplementary information)
31. TID-26488, December 1973 (serial highway)
32. TID-26614 (analog signals)
33. TID-26615, January 1975 (IML language)

For an introduction to CAMAC, see

34. CAMAC Tutorial Issue, *IEEE Trans. Nucl. Sci.*, April 1971.
35. Costrell, L.: Highways for CAMAC Systems, *IEEE Trans. Nucl. Sci.*, February 1974.

IEC/Hewlett-Packard Bus System

36. Ricci, D. W., and G. E. Nelson: Standard Instrument Interface, *Electronics*, Nov. 14, 1974.
37. Loughry, D. C.: The Hewlett-Packard Interface Bus, *Hewlett-Packard J.*, January 1975.
38. Schultz, S. E., and C. R. Trimble: Modular Accessories for Instrument Systems, *Hewlett-Packard J.*, January 1975.

Noise, Shielding, and Grounding

(See also Ref. 2)

39. Demrow, R. I.: Protecting Data from the Ground Up, *Electronics*, Apr. 29, 1968.
40. Brown, H.: Don't Leave System Grounding to Chance, *EDN*, January 1972.
41. Jones, J. P.: *Causes and Cures of Noise in Digital Systems*, Computer Design Publication Company, West Concord, Mass., 1964.
42. Heniford, B.: Noise in 54/74 TTL Systems, *Appl. Bull. CA-108*, Texas Instruments, Inc., Dallas, 1968.
43. Garrett, L. S.: Integrated-Circuit Digital-Logic Families, Part III, *IEEE Spectrum*, December 1970.
44. Morrison, B.: *Grounding and Shielding Techniques in Instrumentation*, Wiley, New York, 1967.

Miscellaneous

45. Klapfish, M.: Interfacing the Teletypewriter, *Comput. Des.*, June–July 1974.
46. Wold, I., and M. Lindheimer: Acquiring Multipoint Plant Data over a Single Two-Wire Link, *Electronics*, Nov. 22, 1973.
47. Nicoud, J. D.: Peripheral Interface Standards for Microprocessors, *Proc. IEEE*, June 1976.
48. Beckwith, D. C.: Local High-Speed Data Transmission, *DECUS Proceedings*, Digital Equipment Corp., Maynard, Mass., Spring 1973.
49. Mick, J. R.: Using Schottky 3-State Outputs in Bus-Organized Systems, *EDN*, December 1974.
50. Abbott, D. L.: *Microprocessors and CAMAC*, Central Laboratory for Electronics, Nuclear Research Installation Jülich, Jülich, West Germany.
51. Wolff, H.: Data-Communications Protocol Nears, *Electronics*, Aug. 7, 1975.
52. Andelman, S. J.: Real-Time I/O Techniques, *Comput. Des.*, May 1966.
53. Lancaster, D.: *The TV Typewriter Cookbook*, Howard W. Sams, Publications, Indianapolis, Ind., 1976.
54. Fisher, E.: Speed Microprocessor Responses, *Electron. Des.*, Nov. 8, 1975.
55. Smith, L.: USART—A Universal Microprocessor Interface for Serial Data Communications, *EDN*, September 5, 1976.

CHAPTER 5

COMPUTER OPERATION, SOFTWARE, AND PROGRAM PREPARATION

CONTROL-PANEL AND PAPER-TAPE OPERATION

5-1. The Operator's Control Panel. The **control panel** of a minicomputer (or of a microcomputer prototype-development system, Sec. 5-28) will typically have the following controls and indicators (Fig. 5-1):

1. A **key-operated main power switch** with three positions: ON, OFF, and LOCK PANEL. In the latter position, power is ON, but all front-panel controls are ineffective—this keeps visitors from ruining computations by playing with the controls.

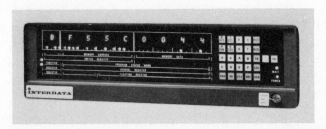

Fig. 5-1. A modern minicomputer control panel. Both hexadecimal and binary displays show either a 16-bit address and a 16-bit data word, or a 32-bit double word (e.g., floating-point data). The traditional bit-switch register has been replaced by a calculator-type hexadecimal keyboard, which enters successive 4-bit groups with each keystroke. Extra keys implement console functions such as SET ADDRESS, RUN, etc. (*Interdata.*)

191

2. **Indicator-light fields,** which display the contents of the principal processor registers for examination. Smaller machines may have only one indicator field, which can display different processor registers selected by a REGISTER SELECTOR switch.
3. A **switch register or registers** for entering binary numbers bit by bit into a processor register selected by a REGISTER SELECTOR switch or by the LOAD ADDRESS, DEPOSIT, and RUN switches.

Many newer machines replace the control-panel light and switch registers by a **numerical (octal or hexadecimal) display** and a set of **numerical keys.**

4. Various switches.
   (*a*) A **REGISTER SELECTOR switch** selects the processor register connected to indicator and/or switch registers.
   (*b*) A **LOAD ADDRESS switch** loads the memory address register with the number set into the switch register.
   (*c*) A **DEPOSIT switch** loads the currently addressed memory location with switch-register contents.
5. An **EXAMINE (FETCH) switch** fetches the contents of the currently addressed memory location into the memory data register for front-panel display.
6. **Controls for starting, stopping, and stepping processor operation.**
   (*a*) The **START (RUN)/STOP switch** starts the program at the memory location set into the address switches.
   (*b*) **SINGLE INSTRUCTION** and **SINGLE CYCLE switches** for "stepping" the program one instruction or one processor cycle at a time; they are used for troubleshooting hardware or programs.

Additional controls and indicators may be provided. Some minicomputers have a **READ IN switch** for starting a paper-tape reader or even for automatic loading (Sec. 5-3*b*). **Sense switches** on the front panel may permit the operator to modify a program while it is running (Sec. 4-7; in other machines, sense lines are available only in peripheral devices). As further aids in troubleshooting, there may be **indicators for the current processor status,** e.g., INSTRUCTION FETCH, EXECUTE, INPUT/OUTPUT, INTERRUPT, etc.

Some minicomputers have a front-panel **CLEAR switch,** which clears a selected processor register or registers and which may also send a clear pulse to the computer peripheral devices for clearing appropriate flags and/or registers.

Some machines (PDP-15) have an I/O instruction to read their front-panel switch register during computation.

5-2. Typical Control-Panel Operations. The operator's control panel serves for starting programs and for troubleshooting through examination of register contents and stepwise program execution. With LSI circuits, panel switches and lights cannot access individual registers directly but require execution of small input/output programs or microprograms. Since registers cannot be checked directly anyway, *one may replace all control-panel operations with keyboard-terminal operations if a teleprinter or other terminal is available.* Dedicated micro/minicomputers can be serviced with a plug-in control panel or keyboard/display carried by a service technician.

Specific front-panel controls and their operation will vary somewhat for different computers—you must consult the operator's manual for your own machine. The following operations are typical:

1. With the computer halted by the START/STOP switch, we can examine and change the contents of registers and memory locations. **To examine a memory location,** we set its address into the switch register and press the LOAD ADDRESS switch. The EXAMINE switch will now bring the contents of the addressed location into the memory data register for display.
2. **To load a memory location manually,** we set its address into the switch register and press LOAD ADDRESS. Then we set the desired binary number into the switch register and press DEPOSIT.
3. It will be useful to examine or load *successive* memory locations. For this purpose, we must increment the memory address register between successive EXAMINE or DEPOSIT operations. Different mini-computers do this in different ways, e.g.,

   (a) In the PDP-8I, LOAD ADDRESS sets the address into the program counter as well as in the memory address register. Program counter and memory address are incremented after *every* EXAMINE or DEPOSIT operation.
   (b) The more elaborate PDP-15 has *special switch positions* (EXAMINE NEXT, DEPOSIT NEXT) which step the memory address before fetching or depositing.
   (c) In the PDP-11, *repeated* operation of the EXAMINE or DEPOSIT switch steps the memory address register.

5-3. Loading and Running Simple Programs with Paper Tape. (a) Manual Loading. An **executable program** (which may or may not have some data attached to it) is, as we have seen, a sequence of multibit computer words. We might have such a program in binary form (or in the more convenient octal or hexadecimal form) (Sec. 1-6) on a sheet of paper; **we must enter the program words into appropriate (usually consecutive) memory locations in the computer.** A simple-minded way to *load the program* is to use the front-panel controls:

1. Select a memory location for the first program word (which could be an instruction or a data word) via the switch register and the LOAD ADDRESS switch.

2. Load successive program words into consecutive memory locations with the aid of the switch register and the DEPOSIT switch, as shown in Sec. 5-2.

3. Set the actual starting address (address of the first instruction) into the program counter via switch register and selector or DEPOSIT switch.

The program is now ready to run if we press the RUN switch.   As the program runs, it will *output data* via the teletypewriter, paper-tape punch, or other peripherals.   The program may also *read input data* (or additional input data) from the teletypewriter, paper-tape reader, measuring instruments, etc.

(b) Paper-Tape Systems and Bootstrap Loaders.   Practical programs can have hundreds or thousands of words.   Manual loading is clearly impractical, and programs are prepared (and stored for repeated use) on a **computer-readable storage medium,** such as punched cards, punched paper tape, magnetic tape, or a disk (Secs. 5-8 and 5-9, Table 5-1).   Many small computer systems can still be bought with paper tape, because this requires minimal peripheral equipment (only an ASR-type teleprinter with built-in paper-tape reader/punch, Sec. 5-7).   We note right here that such systems are inconvenient and slow and ought to be used only where programs will be entered infrequently.

The operations required to load words from paper tape into the computer memory, starting at a specified location, will themselves constitute a computer program, an **absolute loader (paper-tape loader),** which may be supplied on its own paper tape or may form the starting section of a system program such as an editor or assembler (Sec. 5-4).   A suitable loader will read and load its own tape provided that its first 10 to 32 instructions are in memory **(bootstrap loading).**   The initial loading instructions can be loaded manually (some computers protect them from overwriting through a special front-panel switch), but the best scheme is to have the initial loading sequence in read-only memory **(ROM bootstrap loader,** see also Sec. 5-15).   To load the entire paper-tape loader (with or without an associated system program), we set the address switches to the first loading-instruction address and press RUN (or READ IN, depending on the computer).

With a separate loader in memory, we can load any program or data tape:

1. Place the tape in the reader (*consult your manual*)
2. Set the address switches to the first address to be loaded
3. Press RUN, or READ IN (*consult your manual*)

An executable program thus loaded can now be started with the RUN switch as soon as we set the address switches to the appropriate starting address.   Some programs include a jump to the starting address as the last instruction loaded; so we can simply press RUN and go.

5-4. Simple Program Preparation, Editing, and Translation. (a) Source Programs and Object Programs. In Sec. 5-3, we did not discuss preparation of new programs but only the loading and running of executable machine-language programs. Indeed, *with many special-purpose computer systems we may never have to prepare a program*, for the system may come with "canned" programs on tapes, kindly furnished by the computer manufacturer or by a software house, for a variety of jobs. All we do is supply the data inputs, load, and run.

Less specialized applications require us to create our own programs. It would be a cruel job to write programs in binary or even octal machine language, so we type and/or punch a **source program** in a **programming language** admitting a restricted set of stylized English and mathematical statements. A **translator program** then employs the computer itself to read the source-program character code and to translate our source-program statements into machine-language instructions and data words of an executable **object program.**

(b) Program Preparation and Editing. Source programs can, in principle, be typed onto a paper tape **(source tape)** from any keyboard terminal capable of driving a tape punch (with or without the aid of a computer; e.g., an ASR-tape teleprinter, Fig. 5-3a). But it is impossible to make corrections or modifications on our tape, other than deleting the last-typed character or characters (DELETE or RUBOUT key), or the current line (control key, Sec. 5-7). To correct or modify new text, or text read from an existing source tape, we load an **editor program.** The computer now becomes a special-purpose machine for text editing (Fig. 5-2a). The machine enters newly typed or tape-read text into a *text buffer in memory.* Typed commands then permit us to find and modify selected portions of the text (ASCII-character array) in the text buffer, to print edited text, and to produce an *edited source tape* when we are finished. The operation and features of practical editor programs will be discussed in Sec. 5-18.

In contrast with paper-tape systems, source programs punched on conventional punched cards can be edited through replacement of individual cards.

(c) Assemblers, Compilers, and Interpreters. Translators are rather formidable system programs supplied (one hopes) by the computer manufacturer. There are three types of translators.

1. An **assembler** translates an **assembly language,** most of whose statements correspond to machine-language instructions on a one-to-one basis (e.g., **LOAD ACCUMULATOR WITH CONTENTS OF MEMORY LOCATION A,** or **LAC A**).

2. A **compiler** translates a **compiler language,** which is closer to English-cum-mathematics and can include statements (e.g., formulas) which will each be translated into *many* machine-language instructions (e.g., FORTRAN, ALGOL, Sec. 5-24).

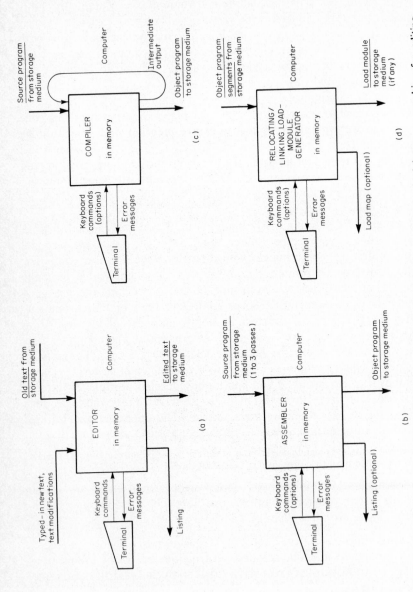

Fig. 5-2. Each of the *system programs* shown makes the computer into a special-purpose machine for editing (*a*), translation (*b*), (*c*), and program linkage (*d*).

196

Each new computer type needs a new assembly language, and relatively simple mathematical and input/output operations can require substantial numbers of assembly-language instructions. But **assembly-language programming** (Chap. 3) **can take the most efficient advantage of minicomputer hardware to save memory and time during execution.** By contrast, some minicomputer compilers generate slow-executing code because both compiler and object programs are compromised by the small amount of memory available (see also Chap. 3).

With our simple computer system, assembler and/or compiler programs come on paper tape. Once the **assembler tape** is loaded, our computer becomes a special-purpose machine for translating properly written assembly-language source programs into binary machine code (Fig. 5-2b). The machine will now read a source-program tape and produces the object program (on paper tape) either in one pass, or after rereading the source tape in a second pass (**one-pass** or **two-pass assembler,** Secs. 3-1 to 3-3). A third pass over the source tape can produce a teleprinter listing of both source program and actual or hexadecimal machine code (Fig. 3-3).

If we have made a mistake in our source-language syntax, exceeded the available memory storage, used too large numbers, etc., the translator program will notify us of the fact by stopping and printing an appropriate **error message** on the teleprinter. At this point, we will have the pleasure of doing the job over. If the program works correctly, however, the translator produces a storable binary-coded object tape, which can be used again and again with new data, without any need for retranslation of our source program.

Compiler translation (*compilation*) of, say, a FORTRAN source program works quite similarly, except that the compiler's first pass may produce an *intermediate* paper tape, which must be read in to be processed by a second compiler pass (Fig. 5-2b).

Some compilers require more than two passes, and some translate the source program into assembly language (which must then be assembled).

Assemblers and compilers generate complete object programs for execution. Our third translation scheme works differently:

3. An **interpreter** translates one source-language statement at a time, executes the resulting machine instruction or instructions at once, translates the next statement, etc.

Interpreter translation is inefficient for "production programs" which are to be executed many times, since each execution will be slowed by translation. This is not objectionable in **on-line conversational computing,** where interpreter systems translate compiler-type source languages like BASIC and FOCAL (Secs. 5-25 and 5-27). Interpreters can also implement step-by-step emulation of computer instructions by the instruction set of a different computer.

5-5. Loading and Combining (Linking) Binary Object Programs (see also Sec. 3-17).   An independent binary object program loaded into core with our paper-tape loader should be ready to execute.   *Data* for such a program may have been loaded together with the program, or the program contains instructions to get its data from peripheral devices, e.g., from typed input, from another paper tape placed in the paper-tape reader, or from instruments such as analog-to-digital converters.   Program output will be obtained on the teleprinter, display, tape punch, etc., as specified by the program itself. Very often, though, *we should like to combine a binary object program with other such programs.*   These may be user programs, perhaps modules of a larger program, or **library subroutines** supplied by the computer manufacturer (e.g., floating-point arithmetic routines, sine/cosine generators, input/output routines).   With a paper-tape operating system, all these programs and subroutine libraries will be on various pieces of paper tape; we would like to load them for combined execution.   This will practically always impose two requirements:

1. We must **relocate** binary programs so that they can be loaded into successive core-memory areas.   This will mean *changing both instruction addresses and memory-reference addresses.*
2. Since the combined programs will refer to one another (by supplying data and/or through jump instructions), we must find all such **external references** and provide them with the correct memory addresses.

To satisfy the first requirement, the object programs to be relocated must have been prepared by an assembler or compiler which generates **relocatable code** (Sec. 3-18).   That is, all memory references to addresses needing relocation are either specially marked—say with an extra word—or they are relative to the current program-counter reading (Sec. 3-19).   To satisfy the second requirement, **each program segment must list all its external references according to a specified convention.**

   To combine program segments satisfying these requirements, we first load a new system program called a **linking loader** and then the various object tapes.   **The linking loader will note the final address of each program segment, relocate the succeeding program, and supply the necessary linkage references.** The combined program will be left in core ready for execution.   Options, usually selected by front-panel register or sense switches, will run the combined program as soon as it is loaded ("load and go") and/or punch a binary tape for the combined object program.   The linking loader will also type out *error messages* if it is prevented from doing its job by user errors such as faulty or missing external references, and it can print out a **load map** listing the starting address and the number of memory locations used for each of the linked programs.

MICRO/MINI PERIPHERAL DEVICES
AND MASS STORAGE

5-6. Introduction. Paper-tape operation is practical only if the paper-tape system need not be used to prepare, translate, or modify extensive new programs. This is true even with high-speed paper-tape reader/punches; with the 10 characters/sec reader/punch on an ASR teleprinter, editing and translation of even small programs can take *hours*. Since paper-tape is a fairly standardized storage medium, it is acceptable for loading programs prepared by *cross translation* on another computer (Sec. 5-29), and also for loading *interpreter programs* (Secs. 5-25, 5-27). But **efficient program preparation requires a system which can quickly read, store, combine, retrieve, and run system programs (editor, translators, etc.) and user programs in response to simple keyboard commands, with a minimum of manual loading operations.** This is achieved by an **executive program (monitor, operating-system executive)** in conjunction with a magnetic disk, drum, or tape **mass-storage system** and a convenient **keyboard/printer** and/or **CRT terminal).** Sections 5-7 to 5-9 will describe low-cost peripheral devices designed for minicomputers and for microcomputer prototyping systems.

5-7. Printers, CRT Terminals, and Keyboards. (a) Teleprinters and Line Printers. Many early minicomputers were furnished with an ASR-33, ASR-35, KSR-33, or KSR-35 **printer/keyboard (teletypewriter)** manufactured by the Teletype® Corporation (Fig. 5-3a).[1] With the OFF/LINE/LOCAL switch in the LOCAL position, the teletypewriter is disconnected from the computer and acts like a typewriter with the special character set shown in Fig. 5-4b. In the LINE position, the keyboard transmits 8-bit ASCII character sequences (Table B-9) to the computer, and the printer can accept and output ASCII characters. These machines can print up to 10 characters/ sec. They produce only capital letters but do have two shift keys (SHIFT and CTRL), which produce special characters or control functions when depressed simultaneously with other keys (see also Fig. 5-4b). Some of these special functions will depend on specific computer programs; conventional interpretations are listed in Table B-7.

The ASR models have a slow (10 character/sec) **paper-tape punch** and *reader*, an important reason for their early popularity. In the LOCAL mode, we can punch the tape from the keyboard or get printed output through the paper-tape reader. In the LINE mode, we can read paper tape into the computer or let the computer punch paper tapes. Program preparation with the console typewriter will be further discussed in Sec. 5-18.

---

[1] ASR stands for Automatic Send/Receive, while KSR stands for Keyboard Send/Receive. ASR-37 has both uppercase and lowercase characters and permits 15 character/sec operations, but it is substantially more expensive.

Fig. 5-3a. Teletype Corporation ASR-33 teletypewriter.   The paper-tape reader/punch is at the left.

Fig. 5-3b. Digital Equipment Corporation DECwriter II is an example of a modern matrix-needle printer.   This unit prints up to 132 columns of upper- and lowercase characters at 30 characters/sec and costs under $2,000.   (*Digital Equipment Corp.*)

ASR-33 and KSR-33 are designed "for intermittent light duty," and this means exactly what it says. Teletypewriters will not last long if you use them as line printers for long listings. Even the "continuous-duty" ASR-35 and the KSR-35 teletypewriters are really designed for use in communications offices, where they are rebuilt on a regular schedule.

Modern computer systems employ faster, quieter, and more reliable **character-wheel printers** (Interdata), **character-ball printers** (IBM), and especially **matrix-needle printers** (e.g., OKI, Singer, Digital Equipment Corp.) to print between 30 and 100 characters/sec. Matrix-needle printers use a ROM character generator to actuate a vertical column of needles in a printhead which moves horizontally to compose the character patterns (Fig. 5-3b).

For faster printing of long listings, it pays to have a small **line printer,** which will print up to about 500 80- to 132-column lines per minute. Line printers suitable for small computer systems cost between $4,000 and $13,000.

Nonimpact printers (thermal or electrolytic) serve where noiseless operation with little mechanical wear is important, but they require costly special paper and cannot print carbon copies. Some nonimpact printers can be used as graphic plotters.

(b) CRT Terminals. Computer operation becomes much faster and more convenient if we substitute a **cathode-ray-tube/keyboard terminal (CRT terminal,** Fig. 5-4a) for the slow, noisy, and maintenance-prone console teleprinter (see also Sec. 5-18).

Inexpensive CRT terminals display about 20 to 40 character lines on a standard television monitor. If much text or tabular material must be displayed, then 80-character lines (which require a wideband TV monitor)

Fig. 5-4a. A CRT/keyboard terminal for alphanumeric input/output. The unit shown has an optional electrolytic printer for hard-copy output. Some TV-raster terminals even have limited graphic-display capabilities, as shown here. (*Digital Equipment Corp.*)

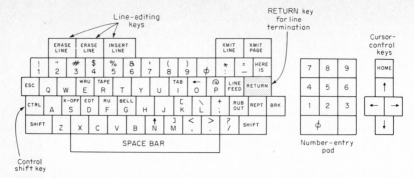

Fig. 5-4b. A CRT-terminal keyboard. The keyboard section on the left is, essentially, a teleprinter keyboard, with the addition of line-editing keys for the CRT display. RETURN keys may combine the functions of LINE FEED and RETURN. The nomenclature on the extra keys shown is intended for communications applications rather than for computing, but the extra keys are useful.

are preferable. An 80-character line can display a complete 80-column punched-card image or a 72-character teletypewriter line.

ASCII-character patterns are generated by table lookup in a MOSFET ROM (Sec. 1-23). The display character sequence is periodically refreshed, usually by a serial memory (MOSFET shift register, Sec. 1-22). Most CRT terminals are *teletypewriter-compatible;* i.e., they connect to the serial teletypewriter interface on a minicomputer or communication system. It is usually possible to speed up the shift pulse rate of such an interface from the 110 to 330 bps teleprinter rate to 2,000 to 9,600 bps, so that a 1,000-character page is written in little over one second. CRT-terminal keyboards are similar to teleprinter keyboards. A blinking **cursor,** which can be moved up, down, left, or right by control keys, indicates the character-entry point on the CRT screen (Fig. 5-4b).

Simple teleprinter-replacement CRT terminals cost between $500 and $1,800. More elaborate ("smart") CRT terminals comprise a microprocessor with enough random-access memory to store and refresh several screen "pages" and permit convenient screen editing

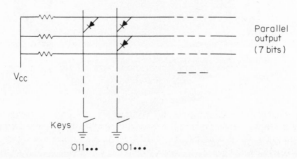

Fig. 5-5a. ASCII keyboard interface with diode encoding matrix and 7-bit parallel output.

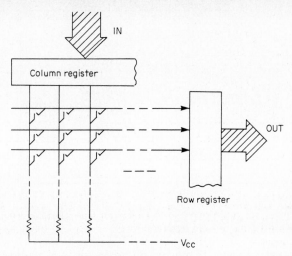

Fig. 5-5b. The columns of this keyboard-interface matrix are scanned by a microprocessor or calculator *program* which successively writes 0111 ..., 1011 ..., 1101 ... into the column register and then reads and decodes the resulting row-register outputs. The program can easily take care of keystroke overlaps (multiple-key rollover), inadvertent short key depressions, etc.

(character and line insertion/deletion, Sec. 5-18), margin justification, and even syntax checking and rescaling. Prices start at $2,000. Some CRT terminals have special hardware for displaying graphs.

   (c) Keyboard Interfaces. Teleprinters and CRT terminals use keyboard-encoder circuits similar to Fig. 5-5a, followed by a UART (Sec. 4-29) for parallel/serial conversion. Calculators and simple instruments use serial encoders similar to Fig. 5-5b. Special hardware or software guards against errors due to inadvertent multiple-key operations (two- and three-key "rollover").

5-8. Paper-Tape and Card Equipment.

Primitive minicomputer systems and microcomputer program-preparation systems employ **punched paper tape** (Fig. 5-6a) for source-program preparation and for source- and object-

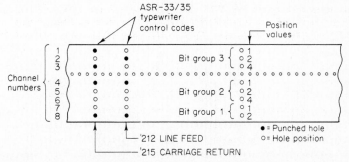

Fig. 5-6a. Paper tape with eight-channel ASCII code. This format is commonly employed for *source-program* tapes. *Binary object programs* are punched in different formats depending on the minicomputer word length. Block header and terminator sections can contain identifying information and a *checksum* (complement of the modulo 2^8 sum of the 8-bit binary numbers in a block).

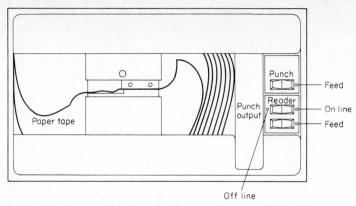

Fig. 5-6b. Medium-speed reader/punch for fanfold paper tape. Read at 300 characters/sec; punch at 50 characters/sec. (*Digital Equipment Corp.*)

program storage. Even with modern photoelectric tape readers, paper-tape equipment is slow and not really cheap (Table 5-1). But paper tape is still widely used as a *transfer medium* for moving computer or teletype-writer-punched information to ROM programmers, numerically controlled machine tools, typesetting machines, or other computers. In this connection, punched-tape *readers* are faster, cheaper (prices start at $250), and more reliable than punches.

As noted in Sec. 5-3, ASR-type teletypewriters have built-in 10-character/sec tape punches and readers. These will do for loading (binary) program tapes and for infrequent problem preparation in applications requiring few such operations (e.g., special-purpose-system start-up, interpreter systems). For faster work, *one usually buys a 300 character/sec reader and a 50*

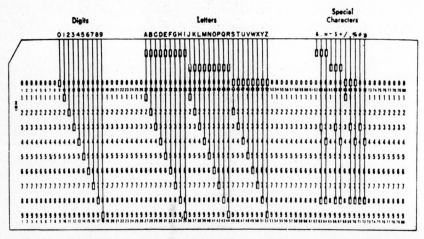

Fig. 5-7. International Business Machines Corporation 80-column punched-card code.

character/sec punch (Fig. 5-6*b*), *both for fanfold paper tape, which does not require rewinding* (see also Table 5-1 and Sec. 5-3). *Faster reel-type readers* serve in special applications with long program or data tapes.

Each of these electromechanical character-handling devices has an 8-bit device register (character buffer), which can be read or loaded by a processor I/O instruction. Each data transfer must wait until completion of a relatively slow electromechanical reading, punching, or printing operation is signaled by a device-flag interrupt (Sec. 4-27).

Punched cards (Fig. 5-7), widely used for source-program preparation and storage with larger digital computers, permit simple off-line editing, since each card usually represents a single 80-character line. Since card punches and readers tend to be expensive, complicated, and slow, they are rarely used with mini-microcomputer systems. **Mark-sense cards,** which do not require a punch, are used in some educational applications.

5-9. Magnetic Disk, Drum, and Tape Storage. (a) Storage Requirements and Operations. Minicomputer system programs, such as assemblers and compilers, typically require several thousand words each. Additional thousands of words will be required for library programs (frequently used arithmetic, function-generator, and input/output routines), stored user programs, and user programs in the intermediate stages of a translation process. For general-purpose computation on minicomputers with 8K to 32K of core memory we will, moreover, "chain" successive segments of longer user programs stored on a disk or tape: we load and execute the first program segment, keep some intermediate results in core, load and execute a second program segment, etc.; such program segments are known as successive *core overlays.* Many applications also involve creation of permanent or intermediate **text or data files** with many thousands of words. Altogether, general-purpose minicomputation will require between 30K and several million words of mass storage, which should be accessible without manual loading operations.

Table 5-1 compares minicomputer mass-storage systems with respect to storage capacity, data-transfer rate, access time, and cost. Rotating magnetic disks and drums have the highest data-transfer rates and the shortest access times, but magnetic tape, on removable reels, is cheaper for larger amounts of storage. Small and larger disks are often combined with magnetic tape so that different programs or data can be loaded from removable tape reels. There are also disk systems with removable disks or disk cartridges, and combinations of fixed and removable disks (Fig. 5-7).

Magnetic mass-storage systems usually transfer 16- to 2,048-word **blocks** directly to and from **buffer areas** in the computer memory (Sec. 4-18). Each buffer is identified by its **starting address** and **size (word count); header words** in each storage block may identify the block by a name and specify word count and addresses of succeeding or preceding blocks (Sec. 5-14). To safeguard the large amounts of information handled, mass-storage

TABLE 5-1. Comparison of Minicomputer Storage Media and Peripherals.

	PAPER TAPE		MAGNETIC TAPE (continuous operation)				MAGNETIC DISKS		
	ASR-33 teletype-writer	Medium speed reader/ punch	Cassette tape	Cartridge tape	LINCtape/ DECtape	Industry-compatible tape	Floppy disk	Moving-head	Fixed-head
8-bit characters/sec	10	300 read, 50 punch	500 –1,600	5,000 –6,000	8,000 –10,000	6,000 –60,000	20,000 –50,000	40,000 –1,000,000	40,000 –1,000,000
16-bit words/ sec	5	150 read, 25 punch	250 –800	2,500 –3,000	4,000 –5,000	3,000 –30,000	10,000 –25,000	20,000 –500,000	20,000 –500,000
Time to read 1,000 16-bit words (object programs)	200 sec	7 sec	1.25 –4 sec	330 –400 msec	200 –250 msec	30 –300 msec	40–100 msec	2–50 msec	2–50 msec
Time to read 1,000 typical 20-character lines (source programs for assembly or compilation)	2,000 sec	70 sec	12.5 –40 sec	3.3 –4 sec	2–2.5 sec	0.3 –3 sec	0.4–1 sec	20 –500 msec	20 –500 msec

			to 150 sec	to 200 sec	to 100 sec	to 240 sec	200 -400 msec	50 -200 msec	8-17 msec
Access time (max)	...	...	...	...	...	...	200 -400 msec	50 -200 msec	8-17 msec
Total storage (16-bit words)	...	...	50K -100K	400K -1.4M	100K -300K	200K -20M	100K -400K	1M -50M	30K -600K
Typical price (combined input/output unit and interface)	$300 more than KSR-33	$1.500 -$3500	$800 -$3,000*	$800 -$3,000*	$2,000 -$10,000*	$5,000 -$14,000*	$1,000 -$4,000*	$3,000 -$30,000*	$6,000 -$30,000*
Typical price of storage medium	$1.50	$1.50	$8-$15	$12-$18	$10-$12	$10-$20	$6-$18	$70-$100†	

* One controller can serve several drives.
† Disk cartridge, 1.5M words.

systems perform *check computations on each block of words transferred* as well as parity checks (Sec. 1-8) on individual bytes.   The system can try repeated rereading or rewriting when an error is detected and will signal read or write failures.   All in all, disk and tape system interface logic is relatively complicated and often incorporates a microprocessor in its own right.

(b) Disk and Drum Systems.   A disk or drum rotates continuously. Computer words are recorded serially along numbered tracks; i.e., successive bits are read or recorded as the magnetic film passes under a read/write head.   Magnetic drums and fast-access disks have **fixed heads** for individual tracks.   **Moving-head disks** can have more tracks, and thus much more storage capacity; but the head-positioning operation increases access time (Table 5-1).   Typical head-positioning actuators employ a moving-coil mechanism similar to that of a dynamic loudspeaker (Fig. 5-8).

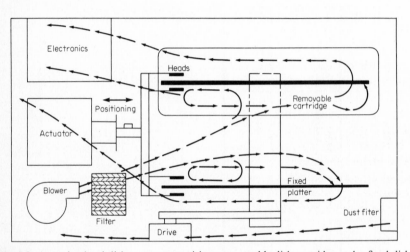

Fig. 5-8. A moving-head disk system comprising a removable-disk cartridge and a fixed disk, showing the moving-coil head-positioning actuator and the positive-pressure air-filtration system.   (*Hewlett-Packard Corporation.*)

A typical 1.25M-word moving-head minicomputer disk might have 203 tracks (3 are spares) on each side, with 12 256-word segments (sectors) and an end-of-track gap on each track.   Block or word addresses are specified by *disk number, track number,* and *segment address.*   Segment addresses are prerecorded on an **address track.**   Each segment address is read before the corresponding words pass under the read/write heads.   Word sequences can be read or written consecutively along each track, switching to the next track when the end-of-track gap is reached ("spiral" reading or writing).

Data transfers are DMA transfers via a *disk buffer register* which buffers a *shift register* implementing parallel/serial conversion (see also Sec. 4-26). To initiate a data transfer, programmed instructions set a *disk control register* to WRITE or READ and preset the *current-address register*, the *word counter*, and the *disk address register*. The latter (which may be a two-word register) specifies the disk, track, and segment address for the first word of a data block. When the segment address matches that read on the address track, the disk controller initiates the block transfer, which stops when the word counter runs out; this will also cause a program interrupt (Sec. 4-18).

Besides WRITE and READ, disk systems have a CHECK (COMPARE, SEARCH) mode which *compares* a word set into the disk buffer register with the word currently read from the disk into the shift register, and which sets an interrupt flag when the words agree. This mode is used for checking purposes, and can also find words on the disk.

Other interrupt flags detect *parity errors*, *missing prerecorded-track bits*, illegal addresses, etc. Front-panel *write-lock switches* can protect selected tracks from overwriting, e.g., to protect system programs. On multidisk systems, one disk can read or write while others search for a specified track and segment.

Disk read/write heads usually float on air, and some care is necessary to prevent track-damaging *head crashes* due to power-supply failures. **Consult your manual for the proper method of removing power;** some disks are never turned off. *Disk operation is sensitive to small dust particles*, which can become a problem especially with removable-disk cartridges. Disk *air filters* require periodic maintenance. Disk surfaces can be *cleaned* with Freon (Miller-Stevens No. 280) and *lint-free* wiping pads.

(c) Floppy Disks. Floppy-disk systems are small magnetic-disk systems (usually of the moving-head type) employing removable flexible disks as storage media. Although they are slower and hold less information than regular disks, floppy-disk systems are very inexpensive and have much faster access times than tape systems (Table 5-1). Floppy disks are, then, a good choice as operating-system devices for small computer systems (Fig. 5-17). The main disadvantage is that most floppy-disk read/write heads are not air-supported and contact the magnetic oxide during reading and writing. A floppy disk must, then, be replaced after the equivalent of about 30 hours of continuous reading or writing. Some late-model floppy disks have air-supported heads. Post-1976 models have twice the storage capacity (400K 16-bit words) of earlier models.

(d) Magnetic-Tape Systems. Unlike disks and drums, magnetic-tape systems store several bits of a partial word (byte) *in parallel* across the tape. Parity can be checked across the tape (*transverse parity*) and for blocks of data along the tape (*longitudinal parity*). **Formatted tape** employs a **prerecorded timing track or tracks** to find blocks of data by reference to a directory table, just like a disk. **Unformatted tape** has no timing track, and the header word of a desired block must be found by scanning the tape. **Incremental-tape** systems start and stop the tape for individual words, but most magnetic-tape units stop only at *record gaps* between blocks of words. Start and stop times are between 1 and 20 msec. The better tape transports can read or write backward as well as forward. The beginning and end of each tape are usually marked by reflective markers sensed by tape-transport hardware.

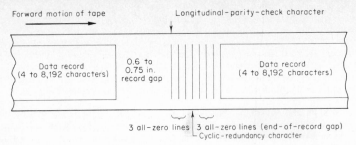

Fig. 5-9. Data arrangement on nine-track magtape. 8-bit bytes are recorded across the 9 tracks together with a ninth *transverse-parity-check bit*. There are either 800 or 1,600 bytes per inch of tape. Tape *records* correspond to memory buffers accommodating some convenient number of bytes (typically 18 to 2,048 bytes, some of which may be reserved to represent a file number). Each record is terminated with the *check-byte sequence* shown (omitted in some systems) followed by an interrecord gap at least 0.5 in long. A *file* (see also Sec. 5-13) appears as a group of records terminated by a 3-in gap followed by a *file mark* comprising an *end-of-file character* and a longitudinal-parity-check character. *Seven-track* magtape either requires 4 lines per 8-bit byte, or 6-bit bytes are used.

Blocks of data on tape can be of fixed or variable length. To **update** a block of data on tape will require *two* tape transports unless one is sure that the new data will fit the old block.

Tape-transport-controller logic "repacks" 8- to 18-bit computer words into 7-bit or 9-bit tape words, adding extra parity bits and check characters as needed (Fig. 5-9).

Data transfers to and from magnetic tape are usually direct-memory-access block transfers; so the controller has a *current-address counter* and a *word counter* (Sec. 4-18), which can be preset by processor instructions. Since tape keeps moving once a transfer is initiated and may transfer as many as 50,000 bytes/sec, the tape-transport controller employs double buffering (Fig. 4-4d) between tape and memory. Only one transport at a time transfers data, but others can wind or rewind at the same time.

The controller has a *control register* (Sec. 4-6) whose control bits are set by processor instructions which implement (and possibly combine) functions like:

Select one of 4 to 16 transports   Write (read) forward
Select binary or character format   Write (read) backward
Select tape speed   Rewind
Select record density   Backspace
Write end of file   Advance to end of file

The current-address counter and the status of the control register can also be *read* by processor instructions. In addition, tape-transport flag flip-flops can be sensed or cause interrupts to detect conditions such as:

Transport not ready (no power, no tape)   End (or beginning) of tape
Transport busy   Parity or check-sum error
Word-counter overflow

Industry-compatible 7- and 9-track unformatted-tape systems have the highest data-transfer rates and storage capacities (Table 5-1), but transports and controllers are relatively complicated and expensive. We would use them with minicomputers only if (1) *very large storage capacity is needed* and/or (2) *tapes must be transferred from or to a larger digital computer.*

(a)

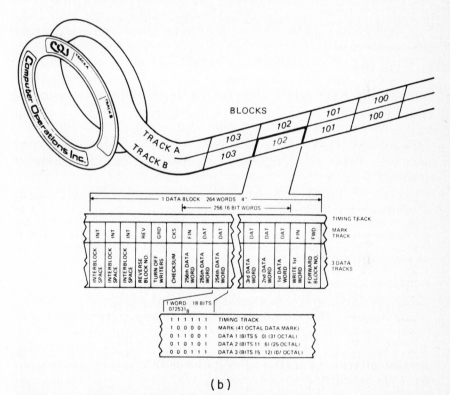

(b)

Fig. 5-10. A LINCtape II transport (*a*), and duplicate data/timing-track format (*b*). 4-in reels hold about 100,000 16-bit words on 150 feet of tape, or about 168,000 words on 260 feet. Prerecorded timing tracks address 256-word blocks of data. Transfer rate is 4,200 words/sec at 60 in/sec, with less than 70 sec total access time. A thin Mylar layer over the tape oxide protects both oxide and heads. Phase recording on nonadjacent duplicate tracks and capstan-less simplicity make such systems very reliable. A single transport and controller cost about $2,000. LINCtape options permit one to trade track duplication for double capacity, or to make the system completely compatible with the similar (but more expensive) Digital Equipment Corporation DECtape, which has timing and mark tracks on the outside. (*Computer Operations, Inc.*)

Phillips-type cassette tape, very convenient to mount and change, is used as a paper-tape replacement in many small computer systems (see also Sec. 5-28). Many different cassette systems exist. A few employ formatted tape, which does not require a capstan for speed control. In general, you should critically check any proposed cassette system for problems with tape wear due to capstan and/or tape-handling rollers. The **Minnesota Mining and Manufacturing Corporation (3M) type of tape-cartridge system,** only a little larger and more expensive than typical cassette systems, is faster and has more capacity. Cartridge systems obtain constant-speed drive through an endless belt which contacts the back (not the oxide) of the tape, so that there is no capstan-caused wear. The Hewlett-Packard Corporation markets a smaller version of the 3M tape-cartridge system, with about one-half the tape capacity. Low-cost cartridge drives are making cassette systems obsolete.

Small capstan-less formatted-tape systems like that shown in Fig. 5-10 employ duplicate tracks for redundancy checks, have very handy small reels, and are simple and reliable, an excellent choice for minicomputers (see also Table 5-1).

All small tape systems must compete against floppy disks which have faster access times but tend to wear faster than 3M cartridges and capstan-less tape. *Future minicomputer systems may well combine cartridge or capstan-less tape for mass storage with about 100K words of magnetic-bubble shift registers or even MOSFET RAM used as a "swapping memory" for program translation and data storage.*

ELEMENTS OF INPUT/OUTPUT SOFTWARE

5-10.   I/O-Software Requirements.   We have already exhibited some simple I/O routines in Chap. 4. Most applications involve *multiple* data transfers, say an array of 1,000 ADC readings or a 72-character teleprinter line taken from an array of two-character 16-bit words in memory. Memory storage areas thus intended for I/O are known as **buffers.** Since peripheral devices generally process data at rates different from that of the computer program, one often provides *two or more* buffers: ADC readings, for instance, may be recorded in one memory array while the program operates on earlier data in a second buffer (Fig. 4-13b and c).

In addition to *buffer management*, I/O routines require careful *interrupt-service programming* (processor-status saving/restoring, priority allocation, Secs. 4-8 to 4-13). DMA transfers are usually terminated and reinitiated by interrupts. Numerical-character I/O requires *formatting routines* relating numerical input or output data to binary fixed-point or floating-point number representations used in the computer. Character packing/unpacking (Sec. 3-11c) is in a similar category. Formatting and packing/ unpacking are not themselves I/O operations, but are often combined with I/O. Finally, input/output programs often include error routines which advise the programmer of incorrect I/O requests (e.g., calls to devices which do not exist or are assigned to other jobs), parity errors, etc.

It follows that I/O programming involves much tedious but important detail. To relieve applications-oriented computer users, computer manufactures furnish "canned" I/O and formatting routines for standard peripherals.

5-11. FORTRAN and Interpreter-Language Formatting and I/O. Many readers will be familiar with FORTRAN formatting and I/O statements like

$$12 \quad \textsf{FORMAT} \quad (\textsf{E 10.4})$$
$$\textsf{READ} \quad (2, 12) \quad \textsf{X}$$

where **E 10.4** calls for a floating-point conversion, **2** is the number of the peripheral device to be read, and **12** refers to the associated **FORMAT** statement. *Unformatted* **READ** or **WRITE** statements like

$$\textsf{WRITE (7) X, Y, Z}$$

call for input or output of the listed quantities in *binary* form (e.g., for ADCs and DACs).

Minicomputer FORTRAN compilers recognize such statements and automatically generate the appropriate formatting and I/O routines without further effort on the part of the programmer. **With programs written in assembly language, the easiest way to produce formatted numerical input/ output is still to link the assembly-language program to a short FORTRAN program for FORTRAN I/O** (Sec. 3-20). The time consumed by the (unseen, but quite formidable) FORTRAN-generated formatting and I/O routines will rarely bother you with slow keyboard/printer I/O, although you might notice the time lost with alphanumeric cathode-ray-tube displays supervising real-time computations.

Interpreter systems (e.g., BASIC and FOCAL, Sec. 5-25) include formatting and I/O commands used much like the corresponding FORTRAN statements, plus special commands for simple cathode-ray-tube and plotter graphics output. Several minicomputer manufacturers supply special versions of interpreter systems such as BASIC with greatly enhanced I/O capabilities for "conversational" programming of instruments, test systems, and process controllers (Sec. 5-25).

5-12. Device Drivers. At the assembly-language level, a complete I/O routine is known as a **device driver** or **device handler.** The most important drivers implement block transfers, and any one device driver can involve all or most of the I/O-related jobs listed in Sec. 5-10, including formatting.

The same peripheral device (a paper-tape punch, say) could have two, three, or more associated drivers for different jobs or formats (e.g., binary and ASCII output).

Most device drivers involve interrupt service and can, therefore, be separated into two sections. The **initiator** subroutine reserves buffer space in memory through pseudo instructions like

BUFFR   •BLOCK   SIZE / Saves SIZE locations
/   starting at BUFFR

initializes buffer pointers, and prepares a peripheral device by clearing flags, setting control registers, and checking status.

The **continuator** section of the device driver typically initiates data transfer (e.g., **START ADC CONVERSION** or **ENABLE DATA CHANNEL**) and returns to the main program to wait for an interrupt. The continuator section of the device driver also comprises the interrupt-service routine(s) needed for data transfer and/or its termination (as in DMA block transfers, Fig. 4-13*b, c*). Both initiator and continuator routines will, in general, have exits to the main computer program and to *error printout or display subroutines* (in case we have called for a nonexistent, illegal, or unready device; if there is no buffer space left; etc.).

Frequently needed device drivers (e.g., for reading and printing a line of text, reading and writing ASCII and binary tape records, etc.) are practically always furnished by the computer manufacturer as library routines. Complete device drivers for specific systems, including some DMA drivers, will be found in each minicomputer manual. They can often be used as models for new or modified drivers.

5-13. Files and Directories. Device drivers for paper-tape reader/punches, keyboards, and printers simply read or write the next available byte or block of bytes. Data on mass-storage devices (tape or disk) can be addressed by block numbers, but it is usually preferable to address specific sets of data or programs as **files** which are treated rather as if each file were a separate device. Each file on a specified device is identified by a **file name** (or number) with an **extension** which specifies the type and thus the data format of the file (e.g., source file, binary assembler output, load module, BCD data, etc.). A **user number** and **protection code** can be appended to the file name to permit reading and/or writing only to specified users. For example,

DISK 1:MYFIL • SRC (1812;11)

might specify a source program called **MYFIL** on disk 1, accessible for reading and writing only to user No. 1812.

Each file stored on a mass-storage device has a header specifying the file-name information. The file may be **contiguous** (stored "in one piece" along a tape or along a spiral disk-track sequence), or it may be a **random**

file stored in segments as blocks are available.[1]   Segments may contain pointer words giving the block addresses of adjacent file segments **(linked file),** or segment boundaries may be in a directory read into memory. Random files utilize storage space more efficiently, but contiguous files can *be accessed more quickly and require less complicated software.*   In either case, a special *storage-compacting program* can be used to recopy files so as to eliminate empty blocks between files.

Each disk or formatted tape (Sec. 5-9) has a **directory.**   This is a file, in a known location, which lists the names, starting addresses, and sizes of all files currently stored on the device.   There may also be **subdirectories** for different users, user groups, or file categories.   Unformatted tapes do not have directories; the device-driver routine searches the entire tape until it finds the file header.

Named files are created by *editor programs* (Sec. 5-4), as *translator output files* (Sec. 5-18), or by keyboard or programmed **file-manipulation commands.** These are furnished as part of an operating system (Sec. 5-16) or in special **file-manipulation programs** and call routines for

Assigning or changing a file name, extension, and/or user/protection code for a set of data
Deleting and/or concatenating files on a specified device (and in its directory, if any)
Moving files from one device to another
Printing or displaying directories

5-14.   I/O Macros, File I/O, and Device-Independent Input/Output Control Systems.   (a) I/O Macros.   Most minicomputers come with a package of I/O routines, including file-access routines, which can be called as subroutines or macros (Sec. 3-21) from assembly-language programs.   These I/O routines are usually furnished as part of the operating system (Sec. 5-16); their names and functions will differ from system to system.   We will discuss typical I/O routines called as **I/O macros** with appropriate arguments.

One may wish to conserve memory by loading only the I/O routines for a specific device from the system disk.   This is done by a macro call

FETCH (device, error return)

to a memory-resident I/O routine before any I/O is programmed.   The corresponding **RELEASE** (device) call permits the I/O routines for the specified device to be overwritten when they are no longer needed.

Typical disk or tape DMA interfaces transfer *blocks* (sometimes referred to as *physical records*) of, say, 256 bytes to and from buffer areas in

---

[1] For this purpose, disk directories have **bit maps,** i.e., words whose bits correspond to free and occupied disk blocks.   Device-driver routines can refer to a bit map and update it as needed.

memory. High-speed user programs can deal with data in such "physical I/O" buffers *directly* (see also Sec. 4-18), and appropriate I/O routines can transfer a specified block, or a number of blocks, to or from memory in response to the call

BLOCK READ/WRITE (device, starting block,
number of blocks, buffer address, buffer
size, error return)

With unformatted tape, there may also be a similar **WORD READ/WRITE** macro.

The argument **error return** in each I/O macro call represents the address of an **error routine** programmed to circumvent the problem and/or to notify the operator if the I/O operation (initialization, directory access, reading, writing) fails because a device is unavailable or has malfunctioned, or because a file is protected from access.

(b) File I/O. Before accessing a file on a specific device, we must *link the file to an I/O channel*, i.e., reserve a data buffer for the appropriate device-driver routines; the device-buffer combination will be identified by a **channel number** or **logical-device number.** Linking can be accomplished through a call

ASSIGN (device, file specification, channel number, error return)

which also creates a **file control table** in memory. The file control table stores device name, channel number, and buffer address/size for use by the device-driver routine and also has pointer locations for the disk or tape address of the file header and of the currently accessed block or word.

We must next **open the file**[1] through a call

OPEN (channel number, error return)

which initializes device functions (e.g., rewinds tape) and obtains the file starting address from the device directory (if any).

With this information in hand, we can read successive data blocks from the device into the buffer by calling

FILE BLOCK READ (channel number, error return)

This routine will update the disk or tape block address in our file control table as successive blocks are read. The macro **FILE BLOCK WRITE** calls the equivalent writing operation; there may also be **FILE WORD READ/WRITE** macros.

Users desiring programming convenience more than speed, however, deal with file data in "logical I/O" buffers sized to hold a **logical record** con-

---

[1] Some minicomputer systems combine the **ASSIGN** and **OPEN** macros.

venient for the user.   A typical logical record is a program or data line terminated by a carriage-return or null character, and fitting into a 72-byte or 132-byte **line buffer.**

The I/O routine called by

READ LOGICAL RECORD (channel number, user-buffer address, user-buffer size, error return)

employs a user-defined logical-record buffer in addition to the channel buffer.   Starting with the first call, the channel buffer is filled (usually by DMA operations) as needed; each call transfers one logical record to the user buffer.   The macro **WRITE LOGICAL RECORD** calls the analogous writing operation.

User programs must not operate on user buffers until a **READ** operation completes, or attempt to refill a buffer until a **WRITE** finishes.   Some manufacturers' I/O routines automatically stop program execution until a buffer is ready, but it is preferable to have a separate call

WAIT (channel number)

which can be programmed to precede only program sections which could actually bother the buffer data.

Another type of **WRITE** or **READ** routine specifies the location of a *completion routine*, which will be called (typically by a DMA end-of-block interrupt, Sec. 4-18) as soon as the I/O operation is complete.   In the meantime, control is returned to the user program.

When a program is finished with a file, the **file is closed** with a call

CLOSE (channel number)

to a routine which updates file header and device directory (if any) after **WRITE** operations and releases the file-control-table area and the channel buffer.

(c) Buffered I/O and Device-Independent Input/Output Control Systems. While the simplest I/O-request calls will simply return an error if a requested I/O device is busy with another request, **more elaborate minicomputer systems save (queue) a number of unfulfilled requests until they can be honored.** To save data as well as requests, the software provides *multiple* channel buffers for each device, so that a calling program can transfer data to or from a buffer while another buffer is filled or emptied by, say, a DMA transfer **(buffered I/O).**   A pool of buffers can serve different devices if their block sizes are integral multiples of some basic unit.   The I/O-request routines implement **buffer management.**

A well-designed system of I/O requests and device drivers **(input/output control system, IOCS)** is, moreover, **device-independent.**   As far as source programs are concerned, IOCS macros look the same for all physical-device/ file combinations, which are identified only by the channel numbers (logical-device numbers) assigned to them. *It is, therefore, possible to let a program transfer data to or from any appropriate device and/or file by simply changing channel-number assignments*, either by a programmed **ASSIGN** or by an operating-system keyboard command. To maintain device independence, we use **OPEN/CLOSE** calls even with nondirectory devices and, in fact, with non-file-oriented devices such as teleprinters; in the latter case, the device name replaces the device/file specification in the **ASSIGN** call. It is then possible to direct, say, a source file to a tape or disk for storage or to a printer for printout by simply changing channel numbers; in particular, *the better minicomputer systems permit one to link named files to logical-device numbers for FORTRAN I/O.*

NOTE: Elaborate packaged IOCS routines do exact a price in computing time. This is especially true of logical-record I/O routines, which must manage the loading/unloading of an extra buffer. Non-file-oriented block I/O operations are faster than file I/O, but **BLOCK WRITE** *must be used with great care: with faulty arguments, they can overwrite any area on a disk or tape, including protected files.* A faulty *file-oriented* writing operation can, at worst, destroy the currently accessed file, and suitably protected files cannot be written into at all. For the highest possible execution speed, users may still write simple I/O routines for their own programs.

I/O macros automatically insert the required external references (Sec. 3-19) to IOCS, which can be implemented as a library (Sec. 3-19) or as a single subroutine with different arguments for different I/O macros, to save external references. The more advanced minicomputer systems implement I/O macros with software interrupts (Sec. 4-13), which require no external references, automatically save the processor status, and facilitate interrupt-priority management.

DISK OPERATING SYSTEMS AND UTILITY PROGRAMS

5-15. Introduction. Interactive Keyboard Operation. A **disk operating system** is a package of service programs designed to simplify program preparation, translation, execution, storage, and retrieval. Above all, the operating system has a **keyboard-monitor program (keyboard executive)** which replaces the troublesome manual fetching and loading of paper-tape programs and data with convenient automatic operations (see also Sec. 5-6). Source and binary programs, data collections, and system programs (editor, compiler, etc.) all become named files (Sec. 5-13). These can be stored on a **system disk** and are loaded into the computer memory, as needed, in response to **keyboard commands from the system terminal** (teleprinter or CRT terminal). Other typed commands can produce input and output on other computer peripherals (Figs. 5-11a and 5-11b).

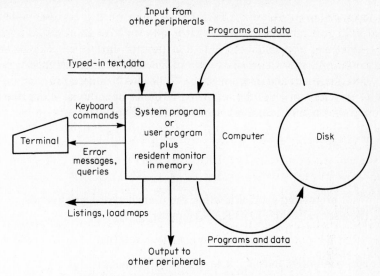

Fig. 5-11a. Computer with disk operating system.

The keyboard monitor includes keyboard-interpretation routines and some I/O routines, and is loaded from the disk with the help of a ROM bootstrap-loader program and control-panel switches (Sec. 5-3b). In multi-

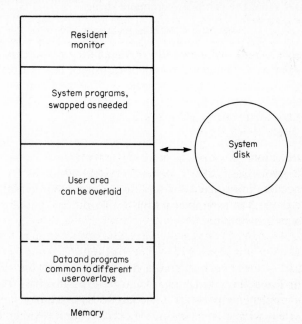

Fig. 5-11b. Memory allocation for a simple disk operating system.

user installations, a user may have to **log in** by typing his **user number,** which will give him access to his own files and to unprotected system files. One may also enter the **date** and **time of day,** which can be used for accounting and to label newly entered files for future reference.

To compile, load, and execute, say, a FORTRAN source program called **MYFILE** typically involves the following terminal operations, which replace the program-preparation sequence of Sec. 5-4 (Fig. 5-2).

1. When the executive is loaded, the computer prints

   EXEC READY
   $

   $ is a **prompting symbol** inviting the user to type a command.
2. The user **calls the FORTRAN compiler** by typing

   RUN FORTRAN (carriage return)

3. The computer finds the compiler on the system disk, loads it into memory, and types

   FORTRAN READY
   #

   # is another prompting symbol.
4. The user types the **compiler command string**

   MYFILE < MYFILE (carriage return)

5. The system **finds the source file MYFILE.SRC** on the disk and feeds it into memory. Now the compiler translates the source file into a binary object file, which is stored on the disk under the name **MYFILE.OBJ**; note the use of *file extensions* (Sec. 5-13) for labeling source and object files.

The compiler may make two or more passes, transferring intermediate results to and from the disk as needed; the user does not notice this directly. Error messages, if any, go to the system terminal. An *assembler* would be called and instructed to translate a source file in exactly the same way. If we desired an assembler output listing on, say, a line printer, the proper command string might be

   MYFILE, LP: < MYFILE (carriage return)

If **MYFILE.SRC** is to be fetched from a device other than the system disk, say tape unit 2, the file specification would be expanded into **TU2:MYFILE** (the extension **.SRC** is implied for any compiler or assembler input). In a multiuser system with user numbers, we can also access other users' files by specifying the user number, provided that his file is not read-protected

(Sec. 5-13).   To get a file from a non-file-oriented device, say a paper-tape reader, we replace the file specification by the device code, viz., **PR**:.

6. When compilation is finished, the compiler requests more input with its prompting symbol

$$\#$$

7. Assuming the user wants nothing else compiled, he **returns control to the executive** by typing a control key, typically

$$\text{control} - \text{C}$$

(in some systems, this must be followed by typing **KILL** to close any open files).

8. The executive acknowledges with its prompting symbol

$$\$$$

9. The user **calls the linking loader** by typing

RUN LOADER (carriage return)

10. The loader is loaded into memory and announces itself by printing,

LOADER READY
*

11. The user now types a **loader command string,**

MYFILE, FFT, SINTAB, FRTRNLIB (carriage return)

plus the **command string switch/GO** if he wants his programs to run as soon as it is loaded ("load-and-go").

The system fetches the object programs **MYFILE.OBJ** and **FFT.OBJ**, the data file **SINTAB.DAT**, *plus any FORTRAN library routines referenced by the programs* (Sec. 3-19).   All these items are linked and loaded into memory.   The loader program will be partially overlaid by the loaded program, and control returns to the executive.   The user programs runs at once if **/ GO** was typed; otherwise, it waits for the keyboard command **RUN**, which is also used for repeated runs.   The loader will print error messages (if any) on the terminal teleprinter if appropriate terms are added to the loader command string.

If the user wants to *save* his linked load module ready for reuse, he assigns a file name and a storage device by typing, say,

SAVE TU1:PROG (carriage return)

which will save the load module as **PROG.LDA** on tape unit 1.   The load module is retrieved, loaded, and run again if we type

RUN TU1:PROG (carriage return)

Many newer minicomputer systems replace the linking loader with a *load-module generator* (Sec. 3-17) which does not load the linked load module, but creates a load-module file (in our case **PROG.LDA**) on a specified storage device.   This file is then loaded and run with the **RUN** command.

The disk operating system is a convenient user/machine interface permitting computer operation from a terminal.   Additional keyboard commands can replace control-panel operations, in particular *loading and examining selected memory locations.   File-manipulation commands* (moving, renaming, deleting, directory output, etc., Sec. 5-13) are part of some keyboard monitors, but most systems save core by calling a special **file-manipulation program** for providing these services.

NOTE: Until you are familiar with the keyboard commands for the operating system, editor, language translator, and load-module generator, use three or four file cards listing the most important commands.

Rapid file access and program translation put a premium on fast disk-access time.   If you can afford it, combine a *fixed-head* system disk (for fast swapping) with moving-head disk and/or tape mass storage (Sec. 5-9b).   Cassette tape and formatted reel tape (Sec. 5-9d) have been used as cheap system-disk substitutes but are not recommended because of their long access times; modern low-cost systems employ floppy disks.

5-16.   Programmed Requests and Overlays.   Operating-system services are not just restricted to keyboard operations but can be called by **programmed requests** (macros or subroutines) *in user programs.*   The most frequent requests are for I/O *service and buffer management*, as described in Sec. 5-14; the input/output control system (IOCS) is usually an integral part of the operating system.   Some *file-manipulation requests* can also be programmed.

A second type of programmed request calls for **loading and/or running an object program.**   *It is, then, possible to execute large programs in a relatively small minicomputer memory by letting successive program segments call and overlay each other* (**chaining**).   The program segments can communicate through a "root" segment which is not overlaid and contains data, subroutines, and program flags (Sec. 3-11b) common to different overlays.   Facilities for creating and cross-referencing overlays must be included in the system's load-module generator.

The overlay facility also makes it possible for a user program to call system programs (e.g., a translator).   Jobs of this type are, however, managed more neatly with the aid of a suitable batch-control language (Sec. 5-17).

5-17.   Batch Operation and Batch-Control Language.   **Batch operation** of a computer system typically involves source-program entry on punched cards (which are prepared and edited off-line), although other media are

admissible.   Programs are then translated, linked, and run according to
some scheduling algorithm designed to optimize throughput or response
time.   There is usually an output file logging the time and facilities used
by different programs.

The larger minicomputers can do fairly respectable number crunching in
the batch mode.   Most minicomputer operating systems permit batch
operation with simple first-in–first-out scheduling.   This amounts simply to
a facility **(batch monitor)** for reading, and acting on, **control cards** sub-
stituting for keyboard-monitor commands, such as **GET THE COMPILER,**
COMPILE THE FOLLOWING CARDS (up to an **end-of-file card**), **LINK** (specified files), **RUN,** etc.   Control cards, program cards, and data cards
pertaining to a given **job** constitute a sort of superprogram executed by the
batch monitor, which calls other system programs and does everything
necessary to complete the job.

*An advanced type of batch monitor can be very useful even if you would
never dream of using your minicomputer as a batch facility with punched-card
input.*   A batch-control language permits composition of a **job file** consisting of *batch-control statements* with references to various user- and
system-program files from the terminal keyboard.   Such a job file can be
stored on a disk or tape and may be repeatedly executed.   *This is a real
help in program development,* where a source program may have to be edited,
translated, linked to a number of other programs, and executed hundreds
of times until all source statements are satisfactory.   *The entire keyboard
sequence of Sec. 5-15 can be replaced by the single command*

RUN MYJOB.JOB (carriage return)

where the file extension **.JOB** refers to a job file.

Advanced batch monitors (e.g., that of the Digital Equipment Corp. RT-11 operating
system) can do even better.   Their batch-control language admits ɪ𝐅 statements conditioning
batch execution on user-program results and keyboard commands.   This greatly simplifies
the creation of sophisticated interactive programs involving multiple languages, generation of
files and displays, with easy operator intervention.

**5-18.   Editing, Debugging, and Other Utility Programs.   (a) Corrections
and Editing.**   *Operating-system command lines* can be corrected with the
RUBOUT (DELETE) key, which echoes the deleted characters bracketed
with reverse slashes, e.g.,

THIMK\KM\NK

A control key can also delete the entire command line before the CAR-
RIAGE RETURN key causes the computer to read and execute the
command.

In principle, the same technique will also *edit a program or data line*
entered into a computer or punched on paper tape with an *ASR-type*

teleprinter, but only before the line is terminated with a carriage return (the computer program accepts a typed or punched line only after it senses a carriage return). *Conventional CRT terminals* permit editing operations (character and line insertion/deletion) on the text displayed on the CRT screen, but again only *before* this text is entered into a computer or recorded on a disk or tape. Note that punched-card systems permit *off-line* program preparation and editing.

Editing of files already entered into a computer, or on a disk or tape, requires the use of a computer loaded with an **editor program.** A minicomputer or microcomputer can thus edit its own programs, but any other computer can be used with a suitable editor program. *Text editing is a very important computer application in its own right.* Much future text editing will be done by microprocessors in CRT terminals designed specifically for editing and costing about $5,000, including a printer and a floppy disk or dual cassette or cartridge drives for storing input and edited files.

(b) Teleprinter and CRT Editors.   An **editor program,** loaded from paper tape (Sec. 5-4) or from mass storage, can be used to edit and combine newly typed text and/or unedited source files. The editor program moves such input text into a working area (**editor text buffer**) in the computer memory, where the text can be modified, and then to an **edited output file.**

The simplest type of text editor requires each text line to be labeled with a **line number,** say 10, 20, 30, . . . to leave space for insertions. The only editing commands needed are to *delete* and *insert* numbered lines, and to *print* specified sections of text. Such an easy-to-use text editor is furnished with the BASIC language system (Sec. 5-25).

More elaborate editors start in **command mode** (as opposed to **text-input mode**) and will then accept **keyboard commands,** typically

1. **Open a named source file** to be edited and **read it** (as far as it will go) **into the editor text buffer.**
2. **Open a named output file.**
3. **Move an editing pointer** indicating a line and character within the text buffer
    (*a*) to the **top** or **bottom** of the text buffer
    (*b*) **up or down n lines**
    (*c*) **up or down m characters**
    (*d*) **to the end of a specified text string**
4. **Print the line containing the editing pointer** (and possibly a specified number of preceding or following lines).
5. **Delete the line or character labeled by the pointer** (and possibly a specified number of preceding or following lines or characters).
6. **Save** a specified number of lines beginning at the pointer, and later **insert** the saved text ahead of the pointer.

7. **Enter text-input mode.** Typed input will now be **inserted** ahead of the pointer; **a control key will restore command mode.**

NOTE: If you forget to type this control key, subsequent keyboard commands will be inserted as text!

8. **Output** text buffer contents into the output file and load **the next input-file section** into the buffer.
9. **Output the text buffer and the remaining input file and close input and output files.**

These editing operations permit any desired text modification. Unfortunately, such **teleprinter editing** does not permit us to see the location of our editing pointer in the text buffer: **we must necessarily edit blindly.** To avoid editing the wrong line or character, we suggest the following useful precautions:

1. *Print the current line after every pointer move and editing operation* (some editor programs do this automatically).
2. Beginners might well *avoid all character-counting pointer moves and editing operations*, and *work only on entire lines*.

Good editor programs will have a command CHANGE *string* 1 TO *string* 2 (on the current line) which permits text corrections without any character counting.

When such a teleprinter-oriented editor program is used with a *CRT terminal*, editing becomes faster, and it may be possible to compose several lines of text on the CRT screen before inserting them. *But editing is still blind.* By contrast, **a true CRT-editor program displays a section of the text buffer on the CRT screen, and the editor pointer appears as a blinking cursor. Editing keys permit text insertion and deletion at the cursor position.** The text "scrolls" up or down as the cursor reaches the top or bottom of the screen. A control key still permits access to editor-command-mode operations, e.g., finding or replacing specified text strings, or moving different text sections to the screen. *CRT editing is surely the only right way to do extensive editing.*

(c) Debuggers and Other Utility Programs. An **on-line debugging program,** loaded together with a user load module, permits the user to run his program, stop it at predetermined **breakpoints,** and examine and modify register and memory contents. The debugger implements keyboard commands to

1. Insert or remove breakpoints (**HALT** instructions or software interrupts, Sec. 4-13) at specified memory locations.
2. Start or restart the program at a specified location, e.g., after a breakpoint.

3. Print or display the contents of specified registers and memory locations, including indirectly addressed locations. Addresses can be stepped up and down.
4. Modify the contents of registers and memory locations.
5. Output corrected program sections to a named file.

Octal-code program addresses are referenced relative to the load-module starting address with the aid of an assembly listing and the assembler and load module–generator symbol tables (Secs. 3-2 and 3-19). Debugging programs work with both FORTRAN and assembly language. They usually disable interrupts, so that interrupt-service routines must be tested separately.

Symbolic debuggers (e.g., PDP-8 and PDP-15 DDT) can read symbol-table files and will then *reference memory locations in terms of symbolic expressions*, which is very convenient. Reference has an example of an actual symbolic debugging session.

Other manufacturer-furnished utility programs include a **file-manipulation program** (Secs. 5-13 and 5-15), a **library-maintenance program** (Sec. 3-19), programs for quickly copying and checking tape and disk records, and **diagnostic programs** for checking computer hardware and peripherals.

(d) System Generation. A **system-generator program** tailors the operating system to a specific minicomputer configuration when the system is installed or modified. This program, supplied by the computer manufacturer or paper tape, on magnetic tape, or on a removable disk, loads the skeleton executive program and completes it through a conversational sequence in which the user is asked to type in his memory size, his system options, and a list of his peripheral devices.

REAL-TIME OPERATING SYSTEMS AND TIME SHARING

5-19. Real-Time Operating Systems: Definition and Requirements. Any sufficiently fast computer dedicated to a single task can handle **real-time operations,** i.e., operations which require appropriate responses to volatile instrument data or time-critical external events. A **real-time operating system** implies programming and management of **multiple tasks,** with at least one real-time task. A **real-time operating system must be designed so that it is impossible for any program, and for any user other than the system manager, to interfere with the execution of critical tasks by halting the machine, by changing interrupt priorities, or by inappropriately overwriting memory.** The operating system will keep and update tables representing the execution status of all tasks and the availability of peripheral devices, computer memory, I/O buffers, and shared program sections (if any). An executive program, with access to an appropriate I/O-routine package, can then

1. **Schedule different tasks** at preset times, or in response to external events and/or requests by other tasks. The most time-critical programs may be memory-resident, while others will be overlaid from mass storage.
2. Correctly **assign and change interrupt priorities** for different tasks.
3. Arbitrate and implement **requests from one task to start, suspend, or terminate another task.**
4. **Pass data from one task to another,** e.g., through a system COMMON area in memory.
5. **Manage nonconflicting memory assignments** for the different tasks.

NOTE: Subroutines which can be interrupted and reentered by another task (e.g., I/O routines, FORTRAN library routines) must be *reentrant* (Sec. 3-16).

5-20. Scheduling Multiple Tasks. As an example of a multiple-task job, consider computer supervision of a laboratory or process plant. Real-time "foreground" tasks, in the order of decreasing priority, might include

1. Instrument reading, some data processing, and file output in response to random interrupts from a detector (pulse detector, counter overflow)
2. Periodic direct digital control of a process temperature
3. Periodic instrument reading and file output (data logging)
4. Operator requests for current-data output (management-information output)

In addition, the job might involve non-time-critical **background tasks,** viz., batch or interactive editing and compilation of programs, plus preparation of reports about the logged data when there is nothing else to do.

In principle, such a job could be programmed as a single program with interrupt-service routines at appropriate priority levels, and programmed requests for I/O service (Sec. 5-14) and disk swapping (Sec. 5-15) of different program segments. The time-critical asynchronous task 1 above might be made memory-resident, while periodic tasks are swapped into memory when or just before they are needed. *Real-time operating systems simplify programming and reprogramming of such multitask jobs.* Packaged software now will not only do routine I/O; essentially all detector, timer, and terminal interrupts trap to a **scheduler** program which also responds to programmed requests (macros, FORTRAN calls) to run, suspend, or delay different tasks (Fig. 5-12).

A **task** is a named user program (usually involving a main program and interrupt service), typically placed into mass storage as a load module or a set of overlays with an absolute starting address.[1] Each task is assigned a

---

[1] At least one minicomputer operating system allocates starting addresses "dynamically" as memory is available. This saves memory (which is cheap) at the expense of software overhead and time, which is usually at a premium.

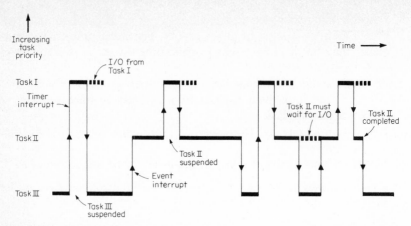

Fig. 5-12. Real-time scheduling of three tasks. Task I is a periodic high-priority data-acquisition task. Task II is an event-actuated computation, e.g., due to an operator keyboard request. Task III is a low-priority task to proceed concurrently with I/O data transfers required by a higher-priority task.

task priority (this is *not* an interrupt priority, although it may affect the latter).

Tasks are introduced into the operating-system scheduler program through the keyboard command or programmed request (in another task),

    CREATE (task identification, priority, memory starting address)

For each task, the memory-resident scheduler maintains a **task control table** containing the above parameters and the current **task status (dormant, ready or executing, or suspended),** plus locations for saving the program counter and other processor registers while a task is suspended (this is *not* the same as interrupt status saving).

The scheduler keeps a list **(queue)** of all tasks with status and priorities and scans this queue whenever a "critical event" (detector, timer, or terminal interrupt; I/O or task completion) occurs. *A typical scheduler algorithm will then run the highest-priority ready task* (some relative order must be defined for tasks having equal priorities). Exceptions will be allowed for "completion routines" of certain tasks, which must be allowed to finish in order to avoid data losses or equipment problems (typically I/O completion routines, Sec. 5-14*b*).

The actual schedule is not simply determined by preset priorities and external interrupts, but is tailored by calls to **scheduling macros or subroutines** programmed within the different tasks themselves. Typical calls are

    READY
    READY PERIODICALLY (starting time, period, number of times)

SUSPEND

RESUME

DELAY (time interval)

OVERLAY (number in current task)

KILL

SET TASK PRIORITY (new priority)

Each such request can specify a task as an argument; READY, SUSPEND, RESUME, and KILL may apply to all tasks of a specified priority. SUSPEND and DELAY may apply to the calling task, which thus gives control to the scheduler.

> Disk-overlay strategies for efficient multitask operation are complicated by the fact that I/O routines may have to complete, and buffers may have to be preserved, while a task is suspended (Ref. 8).
>
> NOTE: Users must take care not to make high-priority tasks unnecessarily long, to lower the priority of less critical subtasks, or to include DELAY requests to give lower-priority tasks a chance. Reference 8 discusses various scheduling algorithms.

5-21. Intertask Communication. Different tasks can pass data to one another through file access and through COMMON areas in memory. Special operating-system calls may also pass one-word messages to another task through a specified memory location, e.g.,

TRANSMIT (word, address)   RECEIVE (address)

5-22. Multiuser Systems and Memory Management. Even simple real-time operating systems admit non-time-critical **background operations** by one user while another user's higher-priority tasks operate **in the foreground.** Typically, only the background user accesses the editor, language translators, and load-module generator for problem preparation.

With multiple users programming their tasks independently, memory protection is necessary. While system software controlling assembly, load-module generation, and block-transfer operations (Sec. 5-14) can prevent the worst, a user program can still write outside of its assigned area unless all write accesses to memory are checked in the program itself. This is not acceptable in critical systems. **Most minicomputer multiuser systems employ a memory-mapping system** (Sec. 2-30) **to map each user's programs into a separate memory partition fixed through preassignment of mapping-register contents by the operating system.** Each user can run and overlay multitask jobs within his own partition. The multiuser operating system provides resources (CPU and I/O channels) on the basis of priorities assigned to all user tasks or, for less time-critical jobs, on a time-slice basis. Different users can access a common data base, and even communicate with other users, as in any multitask system (Sec. 5-21).

A multiuser real-time operating system can be used for **general-purpose interactive time sharing** if the editor, language translators, and load-module generator are accessible to all user terminals.   Many minicomputer time-sharing systems do *not* have this **multilanguage time-sharing capability**, but can only load a BASIC interpreter into each user partition.

More advanced multiuser systems can allocate user partitions dynamically (demand paging, virtual memory, see also Sec. 1-19).   Really efficient systems of this type may require special hardware (Refs. 8, 9).

5-23.   Software Overhead, Context Switching, and Multiprocessor Systems. System programs (Refs. 6 to 8) satisfying the complex requirements of real-time, multitask operation, not to speak of multiuser operation, will exact very substantial overhead costs in computing time and memory.   In particular, most interrupts will trap to time-consuming operating-system arbitration routines before a task's own service routine is entered.   As a result, true interrupt-service delays may be measured in milliseconds rather than microseconds.   Periodically scheduled tasks can force the scheduler to scan its entire ready-task queue on each clock tick.   Since disk swapping is time-consuming, large multiuser systems keep many system routines (e.g., I/O routines) memory-resident and may require as many as 50K bytes just for the system software and buffers.   *It is difficult or impossible to judge the performance of a real-time operating system from the manufacturer's literature;* it is best to inquire among other users.

Modern hardware helps.   Minicomputers with context-switching registers (Sec. 4-9) reserve one set of processor and memory-mapping registers for fast operating-system interrupt service.   The processor may be designed so that "privileged" instructions, such as **HALT** or interrupt-priority allocation, are possible only in this "supervisor state" of the machine (e.g., DEC PDP-11/45).   If there are more than two sets of registers, they can speed up other important service routines.

Large real-time systems using cumbersome software to support multiple memory partitions, multiple context register sets, and a single CPU are badly out of balance as processor costs keep decreasing.   *Without question, future real-time systems will employ multiple processors*, communicating through multiport memories, for different groups of tasks, and especially for system and I/O operations.   This is one of the "natural" application areas for multi-microprocessor systems.   But general-purpose software for such systems still remains to be written.

HIGHER-ORDER LANGUAGES FOR MINI/MICROCOMPUTERS

5-24.   Minicomputer FORTRAN systems.   Real-Time Operations.   Most engineers and scientists are familiar with FORTRAN.   Minicomputer FORTRAN compilers often minimize memory requirements at the expense of execution speed and may implement only a subset of FORTRAN IV. On the other hand, some minicomputers (e.g., DEC PDP-11) provide very elaborate FORTRAN through multiple compiler overlays (and increased compilation time). Consult your minicomputer manual and check the FORTRAN features provided against the check list of Table A-1 (Appendix).

Some minicomputers have optional multipass compilers designed to improve execution speed at the cost of extra compilation time (e.g., Data General FORTRAN V). Some FORTRAN operations can be speeded up by special microprograms (Sec. 2-33).

Good minicomputer FORTRAN systems have special features designed for real-time operations. Library subroutines are **reentrant,** so that they can be reentered by successive interrupt routines (Secs. 3-16 and 4-15), and compilers and other system programs are written so they can be easily relocated in different user partitions (Sec. 5-22). Augmented FORTRAN libraries contain calls requesting *special I/O and task-scheduling operations* (Sec. 5-20). A set of these calls has been standardized by the Instrument Society of America (ISA). **ISA FORTRAN** also has calls for bit-by-bit *logical operations* (**AND, OR, XOR, COMPLEMENT, BIT SET, BIT CLEAR, BIT TEST**) and *bit-shifting operations* just like the corresponding assembly-language operations (Secs. 2-6 and 2-9).

5-25. Conversational Computing and Real-Time Operations with Interpreter Languages. Extended BASIC. Conversational interpreter systems (Sec. 5-4) are especially useful for microcomputers, small minicomputers, and simple time-sharing systems: *there is no need to load a translator and load-module generator* once the interpreter is in memory. Simple interpreters can be supplied on ROM chips for microcomputers (Sec. 6-3). The program itself will be typed in from a terminal, with program and data storage on a disk, tape, or paper tape.

The most popular interpreter language is **BASIC,** followed by the Digital Equipment Corporation's rather similar **FOCAL** (all DEC machines come with BASIC interpreters as well). BASIC and FOCAL are easy to learn and supply their own conversational operating system, including a simple *numbered-line editor* (Sec. 5-18a) and commands to read, run, and store numbered-line programs. BASIC statements *without* line numbers, say

$$\text{LET A} = 1.573 - \text{SIN } (0.35)$$
$$\text{PRINT B} = \text{A} - 0.333$$

are executed *immediately*, as on a sophisticated calculator.

NOTE: The two-word floating-point format used with many 16-bit minicomputer BASIC systems yields only 6 to 7 decimal digits resolution (Fig. 1-7), which produces less accuracy than a pocket calculator. A good BASIC system ought to provide for double-precision arithmetic, or use at least a three-word floating-point format.

Program	Comment
100 CALL (8, 1, 0, 1)	Sets power supply 1 to zero
110 CALL (8, 2, 0, 1)	Sets power supply 2 to zero
120 PRINT "PLUG IN AMPLIFIER"	Instructs operator
125 PRINT "SERIAL NUMBER IS"	Asks operator for information
130 INPUT S	Operator types in serial number
140 CALL (6, 4, 3, 0, 0)	Connects supply #1 to output 4, supply #2 to output 3
150 CALL (8, 1, −12, 100)	Sets supply #1 to −12, 100 mA max
160 CALL (8, 2, 12, 100)	Sets supply #2 to +12, 100 mA max
170 FOR F = 1000 TO 5000 STEP 1000	Establishes loop for changing frequency
180 CALL (5, F, .10)	Sets oscillator to 1,000 (then 2,000, 3,000, 4,000, 5,000) Hz, 0.1 V
190 CALL (7, 7, 0, 0, 0)	Connects oscillator to output 7
200 CALL (9, 5)	Connects oscillator output to DVM
210 WAIT (30)	Delays 30 msec to allow settling
220 CALL (10, 2, .1, 1)	Measures input ac voltage on 0.1 range
230 CALL (9, 23)	Connects amplifier output to DVM
240 WAIT (30)	Delays 30 msec to allow settling
250 CALL (10, 2, 10, V)	Measures amplifier output
260 LET G = V/I	Calculates gain
270 IF G < 5 THEN 320	Checks for low gain
280 IF G > 10 THEN 340	Checks for high gain
290 NEXT F	Return to 170 for next frequency
300 PRINT "AMPLIFIER SERIAL" S "GAIN OK, GAIN =" G "AT 5000 HZ"	
310 GO TO 290	
320 PRINT "AMPL SERIAL" S "GAIN LOW, GAIN =" G "AT" F "HZ"	
330 GO TO 290	
340 PRINT "AMPL SERIAL" S "GAIN HIGH, GAIN =" G "AT" F "HZ"	
350 GO TO 290	
360 END	

Fig. 5-13. Program for testing an audio amplifier, written in Hewlett-Packard extended BASIC. The test itself is automatic, but the computer types requests to plug in the amplifier and to enter its serial number. (*R. H. Grimm, Hewlett-Packard J., August 1969.*)

Table A-2 (Appendix) lists the statements available with an advanced BASIC system (Hewlett-Packard BASIC), which permits *matrix operations* and includes *character-string manipulation, file operations,* and *chaining (overlays) of large programs.* Above all, such advanced or **extended BASIC systems** permit calls to efficient subroutines written in assembly language, so that *completely general I/O operations are possible.* Some of the most useful minicomputer applications employ BASIC (and also FOCAL) interpreters extended to incorporate I/O commands which operate graphic displays, measuring instruments, test-signal sources, and process-control equipment.

Figure 5-13 shows an example of such a program; the statement

220   CALL (10, 2, 0.1, 1)

uses a digital voltmeter (Instrument 10) to make an a-c measurement (Mode 2) on the 0.1-V range and to label the result as 1.   The statement

WAIT (30)

delays the program for 30 msec to allow an instrument to settle.   Such programs permit *branching* to additional statements, such as

IF G LESS THAN 5 THEN 320

Such programs are widely used for automated testing operations.   Timed measurements can be performed through **IF** statements tied to real-time-clock operation.

Other higher-order languages implemented on minicomputers are **APL** and **FORTH,** both of which require Polish-reverse-order entry of numerical expressions.   FORTH, less well known than APL, permits ready addition of user I/O routines and has been widely used for astronomical instrumentation (Ref. 28).   FORTH has also been used by FORTH, Inc. (Manhattan Beach, Calif.) to implement *microcomputer* programs.

A subset of BASIC called **LLL** (Lawrence Livermore Language) is used at the Lawrence Livermore Laboratory for interactive generation of microcomputer programs.

5-26. PL-1 Subsets for Microcomputer Programming.   To simplify microcomputer system development for nonprogrammers, several chip manufacturers provide subsets of the PL-1 programming language.   Microcomputer source programs written in such a higher-order language must be *cross-compiled* on a larger computer which produces the microcomputer object program, usually on paper tape (Sec. 5-29).   Cross compilers for PL-1 subsets are available for several microcomputers (Intel's **PL/M** is the best known such language), and also for the Microdata 3200S minicomputer, which is specially microprogrammed for more efficient execution of the PL-1 derivative MPL.

PL/M language features are summarized in Appendix A.   Compared with FORTRAN (the best-known compiler language) PL-1 has more convenient control statements (e.g., **DO . . . WHILE, IF . . . ELSE,** Appendix A), and microcomputer PL-1 subsets have been chosen to facilitate hardware-related operations (logic operations on bits, shifting, reserving memory). On the other hand, typical PL-1 subsets admit only single- and double-precision *integers* (8-bit **BYTE** and 16-bit **ADDRESS**) in expressions like $A = B^*(C - D)$, so that we cannot use floating-point expressions as in FORTRAN.   But PL-1 subsets permit definition and calling of *macros written in the PL-1 type language* (similar to the *assembly-language* macros introduced in Sec. 3-21) and also admit assembly-language subroutines, so that it is possible to define floating-point and BCD operations more easily.

5-27. Higher-Order Languages vs. Assembly Language. As noted in Chap. 3, assembly-language programs, which correspond more or less directly to hardware operations, use time and memory more efficiently than higher-order languages (microprogramming special instructions can be even more efficient, Sec. 2-33). This efficiency advantage becomes decisive where

a minicomputer program will be executed many times, or

a microcomputer system will be produced in large numbers, so that hardware cost is critical (see also Sec. 6-1).

On the other hand, *higher-order languages simplify and shorten program development, checkout, and modification. Higher-order languages also permit applications-oriented nonprogrammers to use minicomputers and to develop microcomputer systems.* These advantages often outweigh execution efficiency, or pay for the extra cost of faster hardware and/or more memory.

Unfortunately, the comparative efficiencies of FORTRAN or PL-1-subset programs and assembly-language programs are so problem-dependent that few quantitative comparisons exist. Factors usually mentioned range between 2 and 5. Similarly, the relative efficiencies of different FORTRAN compilers are usually biased by the demonstration problems chosen by different manufacturers. Few independent benchmarks have been run, and their results are valid only for specific problems. A few minicomputers have optional code-optimizing multipass FORTRAN compilers (Secs. 6-23 and 6-28). **There is an industry-wide, crying need for better, code-optimizing microcomputer PL-1 subset compilers.**

Note carefully that both FORTRAN and PL-1 subset execution is often speeded up dramatically if critical subroutines are written in assembly language (Sec. 3-20). Finally, the block-diagram languages described in Secs. 3-22 and 3-26 provide an excellent compromise between programming simplicity and execution speed (Ref. 27).

Minicomputer fixed-point assembly-language programs will, of course, execute much more rapidly than *floating-point* FORTRAN programs. The differential-equation benchmark described in Ref. 18 indicates a speed advantage between 10 and 50; fixed-point minicomputer operation was, in fact, faster than FORTRAN execution on a CDC-6400!

MICROCOMPUTER PROGRAM PREPARATION AND SYSTEM DEVELOPMENT

5-28. Problem Statement. Simple Prototyping Systems and Microcomputer Kits. Most microcomputers serve as dedicated subsystems. Once a suitable microprocessor has been selected, **system development will require closely related program preparation and interface design, including**

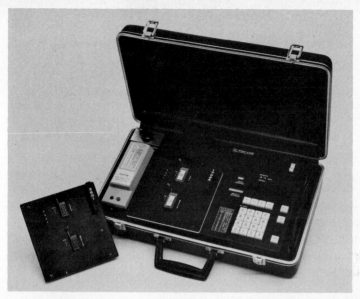

Fig. 5-14. This PROM loader lets users duplicate, program, and list PROMs under control of a hexadecimal keyboard, keyboard terminal, paper-tape reader, or computer. Different plug-in "personality cards" permit programming of different types of MOS and bipolar PROMs (fusible-metal links, polycrystalline-silicon links, avalanche-shorted junctions, EPROMs) with precise control of timing and current. The ultraviolet light on the left is for erasing EPROMs; they may be reused about 40 times. (*Pro-log Corporation.*)

repeated checkout and test cycles.   Since the per-unit cost of a micro-computer is low, the development budget will be an important system-design parameter (Sec. 6-2).

A surprising number of microcomputer systems need only of the order of 100 instructions and are simply **hand-programmed in hexadecimal machine language.**   A breadboard system is built, **with plug-in erasable PROMS (EPROMs, Sec. 1-23) for the program memory.**   Microcomputer programs can now be loaded with a keyboard-operated **PROM loader** (Fig. 5-14), erased with ultraviolet light, and modified as needed.   In such a simple environment, program and interface development may proceed concurrently.

Practical microcomputer checkout and troubleshooting requires simultaneous display of multiple data, address, and control signals.   This has led to the development of **special test instruments:**

1. **Multichannel logic probes,** which clamp onto dual-in-time (DIP) integrated-circuit packages for in-circuit testing of logic levels.   The clamp-on probe may incorporate light-emitting-diode readouts for

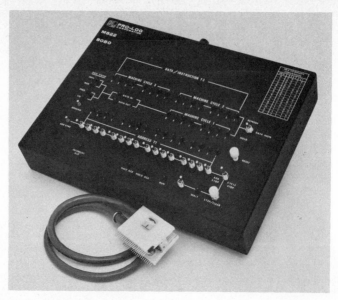

Fig. 5-15. This portable system analyzer clips to the microprocessor dual-in-line package for system development, testing, and troubleshooting.   The analyzer provides computer front-panel functions, permits program stepping, and displays address, data, and status bits for three sequential cycles of an Intel 8080A microprocessor.   (*Pro-log Corporation.*)

cycle-by-cycle logic checks, or it may connect to a **system analyzer** which permits address selection, program stepping, and readout much like a minicomputer control panel (Fig. 5-15).

2. **8- to 16-channel oscilloscopes for simultaneous display of bus signals.** The oscilloscope may be triggered by a clock signal, by an interrupt signal starting a desired instruction sequence, or by a recognition gate (Sec. 1-22) triggered when a specified address or data word appears on a bus.   Nonrepetitive logic-level sequences can be captured with a storage oscilloscope or, preferably, by a fast recirculating shift-register memory, which can record events *before*, as well as after, a trigger pulse (**dynamic logic analyzer,** Fig. 5-16).

A more grown-up prototyping system employs permanently card-mounted processor, memory, and I/O chips of the type proposed for the final project in a separate complete microcomputer.   Such a prototyping system accepts enough RAM and ROM cards for system programs and test routines and can be used for many different projects.   *The prototyping system connects to each project chassis through an I/O cable plugged into a circuit-card socket or DIP socket to substitute the prototyping computer for a dedicated microprocessor* (Fig. 5-17).

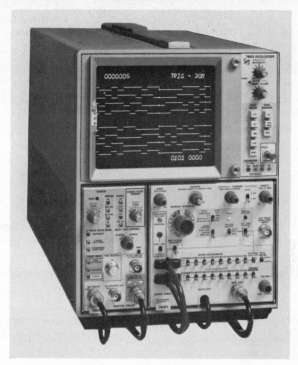

Fig. 5-16. A dynamic logic analyzer captures and displays logic-level sequences on multiple microcomputer bus lines. (*Tektronix, Inc.*)

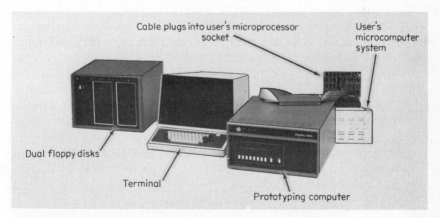

Fig. 5-17. Intel MDS microcomputer prototyping system. An Intel 8080A microcomputer system with random-access program and data memories and a floppy-disk operating system is substituted for the user's microprocessor through a plug-in cable. Either user or MDS memories can be used for tests. (*Intel Corporation.*)

A prototyping computer needs the equivalent of the minicomputer control-panel operations (Secs. 5-1 and 5-2) for reading and loading registers and memory locations, for stepping memory addresses, and for starting and stepping program execution.   *Since microprocessor registers are not directly accessible, all this is done with interrupt-service routines responding to switch closures or keyboard commands.*   These programs are supplied as a ROM-stored **debug package** or "resident monitor," which can usually also interface a keyboard terminal and paper-tape or cassette-tape equipment.   Some microcomputer prototyping systems still affect minicomputer-type control panels with switch and light registers, but it is usually better to control the system from a keyboard terminal.

The simple prototyping microcomputer is often furnished with a rudimentary *line-editing program* (Sec. 5-18*b*) and a primitive *assembler*, thus permitting program preparation and modification in the manner of the paper-tape systems described in Secs. 5-3 to 5-5.   Just as in the case of minicomputers, this is really suitable only for occasional problem modifications.   The system is too slow for extensive program preparation, which will require either *cross translation* (Sec. 5-29) or a prototyping computer with a disk operating system (Sec. 5-30).

Simple prototyping computers are, then, most useful if a user program is already available in object form on a plug-in ROM or on paper tape.   We may then test interface operations and use a ROM-stored **trace program** to step the prototyping microcomputer through the user program, printing the contents of processor registers, selected memory locations, and/or I/O registers at each step.   Such a printout looks just like the emulator printout in Fig. 5-18 and can produce useful insight into system operation.   The prototyping computer may also have a **ROM-programmer card** which can transfer and "burn" a program into PROMs after it has been checked out in the prototyping computer's RAM.   This eliminates the need for a separate ROM loader.

Prototyping systems sold by semiconductor manufacturers for their own chip sets are produced in relatively small quantities.   *You may be able to obtain an equivalent prototyping system more cheaply by buying a mass-produced end-user microcomputer using the same chip set*—if such a microcomputer exists.   In particular, several manufacturers sell useful and inexpensive **microcomputer kits,** including checkout ROMS and software, for the popular Intel 8080A, Motorola 6800, and MOS Technology 650X chips (Fig. 1-16).

NOTE: As a cheaper paper-tape substitute, the audio output of a 110- to 1,000-bps LSI modem can be recorded and reproduced by an *audio cassette recorder* if the UART transmitter timing signals (Sec. 4-26) are also recorded and reproduced to time the receiver (Ref. 21).

```
IMPSSIM                                                          Call the simulator and cause it to run.

MOTOROLA SPD, INC. OWNS AND IS RESPONSIBLE FOR MPSSIM            Enter the MF (machine file) filename of the
   COPYRIGHT 1973 & 1974 BY MOTOROLA INC                        machine file to be simulated

   MOTOROLA MPU SIMULATOR, RELEASE 1.3B                         The contents of the Label Buffer Area from
                                                                the machine file MEMFI.
   ENTER MF FILENAME
                                                                Register heading.
?MEMFI                                                            HH  Input and output base hexadecimal
FILE'S LABEL.                                                     IA  Instruction address
SOURCE FILENAME, PGM                                              OC  Operator mnemonic code
AUTHOR: JOHN DOE                                                  EA  Effective operand address
HH IA   OC  EA  P   X   A   B   C   S   T                         P   Program counter
*000  *0000*0000*0000*00 00 00 0000*0000 0000000                 X   Index register
                                                                 A   Accumulator A
                                                                 B   Accumulator B
                                                                 C   Condition code register
                                                                 S   Stack pointer
                                                                 T   Time cycles (always decimal)

?SM 0A,54.SR P 100.T 0C                                          Simulator commands separated by period
*0100 LDS  *0102*0103 0000 00 00 000000*0132 0000003              SM 0A 54   Set memory location A to
*0103 LDX  *0137*0105*0138 00 00 000000 0132 0000008                        contain 54
*0105 LDA B*0107*0108 0138 00*03 000000 0132 0000010
*0108 LDA A*010A*010B 0138*54 03 000000 0132 0000013              SR P 100   Set register (Program Count-
*010B CMP A*010C*010D 0138 54 03 000200 0132 0000018                        er) equal 100
*010D BEQ  *010D*0113 0138 54 03 000200 0132 0000022
*0113 JSR  *0137*0119 0138 54 03 000200 0130 0000031              T 0C       Trace C instructions
*0119 TAB  *0119*011A 0138 54*54 000000 0130 0000033
*011A ORA A*0133*011D 0138*D4 54 00N000 0130 0000037
HH IA   OC  EA  P   X   A   B   C   S   T                        Simulator command Display Memory, begin-
*011D RTS  *0132*0116 0138 D4 54 00N000*0132 0000042             ning with location 100, display 3B (hex)
*0116 JMP  *0118*0100 0138 D4 54 00N000 0132 0000045             bytes (note the right margin contains the
*0100 LDS  *0102*0103 0138 D4 54 00N000 0132 0000048             literal equivalent of the printable characters,
                                                                the periods show nonprintable characters).
?DM 100,3B
0100 8E 01 32 FE 01 36 C6 03 96 0A A1 02 27 05 09 5A  .2.6......,'.Z
0110 26 F6 3E 8D 01 19 7E 01 00 16 BA 01 33 39 00 00  &.>...~.....39..
0120 00 00 00 00 00 00 00 00 00 00 00 00 00 00 00 00  ................
0130 00 01 16 B0 10 04 01 38 53 45 54           ........8SET

?RS.D                                                           Simulator commands  RS restore registers,
*0000 *** *0000*0000*0000*00*00 00 000000*0000 0000000          D display registers

?EX                                                             Simulator command EX exit simulator

*** RUN COST    XXX  I/O    YYY TOTAL COST    ZZZ ***           NOTE  Hexadecimal input to the simulator
                                                                requires the first character be numeric (i.e.,
*STOP* 0                                                        to enter the hex value "C" enter "0C")
```

Fig. 5-18. A microprocessor-emulator program causes a host computer to emulate microprocessor operation. Microprocessor-register contents produced by successive instructions are printed to trace the program execution. (Motorola, Inc.)

5-29. Program Preparation with Cross Translators and Emulators. Extensive program preparation on microcomputers (or minicomputers) without disk operating systems is not practical. *One may, however, transfer the entire editing/translation process to larger general-purpose computers with good editing, file-manipulation, and program-listing facilities by using* **cross translation.** **Cross assemblers** and **cross compilers** are translator programs which run on a **host computer** to produce object programs for a **target machine** (microcomputer or minicomputer), usually on paper tape. Microcomputer cross translators, available from semiconductor manufacturers, are usually written in FORTRAN, so that they will run on a wide variety of host computers, typically time-sharing systems or larger minicomputers. Cross assemblers are also easy to write in BASIC (Ref. 26). **Existing macroassemblers** (Sec. 3-21) **will readily translate assembly language for other machines** if word or byte sizes can be matched. Each assembly-language statement will be translated into binary code by a suitably defined macro; the host-computer operation-code symbol table is not used. Cross assemblers permit the use of elaborate and convenient assembly languages. Microcomputer cross compilers usually translate a PL-1 subset (Sec. 5-26); some microcomputer systems also provide FORTRAN.

For target-machine-program checking and debugging, the host computer can run an **emulator program** which interprets the cross-translated microcomputer code to *simulate microcomputer operation.* Host-computer memory locations represent target-machine registers, buses, device registers, and memory. The cross-translator output file (binary microcomputer program) is scanned and generates successive operations which simulate execution of successive microcomputer instructions. Contents of the simulated target-machine registers and other locations can be output (**program trace file,** Fig. 5-18), and program breakpoints may be inserted for debugging (Sec. 5-18c).

5-30. More Elaborate Prototype-Development Systems. Cross translation/emulation permits program preparation with a convenient operating system, *but tends to separate hardware and software development* (Fig. 5-19). Each program correction (perhaps needed because of a hardware modification) requires us to return to the host computer and to prepare a new paper tape for the prototyping system. This is inconvenient if the host-computer terminal is not close by the prototype microcomputer system.

A good alternative is to provide the prototyping microcomputer with more memory, peripherals, and software. The most important addition is a *disk operating system* to replace paper-tape operation (see also Sec. 5-15), followed by more elaborate editing and translator programs (Refs. 12 to 14). Most manufacturers use floppy disks to keep the cost down. As a further improvement, *system programs can run on a separate processor*

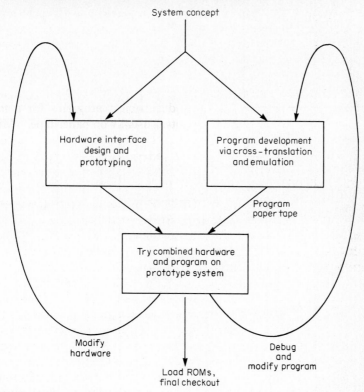

Fig. 5-19. Microcomputer system development using cross translation and emulation separates hardware and software development.

which shares a two-port memory with the microcomputer (as in Fig. 5-20) (Refs. 11, 27). Thus, system programs can still directly load memory locations reserved for the microprocessor, but test-system I/O will not interfere with the execution of real-time microcomputer programs (see also Secs. 5-23 and 6-3). Such a prototyping system can, moreover, work with different types of microprocessors, so that the investment is not lost as new LSI chips are introduced. The Intel MDS (Ref. 11), which pioneered these techniques, is an advanced prototyping system using the Intel 8080 microprocessor as the operating-system processor.

NOTE: Cross translation, and possibly emulation, on a time-shared computer may still be needed if microcomputer program development requires more than, say, two persons.

Software costs and a relatively limited market make specially developed advanced prototyping systems as expensive as respectable end-user minicomputers. **It makes good sense, then, to design an advanced prototyping system around a mass-produced minicomputer whose operating system and**

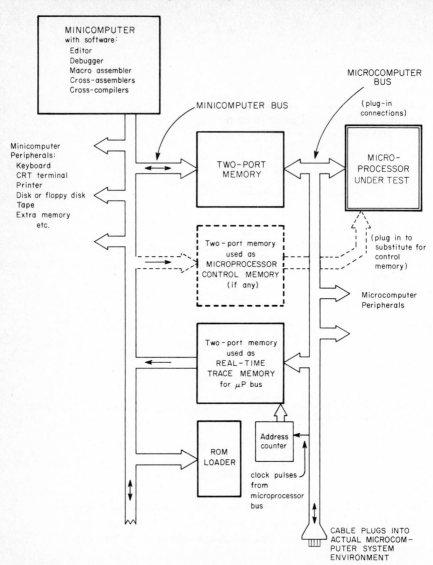

Fig. 5-20. Advanced microcomputer-system-development facility using a minicomputer with elaborate peripherals and software. Two-port memories loaded by minicomputer programs can substitute for microcomputer RAM and ROM, and can also provide control memory for microprogram development. The minicomputer program can also load ROMs, which can be substituted for the two-port memories as needed. Another two-port memory stores real-time bus signals for the last 40 to 100 instruction cycles for display and printout by the minicomputer.

macroassembler are readily adapted to cross assembly, emulation, and block-diagram-language translation (Secs. 5-29, 3-22, and 3-26). Cross translators written in FORTRAN will also run on such minicomputers (cross compilers might require multiple overlays).   Figure 5-20 suggests an advanced system of this type (Ref. 27), which will also load *microprograms* micro-assembled by the minicomputer into a two-port microcomputer control memory (Sec. 6-21).   A ROM loader on the minicomputer bus can load microcomputer program-memory and control-memory PROMs once programs are developed.   As an added feature, a "trace memory," like that in the Intel MDS (Ref. 11), can store real-time microcomputer bus signals for 50 to 100 instruction cycles for display or printout by the minicomputer. The system thus functions also as an advanced logic tester for hardware checkout (Sec. 5-28).   Last but not least, the minicomputer can translate block-diagram languages (Sec. 3-26) (Ref. 27).

REFERENCES AND BIBLIOGRAPHY

The material in this chapter ought to be read together with the operation and software manuals for the reader's existing or proposed computer system.

Peripheral Devices

Commercially available computer peripherals like printers, terminals, and tape transports are periodically reviewed and listed in journals like *Digital Design, Computer Design, Modern Data, EDN,* and *Electronic Products.*

1. Davis, S.: Disc Storage for Minicomputer Applications, *Comput. Des.,* June 1973.
2. Solomon, L., et al.: The Cartridge-Cassette Confrontation, *Digital Design,* May 1975.
3. Rasmussen, D.: Tape Cartridges, *Electron. Prod.,* June 1975; see also *Hewlett-Packard J.,* May 1976.
4. Caswell, S. S.: Floppy-Disk Drives and Systems, *Modern Data,* August 1975.
5. Special issue on Printer Technology, *Computer,* September 1975.

Operating Systems

(See also minicomputer manufacturers' operating-system manuals.)

6. Katzan, H.: *Operating Systems,* Van Nostrand Reinhold, New York, 1973.
7. Donovan, J. J.: *Systems Programming,* McGraw-Hill, New York, 1972.
8. Schoeffler, J. D.: *Minicomputer Real-Time Executives,* IEEE, New York, 1974.
9. ———— and L. R. Bronner: Data-Management Software for Minicomputer Production Monitoring and Control Systems, *Proc. IEEE,* November 1973.

Microcomputer Prototyping Systems

Byte (a magazine for computer amateurs) is a good reference on inexpensive computer kits.   Refer also to manufacturers' manuals on prototyping systems, cross-translators, and emulators.

10. Davidow, W.: The Coming Merger of Hardware and Software Design, *Electronics,* May 29, 1975.
11. Garrow, R., et al.: Microcomputer Development System, *Electronics,* May 29, 1975.
12. Casilli, G., and W. Kim: Microcomputer Software Development, *Digital Des.,* July 1975.

13. Martinez, R.: A Look at Trends in Microprocessor/Microcomputer Software Systems, *Comput. Des.*, June 1975.
14. Session on Microprocessor/Microcomputer Hardware and Software Support Systems, *Proc. WESCON*, 1975.

Miscellaneous

15. *Introduction to Programming*, Digital Equipment Corp., Maynard, Mass. (current edition).
16. *Programming Languages*, Digital Equipment Corp., Maynard, Mass. (current edition).
17. Evans, T. G., and D. L. Durley: On-Line Debugging Techniques: A Survey, *Proc.FJCC*, 1966 (contains further bibliography on debugging).
18. Korn, G. A., and J. V. Wait: *Digital Continuous-System Simulation*, Prentice-Hall, Englewood Cliffs, N.J., 1976.
19. Gray, M. T.: Microprocessors in CRT-Terminal Applications, *Computer*, October 1975.
20. Floyd, W.: When It Comes to Floppies, *EDN*, Jan. 5, 1976.
21. Lancaster, D.: *The TV Typewriter Cookbook*, Howard W. Sams Publications, Indianapolis, Ind., 1976.
22. *Draft Standards, Industrial Computer System FORTRAN*, Instrument Society of America, Pittsburgh, Pa., 1975.
23a. Kildall, G. A.: High-Level Language Simplifies Microcomputer Programming, *Report*, U.S. Naval Postgraduate School, Monterey, Calif., 1974.
23b. Borchert, M.: 16-Channel Logic Analyzer, *Tekscope*, Tektronix, Inc., Beaverton, Ore., 1975.
24. *A Guide to PL/M Programming*, Intel Corporation, Santa Clara, Calif. (current edition).
25. Barnes, J., and V. Gregory: Basic μP Test Tool: The Portable Debugger, *EDN*, Aug. 20, 1975.
26. Conley, S. W.: Portable Microcomputer Cross-Assemblers in BASIC, *Computer*, October 1975.
27. Korn, G. A.: A Proposed Method for Simplified Microcomputer Programming, *Computer*, October 1975.
28. Ewing, M. S.: *The Caltech FORTH Manual*, Owens Valley Radio Observatory, California Institute of Technology, Pasadena, Calif. (current edition).
29. Popper, C.: SMAL—a Structural Macro-Assembly Language for a Microprocessor, *Proc. COMPCON*, Fall 1976.
30. Small, C. T., and S. J. Morrill: The Logic State Analyzer, *Hewlett-Packard J.*, August 1975.
31. Robin, N. A.: The Logic Analyzer: A Computer Troubleshooting Tool, *Comput. Des.*, March 1976.
32. Santoni, A.: Testers are Getting Better, *Electronics*, December 23, 1976.
33. Gladstone, B.: Monitor/Debugger Saves Time, *EDN*, September 20, 1976.
34. Catterton, R. D., and G. S. Casilli: Universal Development System, *Electronics*, September 16, 1976.

CHAPTER 6

MICROCOMPUTER SYSTEMS AND DESIGN DECISIONS

SYSTEM DESIGN

6-1. Introduction. Micro/Minicomputer Applications. The progress of small-computer design, propelled by inexpensive logic circuits and fierce competition, is made more deliberate by the need to spread software costs over as many machines as possible. Hardware and software, in any case, must be designed and evaluated together. Their development is the system designer's response to widely divergent markets, whose requirements are not always well defined for him. The enormous versatility of mass-produced processor chips is the key to their success, but consider just how widely the applications differ:

1. *Replacement of random logic, relay systems, and mechanical linkages, cams, gears, etc.* Relatively short ROM-stored programs implement *logic, sequencing, counting,* and *timing.* Individual operations are simple and need not be very fast.
2. *Direct digital control of machine tools, rolling mills, chemical processes, etc.; often combined with report preparation (plant-data logging).* A wide range of applications, with a trend to replacement of larger minicomputers with a hierarchy of smaller distributed processors.
3. Applications combining data gathering (simple tallying, measurements, automatic testing, business-data acquisition) *and* the need to communicate with higher-level computers and programs.

4. *Simple logic or character-string operations, but with a requirement for fast service and/or large volume* (communications handling, front-ending larger computers, supervision of time-critical operations or measurements). Such applications favor powerful interrupt systems, direct memory access, and fast processing—but simple instruction sets will do.
5. *More complicated on-line numerical computations* (data processing, digital filtering, simulation). Here one needs more advanced arithmetic—even accessory array or floating-point-arithmetic processors; or one tries to pass the load to a larger computer.
6. *Sophisticated special-purpose applications* (e.g., display control, computer-aided design, automated drafting, text editing, typesetting.
7. *"End users"* (as opposed to original-equipment manufacturers or OEMs) such as research groups whose not-so-secret desire is a private computer center, complete with advanced operating system and conversational input/output.

In addition, there is a growing market for *amateur microcomputer kits.*

Applications in classes 5 to 7 are typically the province of "minicomputers." As noted in Sec. 1-2, modern minicomputers do not differ physically from microcomputers (similar LSI components are used), but they are sold as complete subsystems with reasonable software. Such machines will be described in Chap. 7.

Most "microcomputer" applications proper are *not* high-technology research projects, but down-to-earth attempts to extend the range of low-cost automation. *Much specialized design is replaced with programming of mass-produced general-purpose processors.* This reduces development, manufacturing operations, and testing as well as hardware costs and can improve product reliability.[1]

The faster/redesign cycle of the microcomputer approach, moreover, may permit a new product to be marketed before competition limits sales and prices, and faster recovery of development costs becomes possible. Relatively simple reprogramming permits *prompt modification and/or addition of product features* in response to new requirements or competitive pressure.

Many microcomputers replace slow subsystems (relays, gears, pneumatic controllers) so that there is no need for high processor speed as such. But higher processor power—faster logic, longer word length, more registers, address modes, and instructions—can dramatically reduce programming costs. This is so either because assembly-language programs become

[1] 8080A failure rate was measured by Intel Corp. at 0.04 percent per 1,000 hours at a 90 percent confidence level. Mean time between failures of checked-out memory chips can be of the order of millions of hours.

shorter (this also reduces program-memory requirements) or because faster computation makes up for the code inefficiency of a higher-order language, which is easier to write and debug (see also Sec. 6-2).

6-2. Hardware/Software Costs and Other Design Considerations.
Microcomputer-system cost is determined by the fundamental relation

$$\text{COST PER SYSTEM} = \text{HARDWARE COST PER SYSTEM}$$
$$+ \frac{\text{DEVELOPMENT COST}}{N} \qquad (6\text{-}1)$$

where N is the *number of systems produced.*

Hardware cost includes ICs, cards, wiring, interconnections, boxes, and power supplies, plus labor and overhead for manufacturing and testing. Relative costs of these items differ from those in earlier, larger computer systems. Remember that 400 bytes of ROM or 200 bytes of RAM may cost more than an 8-bit microprocessor: *in many systems, memory requirements dominate IC costs.* Power supply and cables, too, may well cost more than the central processor!

Development cost is usually largely *programming* and *program checkout,* plus some interface design and prototype tests. This includes part of the cost of a prototype-development system (Secs. 5-28 to 5-30). Program checkout and debugging can easily take more time than program design.

NOTE: It is not usually cost-effective to program for the highest feasible efficiency in the use of processor speed or memory (Fig. 6-1). It is usually cheaper to buy a more powerful processor and/or more memory. The high cost of efficient programs can be especially damaging when the program must be modified or expanded, or when the superefficient programmer leaves your organization.

Quite in general, *all computer projects ought to provide for expansion.* We cannot predict *how* requirements will change; but we can be virtually certain that they *will* change.

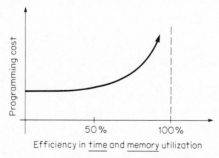

Fig. 6-1. It is rarely cost-effective to program for the highest feasible efficiency in the use of processor speed or memory. It is usually cheaper to buy more memory or a faster processor. (*Based on Ref. 3.*)

TABLE 6-1a. Register/Register ADD Times (μsec).

4-BIT PROCESSOR		**12-BIT PROCESSOR**	
Intel 4040	11	Intersil 6100 not applicable; memory/register ADD is 5 μsec, 2.5 μsec for 6100A	
8-BIT PROCESSORS		**16-BIT PROCESSORS**	
Intel 8080A	2	National Semiconductor PACE	8.5
Intel 8080A-1	1.3	General Instruments CP 1600	2.5
Intel 8080A-2	1.6	Western Digital MCP 1600 (LSI-11)	3.5
Intel 8085	1	Data General MICRONOVA	2.4
AMD 9080A-4	1	Texas Instruments TMS 9900	4.7
Zilog Z-80	1.6	SBP 9900	$\leq$4.7
Motorola 6800	2		
Motorola 6800A	<1.2		
MOS Technology 650X	2		
Signetics 2650	4.8		
2650X	3		
Fairchild F-8	2		
RCA CDP 1802D	2.5		
National Semiconductor SC/MP	16		
Scientific Micro Systems SMS 300	0.25		

TABLE 6-1b. Register/Register MULTIPLY
Times for 16-Bit Microprocessors (μsec).

Western Digital 1600 (LSI-11)	24 to 64
Data General Micronova	41.3
Texas Instruments TMS 9900	17.3

TABLE 6-1c. Power-Supply Requirements
(watts).

1. Single + 5 V Supply*	
Motorola 6800	1
MOS Technology 650X	0.7
RCA 1802D (3 to 12 V)	0.5
Signetics 2650	1.6
Texas Instruments TMS 9900	1
Texas Instruments SBP 9900	0.5
2. ± 5 V and + 12 V	
Intel 8080A	1.5
3. + 15 V and + 12 V	
Fairchild F-8	0.33

* Note that memory chips may require extra power-
supply voltages even if the CPU chip does not.

ICs are cheap, so that *development cost dominates if N in Eq.* (6-1) *is small*,
say for a run of 12 specialized instrumentation controllers. In such a
situation, *we minimize development cost at the expense of hardware*:

program in a higher-order language
use more memory and/or a more powerful processor (perhaps 16 bits
   instead of 8 bits) to make up for the resulting program inefficiency
buy microcomputer cards (Sec. 6-3*b*) rather than chips.

Another related approach is to *buy a microprocessor which belongs to a minicomputer family with lots of software and support* (Sec. 7-1; this usually also
means more expensive hardware).

On the other end of the spectrum, *hardware cost is critical in mass-produced
systems*, where development cost is divided by a large *N* (this would be several
million in the case of, say, an automobile-ignition controller!).   In such a
situation, *we will gladly spend money on optimized assembly-language programs*
and *expensive prototype-development systems* in order to

use as little memory as possible
try to make a cheaper processor do

To minimize manufacturing and testing, we may try to squeeze the job into
a *one-chip microcomputer*, and we may even go so far as to develop special-
purpose LSI.

Most projects lie between these two extremes and require cost comparisons for different hardware/software compromises.

NOTE: All LSI for any system produced on a continuing basis ought to be *second-sourced.* This attenuates surprises with delivery problems and also introduces an element of competition. Table 6-1*d* lists second sources. Only a few minicomputer-family microprocessors (Data General, Texas Instruments) are single-source items.

TABLE 6-1d. Second Sources.

Intel 4040	National Semiconductor
Rockwell PPS-4	National Semiconductor
Rockwell PPS-8	National Semiconductor
Intel 8080	Texas Instruments, AMI; NEC, Siemens; National Semiconductor
Zilog Z-80	Mostek
Motorola 6800	AMI Fairchild, Hitachi
MOS Technology 650X	Synertek
Fairchild F-8	Mostek
RCA CDP 1802	Adv. Memory Systems, Hughes
National Semiconductor SC/MP	Rockwell?
Intersil 6100	Harris Semiconductor
National Semiconductor PACE	Rockwell
General Instruments CP1600	SEMI (EM and M)
Scientific Microsystems SMS 300	Signetics
Intel 3000	Signetics
AMD 2900	Motorola, Raytheon; Hitachi, Thompson CSF Signetics
Monolithic Memories 6701	
Western Digital MCP 1600	DEC; National Semiconductor

6-3. The Microcomputer System.   (a) System Components and Chip-Count Considerations.   A complete microcomputer system (Fig. 6-2) comprises, as major components,

LSI microprocessor (CPU chip or chips)
Program memory (usually ROM)
Data memory (RAM)
I/O ports (interfaces) for parallel and/or serial data

plus accessory logic such as

processor clock
buffer amplifiers and latches for bus signals
extra memory or interface address decoders
refresh logic for dynamic MOSFET memories
start-switch-debounce flip-flop

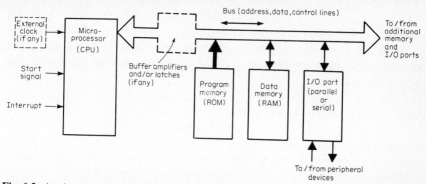

Fig. 6-2. A microcomputer consists of a *microprocessor CPU* and program memory (usually ROM), plus *data memory* (RAM) and *I/O ports* as needed. Accessory chips may include *buffer amplifiers, a clock, and a start/reset flip-flop.*

The cost of designing, manufacturing, testing, and maintaining interconnections makes **chip count** an important design factor, especially in small mass-produced systems. Chip count is reduced by clever one-chip combinations of processors, clocks, ROM, RAM, and I/O ports (Sec. 6-5 and 6-11). In a small system, a processor with an on-chip subroutine-address stack (Sec. 2-23) and enough scratchpad registers may not need any RAM. In general, small microcomputer memories employ *word-oriented* memory chips, while larger memories use general-purpose memory chips *fully decoded at the bit level* (Fig. 1-22). Designers must also try to minimize the number of the accessory-logic items listed above. Small systems usually employ static RAM, which needs no refresh logic.

Complete single-chip 4-bit and 8-bit microcomputers are commercially available. As an example, **Rockwell PPS-4/1** has a 1,344 × 8-bit ROM, 96 × 4-bit RAM, parallel and serial I/O port, an interrupt facility, and an on-chip clock. On-chip ROMs are usually mask-programmed during processor manufacture, although on-chip PROMs exist (Ref. 26).

(b) Microcomputer Card Sets and Kits. Without question, the simplest way to start a microcomputer-development project is to use commercially available **microcomputer cards** and **card sets** (Fig. 1-1*b*). These are available from chip manufacturers and firms making various microcomputer kits, and can save much trouble with initial circuit layout, noise, bus loading, and bus timing. Users can still go on to make their own circuit cards after the first prototype works.

NOTE: **Microprocessor systems which are unplugged and handled ought to have TTL buffers on all bus interconnections to prevent static-charge destruction of MOSFET circuits.**

Card and kit manufacturers usually furnish a rudimentary operating system on a **monitor or debug ROM**. This typically contains I/O routines for a keyboard terminal and an audio-cassette interface, simple programs for reading and loading keyboard-selected RAM locations, for inserting program breakpoints (Sec. 5-18c), and for running and single-stepping computer programs. Some kits have simple ROM-implemented assemblers and even BASIC interpreters.

6-4. Microcomputer Bus Systems. Each microprocessor communicates with memory and I/O ports through a **microcomputer bus,** which transmits **data, addresses,** and **control signals** (Fig. 6-2). Most microcomputer buses are compatible with TTL or CMOS logic; processors usually need buffer amplifiers in all but the smallest systems (consult your manual).

Referring back to our discussion of computer buses in Secs. 4-1 to 4-5, microcomputers have **synchronous** buses; i.e., bus signals are synchronized with processor-clock pulses. A **bus cycle** is a bus transaction which moves one instruction word or data word (say one 8-bit byte) between processor, memory, and I/O ports. In some computers, a bus cycle transfers *two half-words* (4-bit "nibbles," 8-bit bytes) from or to two adjacent memory locations (Sec. 6-5). In any case, each bus cycle typically involves *several microoperations* during successive processor-clock cycles (microcycles, Secs. 2-8, 2-20, and 2-31).

Every computer instruction requires at least one bus cycle (FETCH cycle, Sec. 2-5), which addresses the program memory and moves an instruction word to the processor instruction register. Simple register-operation instructions are executed in one bus cycle. The execution time for such an instruction (e.g., register/register **ADD**) is often used as a *rough* measure of processor speed. Other instructions use successive additional bus cycles to

address program memory again to fetch more instruction words
address RAM or an I/O port, and move a data word
actuate device functions through address and control-signal lines (without moving data)

Most microcomputer buses have as many *bidirectional data lines* as the computer word has bits. A few systems have separate input and output data lines. Memory and I/O *addresses*, and some of the *instructions* typically require more bits than one computer word. We will present examples of **three basic bus systems:**

1. For each bus cycle, **time-shared data lines** transmit one to three address words and then one data or instruction word during successive sub-cycles, using different strobe pulses (Secs. 4-3, 6-5, and 6-16 to 6-18).

This reduces the number of processor-chip connections. A time-shared bus requires either *address latches* on each memory chip or a common *bus address register* outside the processor. Time sharing does not necessarily take much extra time, for addresses must settle before data transfers in any bus system.

2. **Complete addresses are transmitted over separate address lines.**

This method is used in many 8-bit systems, which typically have 8 bi-directional data lines and 16 separate address lines (Secs. 6-6 and 6-7).

3. **The program memory, possibly using a word length longer than the computer data word, has a separate bus system** (e.g., for 16-bit instructions in an 8-bit machine, Sec. 6-14).

This can yield very high computing speed, especially since instruction and data accesses may be partially overlapped.

Since some memories and/or I/O devices may be too slow to operate within a processor's usual bus cycle, *most microprocessors permit one to "extend" the bus cycle by stopping processor operation for an extra microcycle or more with a special control-signal output.* This approximates asynchronous-bus operation (Figs. 4-7c and 6-11b).

References 7 and 9 illustrate useful bus-layout procedures.

4-BIT AND 8-BIT MICROCOMPUTERS

6-5. A 4-Bit PMOS System: Intel 4040. 4-bit PMOS microprocessors, though relatively slow (11 to 16 μsec for a *4-bit* register/register **ADD**), are surprisingly powerful in suitable applications (mass-produced logic replacement, sequence control, BCD operations). Note, however, that an 8-bit processor and bus system costs only a little more and may substantially reduce the number of program steps, and thus memory and development costs. Hence 4-bit microprocessors are usually restricted to small, mass-produced systems, where processor cost is a significant item (Sec. 6-2).

The **Intel 4040**[1] microprocessor has a **4-bit accumulator, 24 4-bit scratchpad registers** which can be combined into **twelve 8-bit pointer registers** (Sec. 2-15), and a **four-level hardware program-counter stack** for subroutine and interrupt-return addresses (Sec. 2-23). Eight of the scratchpad registers (and thus four pointer registers) can be context-switched (Sec. 4-9). The 4040 system includes word-organized ROM and RAM chips with on-chip I/O ports.

Table 6-2 illustrates the 4040 **instruction set.** Only instructions which address program memory (ROM) like **LOAD IMMEDIATE, JUMP,** use 12-bit addresses. *All data-memory (RAM) references are via an 8-bit register pair.*

---

[1] The predecessor model, **Intel 4004,** is slower, has fewer registers and instructions, and no explicit interrupt, but is still widely useful. Intel 4040 will execute 4004 programs without change. 4004 fits a 16-terminal dual-in-line package, while 4040 has 24 terminations.

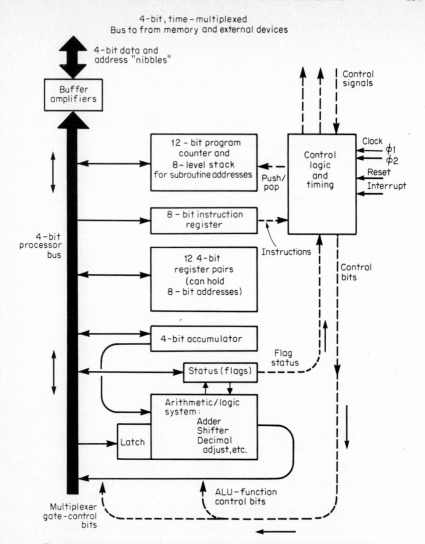

4-bit, time-multiplexed
Bus to from memory and external devices

4-bit data and
address "nibbles"

Fig. 6-3. Block diagram of the Intel 4040, a single-bus, 4-bit microprocessor.

To fit such memory-reference operations into an 8-bit instruction format, they are split into several instructions:

SELECT MEMORY BANK (selects a 256-word page determined by accumulator contents)

SELECT REGISTER BANK (context switching)

SEND REGISTER CONTROL (selects a pointer-register pair and loads the 8-bit address into an address register on the bus, usually on the selected memory chip)

TABLE 6-2. Intel 4040 Instructions.

1. Accumulator Operations (4-bits)

LOAD, STORE	from/to register; via designed register pair; from/to I/O port; immediate
ADD WITH CARRY, SUBTRACT WITH BORROW	from register; via designated register pair
AND	from register 4 or 5
OR	from register 6 or 7
EXCHANGE	register
INCREMENT, DECREMENT, COMPLEMENT, DECIMAL ADJUST	
ROTATE WITH CARRY (left or right)	
KEYBOARD-CODE CONVERSION	

2. Pointer-Register Operations (8-bits)

LOAD IMMEDIATE	immediate; via register pair 0
INCREMENT	(4-bit register, *not* pair)
INCREMENT, SKIP IF ZERO	

3. "Preaddressing" Instructions for Selecting Registers, Memory Banks, and I/O Ports

SELECT POINTER REGISTER BANK	
SEND REGISTER CONTROL	(designates pointer for subsequent memory references)
SELECT MEMORY CHIP or I/O PORT	

4. Program Control

JUMP	direct, 12-bit address; via register pair
JUMP ON CONDITION	direct, 8-bit address (combinations of accumulator $= 0$, $\neq 0$; carry $= 0$, 1; test signal $= 0$, 1)
JUMP TO SUBROUTINE	direct; 12-bit address
RETURN FROM INTERRUPT	
NO OPERATION, HALT, ENABLE/DISABLE INTERRUPT	

5. Other Operations

CLEAR, SET, COMPLEMENT CARRY	
CLEAR ACCUMULATOR AND CARRY	
SET ACCUMULATOR TO VALUE OF CARRY AND CLEAR CARRY	
TRANSFER CARRY SUBTRACT	(set accumulator to BCD 9 or 10 if carry is 0 or 1, clear carry)

Last comes the memory-reference instruction proper, e.g., **LOAD ACCUMULATOR** (from the previously determined address). Note that several instructions in a program may use the same address, so that **SEND REGISTER CONTROL** need not be repeated. Figure 3-15 shows examples of such 4040 programs. I/O ports are similarly addressed with multiple instructions.

As a result of preaddressing, most 4040 instructions (exceptions noted below) are simple 8-bit instructions executed in one cycle of the **time-shared 4-bit bus**. Referring to the timing diagram of Fig. 6-4, each bus cycle follows a SYNC pulse and first transmits three 4-bit address words (time intervals A_1, A_2, A_3 in Fig. 6-4). Three clock pulses strobe these address

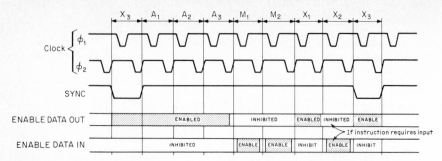

Fig. 6-4. Multiplexed-bus timing for one 8-bit instruction of a 4040 microprocessor. Special-purpose ROMs and RAMs for this system comprise sequential logic which generates address/data enabling strobes by counting clock pulses after each processor SYNC pulse. General-purpose memory chips can be used with a *4289 memory-interface* chip which provides these enabling functions.   Separate instructions select lines in larger memories.

"nibbles" into an address register, which must be provided either on the memory chip or as a separate IC.   The bus next fetches the two 4-bit instruction words (M_1, M_2) and then executes the instruction, which may involve more 4-bit data transfers (X_1, X_2, X_3).

The only 16-bit instructions are **LOAD POINTER-REGISTER PAIR, IM-MEDIATE** (8-bit operand) and direct-addressing **JUMP** and **JUMP TO SUB-ROUTINE** instructions, which require a second bus cycle.

4040 has a single interrupt, and a RESET input which starts or restarts program operation at location 0.   Chip-select bits and the contents of the currently used pointer, as well as the carry flag, must be saved on interrupt.

6-6.   8-Bit NMOS Chips: Intel 8080A and Motorola 6800 (see also Sec. 6-9).

(a) The Intel 8080A Processor.   A block diagram of Intel's pioneering **8080A** (Fig. 6-5*a*)[1] illustrates common features of many monolithic NMOS 8-bit CPU chips:

1. A simple **8-bit ALU/accumulator subsystem** implements logic and arithmetic functions (including **DECIMAL ADJUST** for BCD operations, Sec. 2-26) on 8-bit data bytes and communicates with memory and I/O ports through a **bidirectional 8-bit data bus.**
2. An **8-bit instruction register** receives instruction opcode bytes from the program memory (usually ROM) over the same data bus.
3. A **processor status register** comprises processor flags (Sec. 2-7).
4. Six **8-bit scratchpad registers** can be paired to form **three 16-bit pointer registers** (Table 6-3).   **Program counter, stack pointer, and pointer registers all have 16 bits.**   They can receive address bytes, as needed, over the data bus and transmit **16-bit addresses** to memories and I/O devices through a **16-bit address bus.**

[1] The 8080's PMOS predecessor **8008**, slower, less powerful, and needing more accessory chips, still serves in many systems.   8080 executes all 8008 software, plus new instructions.

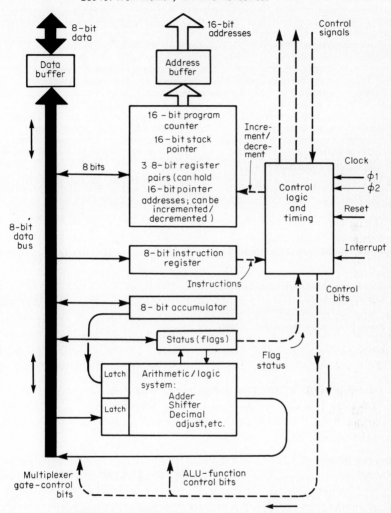

Bus to / from memory and external devices

Fig. 6-5a. Block diagram of an 8-bit microprocessor with a separate 16-bit address bus (Intel 8080A). Motorola 6800, MOS Technology 650X, and Zilog Z-80 are similar, except for different register complements (Table 6-5).

Table 6-4 describes the 8080A instruction set. Register/register **ADD** times of 8080-type processors vary between 1 and 3 μsec (Table 6-2a). Subroutine and interrupt return addresses go on a **software stack.** There is no indirect addressing. The 8080A lacks a 2s-complement overflow flag. The large instruction set is quite powerful but is difficult to learn, since the various registers have different properties, and instruction mnemonics are confusing (Table 6-3).

TABLE 6-3.   Intel 8080A Instructions and Addressing Modes.

Pairs of **8-bit scratchpad registers** H, L, B, C, D, E form **16-bit pointer registers** HL, BC, DE. **Memory-addressing modes** are

   direct addressing of 64K bytes (3-byte instructions, 2 address bytes)
   pointer-register addressing (1-byte instructions)
   stack addressing (1-byte instructions transfer 16 bits, i.e., *two* bytes, between HL, BC, DE, or SP and memory stack; SP is incremented or decremented by 2)
   immediate addressing (2- and 3-byte instructions with 8-bit or 16-bit operands)
(see also Secs. 2-10 to 2-18).   In addition, there is a one-byte instruction for subroutine jumps to 8 3-bit addresses on page 0, used mostly for vectored interrupts.   Peripheral-device registers are addressed either as memory locations or with special 2-byte INPUT and OUTPUT instructions.   The remaining 8080A instructions are 1 byte long.   There is no indirect addressing.

1. Accumulator Operations (8 bits)

LOAD	direct; via HL, BC, or DE; immediate
STORE	direct; via HL
MOVE	to/from scratchpad
INPUT, OUTPUT	to/from devices (with 8-bit address)
PUSH, POP	(accumulator and flags)
ADD, ADD WITH CARRY	
SUBTRACT, SUBTRACT WITH BORROW	scratchpad; via HL; immediate
AND, XOR, OR	
COMPARE	
INCREMENT, DECREMENT, COMPLEMENT, DECIMAL ADJUST	
ROTATE (left, right; with/without carry)	

2. Scratchpad MOVE Operations (8 bits)

LOAD	via HL; immediate
STORE	via HL
MOVE	to/from other scratchpad registers or accumulator

3. Operations on HL, BC, DE Pointer Registers and Stack Pointer (16 bits)

LOAD	direct; immediate
STORE HL	direct
PUSH, POP	
EXCHANGE HL with DE or 2 bytes at top of stack	
MOVE HL TO SP	
ADD INTO HL	(BC, DE, SP, or HL; the last is equivalent to a left shift)
INCREMENT, DECREMENT	

4. Program Control (conditional jumps are on carry, zero, sign bit, parity bit clear or set)

JUMP	direct; via HL
JUMP ON CONDITION, JUMP TO SUBROUTINE, JUMP TO SUBROUTINE ON CONDITION	direct
RETURN, RETURN ON CONDITION	
JUMP TO SUBROUTINE ON PAGE 0	(1-byte instruction, 3-byte address)
NO OPERATION, HALT, ENABLE/DISABLE INTERRUPT	

5. Other Operations

INCREMENT, DECREMENT MEMORY	via HL
LOAD MEMORY IMMEDIATE (8 bits)	via HL
SET CARRY, COMPLEMENT CARRY	

TABLE 6-4. Motorola 6800 Instructions and Addressing Modes.

Memory-addressing modes are
>**direct addressing on page 0** (256 bytes; 2-byte instructions, 1 address byte)
>**direct addressing** of 64K bytes (3-byte instructions, 2 address bytes)
>**indexed addressing** (2-byte instructions, 1-byte offset only)
>**immediate addressing** (3-byte instructions, 16-bit operand)

In addition, 2-byte *branching instructions* employ **relative addressing** (Sec. 2-14) with a 1-byte offset address (-128 to $+127$). The remaining instructions are 1 byte long. There is no indirect addressing. Peripheral-device registers are always addressed as memory locations.

---

1. Accumulator Operations (8 bits)

LOAD, STORE	direct, page 0; direct
ADD, ADD WITH CARRY	indexed; immediate
SUBTRACT, SUBTRACT WITH BORROW	
AND, XOR, OR, BIT TEST	
COMPARE	
PUSH, POP	
MOVE A TO B; B TO A	
ADD, SUBTRACT B TO A	
COMPARE A, B,	
MOVE STATUS REGISTER (FLAGS) TO/FROM ACCUMULATOR	
DECIMAL ADJUST ACCUMULATOR A	

---

2. Operations on Accumulators or Memory

CLEAR, INCREMENT, DECREMENT, COMPLEMENT,	accumulators;
NEGATE, TEST	direct; indexed
ROTATE, ARITHMETIC SHIFT (left or right)	

---

3. Operations on Index Register and Stack Pointer (16 bits)

LOAD, STORE	direct, page 0; direct
COMPARE INDEX WITH MEMORY	indexed; immediate
INCREMENT, DECREMENT	
MOVE X TO SP, SP TO X	

---

4. Program Control

JUMP, JUMP TO SUBROUTINE	direct; indexed
BRANCH, BRANCH TO SUBROUTINE, BRANCH ON CONDITION	relative

6800 has a *complete* set of explicit conditions for signed and unsigned comparisons (Sec. 2-22).

RETURN FROM SUBROUTINE, RETURN FROM INTERRUPT
ENABLE/DISABLE INTERRUPT
SOFTWARE INTERRUPT (Sec. 4-13)
NO OPERATION, HALT, WAIT FOR INTERRUPT (save registers)

---

5. Other Operations

CLEAR, SET carry, overflow flag
ADD, SUBTRACT B TO A
COMPARE A, B
MOVE STATUS REGISTER (FLAGS) TO/FROM ACCUMULATOR
DECIMAL ADJUST ACCUMULATOR A

(b) The Motorola 6800 Processor. *The* **6800** *is also built around a bidirectional 8-bit data bus and a 16-bit address bus as in Fig. 6-5b, with a different register complement:*

two 8-bit accumulators

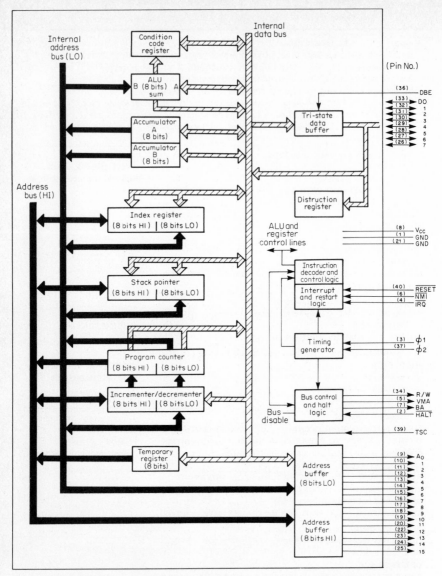

Fig. 6-5b. Motorola/AMI 6800 microprocessor.   (*American Microsystems, Inc.*)

a true 16-bit index register
a 16-bit stack pointer
a processor status register including a 2s-complement overflow flag

6800 has the straightforward minicomputer-like instruction set described in Table 6-5. There is no indirect addressing.

TABLE 6-5.   Comparison of Registers and Addressing Modes.

	Accumulator(s)	Scratchpad or pointer registers	True index register(s)	Stack pointer
Intel 8080A, AMD 9080A	1 8-bit	3 8-bit pairs (or 16-bit pointers)	....	16-bit
Motorola 6800	2 8-bit	....	1 16-bit (8-bit offset)	16-bit
MOS Technology 650X	1 8-bit	....	2 8-bit (16-bit offset); limited pre-indexing and postindexing	8-bit
Zilog Z-80	2 8-bit, context-switched	2 sets of 3 8-bit pairs (or 16-bit pointers), context-switched	2 16-bit (8-bit offset)	16-bit

(c) Interrupt Systems. The 8080A interrupt-enable bit is not part of the processor status register but is cleared by each interrupt; it must be re-enabled by the interrupt-service routine as needed. An interrupting device, or an associated **Intel 8214 interrupt-controller chip** will gate an interrupt-address code onto the bus data lines with the bus-control signal INTA (INTER-RUPT ACKNOWLEDGE).

NOTE: The 8080A actually interprets this code as a 1-byte *instruction* and executes this instruction. The instruction code chosen is normally that for a 1-byte subroutine jump to one of eight vector addresses on page 0. This saves the return address on the stack; the *program* must save status flags and/or registers as needed.

In addition, the processor input RESET clears the program counter and acts like an interrupt trapping to location 0. This is usually employed to start processor operation.

A 6800 interrupt automatically saves return address, status register (which includes an interrupt-enable bit), and all processor registers on the processor stack in memory. Four fixed vector locations contain starting addresses for four interrupts (external RESET, INTERRUPT, and NONMASKABLE INTERRUPT inputs and SOFTWARE INTERRUPT; the latter amounts to a subroutine jump with automatic register saving). To obtain more vectored interrupts, *a special interrupt-controller chip* intercepts memory-address lines to modify the vector address for each interrupt (Fig. 6-6d; Ref. 7).

6-7. Bus Signals and I/O Ports. The operation of the Motorola 6800 bus (Fig. 6-6) illustrates typical 8-bit microcomputer bus operations during any one bus cycle (see also Sec. 6-4).

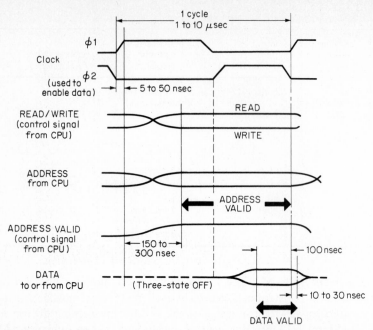

Fig. 6-6a. Bus-signal timing for an NMOS 8-bit processor with bidirectional data lines and a separate address bus (Motorola 6800). Instructions transferring multiple 8-bit bytes use multiple cycles.

1. The processor places an address (ROM, RAM, or I/O) on the bus address lines and advises memory and devices of this fact by raising the VALID MEMORY ADDRESS line.
2. When the address levels are "stable," a clock or control pulse gates one instruction byte or data byte to or from the processor over the bus data lines.

Fig. 6-6b. A Motorola 6800 microcomputer system. The 40 processor terminations are

AO-15	16 address lines (out)	3-state buffers
DBO-DB7	8 bidirectional data lines	drive one TTL load plus 130 pF

R/W (Read/write, *out*)	READ is high. Off when CPU is halted
DBE (Data Bus Enable, *in*)	Usually connected to $\phi2$ clock, enables tri-state bus drivers. Can disconnect bus for DMA
TSC (Three-state Control, *in*)	Disconnects address lines after 500 nsec; used for DMA
VMA (Valid Memory Address, *out*)	Indicates address on bus
BA (Bus Available, *out*)	High when processor stops and releases bus

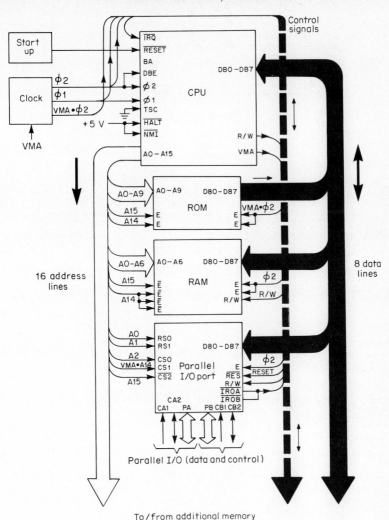

To/from additional memory
and/or I/O ports

$\overline{\text{RESET}}$ (*in*)	Starts processor from location stored in memory locations FFFE, FFFF
IRQ ($\overline{\text{Interrupt Request}}$, *in*) NMI ($\overline{\text{Nonmaskable Interrupt}}$, *in*)	Interrupt inputs
$\overline{\text{HALT}}$ (*in*)	Halts processor at the end of current instruction, with BA = 1, VMA = 0, bus off; $\overline{\text{HALT}}$ must not occur during the last 250 nsec of $\phi1$
$\phi1$, $\phi2$, + 5 V, Ground (*in*)	Clock, power, and ground

Two pins connect to + 5 V; there are two spare pins.   Chip-enable terminations on memory and I/O chips are marked E, $\overline{\text{E}}$.   (*Based on Ref. 7.*)

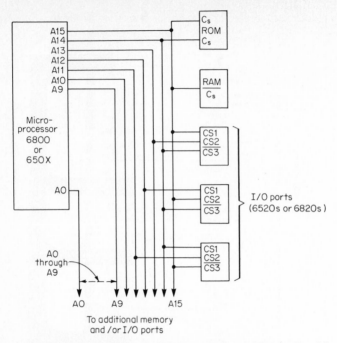

Fig. 6-6c. Typical chip-select connections for ROM, RAM, and I/O ports in a Motorola 6800 or MOS Technology 650X microcomputer system. (*MOS Technology, Inc.*)

A control signal tells the memory or I/O port whether a read or write operation is wanted.

The 6800 processor connects to the bus through tri-state gates (Sec. 4-1). This makes it simple for a *DMA controller* (Sec. 4-18) to *disconnect* processor address and data lines from the bus and to move data between memory and I/O ports by supplying memory addresses during "stolen" cycles. To steal a cycle, raise the address-bus three-state-control (TSC) input on the leading edge of the $\phi 1$ clock; then stop the clock ($\phi 1$ high, $\phi 2$ low, Fig. 6-6). Stopping the clock for over 5 μsec will lose data in the dynamic CPU logic.

Intel 8080 bus operations are more complicated. Instructions involve bus cycles of unequal lengths and more bus control signals than available processor-chip terminations. The 8080A, therefore, transmits 8 control-signal bits over the *data lines* at the start of each bus cycle. Some or all of these control bits must be latched into an external *bus status register* by a special clock pulse to determine bus operations during the cycle (Fig. 6-7). This extra hardware permits the 8080A to address peripheral devices either as memory or with (possibly more efficient) two-byte I/O instructions, simplifies interrupt vectoring (Sec. 6-6c), and may provide for future contingencies. The **Intel 8228 system-controller chip** combines the

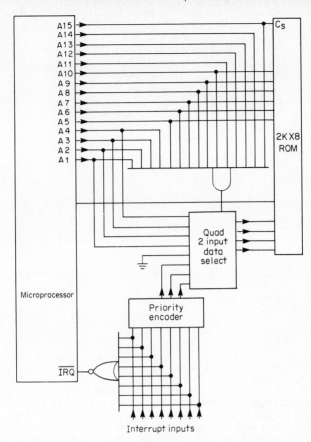

Fig. 6-6d. A multiplexer/selector circuit intercepts four memory-address lines and substitutes the interrupt-priority encoder output whenever the recognition gate reads the primary interrupt-vector address FFFE or FFFF. This modifies the primary vector address to produce eight pairs of vector addresses. (*MOS Technology, Inc.*; the same circuit is also used with the Motorola 6800.)

bus status register with data-line buffer amplifiers, which are usually needed anyway.

Microcomputer device interfaces can be inexpensively configured with ordinary TTL or MOS integrated-circuit flip-flops for data registers and flags (Fig. 6-8 and Chap. 4). With declining LSI costs, though, *more and more systems employ general-purpose I/O chips which, once again, replace special-purpose logic with programmed functions.* As a typical example, Motorola's programmable I/O chip **(6820 peripheral interface adapter, PIA)** has *two complete 8-bit interfaces* essentially identical except for higher-power buffer amplifiers on one I/O port. Users program PIA functions by loading

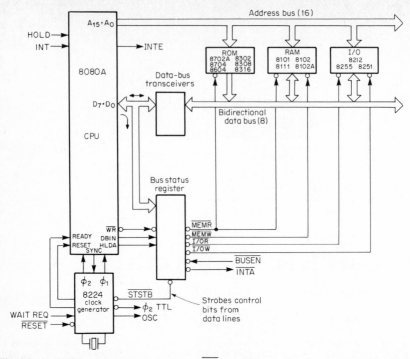

Fig. 6-7. An 8080A microcomputer system. $\overline{WR}$ low indicates that the processor has placed data on the bus.   DBIN high indicates the processor is ready to read data.   SYNC indicates the start of a bus cycle.   The first $\phi1$ clock after SYNC (status strobe $\overline{STSTB}$) strobes eight control-signal bits from the data lines into the *bus status register*, which latches these bits to determine bus operations during the rest of the bus cycle.   I/O ports can be addressed either with *memory-reference instructions* using the $\overline{MEM\ R}$, $\overline{MEM\ W}$ control bits, or with shorter *special I/O instructions* using $\overline{I/O\ R}$, $\overline{I/O\ W}$.   INTA is used for *interrupt vectoring* (Sec. 6-6c).   Other status-latch bits, used for various special operations, are not shown.

or reading four locations which look, to the processor, like memory locations:

1. **Two control/status registers** (Secs. 4-6 and 4-7), each with a control bit usable as a device strobe or handshake signal; a status or interrupt/ request flag; a flip-flop usable for either control *or* status; and additional flip-flops controlling the use of the others (control or status, flag set on positive or negative transition).

2. **Two 8-bit data registers.**   Each individual data-register bit can serve for output *or* input, as determined by the corresponding bit of a **direction register.**   The direction register has the same address as the corresponding data register; the direction register, rather than the data register, can be selected by a control-register bit.

The direction register is usually programmed for a specific combination of input and output bits at the beginning of a program, and control/status-bit

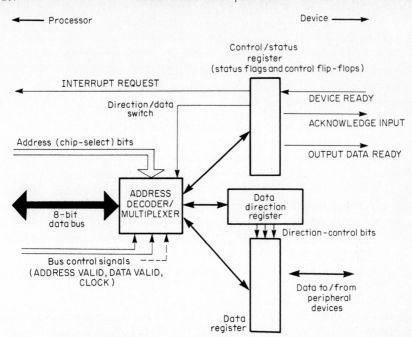

Fig. 6-8. Microcomputer programmable I/O ports are complete device interfaces (see also Fig. 4-17). Commercially available LSI chips may have two or more data registers, direction registers, and control/status registers. Motorola 6820, for instance, accepts three address lines, of which two must be high and one low (Fig. 6-6c). Each of the four chip-select combinations then selects a control register or a data/director-register pair. A control-register bit determines whether data or direction bits are loaded.

functions are also set up. Thus, many different interfaces can be tailored to specific peripheral devices (Fig. 6-8). **Intel 8255,** the corresponding I/O chip for 8080 systems, is similar but has 24 I/O lines. In each system, priorities and vector addresses for *multiple interrupts* are determined by separate **interrupt-controller chips** (Secs. 4-10 to 4-15).

NOTE: A 6820 control bit can be programmed so that it goes low whenever the processor writes into the associated data register (I/O DATA AVAILABLE "handshake" signal). This control bit is then reset by a data-strobing signal from a device. Similarly, a 6820 status-flag bit set by a device request can be reset by a processor instruction reading the associated data register.

Most microcomputer systems also include at least one **parallel/serial interface for asynchronous or synchronous data transmission** (Sec. 4-26), which can communicate with keyboard terminals and audio-type cassette-tape recorders. The simplest microcomputer systems (e.g., SC/MP, Sec. 6-12) let the CPU do parallel/serial conversion at the expense of processor time. Other I/O chips include complete monolithic controllers for DMA, CRT terminals, and floppy disks.

6-8. MOS Technology 650X, Zilog Z-80, and Improved 8080-Type Chips.
The **MOS Technology 650X-series** NMOS processors can execute most of
the Motorola 6800 instruction set and have a similar memory/I/O bus,
although instruction codes, pinout, and some bus signals differ.[1] Note the
following more significant differences between 650X and 6800 (see also
Tables 6-4 and 6-5 and Sec. 6-9):

1. 650X has a **single** 8-bit accumulator and **two 8-bit** index registers;
    indexed/direct-addressing instructions can use a **full 16-bit offset.**
2. 650X permits **preindexed indirect addressing** with one 8-bit index register
    and an 8-bit offset, with the pointer address restricted to the 256-byte
    page 0. The other index register permits **postindexed indirect
    addressing** with an 8-bit address byte pointing to a 16-bit base address
    on page 0, which is added to the 8-bit index.
3. 650X has an *indirect* **JUMP** instruction with a 16-bit indirect address.
    No other instruction permits simple indirect addressing.
4. 650X has only an **8-bit stack pointer,** which restricts the processor stack
    to a single 256-byte page of memory (normally page 1).
5. **STORE ACCUMULATOR** and **JUMP TO SUBROUTINE** instructions are
    faster in the 650X, but it lacks some of the 6800's conditional-branching
    instructions, as well as **CLEAR, COMPLEMENT, NEGATE, TEST,
    ADD/SUBTRACT** without carry or borrow, and **LOAD/STORE/
    INCREMENT/DECREMENT STACKPOINTER.**
6. Special instructions set and clear a **decimal mode,** in which **ADD WITH
    CARRY** and **SUBTRACT WITH BORROW** produce *true BCD addition
    and subtraction.*
7. The 650X interrupt system saves and restores only return address and
    status register, *not* the accumulator and index registers.
8. 650X has an **on-chip clock** needing only an external crystal or *RC*
    timing element.   *650X lacks the 6800's tri-state address-line bus drivers.*

Among the memory and I/O chips complementing the 650X series, **6530** contains 1K
bytes of ROM, 64 bytes of RAM, 16 I/O lines, and a simple real-time clock (*interval timer*).
This permits the design of a simple two-chip computer.   **6520** is a direct replacement for the
Motorola 6820 Peripheral Interface Adapter (Sec. 6-7).

Various improved versions of the classical 8080 and 6800 all employ
depletion-mode NMOS logic (Sec. 1-17 and Table 6-1a).   In particular,
Advanced Micro Devices Am 9080A-4 is, essentially, a faster 8080 (1 μsec
register/register **ADD**) with slightly lower power dissipation (1.1 W vs. 1.3 W)
and somewhat better noise margin (3 V vs. 2.7 V logic).   Intel's **8085,** a software-compatible, depletion-mode replacement for the 8080A, is faster (1.3
μsec register/register **ADD**), works with a single 5-V supply, and has an

---

[1] The **6501,** which was pin-compatible with the 6800, has been discontinued. **6502** has
40 pins; **6503-5** have 28 pins, with fewer address and/or interrupt lines.   650X can use a good
deal of 6800 software if instructions are recoded.

on-chip clock.   While 8080A multiplexes control signals into a bus status register (Fig. 6-7), 8085 has extra control lines and multiplexes bus data and *addresses*.   This requires address latches, but special interface circuits can make 8080 and 8085 systems compatible.

Zilog Z-80 (Table 6-5) is a much more powerful microprocessor. Z-80 executes the entire 8080 instruction set, and can thus adapt to all software developed for the 8080; the Z-80 assembler, moreover, works with a much neater set of instruction mnemonics.   **Z-80 duplicates the 8080's accumulator, flags, and general-purpose registers for fast context switching.**   The parity flags double as **true 2s-complement-overflow flags.** Z-80, moreover, has **two true 16-bit index registers;** indexed instructions have only an 8-bit offset, as in the 6800.   Z-80 also has **ARITHMETIC SHIFT, JUMP VIA INDEX REGISTER,** and permits **relative addressing** for some branching instructions.

As a special feature, Z-80 has explicit single instructions for *transferring an entire block of N bytes* and for *searching a block of bytes until the accumulator contents are matched.*   Finally, Z-80 has an extra nonmaskable interrupt and is faster than the basic 8080A (1.6-μsec register/register **ADD**). Although it is more expensive than 8080A, *Z-80 requires only a single* $+5$-V *supply, needs no control-signal decoder* (as in Fig. 6-5), *and the processor chip contains some of the memory-refresh logic for dynamic MOSFET memories.* This makes it practical to use cheaper dynamic memory even in small systems.

6-9.   System Comparisons.   The 8080 and 6800 systems, backed by substantial software efforts and extensively second-sourced, dominate the international marketplace.   A number of related microprocessor designs capitalize on software and accessories developed for the 8080 and 6800 (Sec. 6-8).   It is, then, important to assess the relative advantages of the 8080, 6800, and related systems.   A number of firms have developed *benchmark problems* suitable for comparing microprocessor speed and memory requirements in "typical" applications.   Manufacturers have fine-tuned programs for such benchmarks; remember, though, that applications differ so much that a user's own program is the only really valid benchmark for his purposes.

The following are *the writer's* interpretations of various benchmark results (Refs. 1, 4, 5).

1. In *complicated multiple-precision arithmetic*, the two-accumulator 6800 is 15 to 30 percent faster.   It uses fewer instructions, but about as much memory as the 8080A.

2. In a simple block transfer (Sec. 3-9) used to test *indexing operations*, the 8080A's three incrementable pointer registers produce twice the speed obtained with the 6800.   The latter's single true index register must be repeatedly saved and restored if multiple pointers are needed.

NOTE: MOS Technology 650X has indexing instructions with a *16-bit* address (rather than 8 bits, as in 6800 and Z-80). *This relieves the multiple-pointer problem*, since each index register can now index several arrays (and also serve as a loop counter) in the manner of Fig. 3-6. Although array sizes larger than 256 require extra operations, *an 8-bit index register with 16-bit offset appears more useful than a 16-bit index register with 8-bit offset. But the 8-bit stack pointer and index registers complicate subroutine-data-passing operations* like those in Fig. 3-12*a*. 650X's indirect-addressing modes, though restricted (Sec. 6-8), are very useful for implementing block-diagram languages (Sec. 3-25). Z-80, of course, has *multiple* index and pointer registers, plus explicit block-transfer and block-search instructions. System designers are also reminded that Signetics 2650 (Sec. 6-10) has more flexible addressing modes than 8080-type or 6800-type machines.

3. 6800 has a more complete set of explicit *conditional-branching* instructions, while 8080A permits *explicit conditional subroutine jumps.*
4. *Interrupt programming* is simpler with 6800 (and 650X) than with 8080A and 9080A, which require an explicit instruction to save even the status register. *Z-80 has context switching.* 8080-type machines have *more and more convenient stack instructions* than 6800 and 650X.

On a more subjective basis, **the 6800's neat, compact instruction set is very easy to learn,** which is not true for the 8080's larger instruction set and clumsy instruction mnemonics. Both Motorola and Intel offer PL-1-type higher-order languages and excellent prototype-development systems.

Hardware-wise, the original 8080A is handicapped by its *multiple power-supply voltages* and possibly by the need for an 8228 command-signal decoder (although this also supplies buffer amplifiers, which may be needed anyway). *6800 and 8080A accessory chips are about equally useful;* Intel's 8255 is a 24-bit I/O port, while Motorola's 6820 has 16 bits, if this is a consideration. The newer 6800 and 8080 derivatives (650X, 9080A, 8085, Z-80, Sec. 6-8) all reduce system chip count.

6-10. 8-Bit NMOS Chips: Signetics 2650 (Ref. 24). The **Signetics 2650** CPU chip has **six 8-bit general-purpose registers in two sets of three context-switched by a status-register bit, plus a common accumulator** and a **seven-level hardware stack** for return addresses. There are zero, negative, carry, and overflow flags, plus a half-carry flat for decimal operations (Sec. 2-7). 15 address bits can address up to 32K bytes divided into 8K pages, with the following **memory-addressing modes:**

Absolute current-page addressing (up to 8K bytes, 3-byte instructions)
Indirect (via current page) addressing (up to 32K bytes, 3-byte instructions)
Indexed and postindexed indirect addressing, using a 13-bit address and

one of six index registers (3-byte instructions).   Index registers have only 8 bits, but **automatic preincrementing** and **predecrementing** can be specified (postincrementing would be even better, Sec. 6-9).
Direct and indirect relative addressing within -64 to $+63$ bytes (2-byte instructions)
Immediate addressing (2-byte instructions)

The NMOS processor needs only **a single 5-V power supply** and **a single-phase clock; all processor signals are TTL-compatible.** There are 8 bi-directional data lines and 15 address lines.   In *small* systems, only a few control signals require buffer amplifiers.

External devices can be addressed either as memory locations (more flexible instructions) or with special I/O instructions (fewer address bits needed).   The 2650 also has *1-bit sense and control lines* for simple logic and for serial I/O operations.   There is **a true vectored interrupt system** with up to 128 levels, and three processor registers may be context-switched by a status-register-loading instruction.

Manufacturer-supplied software includes a two-pass cross assembler (not a macroassembler) and a simulator, both written in standard FORTRAN.

The 2650 instruction set is probably the most flexible among the 8-bit NMOS chips.   It includes **indirect** and indexed addressing (albeit with 8-bit index registers, see Sec. 6-9) and lacks only a one-instruction **PUSH** operation. While the original 2650 was relatively slow (register/register **ADD** 4.8 μsec, memory/register **ADD** 9.6 μsec), the new depletion-mode 2650A-1 is faster (3 μsec and 6 μsec).   A FORTRAN compiler exists.

6-11.   8-Bit NMOS Chips: Fairchild F-8.   Compared to other 8-bit NMOS microcomputers, the **Fairchild F-8** chip set is less concerned with implementing a general-purpose minicomputer architecture than with reducing chip count and chip complexity for small dedicated systems.   Thus, the F-8 **3850** CPU chip includes 64 bytes of RAM ("scratchpad") addressed via a 6-bit "indirect scratchpad address register" (ISAR), and a 16-bit I/O port. Each 1K-byte ROM (**3851** program storage unit, PSV) has another 16-bit I/O port, a vectored-interrupt controller, a real-time clock (interval timer), a pointer register ("data counter," DCO), and its own separate program counter and subroutine-linkage register ("stack register").   **3859** combines 3850 and 3851.   The F-8 chip set further includes static-memory and dynamic-memory interfaces (**3853 SMI** and **3852 DMI**), each containing a duplicate program counter, linkage register, and pointer register, plus an extra register to store pointer-register contents ("data counter," DC1).   There is also a DMA-interface chip.   These memory interfaces work with inexpensive general-purpose memory chips connected to an 8-bit bidirectional data bus.

Program counters, linkage registers, and pointer registers in the various memory interfaces have 16 bits for 64K-byte addressing, but communicate

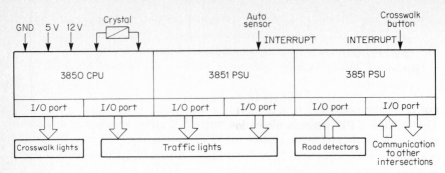

Fig. 6-9. This traffic-light controller illustrates the low chip count possible with small F-8 systems. (*Fairchild Semiconductor.*)

with the CPU through an 8-bit connection to associated 8-bit scratchpad locations. Duplicated program counters, linkage registers, and pointer registers normally contain the same addresses. The *only* addressing mode for external memory is **autoincrement addressing via pointer register DCO.** *There are no explicit stack instructions for subroutine nesting* (Refs. 6 and 28).

Figure 6-9 shows an F-8 microcomputer application to a sophisticated traffic light controller, which requires only three chips (two with 3859). Two power-supply voltages (-5 V and $+12$ V) are needed. The success of the F-8's "distributed" architecture and simple instruction set will depend on final system prices. Programming is unconventional, and it is not a foregone conclusion that simpler chips are significantly cheaper.

6-12. An Inexpensive PMOS Chip: National Semiconductor SC/MP. SC/MP brings a relatively sophisticated and easy-to-learn instruction set to the low-cost mass-production applications area at the expense of speed (16 μsec register/register **ADD**, 38 μsec memory/register **ADD**). The PMOS CPU includes tri-state buffers for 8 bidirectional data-bus lines and 12 address lines. Four additional address bits can set a chip-select (page) register via the data bus. SC/MP has an on-chip clock and can work directly with TTL or 5-V CMOS logic, using a $+5$-V supply in addition to the -12 V required for the CPU. Small systems (say a CPU with a 2K-byte memory) need no external bus-signal amplifiers. A new NMOS SC/MP is twice as fast as the PMOS version.

SC/MP has an **8-bit accumulator** with an 8-bit extension for shifting and serial I/O, plus **six 16-bit pointer registers** and a 16-bit program counter. Status-register bits include two sense flags and three control bits for external devices as well as CPU carry and overflow flags. SC/MP's two-byte memory-reference instructions permit

Relative addressing
Indexed addressing

Pointer-register addressing, with automatic addition of the offset byte to the pointer contents after execution (implements automatic postincrementing/decrementing by the offset)

Immediate addressing

all using an 8-bit address byte (-128 to $+127$). Effective addresses will not cross the boundary of a 2^{12} (4K)-byte page, but will "wrap around." The SC/MP CPU permits **direct low-cost serial I/O** and has a two-byte **DELAY** instruction which implements delays between 13 and 131,593 microcycles (typically 2 μsec each), as determined by the second instruction byte and the accumulator contents.

SC/MP's single **interrupt** interchanges the contents of the program counter and a pointer register previously loaded with the trap address. A similar scheme implements subroutine jumps; there are no explicit stack instructions.

6-13. A CMOS System: RCA COSMAC. COSMAC's really important feature is its **low-power, high-noise-immunity CMOS logic.** A single power supply provides 4 to 6 V (CDP 1802 CD processor) or 3 to 12 V (CDP 1802 D) at only 0.5 to 0.6 W. The 1802 has a built-in scratchpad of **sixteen 8-bit register pairs,** which can serve as **incrementable/decrementable 16-bit pointers** or **program counters.** Unconventional *8-bit* memory-reference instructions use 4 bits to select a 16-bit pointer register for addressing. Most 1802 instructions execute within two 1.25-μsec "machine cycles"; a few instructions take three cycles. Branching instructions can directly test four I/O status flags. Simple DMA transfers can use scratchpad pointer registers as address and data counters ("built-in" DMA). A faster CMOS/SOS COSMAC exists.

6-14. A Fast Bipolar 8-Bit System: Scientific Microsystems SMS 300. The **SMS Microcontroller** is an all-bipolar (Schottky/TTL) 8-bit microcomputer system comprising

a bipolar 8-bit microprocessor ("Interpreter" chip)

entirely separate program and data memories (16-bit instructions and 8-bit data)

a set of 8-bit, tri-state **I/O-port registers** ("interface-vector bytes")

(Fig. 6-10). These chips are sold individually or combined in a 64-terminal hybrid package. **Overlapped access to the separate instruction and data memories makes SMS 300 very fast: every instruction is fetched and executed in 250 nsec** (300 nsec for older models). The instruction set is not designed for general-purpose computation (e.g., negation and subtraction must use **XOR**), but *for fast retrieval, moving, shifting, and masking of data and control bytes in peripheral controllers or communications systems.* If the programming inconvenience can be tolerated, Microcontroller programs, though longer, may still execute more quickly than more efficient NMOS-processor

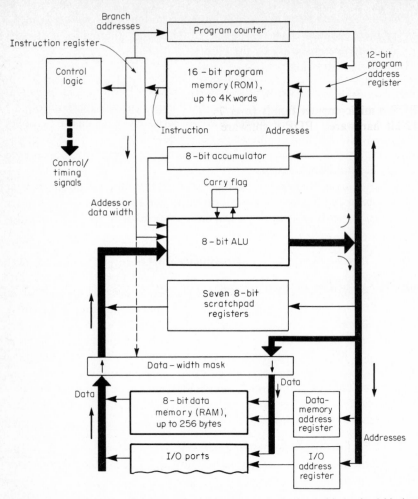

Fig. 6-10. The SMS Microcontroller had entirely separate memories and buses for 8-bit data and for complete 16-bit instructions. This permits the fast bipolar processor to execute every instruction in 250 nsec. I/O-port bits receive and transmit interface status and control signals, as well as data, at program-selected times.

programs.   Some instructions permit clever manipulation of individual data bits.   A fairly advanced assembly language (MCMAC) is available, as are a cross assembler and simulator.

The SMS Microcontroller had no explicit interrupt input.   A RESET input will, however, restart the program at location 0 in program memory.   Such a reset operation can initiate a status-flag-polling sequence (Sec. 4-11), or external priority-arbitration logic could chip-select different program-memory chips containing different starting sequences to simulate vectored interrupts.

SYSTEMS WITH 12-BIT AND
16-BIT PROCESSORS

6-15. Digital Equipment Corporation PDP-8 and Intersil 6100. An enormous amount of useful software developed for the hugely successful PDP-8 minicomputer family (over 70,000 sold) perpetuates its now-obsolete 12-bit hardware. PDP-8 software includes remarkably good operating systems, macroassemblers, FORTRAN, BASIC, and FOCAL developed by various software houses as well as DEC, plus a large user-group library of programs for every conceivable application. DEC's PDP-8 system has been updated several times. The most recent MSI version **(PDP-8A)**, with or without an optional accessory floating-point-arithmetic processor (Sec. 2-27), serves in the company's packaged educational computers, small-business computers, and word-processing systems, and in many industrial-control and laboratory systems. The **Intersil 6100 12-bit CMOS micro-processor chip** executes all PDP-8 instructions except for those associated with the hardware multiply/divide option and is, thus, largely software-compatible with the PDP-8. Intersil also has an accessory 50-μsec multiply/divide chip (6103).

The 6100's bus system, however, time-multiplexes 12-bit addresses and data (and thus requires address latches in its CMOS memory chips), while PDP-8's OMNIBUS® has separate 12-bit memory-address, memory-data, and I/O-data buses. Note that bus signals for different PDP-8 models are not identical. In particular, early-model PDP-8s had separate I/O input and output data lines, and the earliest PDP-8s had negative diode-transistor logic instead of TTL.

Intersil 6100 has an *on-chip clock* and uses *a single +5-V power supply.* 6100A uses +10 V and is twice as fast (2.5 μsec versus 5 μsec memory/accumulator **ADD**), which is as fast as the MSI PDP-8A. An extended-temperature-range version works between $-55°C$ and $+125°C$.

PDP-8/6100 has **a single 8-bit accumulator** and **one extra register** (MQ) which can receive or transmit data only through the accumulator. Figure 2-6b shows the instruction formats. There are only six memory-reference instructions (**ADD, STORE AND CLEAR ACCUMULATOR, AND, INCREMENT AND SKIP IF ZERO, JUMP, JUMP TO SUBROUTINE**). The only addressing modes are **direct and indirect addressing on page 0 and on the current page** (Sec. 2-13). An external page register can be added for addressing more than the $2^{12} = 4K$ locations accessible through simple indirect addressing. I/O instructions are 12-bit instructions incorporating a device address. In addition to transfers to and from the accumulator, *6100 and the newer PDP-8's can read or add I/O data into the program counter to produce absolute or relative jumps.* There is also a skip/sense line (Sec. 4-7).

PDP-8 has single **interrupt** trapping to location 0, which contains a jump to the interrupt-service routine (Sec. 4-9). With multiple interrupts, the service routine can read or add an interrupt-controller address output into the program counter and thus branch to a desired address. There are no provisions for automatic status saving, but PDP-8/6100 memory-extension options provide a storage register to save carry flag and memory page, which are then stored in memory as needed.

Both PDP-8 and 6100 can use DMA. PDP-8 (but not 6100) has a built-in facility to use two memory locations as automatically incremented DMA address and word counters, as described in Sec. 4-22.

6-16. National Semiconductor PACE. 16-bit microprocessors typically time-share bus connections between 16-bit bidirectional data and 16-bit addresses latched in an external address register. 16-bit processors usually

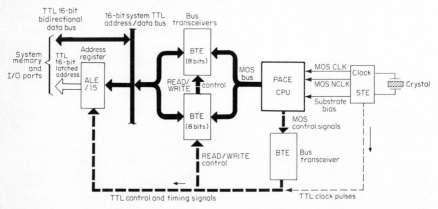

Fig. 6-11a. A 16-bit microcomputer system. A 16-bit address register on the time-shared processor bus is used to create a 16-bit TTL-level address bus. Bus transceivers buffer TTL data-bus and control-signal lines. (*National Semiconductor PACE system.*)

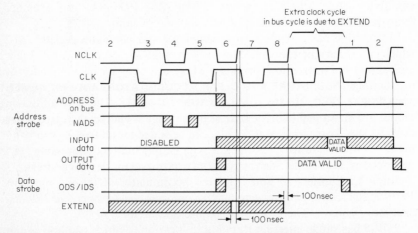

Fig. 6-11b. PACE multiplexed-bus timing. Shaded areas indicate timing tolerances. An EXTEND input to the processor delays the start of the following bus cycle by one clock cycle. (*Based on National Semiconductor PACE manual.*)

use enough memory to require bus amplifiers in any case; *the address register and a set of data-bus amplifiers will create external power-driven address and data buses with convenient TTL or CMOS logic levels* (Figs. 6-11*a* and 6-11*b*).

A **PACE system** thus includes a **CPU chip, address-latch chips (ALE),** and **bidirectional transceivers (BTE),** which also translate PMOS logic levels to TTL levels. PACE requires −12 and +5 V and a **clock chip (STE),** which also supplies a low-current +3 V substrate voltage. Slow PMOS logic (8.5 μsec register/register **ADD**) implements a rather advanced, mini-computer-like instruction set, including

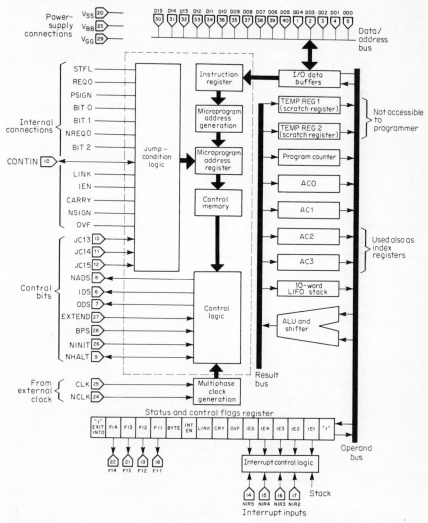

Fig. 6-12. PACE processor block diagram and terminations. (*National Semiconductor Corp.*)

direct and indirect addressing on page 0
direct and indirect relative addressing (-128 to 127 words)
indexed and preindexed/indirect addressing with an 8-bit (-128- to $+127$-word) offset

but not all memory-reference instructions can use all addressing modes.

Word addressing is used, but a status-register bit can be set to make instructions into byte-operation instructions. I/O devices are addressed as memory locations. Page 0 is the first 256 words in memory or, if a control-input bit (BPS) is set, page 0 is split between the first and last 128 words in memory, e.g., between ROM and RAM, memory and devices.

All PACE instructions fit a 16-bit format. There are **four 16-bit accumulators, two of which can serve as index registers,** and a 16-bit program counter. A **10-level hardware stack,** normally used for subroutine and interrupt return addresses, also works with accumulator PUSH and POP instructions. There is an automatic *stack-overflow interrupt*. Conditional branching uses **SKIP**.

PACE has *four built-in control-bit outputs* and *three status-line inputs*, which can be tested with conditional **SKIP** instructions. The CPU chip also has a complete **vectored priority-interrupt controller** with four request inputs. PACE subsystems are also sold as card sets.

Manufacturer-supplied software includes a cross macroassembler, a PL-1-type language (SM/PL), and a floppy-disk operating system for prototype development.

6-17. General Instruments CP 1600. Used in many Honeywell process-control systems, **CP 1600** has a 16-bit program counter and a **16-bit stack pointer,** plus **six 16-bit general-purpose registers** usable as accumulators or pointers. A **status register** has regular N, Z, O, and C flags (Sec. 2-7). The external bus of the 40-pin device is *time-shared* between 16-bit addresses and 16-bit data, so that an external address register is needed. I/O devices are addressed as memory locations. *CP 1600 needs $+12$, $+5$, and -3 V, bidirectional bus-driver amplifiers, and an external two-phase clock.*

Unlike PACE, which has a 16-bit ALU, CP 1600 internally manipulates 8-bit bytes, but fast NMOS logic and clever pipelining (Ref. 15) produce respectable speed (2.4 μsec for a 16-bit register/register **ADD**, 3.2 μsec memory/register **ADD**). With only 10 instruction-register bits, memory references are limited to **direct, via register, stack, and immediate addressing.** Indexing can be simulated with a register/register **ADD** into a pointer register. There is *a full set of relative-address conditional branching instructions* (-128 to $+127$ words), plus **JUMP** via pointer and relative with a 16-bit address. CP 1600 can implement 2-bit as well as 1-bit shifts. There is no byte addressing, but a **SWAP BYTES** instruction. A future model may have a full 16-bit instruction register and more addressing modes.

CP 1600 has provisions for **vectored interrupts** and a **simple DMA interface.** *The processor can also interrogate 16 device-status lines by a special conditional-branch instruction* (**BEXT N**, **N** = 0 to 15), *which transmits a 4-bit address code over four externally decoded sense lines;* a fifth line returns the response from any one of up to 16 sense gates (Sec. 4-7).

6-18. Three Processors with Full Minicomputer Instruction Sets. (a) Western Digital MCP 1600. Unlike other NMOS processors, **MCP 1600** is not a single-chip unit, but a **multichip system** comprising

a 16-bit **register/ALU (RALU) chip (1611B** "data chip")
a **microprogram-control-unit (MCU) chip (1621B** "control chip")
one to four control-memory (CROM) chip(s) (1631B "microm")

(Fig. 6-13). The user can microprogram a complete minicomputer instruction set of his choice by using different mask-programmed CROMs. In addition, two programmed logic arrays (PLAs) in the MCU must be mask-programmed to translate instructions into microprogram starting addresses (Sec. 2-31).

The RALU "pipelines" 16-bit words in terms of successive 8-bit bytes, using 26 8-bit registers and an 8-bit ALU, but the processor is quite fast (3.5 μsec for a 16-bit register/register **ADD**. The external processor bus is time-shared between 16-bit addresses and 16-bit data.

The multichip scheme permits remarkably sophisticated microprogramming. MCP 1600 can implement *the entire instruction set of a PDP-11 minicomputer, including optional floating-point instructions* (Digital Equipment Corporation LSI-11 and PDP-11/03, Sec. 7-6) (Ref. 27).

(b) Data General mN601 and Texas Instruments 9900. Data General mN601 and **Texas Instruments TMS 9900** are single-chip 16-bit NMOS processors which implement the respective instruction sets of Data General NOVA 3 and Texas Instruments 990-series minicomputers, which include **MULTIPLY/DIVIDE** and will be discussed in Secs. 7-13 to 7-15. Texas Instruments **SBP 9900** is a faster I^2L version of the 9900 (Table 6-1; see also Secs. 7-13 to 7-15).

mN601 has a multiplexed 16-bit bus, and 9900s have separate data and address lines (TILINE bus, Sec. 7-15). In addition, both mN601 and 9900s have a novel feature, viz., *an economical serial I/O connection which is fast enough to feed most parallel 8-bit and 16-bit I/O interfaces.* 9900s do this with only three lines (serial input, serial output, serial-line clock) and use 12 regular address-bus lines to select I/O devices for serial data transfers (Fig. 7-13a); serial bit rate is 1.5 MHz for TMS 9900.

The Data General System is more complicated. It transmits device addresses as well as 16-bit data at 8.3 MHz over two differential pairs of

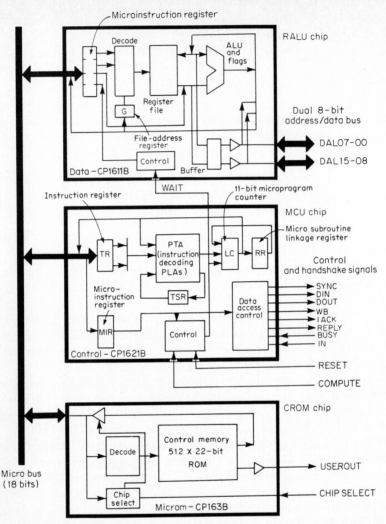

Fig. 6-13. Western Digital MCP 1600 multichip processor.   Two or three CROM chips may be used.   (*Based on MCP 1600 manual.*)

bidirectional serial I/O lines in response to regular NOVA-type I/O instructions (Sec. 7-14).   A 40-pin *I/O controller* (**mN603**) decodes the device address, performs serial/parallel/serial conversion, and also comprises logic for power-up initialization, interrupt masking, and DMA block transfers. The mN602 I/O system further requires *clock amplifiers* and *I/O-line transceivers*, which permit up to 100 ft bus length.

Fairchild **9440** implements the 16-bit NOVA even faster with a modified I²L process.

BIT-SLICE MICROPROCESSORS

6-19. Introduction. The National Semiconductor IMP. To simplify chip-*size* and chip-*termination* problems in larger and faster microcomputers, one uses multichip processors configured to use as few types of LSI chips as possible. Control circuits, viz., a **microprogram control unit (MCU)** and **control ROMs (CROMs),** are separated out to permit flexible microprogramming (see also Sec. 6-18a). Referring to a CPU block diagram like Fig. 2-2, the processor registers, register gates (multiplexers), and the arithmetic/logic unit (ALU) are "sliced" into **2-bit** or **4-bit register/ALU chips (RALUs).** In this way, four 4-bit RALUs can make up a 16-bit processor, six 4-bit RALUs a 24-bit processor, etc., with appropriate MCU, CROMs, and as little extra logic as possible.

The National Semiconductor **IMP series** offered the first bit-slice LSI components. *An IMP uses 4-bit RALUs and a combination PCU/CROM chip in the classical three-bus mincomputer architecture of Fig. 2-2.* The IMP register complement, "sliced" into each 4-bit RALU, is exactly that of the (later) National Semiconductor PACE processor (Sec. 6-16), except that IMP has 16-word hardware stack and no split page 0. In standard 16-bit IMP systems,[1] factory-programmed CROMs implement the 16-bit PACE instructions (Sec. 6-16), plus a number of extra instructions, including *two-word* direct-address and indexed memory references and a few *double-precision* and *byte operations.* Options obtainable with extra CROMs include *multiplication, division,* and even *floating-point operations.* IMP prototype-development systems permit both *computer-controlled PROM loading* and substitution of *writable control memory* for a CROM to implement new instructions, and a substantial amount of software exists. Slow PMOS logic (8 μsec register/register **ADD**), which also necessitates level-changing bus transceivers and latches as for PACE, makes IMP systems obsolescent. A possible bipolar version could benefit from existing IMP software, but would compete against newer bipolar bit slices with more processor registers.

6-20. Bipolar RALUs. Bit-sliced processors can use CMOS (see also Sec. 6-22) and silicon-on-sapphire (SOS), but **most bit-slice chips employ bipolar logic for speed,** mainly Schottky/TTL, I^2L, or combination techniques. ECL bit slices are even faster, but dissipate more power and cost more (Sec. 6-22). *Bipolar bit slices are the basic components of medium- to high-power minicomputers* and of various medium-sized 24-bit to 64-bit

---

[1] 24-bit and 32-bit systems can have longer offset bytes. There are also 4-bit and 8-bit IMP kits with slightly different instructions.

processors.   The second important production application is to *peripheral controllers* and *communications processors* with data rates too high for NMOS microprocessors.   Bipolar bit-slice CPUs need more chips than NMOS microprocessors and must usually be microprogrammed by their users, who tend to be computer designers rather than general-purpose microprocessor users. But some pre-microprogrammed bit-slice kits exist (Secs. 6-19 and 6-21), and more are sure to be available.

Figures 6-14*a*, 6-14*b*, and 6-14*c* show the features of a popular type of 4-bit Schottky/TTL RALU slice, the **Monolithic Memories 6701/5701**[1] and **Advanced Micro Devices 2901.**

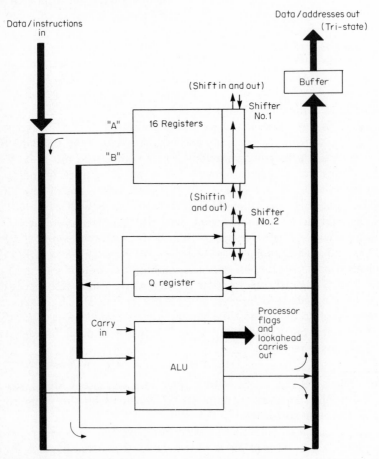

Fig. 6-14a. Functional block diagram of a Monolithic Memories 6701/5701 or Advanced Micro Devices 2901 4-bit RALU slice.

[1] Military or extended-temperature-range ($-55°C$ to $+125°C$) version of 6701, about 20 percent slower.   6701 and 2901 are similar, but not pin-compatible.

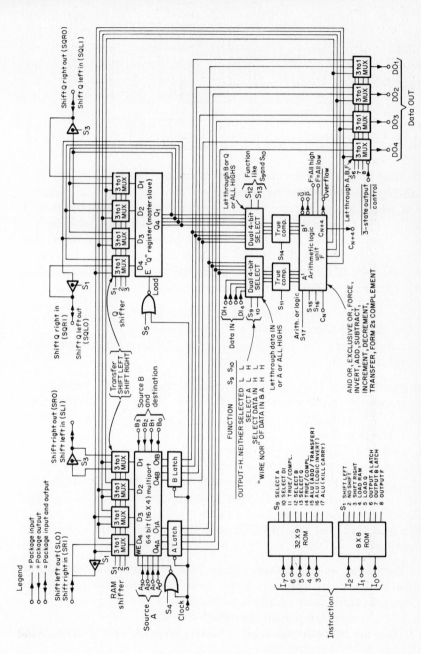

Fig. 6-14b. Monolithic Memories 6701 4-bit RALU slice.   *(Monolithic Memories, Inc.)*

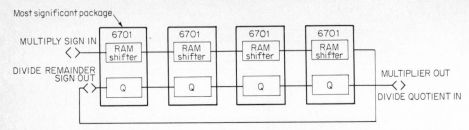

Fig. 6-14c. Interconnection of 6701 scratchpad and Q-register shifters for convenient double-register shifting, multiplication, and division. (*Monolithic Memories, Inc.*)

Tri-state bus transceivers can be used to create a bidirectional data bus; an **off-chip bus-address register is needed.** There are **16 general registers,** two of which normally serve as the program counter and stack pointer (if any). The **Q register** is useful as a register extension for double-register shifting, multiplication, and division; **dual shifters** permit simultaneous shifting of two registers (Fig. 6-14c; see also Fig. 6-17). External **carry-lookahead logic** is recommended for faster addition and subtraction (Sec. 1-15). Referring to Fig. 6-14b, control-word inputs include

4 bits (AO-A3) selecting one of 16 registers as source A
4 bits (BO-B3) selecting one of 16 registers as source B
8 function-control bits (IO-I7), which are *encoded* to save chip terminations
and to simplify microprogramming

The resulting microinstructions conveniently implement all register and register/memory arithmetic/logic instructions of typical minicomputers (Chap. 2). Note that the ALU can access *an arbitrary pair of registers* in one microinstruction.

Each 40-pin 6701 or 2901 chip is equivalent to over 1,000 TTL gates and dissipates about 900 mW from a single +5-V power supply. A typical RALU operation (from receipt of microinstruction to data settled in destination), exclusive of carry- and shift-bit propagation between RALUs, takes at least 130 nsec for 6701 and 100 nsec for 6701-1 and 2901.

The **Intel 3002** 2-*bit* Schottky/TTL RALU chip (Fig. 6-15) has a different architecture:

1. There is an **on-chip address register,** and a separate memory-address bus. There are two data-input buses. Tri-state data inputs and outputs easily create a bidirectional memory data bus.
2. There is no on-chip microinstruction decoding.
3. There are **10 scratchpad registers** and an **accumulator.** *Only one ALU input can access scratchpad registers.*
4. A **mask-bus input** is useful for entering immediate operands from the microprogram.

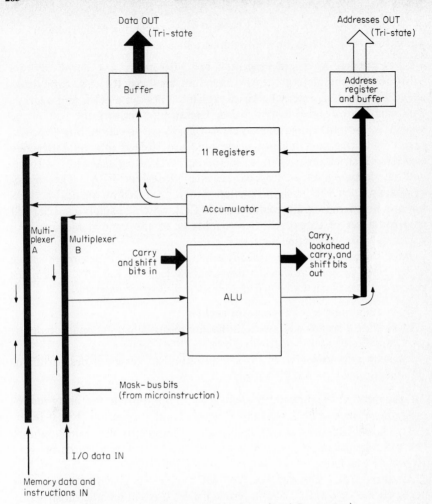

Fig. 6-15. Intel 3002 2-bit RALU slice.   (*Intel Corporation.*)

Items 1 and 2 give the 3002 a speed advantage (operation time as low as 50 nsec) in peripheral controllers and communications processors primarily concerned with data moving. But *6701 and 2901 seem to be more suitable for use in general-purpose CPUs* because, unlike the 3002,

1. They can select different scratchpad registers for *both* ALU inputs.
2. *They have an explicit* **SUBTRACT** *microinstruction.*
3. They have *2s-complement overflow flags.*
4. Their dual shifters simplify double-register shifting, and thus multiplication and division (Fig. 6-14c).

In general, 6701/2901-type RALUs will need fewer microinstructions for general-purpose arithmetic and comparisons than a 3002.

6-21.   Complete Bit-Sliced Processors and Microprogram Control. Figure 6-16 shows a complete processor including **bit-sliced RALUs, carry-look-ahead logic,** and an **external address register.** Besides a **clock** and **address, data, and control-signal buffers and/or latches** (not shown), the rest of the system is the **microprogrammed-control logic.** Instruction bits (opcode, register-selection, and address-mode bits) are latched into an **instruction register.** Instructions generate *microprogram starting addresses* with or without decoding by an **"opcode-cracker" ROM or PLA.** The microprogram sequence for each instruction is then produced by the next-address logic in the **microprogram-control unit (MCU),** which is usually a special LSI chip (or a set of chips). Either the MCU or the control memory will contain a **microinstruction address register.**

Bit-sliced microprocessors typically employ "horizontal" microprogramming, as described in Sec. 2-11. The **next-address logic** of Fig. 2-9 determines successive microinstruction-word addresses in control memory

- by incrementing a **microprogram counter**
- by **reading a branch address from the microinstruction,** unconditionally or conditioned by processor-flag bits
- by using a **hardware stack** for saving return addresses of nested micro-subroutines

An **interrupt-line input** causes branching to an appropriate vectoring microprogram at the end of the current-instruction microprogram (Fig. 6-18*b*).

8 to 12 control-address bits are usually sufficient; typical minicomputer instruction sets can be obtained with 256 microinstruction words between 16 and 64 bits long.

Advanced Micro Devices Am 2909 MCU chips implement the complete next-address logic of Fig. 2-9*b* in terms of *4-bit slices* of the microinstruction address. Less sophisticated next-address logic fits a single-chip MCU. **Signetics 8X02** generates complete *10-bit addresses* and can produce unconditional and conditional branching, conditional-skip microinstructions, and micro-subroutine jumps and returns with a four-level stack, using three control bits and 10 branch-address bits. **Monolithic Memories** 67110 produces a 9-bit address and has no micro-subroutine stack, but only a one-level linkage register. But 67110 has a 5-bit *microloop counter* and *on-chip hardwired control logic for conditional shifting,* which is useful for multiplication and division.

Intel 3001, the single-chip MCU developed for use with the 3002 RALUs (Sec. 6-20), is entirely different. *There is no microprogram counter or stack.* Every microinstruction is in effect a branching instruction which determines

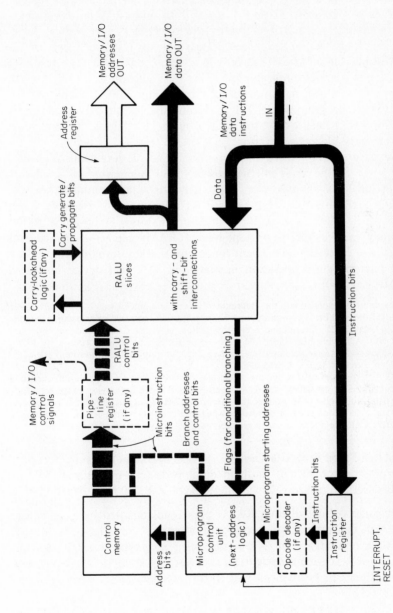

Fig. 6-16. A complete bit-sliced processor. An external address register is shown (not needed with 3002). An external instruction register latches the computer instruction, which may or may not need decoding by a ROM or PLA.

287

the next address in conjunction with instruction bits and flag conditions. 9 control-memory address bits are latched into an on-chip address register divided into 4 *column bits* and 5 *row bits* to address a *two-dimensional array* of control words.   To simplify the single-chip next-address logic, typical microinstruction sequences branch only to restricted *jump sets* in this two-dimensional array (e.g., only in a row or column).   The resulting constraints make microprogramming of the 3001 quite difficult (Refs. 19, 20).

Figure 6-17 shows a complete bit-sliced 16-bit CPU which uses an appropriately programmed ROM to decode the instructions of a simple minicomputer as well as for the control memory.   Simple discrete logic serves for next-address generation.

Manufacturers of bit-sliced microprocessors provide **development software** in the form of the **cross-microassemblers** and **microprogram emulators** running on time-share-service computers or minicomputers.   Small-computer *macroassemblers* can be used for microprogram assembly if the control-word length is a multiple of 8 or 16 bits.   Stand-alone **ROM simulators,** i.e., keyboard- or tape-loaded RAMs replacing the control memory, are especially convenient for microprogram development.   They permit microprogram operation in real time, with real device interfaces (see also Sec. 5-30).

As examples of applications, the Interdata 6/16 minicomputer (Sec. 7-2) employs 2901 chips, and Honeywell Level 6 machines uses 6701s in the CPU and 3002s for communications processing (Sec. 7-12).   Monolithic Memories sells a bit-sliced CPU emulating the Data General NOVA3 architecture (Sec. 7-3) with a 900-nsec register/register ADD, using 6701s. Intel 3000-series chips have been used to emulate a Digital Equipment Corporation PDP-11/40 (Sec. 7-6) at Carnegie-Mellon University.

NOTE: Microprocessor MCUs are themselves microprocessors capable of executing programs (including branches, loops, subroutines, and interrupt-service routines) which produce no arithmetic/logic operations, but only control-word output.   An MCU and control memory can stand alone as a **microcontroller** which can control external devices, experiments, or manufacturing operations *without* a real computer.

6-22.   High-Speed Processor Design.

RALU operation times (from receipt of microinstruction bits to result in on-chip destination register) for the RALUs described in Sec. 6-20 vary between 50 and 200 nsec, depending on

  the specific version of each RALU chip used (denoted by a suffix like 6701-1; consult current specification sheets)
  the time needed for *carry and shift-bit propagation* through multiple RALUs.   This increases with the processor word length; carry-propagation time can be reduced with carry-lookahead logic (Sec. 1-15 and Fig. 6-16)
  worst-case effects of board layout

If we add the time needed for next-address generation and microinstruction fetch, we obtain **microinstruction times** between 120 and 350 nsec.   We can,

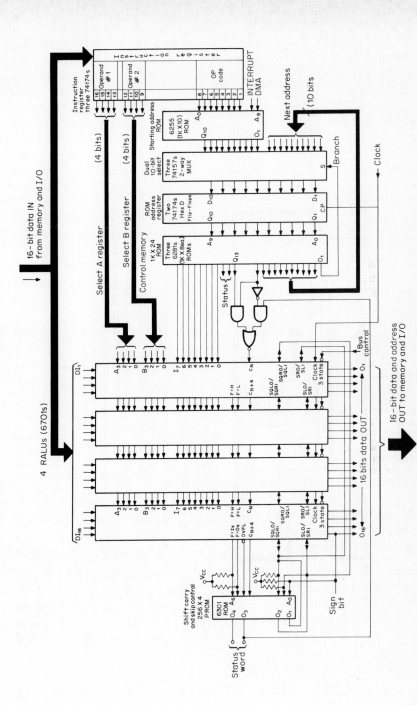

Fig. 6-17. A simple 16-bit processor using a bipolar ROM for instruction decoding. (*Monolithic Memories, Inc.*)

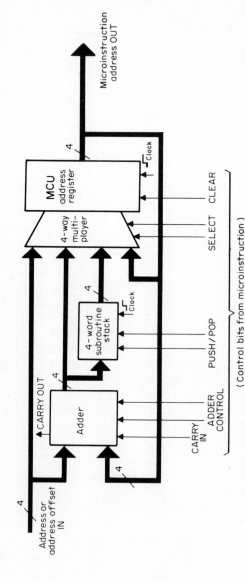

Fig. 6-18a. Texas Instruments SN 54S/74S 482 4-bit MCU slice. 4 bits of the next microinstruction address can be obtained from the current address, as an external branch address (usually a microprogram starting address), from a subroutine stack, or from an adder. The latter can increment the current address, or it can add a positive or negative branch-address offset (relative addressing). This is preferable to the OR-input address modification shown in Fig. 2-10. The next address can also be set to zero (e.g., for initialization).

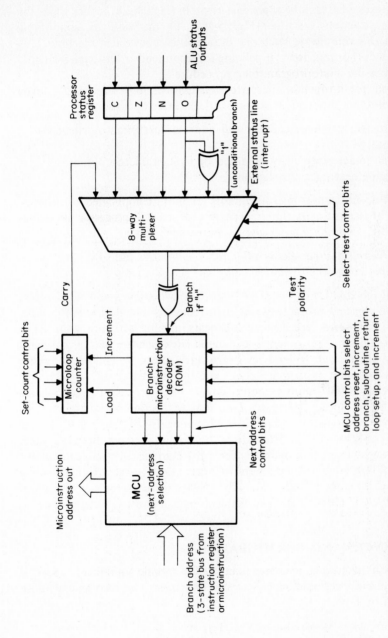

Fig. 6-18b. Used with MCUs like those in Figs. 2-10 or 6-18a, this circuit selects 16 different test conditions for branching, subroutine, and subroutine return. Tests include four status flags, unsigned COMPARE (Sec. 2-22), termination of a microloop, an interrupt-request line (typically checked once per microprogram), unconditional branching, and their logical complements. More elaborate bit-sliced MCUs may contain some or all of this logic on the MCU chips.

291

however, *overlap microinstruction fetch and execution times* by fetching the next microinstruction into a **pipeline register (lookahead buffer)** while the current instruction executes (Fig. 6-16). In the case of conditional branches, one can always fetch one branch and replace it if the branching condition was not satisfied.   Pipelining is recommended, although it slightly complicates the microprogramming procedure.

With simple horizontal-microprogram control logic (Sec. 2-31), even simple computer instructions require at least three operations:

1. Increment program counter and address next (macro)instruction in memory
2. Fetch (macro)instruction and decode it, start microprogram
3. Execute next microinstruction

To speed up horizontal microprograms for more complicated operations, **we try to implement more simultaneous ("concurrent") processor operations** by providing *extra data paths and hardware*, such as

1. *hardware serial/parallel or all-parallel multipliers* (Ref. 18)
2. *a separate adder for address (indexing) computations*

Note that the RALUs of Fig. 6-14, with their two shifters and ALU access to any two registers, promote more concurrency than the RALU in Fig. 6-15. **Fairchild 9400-series processor components** include separate **4-bit ALU slices, 16-register slices, address-arithmetic slices, shifter/masker/constant-generator slices,** and **16-level hardware-stack slices** to enable computer designers to obtain more concurrency and thus higher speed.

Motorola 10800 emitter-coupled-logic microprocessor components provide higher speed (50 to 65 nsec RALU operation) at higher cost. Higher power dissipation requires double-wide IC packages for separate **4-bit ALU slices, 4-bit-register slices,** and **4-bit memory-interface slices** (address register and data buffer).   The ALU chip has only an accumulator and a holding latch.   A minimum of internal microinstruction decoding speeds operation (as in Fig. 6-15).   The 10800 chip set includes an advanced bit-sliced MCU **(10801),** carry-lookahead logic, and a clock chip.

REFERENCES AND BIBLIOGRAPHY

See also manufacturers' reference manuals for specific equipment.   Several journals publish periodic *microprocessor directories;* we recommend those published by *EDN*.

1. *An Introduction to Microcomputers* (2 volumes), Adam Osborne and Associates, Inc., Berkeley, Calif., 1976.
2. Souček, B.: *Microprocessors and Microcomputers,* Wiley, New York, 1976.
3. Boehn, B. W.: Software and Its Impact, *Datamation,* May 1973.

4. Benchmark Program Evaluation of Available Microprocessors, *AHS Report* 75-651, A. H. Systems, Inc., Chatsworth, Calif., 1975. Some programs listed in this report have since been amended.
5. Motorola's 6800 vs. Intel's 8080, *Short-Course Notes*, Integrated Computer Systems, Inc., Culver City, Calif., 1975.
6. Marchin, P.: Multilevel Nesting of Subroutines in a One-Level Microprocessor, *Comput. Des.*, February 1976.
7. *Microprocessor Applications Manual*, Motorola Semiconductor Products, Inc., McGraw-Hill, New York, 1975.
8. Garrow, R., et al.: The " Super Component ": the One-Board Computer with Programmable I/O, *Electronics*, Feb. 5, 1976.
9. Vasques, R. M.: Design Worksheet Can Generate Least-Part System, Best Addressing, *Electronics*, May 27, 1976.
10. Cushman, R. H.: Single-Chip Microprocessors Move into the 16-Bit Arena, *EDN*, Feb. 20, 1975.
11. *Small Computer Handbook*, Digital Equipment Corp., Maynard, Mass. (current edition).
12. *Introduction to Programming*, Digital Equipment Corp., Maynard, Mass. (current edition).
13. *Programming Languages*, Digital Equipment Corp., Maynard, Mass. (current edition).
14. Hilbrun, J. L., and P. M. Julich: *Microcomputers/Microprocessors: Hardware, Software, and Applications*, Prentice-Hall, Englewood Cliffs, N.J., 1976.

Bit-Sliced Microprocessors

15. Rattner, J., et al.: Bipolar LSI Computing Elements Usher in New Era of Digital Design, *Electronics*, Sept. 5, 1974.
16. Wyland, D. C.: Design Your Own Microprocessor, *Electron. Des.*, Sept. 27, 1975.
17. ————: Increase Microcomputer Efficiency with Interrupt and DMA, *Electron. Des.*, Nov. 8, 1975.
18. Mick, J. R., and J. Springer: Single-Chip Multiplier, *Electronics*, May 13, 1976.
19. 3000-Series *Reference Manual* and *Microprogramming Manual*, Intel Corporation, Santa Clara, Calif. (current edition).
20. Wakerly, J., et al.: Placement of Microinstructions in a Two-Dimensional Address Space, *MICRO-8 Proc.*, Catalog CH 1053-86, IEEE, New York, 1975.
21. Muething, G. F.: Designing Maximum Performance into Bit-slice Microprocessors, *Electronics*, September 30, 1976.
22. Gold, J.: Bipolar Controllers, *Electronic Design*, October 25, 1976.
23. Mick, J. R., and J. Brick: *Microprogramming Handbook* (current edition), Advanced Micro Devices, Sunnyvale, Calif.

Miscellaneous

24. Ulman, D.: Using the 2650 Microprocessor, *Electronic Design*, September 1976.
25. Young, A.: Getting to know the COSMAC, *Electronic Design*, October 25, 1976.
26. Raphael, H. A.: Putting a Microcomputer on a Single Chip, *Computer Design*, December 1976.
27. *Microprocessor Handbook*, Digital Equipment Corp., Maynard, Mass. (current edition).
28. Chung, D. H.: Design Principles . . . for Microprocessor Systems, *Electronics*, January 20, 1977.

CHAPTER 7

MICRO/MINICOMPUTER FAMILIES

INTRODUCTION

7-1. Minicomputer-System Selection. As noted in Secs. 1-2 and 6-1, we will regard *minicomputers* as machines suitable for general-purpose computation and costing between $1,500 and $25,000 for one processor, 4K words of memory, power supply, control panel, and some software. Most minicomputers serve original-equipment manufacturers (OEMs), communications applications, and laboratory or process automation as dedicated subsystems, i.e., *not* for general-purpose computation (see also Sec. 6-1). But the larger minicomputers also make excellent number crunchers for scientific and business "end users," and even low-cost models can serve for general-purpose computation if they are provided with at least a floppy disk for operating-system use (Chap. 5).

Almost all new minicomputers are microcomputers; i.e., they have microprocessor CPUs (Sec. 1-2). The larger and faster models employ bit-sliced LSI processors (Sec. 6-20). Manufacturers typically build *families* of software-compatible low-cost, medium, and high-power machines. Table 7-1 surveys the range of minicomputer specifications.

Manufacturers also provide *software, user-group program libraries, documentation,* and (more or less) *application support, installation help, diagnostics,* and *maintenance.* These services are usually priced separately, but at least some of the value of *available* software and *potential* services will be reflected in competitive pricing structures. Note that

1. **Selection of OEM minicomputers is governed by the hardware- versus development-cost tradeoffs of Sec. 6-2.** OEMs will buy a minicomputer

TABLE 7-1.   Range of Minicomputer Specifications.

Price (processor and 4K words)	$1,000–$15,000
Word size (data-path width)	12–18 bits
Memory cycle time	0.3–2.5 μsec
Register/register ADD time	typically 1 cycle
Memory/register ADD time	typically 2 cycles
Register/register MULTIPLY time	2–25 μsec
Number of addressable registers (accumulators and/or index registers)	1–16 ⎫ may be duplicated for
Number of index registers	0–15 ⎭ context switching
DMA transfer rate (maximum)	0.2–3 MHz
Number of external interrupts	1–256
Typical options	Memory parity check
	Memory error correction
	Memory protection and mapping (to 2M bytes)
	Real-time clock
	Automatic bootstrap loader
	Power-failure restart
	Floating-point processor

subsystem instead of microcomputer cards or chips if the minicomputer manufacturer's support lowers per-unit development costs sufficiently.

2. **Minicomputer end-user costs are usually dominated by programming costs, so that software is vital.**   Higher-order-language programming is less efficient, but much cheaper than assembly-language programming.

3. **Uptime constraints may put a high premium on reliability, service or serviceability, diagnostics, and documentation.**

These considerations usually outweigh minicomputer hardware features, which are inexpensive anyway.   We refer again to Fig. 6-1 and remind the reader that

4. **Unless programming cost is divided over a large number of systems, a more powerful computer system is cheaper than superefficient programming.**   This is especially true because **most systems require future expansion.**

A   reasonable   **minicomputer-selection   procedure**   must   consider   the following:

1. **Objectives** (What is the system supposed to accomplish?).   State objectives, as far as possible, in terms of *quantitative measures* (cost, net return) and/or *constraints* (must handle 1,000 data points per second; must cost less than $5,000).

To establish requirements, we must consider **data rates,** do some **rough programming,** and estimate the **amount of memory** needed for some different programs.

2. **Alternatives** (different types and numbers of computers, special-purpose logic, human operators; or *no* system at all)
3. **How will system requirements change over a 2- to 5-year period?** Can the system be modified?
4. **Interface requirements** (I/O ports, interrupts, DMA). Can we use standard interface cards or chips?
5. **Sources and cost of programs** (in-house, manufacturer, customers, software house)
6. **Sources and cost of maintenance** (in-house, manufacturer, customers, service firm). What is the effect of system failure or downtime?

The selection process must *loop back* over these considerations for each possible alternative.

Minicomputer manufacturers also sell *memories, interface* cards, and *computer peripherals* (terminals, printers, disk systems, etc.). Compatible components of this kind can often be bought more cheaply from other manufacturers. Installation is rarely a problem, but service is. Manufacturers of different components are sure to blame one another, and you, if anything goes wrong. "Mixed" systems, then, are only for knowledgeable users, who can reap substantial savings. Minicomputer manufacturers' interface cards, in particular, are often overpriced. Check carefully whether software for "foreign" peripherals is available.

"**Ruggedized**" computer systems (Refs. 9 to 11) designed for demanding industrial, aerospace, or military environments must stand shock/vibration, extended temperature ranges, and possibly radiation. CMOS logic, which also consumes relatively low power, is often a good choice. Plated-wire memories have been popular, but they are expensive. The large printed-circuit cards used in many minicomputers invite vibration-bending troubles and must be stiffened and/or replaced by smaller cards. Ruggedized versions of standard minicomputers are cheaper than full-MIL-spec machines but are, typically, not as easy to maintain in the field.

7-2. Improved "Classical" Single-Address Machines: PDP-15, Hewlett-Packard 21MX, Interdata, and General Automation Families. The still-extant **PDP-8** (Sec. 6-15), usually regarded as the first minicomputer, is a single-address machine (Sec. 2-2) with **a single 12-bit accumulator;** a 12-bit **accumulator extension (MQ) register** serves for multiplication/division. A number of memory locations are used as **autoincrementing pointers.** Early Honeywell and Hewlett-Packard minicomputers upgraded the extension register into a **second accumulator.** Such computers typically used **one-word instructions** with paged direct and indirect addressing (Sec. 2-13), relying on assembler arithmetic for page-boundary crossing. The next improvements added a single 16-bit **index register** and two-word direct, indirect, and indexed addressing (e.g., Varian, Raytheon). Some of these three-register instruction sets (particularly that of the Varian 620 series) were quite powerful and are still kept alive by software compatibility.

Since the advent of cheaper logic and the universal introduction of microprogramming, modern micro/minicomputers have **more general-purpose registers** (accumulators and index registers), and **much more sophisticated addressing modes and instructions sets.** Applications to ever more complicated multiple real-time tasks put a premium on **easy program relocation, fast multi-interrupt systems,** and **reentrant programming** (Sec. 3-16 and Chap. 4) and led to the use of **stack operations** and **context switching** even in microprocessors. Larger memories became more desirable *and* less expensive; most manufacturers now offer a **memory-mapping system** to increase address space (Sec. 2-30) and to protect operating-system routines (Sec. 5-22).

Besides the PDP-8, one single-accumulator machine,[1] the **Digital Equipment Corporation PDP-15,** survives. Interestingly, this is an **18-bit** minicomputer, whose *one-word* memory-reference instructions can address 8K words with a 13-bit address byte. These one-word instructions often permit PDP-15s to match assembly-language execution speeds of more modern 16-bit machines, which require many two-word instructions (Ref. 5). Digital Equipment Corporation **XVM systems** join the old-fashioned PDP-15 CPU, curiously, to an ultra-modern memory/I/O subsystem. XVM memory feeds the processor through a bipolar *lookahead buffer* (Sec. 1-19) and has a second port to a 16-bit PDP-11 minicomputer serving as an *I/O processor* (Ref. 8). There is also an optional *floating-point processor*, which is relatively slow and expensive, and a powerful *graphics system.*

The **Hewlett-Packard 21MX** minicomputer family has made a virtue of the old-fashioned page-addressing system inherited from its predecessors for the sake of software compatibility. The 21MX one-million-word memory-mapping system employs *page registers* rather than the *base registers* used with most memory-mapping systems (Sec. 2-30), and does not impose the 100-nsec time penalty typical of such systems.

Perhaps the main feature of Hewlett-Packard 21MX minicomputers is the company's extensive development of hardware/software interfaces to Hewlett/Packard instruments and instrumentation systems, including the IEC bus (Sec. 4-27c) pioneered by Hewlett-Packard. 21MX hardware is neatly packaged (Fig. 1-2); while the instruction set has been improved, instruction-set architecture is handicapped by the need for software compatibility with predecessor machines.[2] There are **two accumulators** and **two index registers.** Memory is divided into 1,024-word pages. **Addressing modes** are

  direct/(multilevel) indirect on page 0 and on the current page (one-word
     instructions)

---

[1] PDP-15 does have a 16-bit index register, but it can be loaded only through the accumulator and is not very useful.
[2] Future Hewlett/Packard mini/microcomputers will have a completely different architecture based on the advanced stack operations of Hewlett/Packard's larger 3000 series.

direct/(multilevel) indirect (two-word instructions)
indexed and (multilevel) indirect-preindexed (LOAD, STORE, and JUMP
only; 16-bit offset)

LOAD/STORE BYTE and SCAN TO MATCH ACCUMULATOR BYTE use the
second accumulator as a pointer to a byte address (other 21MX addresses
are *word* addresses). JUMP TO SUBROUTINE stores the return addresses
at the subroutine-address location (Sec. 2-23).

Firmware options include various operations for improving FORTRAN
execution, including **floating-point instructions** (Table 2-2a). An optional
user-microprogramming system of modest power (256 words of 325-nsec,
24-bit writable control store, Sec. 2-33) permits access to 12 extra scratchpad
registers and is nicely supported with *microassembler/simulator software*.
21MX has a **true vectored interrupt system,** but lacks automatic stack
operations for saving return address, processor status, and registers.

Interdata[1] minicomputers already had a modern microprogrammed,
multiregister architecture even when this still meant magnetic U-core ROMs,
memory-implemented registers, and low computing speed. Now even the
small 5/16 and 6/16 have bit-sliced microprocessors (2901 RALUs, Sec. 6-20)
with **sixteen 16-bit general registers, of which 15 can serve as index registers
with a 16-bit offset.** Figure 2-6d shows Interdata instruction formats, which
are patterned after IBM 360/370 formats. All memory-reference instructions are multiword instructions. *There is no indirect addressing.* 6/16 has
byte-manipulation instructions and optional MULTIPLY/DIVIDE firmware,
and can be field-upgraded into a Model 7/32. *5/16 is designed to use
inexpensive microprocessor I/O-port chips* (e.g., Motorola 6820, Sec. 6-7) *to
reduce interface costs.*

The relatively inexpensive **Model 7/32** (Fig. 5-1) is one of the most
interesting minicomputers, because it can act as **a small 32-bit computer
capable of addressing up to one million words without memory mapping,**
using two or three 16-bit instruction words (Ref. 7). Partially overlapped
memory accesses and a pipelined arithmetic unit implement microprogrammed *32-bit fixed-point and floating-point arithmetic* as well as 16-bit
operations (see Table 2-2 for floating-point execution times). 7/32 has **two
context-switched sets of 16 32-bit registers** and an optional set of 64-bit
hardware floating-point registers.

The Interdata I/O bus is time-shared between I/O addresses and data
(Fig. 4-6). Interrupt vectoring requires a programmed ACKNOWLEDGE
INTERRUPT instruction (Sec. 4-12). Interrupt return address and two
status words, like subroutine return addresses, are automatically saved in
registers; there is no automatically operated processor stack.

---

[1] A division of Perkin-Elmer Corporation. See also Figs. 1-4a and 5-1.

Interdata **80** and **85** are older top-of-the-line models[1] with fast Schottky-TTL processors, partially overlapped MOS memory, and 32-bit-wide control memories. *Vertical* microprogramming makes the user-microprogrammable Model 85 much easier to use than other machines with writable control store (Sec. 2-32; even multiplication is a single microinstruction). Model 85 has two sets of general registers.

The **General Automation, Inc.,** 16-bit family has an asynchronous tri-state memory bus (Sec. 1-9), but a separate synchronous I/O bus. **GA-16/110, 220,** and **330** are microcomputers based on a proprietary two-chip (RALU and CROM) 16-bit NMOS processor.[2] Its remarkable specifications include 34-bit microinstructions, 2-μsec register/register **ADD**, 2.6 μsec **LOAD REGISTER**, and microprogrammed **MULTIPLY/DIVIDE**. 16/110 is a single-board microcomputer complete with 1K or 2K static RAM on a plug-in subcard and card-edge indicator lights and switches.

The GA-16/440 has a fast MSI processor with 0.8-μsec register/register **ADD** and 1.5-μsec **LOAD REGISTER**. Its optional **20-bit memory-mapping system** can address 2M bytes.

The General Automation instruction set is an improved revision of their older SPC-16 instruction set (Ref. 4). The new machines duplicate the SPC-16's 8-register set for fast context switching. **All eight registers can be used for indexing;** two registers can do **preindexing,** six permit **postindexing,** and one is a **base register** whose contents may be added to other addresses for program relocation (Sec. 2-16) or **double indexing. Stack operations,** which require optional CROMs in the 110, 220, and 330, employ memory locations as stack pointers and stack-limit registers.

General Automation has specialized in factory automation and, more recently, in small business computer systems. Available software includes real-time operating systems, a macroassembler, scientific and business FORTRAN, COBOL, and multiuser BASIC.

THE DATA GENERAL
MICRONOVA/NOVA/ECLIPSE FAMILY

7-3. Instruction-Set Architecture. The **Data General** family ranges from the one-board **MICRONOVA** based on the mN601 16-bit NMOS microprocessor (Sec. 6-18*b*), through various **NOVAs,** to the **ECLIPSE** models, Schottky-clamped-TTL minicomputers with extended instruction sets. Each processor has **four accumulators, two of which can serve as index**

---

[1] The new top model, Interdata **8/32,** is a medium-sized 32-bit computer.
[2] Made by Synertek, Inc., Mountain View, Calif.

registers. There are six simple memory-reference instructions, *which do not implement arithmetic/logic operations:*

LOAD ACCUMULATOR	**STORE ACCUMULATOR**
NO. 1, 2, 3, or 4	**NO. 1, 2, 3, or 4**
INCREMENT, SKIP IF ZERO	**DECREMENT, SKIP IF ZERO**
JUMP	**JUMP AND SAVE RETURN**
	ADDRESS IN ACCUMULATOR 3

Their 16-bit instruction format has an *8-bit address byte* and permits

direct/indirect addressing on page 0 (256 words)
direct/indirect relative addressing (-128- to $+127$-word offset)
indexed/preindexed-indirect addressing (-128- to 127-word offset)

Repeated indirect addressing is permitted; indirect addresses include a mode bit and 15 address bits and can address 32K words. 16 memory locations

TABLE 7-2a. NOVA/ECLIPSE Register-Operation Instructions.

Bit	
0	Identifies this class of instructions
1 2	Specifies **source register**
3 4	Specifies **destination register**
5 6 7	**Operation code:** ADD, ADD COMPLEMENT. SUBTRACT, AND, MOVE, NEGATE, COMPLE-MENT; INCREMENT
8 9	**Rotate** result and carry bit as specified below: LEFT, RIGHT, NOT AT ALL; or SWAP 8-BIT BYTES
10 11	**Select carry** (before rotation): 0, 1, OLD CARRY, COMPLEMENT
12	**Do not actually disturb destination register** if this bit is 1 (skip test only)
13 14 15	**Skip** next instruction*: NEVER, ALWAYS; IF RESULT = 0, ≠0; IF CARRY = 0, ≠0; IF RESULT OR CARRY = 0, IF RESULT AND CARRY = 0

* Note that skip tests are made on the rotated 16-bit result-and-carry. Thus, if the result of an addition is shifted left, SKIP ON ZERO CARRY actually tests the sign of the sum. Note also that skip tests can be made without loading the result into the destination register, thus preserving its current content.

TABLE 7-2b. NOVA/ECLIPSE Instruction Execution Times.

(In microseconds)

Instruction	Micronova	Nova 2	Nova 3 (MOS)	Nova 800	Eclipse (core, 4-way interleave)
LOAD, STORE	2.9	2.0	1.2–1.5	1.6	0.8–1.4
with extended address	...	...	...	...	1.8–2.4
JUMP	2.9	1.0	0.7	0.8	0.6–0.8
with extended address	...	...	...	...	1.6
JUMP AND SAVE	3.4	1.2	1	0.8	0.6–0.8
JUMP AND PUSH	7.7	...	3.3	...	2.2–3.6
RETURN	7.2	...	4.3	...	4.4–5
Register operations	2.4	1.0	0.7	0.8	0.7
with skip	2.9	1.2	0.9	1	0.9
MULTIPLY (unsigned)	41.3	6.3	5.8 (typical)	8.8	7.2
DIVIDE (unsigned)	59.0	7.7	6.7 (typical)	8.8	8.2
I/O READ	7.2	2.4	2	1.4–2.2	2.2
I/O WRITE	4.8	2.4	2	2.2–2.8	2.6
I/O SENSE	7.2	2.4	2	1.4–2.2	0.8

on page 0 serve as *autoincrement and autodecrement pointers* when they are used as indirect addresses.

ECLIPSE also has similar **2-word memory-reference instructions** with a 16-bit address word, and permits explicit **immediate addressing** with 8-bit and 16-bit operands.

MICRONOVA, NOVA 3, and ECLIPSE have **software-stack operations** (PUSH/POP ACCUMULATORS M TO N) with a programmable *stack limit*. These newer machines also have stack-type **JUMP TO SUBROUTINE** and **RETURN FROM SUBROUTINE** instructions. A special *frame pointer* can be used to allocate stack locations for subroutine data passing. The ECLIPSE stack pointer is really a memory location.

Most arithmetic/logic operations are one-cycle register operations—they do not address memory. This frees instruction bits to make these instructions quite powerful. Each such instruction can *combine* an arithmetic or logic operation, an operation on the processor carry flag, a rotation of the resulting register-and-carry, *and* a skip test (Table 7-2).

Compared with similar PDP-11 models (Sec. 7-6), NOVA/ECLIPSE computers have *fewer registers* and *much less useful memory-reference and I/O instructions*, but *more powerful register-operation instructions*.

Inexpensive accessory *floating-point processors*, and an optional optimizing (but relatively slow) FORTRAN compiler ("FORTRAN 5") make NOVA and ECLIPSE minicomputers into *respectable moderate-cost number crunchers* (Table 2-2*b*).

7-4. Input/Output. Data General machines use *explicit input/output instructions* with 6-bit device codes and 2 control bits. These instructions move data to or from a specified accumulator or perform a skip test (Secs. 4-2 and 4-7).

Data General does not provide totally automatic interrupt vectoring. NOVAs use an **ACKNOWLEDGE INTERRUPT** instruction to read the interrupt address (Sec. 4-12) and must do explicit status saving. As an improvement, ECLIPSE has a **VECTOR** instruction, which is programmed to implement a jump to the correct vector address and saves the return address and user-selected status information on the stack.

NOVA DMA operations include the useful memory-increment and add-to-memory modes described in Secs. 4-20 and 4-21.

7-5. ECLIPSE Features. The top-of-the line ECLIPSE models have a Schottky-clamped TTL processor and a number of added instructions, including **DECIMAL ADD/SUBTRACT, SIGNED/UNSIGNED MULTIPLY/ DIVIDE**, multiple shifts, byte manipulation, bit testing, and bit counting. Microprogrammed **BLOCK MOVE** and **BLOCK ADD AND MOVE** respectively operate on an entire N-word array in $1.8 + 1.2N$ to $2 + 1.6N$ μsec once the block size, source and destination starting addresses, and assistant to be added (if any) are loaded into processor registers.

ECLIPSE memory can combine 800-nsec core memory and 700-nsec MOS memory on the asynchronous memory bus, with the following useful options:

1. 8-way *interleaving* of core-memory banks, 4-way for MOS, reducing effective cycle time to about 600 nsec.
2. A small (16-word) 200-nsec bipolar **cache memory** (Sec. 1-19) for *each* 8K MOS memory bank, with a least-recently-used (LRU) cache word-replacement algorithm. This can improve effective memory-access times by 10 to 20 percent.
3. Memory error checking and *correction*, using 5 check bits per 16-bit memory word.

A *memory-mapping option* permits users to address program-protected segments (up to 32K per user only) in up to 128K words of memory, with a 100-nsec time penalty per memory access.

ECLIPSE C/300, intended for medium-sized business-computer applications, has 37 special microprogrammed *editing instructions* for moving, searching, and code conversion of byte strings.

ECLIPSE C/200 has a *user-microprogramming* option. The instruction **ENTER WCS** (*entry-point number*) starts one of up to 16 user microprograms in a 256-word × 56-bit writable control store (WCS). User microprograms can access three extra general registers.

THE PDP-11 AND OTHER ASYNCHRONOUS-BUS MACHINES

7-6. Digital Equipment Corporation PDP-11 Family: Survey. The **PDP-11** 16-bit minicomputer architecture, the first consciously designed for modern real-time, multitask operations, simplifies implementation of computer systems with multiple devices and processors, swapping of relocatable programs, and reentrant procedures. Backed by impressive software and ubiquitous if expensive service, PDP-11s dominate the market; each type of PDP-11, therefore, becomes a standard of comparison for machines in its general class.

PDP-11/03, based on the **LSI-11 microcomputer card** built with Western Digital or DEC MCP 1600 chips (Sec. 6-18a and Fig. 6-13), and the MSI **PDP-11/04** are the smallest PDP-11s and replace the earlier PDP-11/20, 05, 10, and 15. **PDP-11/34** has an integral memory-mapping system, which was optional in the earlier 35 and 40 models. The larger and faster **PDP-11/55** (replacing the earlier 45 and 50) will be discussed in Sec. 7-10; the top model, **PDP-11/70,** cannot be fairly considered a minicomputer. *All current models (03, 04, 34, 55) are software-compatible and execute the same basic instruction set* (20, 05, 10, and 15 had slightly different instruction sets). PDP-11/03 and 40 have *optional microprogrammed* **FLOATING ADD, SUBTRACT, MULTIPLY,** *and* **DIVIDE,** *instructions.* PDP-11/34 and 55 (as well as the older 45 and 50) have optional fast and relatively inexpensive *floating-point processors* (Table 2-2).

7-7. PDP-11 Instructions and Addressing Modes. A PDP-11 processor (Fig. 7-1a) has **8 programmable 16-bit registers,**[1] R0 through R7. R0 through R5 serve as accumulators, pointers, or index registers. **R7 is the program counter,** and **R6 is the processor-stack pointer**—they are not truly general-purpose registers, although the programmer can address them just like R0 to R5.

Table 7-3 shows the basic instruction set. *Single-address instructions* like

INCREMENT   *destination*

---

[1] PDP-11/45, 50, 55, and 70 duplicate register R0 through R6 for context switching, Secs. 4-9.

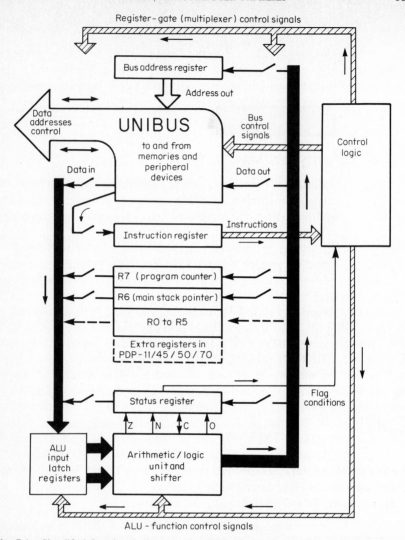

Register-gate (multiplexer) control signals

Bus address register

Address out

Data addresses control

UNIBUS

to and from memories and peripheral devices

Bus control signals

Control logic

Data in

Data out

Instruction register

Instructions

R7 (program counter)

R6 (main stack pointer)

R0 to R5

Extra registers in PDP-11/45/50/70

Status register

Flag conditions

Z   N   C   O

ALU input latch registers

Arithmetic/logic unit and shifter

ALU - function control signals

Fig. 7-1a. Simplified functional diagram of a PDP-11 processor. The various processors actually have more complex additional data paths and internal holding registers invisible to the programmer, but each still has a single ALU input path, with a latch register holding the second input.

operate on a 16-bit word in a *register*, in a *memory location* addressed in a specified address mode, or in a *device register*, which is simply addressed as an absolute location (Sec. 7-9). Analogous **BYTE instructions,** say

INCREMENT (BYTE) *destination*

similarly operate on 8-bit bytes. *All addresses are byte addresses*, with 16-bit words using two byte locations (Table 7-3). Register bytes occupy

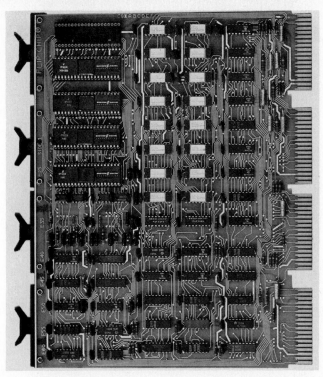

Fig. 7-1b. This LSI-11 card holds a 4-chip Western Digital CPU (upper left; see also Sec. 6-18), a 4K-word memory, and interface and accessory logic. The spare socket is for an extra control-ROM chip to implement floating-point instructions. (*Digital Equipment Corporation.*)

the less significant bits (called bits 0 through 7 in the PDP-11) of a register. There are also *double-register* shifts.

Significantly, PDP-11 has **two-address instructions** like

ADD *source* **INTO** *destination*

SUBTRACT (BYTE) *source* **INTO** *destination*

where both source *and* destination may be memory locations or device registers as well as processor registers.

Each effective address (register, memory, or device) is specified by a *6-bit address field* in the instruction (Table 7-3). Three address-field bits (one octal digit) specify one of 8 registers used in the address computation, and 3 bits specify one of **8 addressing modes** (a two-address instruction would have 64 different combinations of source and destination address modes):

1. **Register addressing:** The referenced register contains the operand.

TABLE 7-3. Basic PDP-11 Instruction Set.

1. Single-Adress Instructions

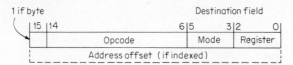

CLEAR	INCREMENT	ROTATE LEFT/RIGHT
COMPLEMENT	DECREMENT	ARITHMETIC SHIFT
NEGATE	TEST	LEFT/RIGHT
SWAP BYTES	ADD/SUBTRACT CARRY	JUMP

2. Two-Adress Instructions

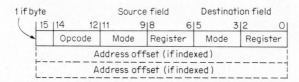

MOVE	BIT TEST
ADD/SUBTRACT	BIT CLEAR
COMPARE	BIT SET

XOR   JUMP TO SUBROUTINE

MULTIPLY/DIVIDE (optional)

MULTIPLE ARITHMETIC SHIFT (single or double register; optional)

Word and Byte Addresses for First 4K Bank (octal)

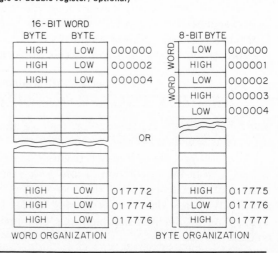

TABLE 7-3. (*continued*)

---

3. Program Control

JUMP (format as in 1 above)
JUMP TO SUBROUTINE (format as in 2 above)
RETURN FROM SUBROUTINE (via register)
RETURN FROM INTERRUPT
SOFTWARE INTERRUPT
HALT, NO OPERATION, WAIT FOR INTERRUPT

BRANCH (-128- to $+127$-word offset)
— unconditionally
— if $=0$, $\neq 0$
— if carry $=0$, $=1$; overflow $=0$, $=1$
— if <0, ≤ 0, ≥ 0, >0 (also for *unsigned* COMPARE, Sec. 2-22).

DECREMENT REGISTER, BRANCH IF NOT ZERO (0 to -63-word offset)

4. Miscellaneous Instructions

CLEAR/SET   individual processor flags
CLEAR   all processor flags; I/O control bits
MARK   (marks stack for data passing)
FLOATING ADD, SUBTRACT, MULTIPLY, DIVIDE (optional in PDP-11/03, 40).

For example,

ADD RO, R3

adds the contents of registers 0 and 3 and places the sum into register 3.

2. **"Deferred" addressing via registers:** The referenced register contains the *address* of the operand.   Thus,

MOVE R1, (R3)

moves the *contents* of register 1 to the memory location *addressed by* register 3.

3. **Autoincrement addressing:** The operand address is taken from the referenced register, which is *afterwards* incremented.

CLEAR (R6) +

clears the memory location addressed by register 6 and *then* increments register 6.

4. **Autodecrement addressing:** The specified register is *first* decremented and *then* used as an address pointer.

ADD R1, −(R2)

adds the contents of register 1 into the memory location addressed by the decremented contents of register 2.

5. **Multiword indexed addressing:** The effective address is the sum of the word in the specified register (used here as an index register) and a

TABLE 7-4a. Effect of PDP-11 Address Modes on Relative Execution Time.

This table is useful for judging execution-time advantages of different programming techniques. Times required for source/destination memory accesses and instruction fetch/execution are given in "*effective memory cycles*" (including bus-access time; about 1 μsec for core, 500 nsec for MOS, and 350 nsec for bipolar—add about 100 nsec for each memory-mapped access). Total time required to execute an instruction is

FETCH/EXECUTION TIME + DESTINATION TIME + SOURCE TIME (if any)

Times computed from this table are correct within 10% for PDP-11/45, 50, and 55. For smaller PDP-11s, instruction microprograms do not fit into integral numbers of memory cycles, but the table still shows *relative* execution times for different address modes roughly. Refer to PDP-11 manuals for exact execution times.

	Address Mode	Source or Destination Time	FETCH/EXECUTION TIME MOVE, INCREMENT, etc.	ADD, SUBTRACT, etc.
0	R	0	1	1
1	(R) or @ R	1	1	2
2	(R) +	1	1	2
4	−(R)	1	1	2
3	@ (R) +	2	1	2
5	@ − (R)	2	1	2
6	X(R)	2	1	2
7	@ X(R)	3	1	2
2	≠A (immediate)	1	1	2
3	@ ≠ A (absolute)	2	1	2
6	A (relative)	2	1	2
7	@ A (indirect)	3	1	2

EXAMPLES:

(a) MOV A, R takes $2 + 0 + 1 = 3$ cycles
  ADD A, R takes $2 + 0 + 2 = 4$ cycles
  MOV R0, B takes $0 + 2 + 1 = 3$ cycles
(b) ADD A, B takes $2 + 2 + 2 = 6$ cycles
(c) MOV (R6)+, R1 takes $1 + 0 + 1 = 2$ cycles
  ADD (R6)+, R1 takes $1 + 0 + 2 = 3$ cycles
  MOV R1, −(R6) takes $0 + 1 + 1 = 2$ cycles

TABLE 7-4b. PDP-11 MULTIPLY/DIVIDE Times (in μsec; register/register, or add source time).

	MULTIPLY	DIVIDE
PDP-11/03	24–64	≤78
PDP-11/34 (MOS)	9–12.2	12.5
PDP-11/40	8.9	11.3
PDP-11/45, 55 (bipolar)	3.3	7–8.6

16-bit word following the current instruction. Two such address words follow if *both* address fields of a two-address instruction are indexed.

In addition, autoincrement, autodecrement, and indexed addresses can be **indirect** (i.e., the addressed memory location is a pointer to the effective operand address). We thus have eight explicit addressing modes.

NOTE: Autoincrementing and autodecrementing of R0 to R5 are automatically done by *byte* addresses for **BYTE** instructions, and by *word* addresses (2 bytes) for word instructions. The program counter R7 and the processor stack pointer R6 are *always* autoincremented/ decremented by word addresses (2 bytes).

The PDP-11 address modes are ingenious and powerful. Note, first, that the predecrement and postincrement modes permit us to use any register except the program counter R7 as a **stack pointer** (Sec. 2-17), e.g., R4:

> MOVE R0,   – (R4) / push R0
> MOVE (R4)+,   R3   / pop into R3

Nor are we restricted to simple **PUSH** and **POP** operations:

> SUBTRACT (R4)+, (R4) / pop top element of stack
>   and subtract it from new
>   top element

Note that memory space must be allowed for the stack; it may be necessary to compare the stack pointer with a limiting address. The *processor stack pointer* R6 will cause an automatic *stack-limit interrupt* when a **PUSH** operation reaches a specified address (programmable in PDP-11/45, 50, and 55).

The program counter R7 is used as a pointer register to produce the two-word (or three-word) address modes typically employed in PDP-11 assembly language:

multiword **immediate addressing**
multiword **direct addressing**
multiword **direct/indirect relative addressing**

(Table 7-5). *PDP-11 assemblers always translate relocatable symbolic addresses into the multiword relative-address mode* to simplify swapping of program sections into different core locations.

One-word *branching instructions* (Table 7-3) have **relative addresses** with − 128- to + 127-*word* offsets. The assembler again translates symbolic addresses into relative addresses.

TABLE 7-5. PDP-11 Addressing Modes Using Program-counter References.

Word (rather than byte) operations are illustrated. R7 = PC is the program counter. . Stands for the current instruction location. Two-address instructions can involve as many as three words.

Addressing Mode	Assembly Language	Assembled Code	
1. **Immediate addressing** with 16-bit operand word	ADD #A,R2	.	ADD (R7)+,R2
		.+2	A (operand)
2. **Direct absolute addressing**	MOV @#A,R3	.	MOV @(R7)+,R3
		.+2	A (operand address)
3. **Direct relative addressing** -used by assembler to generate position-independent code	ADD .+n,R3	.	ADD n – 4(R7),R3
		.+2	n – 4
	ADD A,R3	.	ADD A–.–4 (R7),R3
		.+2	A–.–4
4. **Indirect relative addressing** -used by assembler to generate position-independent code	ADD @A,R3	.	ADD @A–.–4 (R7),R3
		.+2	A–.–4

Note also constructions like

```
            MOV R2, (R7)+
QQ:    .WORD 0
```

for fast intermediate storage at the location QQ; the program automatically skips the storage location.

7-8. PDP-11 Subroutines and Interrupt Service. The PDP-11 instruction

JUMP TO SUBROUTINE *register, destination*

saves the return address (program counter incremented by 2) in the specified register, and pushes the old register contents onto the processor stack.

RETURN FROM SUBROUTINE *register*

appropriately reverses this procedure. This permits nesting of successive subroutines and also provides a linkage register for data passing (Secs. 2-23 and 3-15). Many PDP-11 subroutines, however, do not need a linkage register and use

JUMP TO SUBROUTINE   R7, *destination*
RETURN FROM SUBROUTINE   R7

which simply push and pop the return address (incremented program counter R7).

PDP-11 has an **automatic vectored priority-interrupt system** with four hardware priority levels and four levels assigned to the current program by status-register bits.   Any number of priority sublevels within each hardware level are established by chain-wired controllers (Fig. 4-11), which transmit vector addresses over bus data lines (Sec. 4-14).   Each vector location contains the *interrupt-service-routine address*, and the following location contains the *processor status word* (flags, interrupt priority, and memory-mapping information, if any) for the interrupt-service routine. When an interrupt is recognized, *return address and status word for the interrupted program are automatically pushed onto the processor stack.* Interrupt service ends with the instruction **RETURN FROM INTERRUPT**, which restores program counter and status word from the stack.

The time between completion of the current instruction and the *beginning* of the first interrupt-service-routine instruction fetch is, respectively, 7.7 and 3.13 μsec for a PDP-11/34 and a PDP-11/55 with MOS memory and no memory mapping (see also Sec. 4-15).

7-9. The PDP-11 UNIBUS®.   PDP-11 systems employ **asynchronous buses,** permit **mixing of different memories,** and **treat peripheral devices as memory locations** (Secs. 4-4 and 4-5).

This permits convenient operations with device data.   In particular, PDP-11 *two-address* instructions like

```
ADD         ADC,     X
COMPARE     Y,       ADC
MOVE        ADC,     DAC
```

can avoid much register saving in interrupt-service routines.

Except for PDP-11/03, which has time-shared address/data lines (Sec. 6-18a), PDP-11 systems are packaged around the **UNIBUS®,** with

16 bidirectional data lines for programmed and DMA-type data transfers, and for interrupt-vector addresses.

18 address lines to memories and device-selector logic.   This permits a memory-mapping system (Sec. 2-30) to address 256K byte locations. A processor by itself can address 64K bytes.

22 control-signal lines.

Normally, the processor is *bus master;* i.e., it can initiate bus data transfers (Sec. 4-4).   Interrupt and DMA-type controllers can become master and use the bus after a bus cycle is completed (Secs. 4-14b and 4-16).   DMA-type data transfers need not necessarily address memory but can, for instance, transfer a block of words from a disk to a group of digital-to-analog converters.

7-10. PDP-11 Systems: General Discussion. Even in the medium-priced PDP-11/40, the complicated instruction microprograms do not always fit into a 1-μsec memory cycle, so that PDP-11/03 through 40 cannot take advantage of fast memories or memory interleaving. Asynchronous-bus handshaking also lengthens the effective memory cycle by 10 to 50 nsec, and *memory mapping (if used) takes an extra 90 to 120 nsec per memory access.* Worse, the *PDP-11's single-bus ALU input exacts a full extra memory cycle for each two-address instruction such as* **ADD, SUBTRACT,** *etc.* (*not* **MOVE**) *if a memory location or device is addressed* (Table 7-4).

To improve this situation, PDP-11/45, 50, and 55 employ fast Schottky-clamped TTL to fit instruction microprograms even into 300-nsec bipolar-memory cycles. These machines also provide *faster internal asynchronous buses* to as much as 32K words of fast bipolar memory[1] (and also to the optional floating-point processor, Fig. 7-2). PDP-11/45, 50, and 55 also have *context-switched registers* and a *supervisor mode* which keeps unauthorized users from executing *privileged instructions* (Sec. 4-23).

The asynchronous UNIBUS system makes interfacing and I/O programming flexible and convenient, but DEC-supplied interface cards and cables are expensive. MDB, Inc., makes less expensive PDP-11 interface cards.

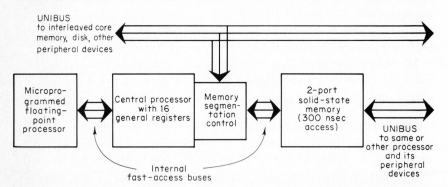

Fig. 7-2. PDP-11/45 or 55 system with special fast buses to a fast solid-state memory and/or a fast floating-point processor. Two-port memories permit multiprocessor interconnections. The Schottky/TTL processor can access up to 124K words of memory-mapped interleaved-core and/or solid-state memory and has two context-switched sets of general registers.

---

[1] Fabri-tek, Inc., supplies an 800-nsec nonvolatile core memory buffered by bipolar lookahead registers (Sec. 1-19) for the fast memory bus, with an effective cycle time of 500 to 600 nsec without memory mapping.

PDP-11 systems benefit from *massive software support* and a large user library.   The *Macro-11 macroassembler*, surely the most powerful furnished for any minicomputer, has excellent macro and conditional-assembly facilities, plus the ability to create labeled COMMON areas.   There are *two elaborate FORTRAN compilers.*   One is an optimizing compiler for use with floating-point processors.   Both have complex-number arithmetic, string processing, and file access.   PDP-11 *load-module generators* permit sophisticated overlays, but run relatively slowly.   *RT-11* and *RSX-11M* are *small real-time disk operating systems* with many advanced features; even the small RT-11 system supports foreground/background operation, computer graphics, batch-file control (Sec. 5-17), and has one of the first no-extra-cost CRT editors.   *RSX-11D*, a large multiuser real-time operating system, requires at least 48K words and seems rather too elaborate.   New REMOTE-11 and *DECNET software* permits users to link minicomputers into networks. There are also *multiuser BASIC systems* and much *business software* supplied by both DEC and various systems houses.   Last but not least, Three Rivers Corporation sells a powerful (80-bit) *writable-control-store accessory* for the PDP-11/40.

7-11.   Other Asynchronous-Bus Machines.   Varian V70-Series Family. Asynchronous-bus systems permit economical mixtures of fast and slow RAM and ROM, simplify device addressing and DMA, and make memory and device logic less time-critical.   **LOCKHEED SUE, Microdata 3200,** and the **Varian V70 series** are all 16-bit asynchronous-bus minicomputers.

Microdata 3200 is available with a routine minicomputer instruction set **(3230),** as an all-user-microprogrammed machine for systems houses **(3200),** and as the **32/S** model specially microprogrammed with stack operations which optimize execution of a PL-1 subset **(MPL).**

Varian 70-series machines are modern 16-bit, asynchronous-bus machines (660-nsec register/register **ADD**, 1.5- to 3-μsec register/memory **ADD**, depending on type of memory).   A fast, flexible 190-nsec, 64-bit horizontal microprogramming system can utilize eight general registers, but only with optional firmware or user microprogramming.   Standard V70 software is restricted to the three-register instruction set of the predecessor machine ($620/f$).   A new "fast FORTRAN" compiler, however, can use the optional firmware as well as *microprogrammed floating-point instructions* or an optional fast *floating-point processor.*   V70s can be had with a *memory-mapping system* and *two-port memories* for multiprocessor systems.   There is a modern real-time operating system (*VORTEX II*) and *user-microprogramming software.*

NEW MICROPROCESSOR-BASED DESIGNS

7-12. Honeywell Level 6 Family. Like the PDP-11, the more recent **Honeywell Level 6 family** was developed as an integrated hardware/software system for modern real-time applications.[1] 16-bit Level 6 processors connect to a variety of memories and to I/O devices through their asynchronous MEGABUS, which is capable of handling 3 million 16-bit words per second. Although device registers can be addressed like memory locations, standard peripheral devices, whether fast or slow, normally use DMA transfers. Their DMA controllers are set up through special I/O instructions using a 10-bit device code corresponding to an *I/O channel number* (Sec. 5-14).

MEGABUS memory-read operations (Ref. 12) do not wait for a memory to return data but release the bus once the address is transmitted (*read-request cycle*). The bus is thus free (e.g., for access to another memory bank) until the memory completes its own cycle and is ready to return data (*read-response cycle*). There are also read/modify/write operations (e.g., **INCREMENT A**). *Error-correcting memories* are available.

Level 6 processors utilize the 16-register complement of Monolithic Memories 6701 microprocessor bit slices (Sec. 6-20) to implement *the most elaborate set of addressing modes for any minicomputer.* Instructions are single-address instructions, except for register/register operations; there are **seven general registers, of which three can be index registers, plus seven base registers** (Sec. 2-16). **Address modes,** specified by 7-bit "address syllable" in each memory-reference instruction, are

two-word **direct/indirect**
two-word **direct/indirect relative**
two-word **indexed** or **indirect-postindexed** by R1, R2, or R3
one-word **direct/indirect via base register** B1 to B7
one-word **direct/predecrement** and **postincrement** via B1 to B7
one-word **via base register B1 to B7, indexed** or **indirect/postindexed** by R1, R2, or R3
one-word **via base register B1 to B7, indexed and predecremented or postincremented** by R1, R2, or R3
one-word and two-word **immediate**

In addition, there are **one-word branch instructions with an 8-bit** ($-$128- to $+$127-word) **relative offset.**

NOTE: The Level 6 MEGABUS has 24 address lines, so that future systems will be able to address over 16M bytes. 16-bit addresses in the program counter, base registers, and address words are *word* addresses capable of addressing 64K words. *Byte* addressing, also possible, is handled with byte counts in an index register.

[1] Only the small 6/06 processor emulates the (modernized) instruction set of the older three-register Honeywell 716 minicomputer.

Level 6 processors have **two status registers.** The **I (indicator) register** has the usual carry and overflow flags, plus special flags for various comparison and bit-testing instructions (greater than, less than, etc.), and an I/O status flag. The **S (status) register** holds the current priority level and a supervisor-state flag (Sec. 5-23), plus spare bits for memory mapping, etc. As a new feature, **a 2s-complement overflow in any of the seven general registers will cause an interrupt** if a bit corresponding to that register in a **mode-control register** is set by the program. **It is then unnecessary to program an overflow-flag test.** An eighth mode-control-register bit, when set by a debugging program, will cause an interrupt when the processor executes any branching instruction **(trace trap).**

Level 6 machines do not use a specific processor stack. Any base register can be a stack pointer for subroutine return addresses. Hardware and software interrupts are handled differently. Each interrupt-vector location points to an associated **save area** in memory, where return address, status registers, and register contents to be saved are stored. Each save area contains a 16-bit location (*interrupt save mask*) which the programmer preloads with a code indicating which processor registers are to be automatically saved for this interrupt. A number of special instructions simplify task scheduling (Sec. 5-20) and the operation of an optional floating-point processor. **Special firmware performs partial hardware tests,** whose results are indicated by test lights.

7-13. Texas Instruments 990 Family (Ref. 9). Begun in 1975 with the **990/4 microcomputer** based on the 16-bit **TMS 9900** NMOS chip and the **MSI/TTL 990/10** and **20,** newer members of this family employ a variety of single-chip I^2L and bit-sliced Schottky/TTL microprocessors[1] with both MOS and bipolar memories. The 16-bit 990 family is, again, designed from the ground up for modern real-time systems. *990 architecture offers CPU simplicity and a profusion of context-switched "registers," which are really memory locations.* This exacts a price in computing speed (one extra memory cycle per memory or *register* access), which is partly compensated by efficient instructions and fast solid-state memories (see also Table 6-1).

A 990 CPU has no real accumulator or index register accessible to the program (Fig. 7-3). A 16-bit **workspace-pointer register** points to a **workspace array** of 16 memory locations WP + 0, WP + 1, ..., WP + 15, which are used as processor "registers" for the currently executing program. In particular, WP + 1 through WP + 15 can all be used for *indexing.*

990s have *word* and *byte single-address* and *two-address instructions*

---

[1] 74S481, a Schottky/TTL 4-bit slice for 990-series processors, can perform register/register multiplication in 2.5 μsec.

somewhat like PDP-11s (Sec. 7-7), but 6-bit address fields can specify 15 workspace registers (4-bits) and only 4 address modes (2 bits):

two-word direct
direct/indirect via workspace register
indirect via workspace register, with postincrement
two-word indexed through workspace register

In addition, there are two-word **immediate-address** instructions and **relative branches** with the usual −128- to +127-word offset. Even the 9900 chips have microprogrammed signed **MULTIPLY** and **DIVIDE** instructions. There are also ROM-implemented programs for **partial self-tests.**

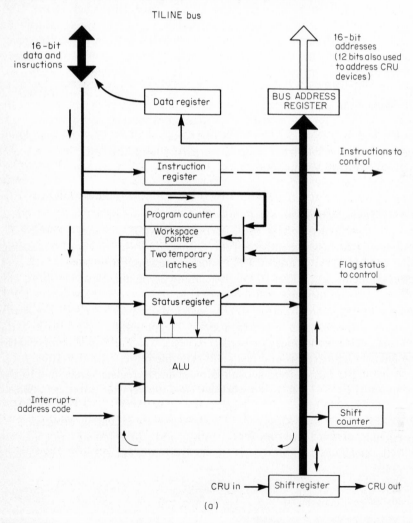

(a)

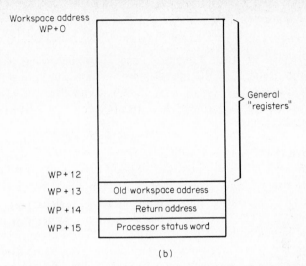

(b)

Fig. 7-3. Texas Instruments 990 series processors (*a*) make up for their hardware simplicity with complicated microprograms.   These implement sophisticated instructions referencing 16 "registers" in the computer memory (*b*).

7-14.   990 Interrupts, Context Switching, and Subroutine Linkage.   990s have **vectored interrupts.**   Even the 9900 microprocessors have special interrupt-address code inputs, which require only simple priority-encoder chips **(74148)** rather than complete interrupt controllers (Sec. 4-12).   990 interrupt-vector locations contain the service-routine address followed by a **workspace address WP assigned to the interrupt.**   When the interrupt is recognized, a microprogram loads the new **WP** into the processor workspace pointer.   **This context-switches the machine to a new set of "registers."** The old registers are still safe in memory; **no explicit register saving is needed.**   Firmware automatically saves the old workspace address in WP + 13 and the return address in WP + 14.   The *processor status word* (flags, priority level, etc.), prestored for each interrupt in location WP + 15 of its workspace, is transferred to the processor status register (note that the old status word is also safe in memory).   The **RETURN** instruction reverses these operations.

990s have a simple **JUMP TO SUBROUTINE (BRANCH AND LINK)** instruction using WP + 11 as a linkage "register" (Sec. 2-23).   But for nested, reentrant subroutines, one employs **BRANCH AND LOAD WORK-SPACE POINTER**, which specifies a new **WP** as well as a subroutine address and is really a software interrupt (Sec. 4-13).   Note that now *both* **WP + 13** *and* **WP + 14** *can serve as index registers* for data passing (see also Secs. 3-14 to 3-16).

Extended instructions (e.g., floating-point instructions) which are not implemented in a 990 processor are coded so as to produce a software-interrupt jump either to a suitable subroutine or to an operation with an accessory processor.

7-15. 990 TILINE Bus, Memories, and Communications-Register I/O. The asynchronous[1] TILINE bus of a 990 system can connect to a wide variety of memories, devices, and DMA controllers. *Error-correcting memories* are available. An optional memory-mapping system can use 20 TILINE address bits.

990 computers (in common with the earlier Texas Instruments 960A minicomputer) have another, *unique low-cost method of interfacing with slow to moderate-speed peripheral devices.* Special two-address I/O instructions can address any contiguous group of up to 16 bits in a block of 2,048 I/O input lines or 2,048 output lines (**communications register unit, CRU**) and transfer these bits to or from a memory location. Other instructions can set or clear individually addressed CRU bits. The microprogrammed bit transfers are actually *serial transfers* (bit following bit) at 1.5 to 4 MHz and can be latched into 8-bit or 16-bit I/O ports. Transferring, say, an 8-bit byte at 1.5 MHz contributes less than 6 μsec to a total I/O-instruction time of 20 μsec.

REFERENCES AND BIBLIOGRAPHY

Minicomputer manufacturers publish extensive hardware and software manuals. Auerbach (Philadelphia, Pa.), D.A.T.A. (Orange, N.J.), and DATAPRO (Delran, N.J.) publish regularly updated computer directories.

1. Eckhouse, R. H.: *Minicomputer Systems*, Prentice-Hall, Englewood Cliffs, N.J., 1975.
2. Perkins, D.: Mini I/O Architecture, *Digital Design*, May 1976.
3. Lofthus, A., and D. Ogden: 16-Bit Processor Performs Like Minicomputer, *Electronics*, May 27, 1976.
4. *The Value of Power*, General Automation, Inc., Anaheim, Calif., 1973.
5. Korn, G. A., and J. V. Wait: *Digital Continuous-System Simulation*, Prentice-Hall, Englewood Cliffs, N.J., 1977.
6. Special Issue on 21MX Minicomputers, *Hewlett-Packard J.*, October 1974.
7. Sweet, W. B.: Addressing Technique Unlocks Extended Memory, *Electronics*, Nov. 8, 1973.
8. Cole, G., and R. Gray: The Hybrid Digital Computer, *EDN*, June 1973.

Ruggedized Minicomputers

9. Session on Military Computer Systems, *Proc. FJCC*, 1973.
10. Jurison, J.: Design Considerations for Aerospace Digital Computers, *Comput. Des.*, August 1974.
11. Rolfe, F.: Designing an Ultrarugged Mini, *EDN*, May 5, 1975. Applicable *military standards* are

MIL-E-5400 (Airborne Electronics)
MIL-E-16400 (Naval Ship/Shore Electronics)
MIL-STD-461A (Electromagnetic Interference)
MIL-S-901C (High-Impact Shock)
12. Conway, J. W.: Unified Bus Architecture, *Computer Design*, January 1977.

[1] NMOS processors simulate true asynchronous data transfers with CYCLE EXTEND operations (Secs. 4-4 and 6-16).

REFERENCE MATERIAL ON HIGHER-ORDER LANGUAGES

A PL/M SUMMARY

A-1. Introduction. PL/M is a subset of the PL-1 language, developed by the Intel Corporation for its 4040- and 8080-series microcomputers. Similar languages exist for several other microcomputers. PL/M permits more direct hardware manipulation than FORTRAN; users can, for instance, reference absolute memory locations (and thus also device registers) explicitly.

A-2. Statements, Declarations, Operations, and Comments. PL/M accepts alphanumeric characters and $=./()+-*,<>;$. Each PL/M **statement** ends with a semicolon. PL/M's **free format** makes entries column-independent and disregards blank spaces which do not delimit words. Dollar signs (**$**) within words are also disregarded and may enhance readability (e.g., LONG$WORD). /* *comment* */ illustrates PL/M **comment delimiters.** The statement EOF (end of file) terminates compilation.

Declaration statements control storage allocation or define **procedures** (subroutines) and **macros.** Declarations within a procedure or DO group have "scope" only within this "block" (**block-structured language**).

Executable statements specify operations. Numerical operands are either 8-bit (type BYTE) or 16-bit words (2 bytes, type ADDRESS). Arithmetic statements usually interpret both as **unsigned binary integers,** even though the user may consider them as fractions, floating-point-number exponents, etc. There is also a very limited set of BCD operations (PLUS, MINUS).

More general operations on different data types must be introduced as procedures (Sec. A-8) on suitably defined arrays. There are no explicit floating-point operations, but user-group libraries contain suitable procedures.

319

A-3. Constants and Variables. 8-bit or 16-bit numbers and **strings** of 8-bit characters are **constants** if they are defined for good at compile time; otherwise, they are **variables.** Constants can be specified by different number codes:

$$000111\text{B} \quad \text{means} \quad 000111_2$$

$$330 \text{ or } 33\text{Q} \quad \text{means} \quad 33_8 = 011011_2$$

$$0\text{F2H} \quad \text{means} \quad F2_{16} = 1111\,0010_2$$

where the leading zero is needed to show this is a number.

$$12\text{D} \text{ or simply } 12 \quad \text{means} \quad 12_{10} = 1100_2$$

Dollar signs may be used to improve readability; e.g., 011011B and 011$011B are equivalent. Numbers must fit 16 binary bits.

Character strings are delimited by apostrophes, e.g., 'B00213B00'. To include an apostrophe, write it as a double apostrophe. Each ASCII character will occupy one byte with a leading zero.

A-4. Data Declarations

DECLARE X1 BYTE; reserves an 8-bit byte named X1

DECLARE PFUI ADDRESS; reserves two bytes (16 bits), which will usually contain an address.

DECLARE Q(50) BYTE; reserves storage for an *array* of 50 bytes, which may be referenced as *subscripted variables* Q(I), where I runs from 0 to 49 (*not* 1 to 50). Multiple symbols or arrays can be declared with a single statement, e.g.

DECLARE (A, B, C) (5) ADDRESS, FOO BYTE; reserves storage for three arrays of 16-bit words labeled A(I), B(I), C(I), where I runs from 0 to 4; and for an 8-bit byte labeled FOO.

Variables and arrays may be given **initial values** at compile time:

DECLARE A (2) BYTE INITIAL (8, 'S'); makes A(0) = 8, A(1) = 'S'. Byte strings may be declared with a DATA declaration:

DECLARE STRING1 DATA ('DATE IS 1/5/79'); which reserves 14 bytes and inserts the given string at compile time.

A-5. Assignment Statements and Expressions. **Assignment statements** like

$$P = A * B + C/D;$$

work much as in FORTRAN, but +, −, *, and / interpret BYTE or ADDRESS operands as **unsigned** integers. If any operand on the right is of type ADDRESS, then so is the result, and 16-bit arithmetic is used. Moreover, all products and quotients are treated as type ADDRESS. −A is the nonnegative number encoded as 0-A. Overflow will produce garbage.

$$A \text{ MOD } B \text{ is the remainder in } A/B$$

Parentheses may be used as in FORTRAN.

Logical operations like

$$\text{NOT 1101B} \quad \text{A AND B}$$
$$\text{A OR B} \quad \text{A XOR B}$$

produce bit-by-bit operations, using 16-bit words if any operand is of type ADDRESS.

$$A,B,C = X + Y;$$

is equivalent to $A = X + Y$, $B = X + Y$, and $C = X + Y$.

Relational operators <, >, = have their usual meaning. ≤ becomes <=, > becomes > =, and ≠ becomes <>.

Precedence in expressions, from top to bottom, is

* / MOD

+ – PLUS MINUS

< <= <> = >= >

NOT

AND

OR   XOR

where operators on the same line have equal precedence.

A-6. DO Groups

```
DO;
    statements ...
END;
```

is not a DO-loop, but may be used to restrict declarations to within the DO-group block, or to reference multiple statements.

```
DO WHILE expression;
    statement(s) ...
END;
```

evaluates its expression and then causes execution of its statements if and only if the rightmost bit of the expression is a 1.

EXAMPLE:

```
DO WHILE (X < = 10) AND (Y > A);
    statements ...
END;
```

```
DO I = expression 1 TO expression 2 BY expression 3; statement(s) ...
END;
```

executes its statements while incrementing an index I from the integer value given by *expression 1* to that given by *expression 2;* expression 3 gives the increment.

```
DO CASE expression;
    n statements
END;
```

evaluates its expression, whose value must lie between 0 and $n - 1$; if expression $= k$, then the $(k - 1)$st statement is executed. Each of the n statements can be a simple DO group of two or more statements.

A-7. IF Statements

```
IF expression THEN statement 1;
ELSE statement 2;
```

respectively executes *statement 1* or *statement 2* if the rightmost bit of the *expression* is 1 or 0. Simple DO groups can again generate multiple statements. The ELSE statement is omitted if *statement 2* is needed after *statement 1* in any case.

A-8. Procedures and Function Procedures. There are two types of PL/M **procedures,** corresponding to FORTRAN *subroutines* and *functions.* A **subroutine** is called with the statement

```
CALL name (argument 1, argument 2, ...);
```

and defined with

```
name: PROCEDURE (dummy argument 1, dummy argument 2, ...); statement(s)
END name;
```

No RETURN statement is needed unless there are multiple exits, for END implies a RETURN.

A **function** *name* (*argument 1, argument 2, ...*) used in any legal statement is defined, and its type is declared with

name: PROCEDURE (*dummy argument 1, dummy argument 2, ...*) *type; statement(s)* ...
RETURN *expression;*
END *name;*

where the value of the *expression* is returned as the desired function value.

A-9. Statement Labels and GO TO statements.   PL/M statements may be preceded by a **label,** as in

START: A = A + B;

Labels serve as documentation references and in GO TO statements.   A statement may be given more than one label:

105: START: QQQ: A = A + B;

A numerical label, if used, specifies an *absolute memory location;* only one label may be a number.   No two statements may have the šame label.   Multiple labels are equivalent.

The statement

GO TO *label;*

transfers control to the labeled statement (unconditional jump), and

GO TO *variable;*

where variable is of type ADDRESS, transfers control to the absolute memory location given by the current value of *variable*.   Users must make sure that each GO TO target is an executable statement.

Modern "structured" programming avoids GO TOs.   In any case, GO TO statements should not transfer control between different procedures, or from a main program to a procedure; we may transfer control from a procedure to the outermost block level of the main program.   Violations of these rules produce stack errors.

A-10. Based Variables and Dot Notation.   The declaration

DECLARE A BASED APOINTER BYTE;

where APOINTER was previously declared to be of type ADDRESS, reserves one byte for A at the address APPOINTER.

Conversely, .A represents the *address* of A.

NOTE: .Q(10) = .Q(0) + 10 if Q(I) is of type BYTE, but .Q(10) = .Q(0) + 20 if Q(I) is of type ADDRESS.

Using . with a *constant*, say .25, automatically reserves storage for the constant and defines its address.   ."STRING" stores the string STRING and returns a pointer to the first character.

A-11. Input/Output and Other "Predeclared" Functions.   The "predeclared" PL/M variables INPUT (*number*), OUTPUT (*number*) refer to 8-bit quantities transferred from/to I/O ports numbered according to a table furnished with the hardware.

LAST (*name*) and LENGTH (*name*) are "predeclared" PL/M functions respectively equal to the highest index value of the array *name*, and 1 + LAST (*name*).

LOW (*expression*) and HIGH (*expression*) respectively return the low-order and high-order byte of an ADDRESS-type expression. DOUBLE (*expression*) makes a BYTE-type expression into an ADDRESS by adjoining a high-order byte of zeros.

ROR (*expression 1, expression 2*) returns the BYTE result of **rotating** the BYTE *expression 1* **right without carry** (Sec. 2-9) a number of times given by the BYTE *expression 2;* the carry flag takes the value of the last bit rotated off the end. *expression 2* must not be zero.

ROL produces an analogous **left rotation without carry.** SCR and SCL produce right and left rotations **with** the carry, and *expression 1* can be an ADDRESS (16-bit word). SHR and SHL similarly produce **right and left logical (not arithmetic) shifts** of 8-bit or 16-bit quantities; the carry flag takes the value of the last bit shifted off the end. In any case, *expression 2* must not be zero.

CARRY, ZERO, SIGN, and PARITY return the 16-bit value $00FF_{16}$ if the corresponding processor flag is set, and 0000_{16} otherwise.

The function MEMORY returns the absolute address following the last program statement and may be a useful indication of the amount of memory still available. STACKPTR refers to the current address of the top of the processor stack.

The *time-delay procedure* CALL TIME (*expression*)*;* returns after expression/10 msec.

BYTE quantities A,B corresponding to valid 2-digit BCD numbers (i.e., each 4-bit "nibble" is less than 10) can be BCD-added in the form

DEC (A + B) or DEC (A PLUS B)

where the second expression will correctly account for the decimal carries into higher-order decimal digits.

EXAMPLE (Ref. 1): To find the sum of two six-digit decimal numbers represented as two 3-byte arrays X1, X2, X3; Y1, Y2, Y3, we use

DECLARE (X1, X2, X3, Y1, Y2, Y3, Z1, Z2, Z3) BYTE;

Z1 = DEC (X3 + Y3) /*LOW-ORDER RESULT*/;
Z2 = DEC (X2 PLUS Y2);
Z3 = DEC (X1 PLUS Y1);

A-12. Interrupt Service. The statements ENABLE; and DISABLE; turn the interrupt system on and off. **Interrupt-service procedures** will be automatically called if they are user-defined in the form

Name: PROCEDURE INTERRUPT *n*;
     statement(s) ...
    RETURN;
    END   (*name*);

where *n* is the hardware interrupt level ($0 \leq n \leq 7$).

A-13. PL/M Macros (see also Sec. 3-21). The PL/M declaration **(macros definition)**

DECLARE *name* LITERALLY '*string*';

will cause *name* to be replaced by *string* wherever *name* appears after this definition. Note that this does not introduce macro *arguments* directly.

EXAMPLE:

DECLARE XSQUR LITERALLY 'X*X';
X = A;
Y = XSQUR;

generates Y = X*X = A*A.

REFERENCE

1. *8008 and 8080 PL/M Programming Manual,* Intel Corporation, Santa Clara, Calif. (current edition).

TABLE A-1. Minicomputer FORTRAN Check List.

In FORTRAN:

1. Specification **statements** *define the properties of, and allocate storage to,* **named variables, functions,** and **arrays.**
2. **Arithmetic statements** define computing operations which assign the value of an expression to a variable, e.g.,

$$VAR = B + 0.1$$

3. **Control statements** determine the sequence of operations in a program, e.g.,

$$GO\ TO\ 17$$

4. **Input/output statements** specify input/output operations.

FORTRAN is "portable"; i.e., the language is to a large extent independent of the processor and compiler used.   Most minicomputer FORTRAN systems are subsets of USASI FORTRAN IV.   But different minicomputers (and even the same minicomputers with different amounts of core) implement more or less complete FORTRAN systems.   It will be necessary to check precisely on your particular minicomputer:

1. Are **logical** and/or **complex** type quantities admissible?
2. **Representation of Real Constants:** How many digits are accommodated?   Are all possible formats, for example,

5E-02	0.05
0.5E-01	0.5E-1
5.0E-02	

admissible?   The same questions should be answered for **double-precision** quantities.
3. **Logical constants** are **.TRUE.** and **.FALSE.** If no logical variables and operations are available, you can still employ the arithmetic IF statement.
4. Check on **specification statements** for declaring variables as real, logical, etc. In general, integer names begin with I, J, K, L, M, or N.
5. Check on the extent to which expressions can be used as subscripts for **subscripted variables.**
6. **Relational Operators:** **.LT.**, **.LE.**, **.EQ.**, **.NE.**, **.GT.**, **.GE.** Are all admissible? Are **logical expressions** admitted?
7. Check on the availability of each of the following **control statements:**
   (*a*) **Assigned** GO TO: ASSIGN 18 TO K
                       GO TO K, (3, 4, 18, 21)
   (*b*) **Computed** GO TO: I = 2
                         GO TO (3, 18, 21), I
   The examples in (*a*) and (*b*) are equivalent to the *unconditional* GO TO 18.
   (*c*) **Arithmetic** IF: IF (arithmetic expression) n_1, n_2, n_3
         Program goes to statement number n_1, n_2, or n_3 if the specified expression is, respectively, less than, equal to, or greater than zero.
   (*d*) **Logical** IF: IF (logical expression) (statement)
         The specified statement, which must be executable and neither a DO nor a logical IF statement, is executed if the logical expression is true; otherwise, control transfers to the following statement.   The logical expression might be a hardware sense line or switch output:

$$IF\ (SENSE\ SWITCH\ 3)\qquad (statement)$$

TABLE A-1. Minicomputer FORTRAN Check List (*Continued*).

(*e*) DO n INDEX $= m_1, m_2, m_3$
  n is a statement number; m_1 and m_2 are the *initial* and *final values* of the integer INDEX, and m_3 is the *increment* of INDEX. If $m_3 = 1$, one may write

$$\text{DO n INDEX} = m_1, m_2$$

(*f*) CONTINUE   STOP   PAUSE n
  PAUSE   END   STOP n

8. Check on the interpretation of READ and WRITE statements and device numbers; minicomputer peripheral devices may differ from those used with batch-processed FORTRAN systems on large digital computers.
9. Check on the **library subroutines** and **special functions** available with your FORTRAN system.
10. **Can FORTRAN programs be linked to assembly-language programs?**
11. Can FORTRAN be used for interrupt servicing?

TABLE A-2. A Quick Reference Guide to BASIC.

This table was prepared by the software staff of the Hewlett-Packard Corporation for their 2000B (time-shared) version of BASIC. The complete BASIC system illustrated here is more than a simple algebraic-interpreter language; it permits array and matrix manipulation, limited string manipulation, some editing, file manipulation, and chaining (overlays) of program segments. Hewlett-Packard BASIC has also been extended to operate with *displays* and *instruments* (Sec. 5-25). Nevertheless, completely untrained operators can use BASIC as a very simple "conversational calculator" by typing statements like

LET V1 = 7.5
LET B = V1 + 2.1

as commands, i.e., *without statement numbers*, and to obtain answers by typing, say

PRINT B, V1

OPERATORS
Operators are used in the statements of a program.

Sample Statement	*Purpose/Meaning/Type*
100 A = B = C = 0	Assignment operator; assigns a value to a variable.
110 LET A = 0	May also be used without LET.
120 Z = X↑2	Exponentiate (as in X^2).
130 LET C5 = (A∗B)∗N2	Multiply.
140 IF T5/4 = 3 THEN 200	Divide.
150 LET P = R1 + 10	Add.
160 X3 = R3 − P	Subtract.

NOTE: The numeric values used in logical evaluation are: "true" = any nonzero number; "false" = 0.

170 IF D = E THEN 600	*Expression* "equals" *expression*.

Example	*Purpose*
180 IF (D + E)#(2∗D) THEN 710	*Expression* "does not equal" *expression*.
180 IF (D + E)< >(2∗D) THEN 700	*Expression* "does not equal" *expression*.
190 IF X > 10 THEN 620	*Expression* "is greater than" *expression*.
200 IF R8 < P7 THEN 640	*Expression* "is less than" *expression*.
210 IF R8 > = P7 THEN 810	*Expression* "is greater than or equal to" *expression*.
220 IF X2 < = 10 THEN 650	*Expression* "is less than or equal to" *expression*.

TABLE A-2.   A Quick Reference Guide to BASIC (*Continued*).

Example	*Purpose*
230 IF G2 AND H5 THEN 900	*Expression* 1 AND *expression* 2 must both be "true" for composite to be "true."
240 IF G2 OR H5 THEN 910	If either *expression* 1 OR *expression* 2 is "true," composite is "true."
250 IF NOT G5 THEN 950	Total expression NOT G5 is "true" when *expression* G5 is "false."
260 LET B = A2 MAX C3	Evaluates for the larger of the two expressions.
270 LET B1 = A7 MIN A9	Evaluates for the smaller of the two expressions.

STATEMENTS

Programs consist of numbered statements.   The statements are ordered by number.

Example	*Purpose*
300 CHAIN PROG	GETs and RUNs the program specified. The current
310 CHAIN $LIBR	program is destroyed, except for COMmon variables.
320 COM A,B1,C(20),C$(72)	Declares variables to be in COMmon; they can then be accessed by other programs. Must be lowest numbered statements.
360 DATA 99, 106.7, "HI!"	Specifies data; read from left to right.
310 DIM A(72)	Defines maximum size of a string or matrix.
400 END	Terminates the program; must be last statement in a program.
375 ENTER #T	Fills the first variable #T with the user terminal number
380 ENTER A,B,C	and/or allows the user a specified number of seconds to
390 ENTER T,A,B,C$	reply (A), returns the actual response time B, and returns the value entered C,C$. On time out, the response time is set to -256. On illegal input type, the response time is negated.
400 FOR J = 1 TO N STEP 3	Executes the statements between FOR and NEXT a specified
500 NEXT J	number of times, incrementing the variable by a STEP number (or by 1 if STEP is not given).
330 GO TO 900	Transfers control (jumps) to specified statement number.
412 GO TO N OF 100,10,20	Transfers control to the Nth statement of the statements listed after "OF."
420 GOSUB 800	Begins executing the subroutine at specified statement. (See RETURN.)
415 GOSUB N OF 100,10,20	Begins executing the subroutine N of the subroutines listed after "OF." (See RETURN.)
340 IF A #10 THEN 350	Logical test; transfers control to statement number if "true."
390 INPUT X$,Y2,B4	Allows data to be entered from terminal while a program is running.
300 LET A = B = C = 0	Assigns a value to a variable; LET is optional.
310 A1 = 6.35	
360 READ A,B,C	Reads information from DATA statement.
350 READ #3;A	See "Files."
320 REM--ANY TEXT**!!	Inserts nonexecutable remarks in a program.
356 PRINT A,B,C$	Prints the specified values; 5 fields per line when commas are used as separators, 12 when semicolons are used.
358 PRINT	Causes the teleprinter to advance one line.
395 PRINT #3;A	See "Files."
380 RESTORE	Permits rereading data without rerunning the program.
385 RESTORE N	Permits data to be reread, beginning in statement N.
850 RETURN	Subroutine exit: transfers control to the statement following the matching GOSUB.
410 STOP	Terminates the program; may be used anywhere in program.

TABLE A-2. A Quick Reference Guide to **BASIC** (*Continued*).

STRINGS

1. A string is 1 to 72 teleprinter characters enclosed in quotes; it may be assigned to a string variable (an A to Z letter followed by a $).
2. Each string variable used in a program must be dimensioned (with a DIM or COM statement) if it has a length of more than one character. The DIM sets the physical or maximum length of a string.
3. Substrings are described by subscripted string variables. For example, if A$ = "ABCDEF," then A$(2,2) = B, and A$(1,4) = "ABCD."
4. The LEN function returns the current string length, for example: 100 PRINT LEN (A$). This length is the logical length.

Example	*Purpose*
10 DIM A$(27)	Declares the maximum string length in characters.
20 LET A$ = "**TEXT 1"	Assigns the character string in quotes to a string variable.
30 PRINT LEN (B$)	Gives the current length of the specified string.
105 IF A$=C$ THEN 600	String operators. They allow comparison of strings,
110 IF B$≠X$ THEN 650	and substrings, and transfer to a specified statement.
115 IF N$(2,2)>B$(3,3) THEN 10	Comparison is made in ASCII codes, character by
120 IF N$<B$ THEN 999	character, left to right until a difference is found.
125 IF P$(5,8)> =Y$(4,7) THEN 10	If the strings are of unequal length, the shorter
130 IF X$< =Z$ THEN 999	string is considered smaller if it is identical to the initial substring of the longer.
205 INPUT N$	Accepts as many characters as the string can hold (followed by a *return*). The characters need not be in quotation marks if only one string is input.
210 INPUT N$,X$,Y$	Inputs the specified strings; input must be in quotes, separated by commas.
215 READ P$	Reads a string from a DATA statement; string must be enclosed in quotes.
220 READ #5; A$,B$	Reads strings from the specified file.
310 PRINT #2; A$,C$	Prints strings on a file.

FUNCTIONS

Functions return a numeric result; they may be used as expressions or parts of expressions. PRINT is used for examples only; other statement types may be used.

Example	*Purpose*
300 DEF FNA (X)=(M*X)+B	Allows the programmer to define functions; the function label A must be a letter from A to Z.
310 PRINT ABS (X)	Gives the absolute value of the expression X.
320 PRINT EXP (X)	Gives the constant *e* raised to the power of the expression value X; in this example, $e+X$.
330 PRINT INT (X)	Gives the largest integer ≤ the expression X.
340 PRINT LOG (X)	Gives the natural logarithm of an expression; expression must have a positive value.
350 PRINT RND (X)	Generates a random number greater than or equal to 0 and less than 1; the argument X may have any value.
360 PRINT SQR (X)	Gives the square root of the expression X; expression must have a positive value.
370 PRINT SIN (X)	Gives the sine of the expression X; X is real and in radians.
380 PRINT COS (X)	Gives the cosine of the expression X; X is real and in radians.
390 PRINT TAN (X)	Gives the tangent of the expression X; X is real and in radians.
400 PRINT ATN (X)	Gives the arctangent of the expression X; X is real, result is in radians.

TABLE A-2. A Quick Reference Guide to BASIC (*Continued*).

Sample Statement	Purpose
410 PRINT LEN (A$)	Gives the current length of a string A$, i.e., number of characters.
420 PRINT SGN (X)	Gives: 1 if $X > 0$, 0 if $X = 0$, -1 if $X < 0$.
430 PRINT TAB (X); A	Tabs to the specified position X, then prints the specified value A. Used for plotting.
440 PRINT TIM (X)	Gives current minute $(X = 0)$, hour $(X = 1)$, day $(X = 2)$, or year of century $(X = 3)$.
450 PRINT TYP (X);	If argument X is negative, gives the type of data in a file as: 1 = number, 2 = string, 3 = "end of file," 4 = "end of record"; or if argument X is positive, gives the type of data in a file as: 1 = number, 2 = string, 3 = "end of file." (For sequential access to files—skips over "end of records.") If argument $X = 0$, gives the type of data in a DATA statement as: 1 = number, 2 = string, 3 = "out of data."

MATRICES

Absolute maximum matrix size is 2,500 elements. Matrix variables must be a single letter from A to Z.

Sample Statement	Purpose
10 DIM A (10,20)	Allocates space for a matrix of the specified dimensions.
15 MAT X = IDN (M,M)	Establishes an identity matrix (with all 1s down the diagonal). A new working size (M,M) can be specified.
20 MAT B = ZER	Sets all elements of the specified matrix equal to 0.
25 MAT D = ZER (M,N)	A new working size (M,N) may be specified after ZER.
30 MAT C = CON	Sets all elements of the specified matrix equal to 1.
35 MAT E = CON (M,N)	A new working size (M,N) may be specified after CON.
40 INPUT A(5,5)	Allows input from the teleprinter of a single specified matrix element.
45 MAT INPUT A(4,7)	Allows input of an entire matrix from the teleprinter; a new working size can be specified.
50 MAT PRINT A;	Prints the specified matrix on the teleprinter.
55 PRINT A(X,Y)	Prints the specified element of a matrix on the teleprinter; element specifications X and Y can be any expression.
60 PRINT #2; A(1,5)	Prints matrix element on the specified file.
65 MAT PRINT #2,3;A	Prints matrix on a specified file and record.
70 MAT READ A	Reads matrix from DATA statements.
75 MAT READ A(5,5)	Reads matrix of specified size from DATA statements.
80 READ A(X,Y)	Reads the specified matrix element from a DATA statement.
85 MAT READ #3; A(I,J)	Reads matrix from the specified file; new working size can be specified.
90 MAT READ #3,5;A	Reads matrix from the specified record of a file.
100 MAT C = A + B	Matrix addition; A and B must be the same size.
110 MAT C = A − B	Matrix subtraction; A, B, and C must be the same size.
120 MAT C = A * B	Matrix multiplication; number of columns in A must equal number of rows in B.
130 MAT A = B	Establishes equality of two matrices; assigns values of B to A.
140 MAT B = TRN (A)	Transposes an *m* by *n* matrix to an *n* by *m* matrix.
150 MAT C = INV (B)	Inverts a square matrix into a square matrix of the same size; matrix can be inverted into itself.

TABLE A-2. **A Quick Reference Guide to BASIC** (*Continued*).

FILES

A FILE = a named storage area of from 1 to 128 records.   Maximum size varies with systems.
A RECORD = 64 words of memory.
A NUMBER = a data item using 2 words of memory.
A STRING = a data item using about $\frac{1}{2}$ word of memory per character.

Example	*Purpose*
OPE-MYFILE,80	Opens a file with a specified name and size.
KIL-MYFILE	Removes the specified file.
10 FILES BUG,GANG	Declares which files will be used in a program. Up to 4 FILES statements with a total of 16 files per program. Files must be OPEned first.
20 PRINT #N A,B	Prints the specified values A,B on a specified file at the current position. Files are numbered from 1 as they appear in the FILES statements.
30 PRINT #X,Y A,B,C$	Prints the specified values on a specified record Y of a file X.
40 PRINT 3,5	Erases the specified record of a file.
70 READ #1 A,B2	Reads the next values of a specified file into the specified variables.
80 READ #2,3 A,B	Reads values from the beginning of a specified record of a file into specified variables.
185 READ #3,5	Resets the pointer for a file to a specified record.
190 IF END #N THEN 800	Transfers control to a specified statement if an end-of-file occurs on a specified file.

COMMANDS

Commands are executed immediately; they do not have statement numbers.

Example	*Purpose*
APP-PROGI	Appends the named program to the current program.
BYE	Logs the user off his terminal.
CAT	Lists the names and lengths of user library programs.
CSA	Saves the current program in semicompiled form.
DEL-100	Deletes all statements after and including the specified ones.
DEL-100,200	Deletes all statements between and including the specified ones.
ECH-OFF	Permits use of half-duplex coupler.
ECH-ON	Returns user to full-duplex mode.
GET-SAMPLE	Retrieves the program from the user's library and makes it the current program.
GET-$PROG	Retrieves the program from the system library.
HEL-D007,BᶜGᶜ	Logs the user onto his terminal. User might give I.D. code and password.
KEY	Returns terminal to keyboard entry after TAPE command.
KIL-SAMPLE	Deletes the specified program from the user's library (does not modify the current program).
LEN	Lists the current program length in words.
LIB	Lists the names and lengths of system library programs.
LIS	Lists the current program, optionally starting at a specified statement
LIS-150	number and stopping at a specified statement.
LIS-100,200	
NAM-SAMPLE	Assigns the name to the current program; name may consist of one to six printing characters.

TABLE A-2. A Quick Reference Guide to BASIC (*Continued*).

Example	*Purpose*
PUN	Punches the current program to paper tape, optionally starting at a
PUN-50	specified statement number and optionally stopping at a specified
PUN-100,200	statement.
REN	Renumbers the current program from 10 (optionally from a specified
REN-50	statement number) in multiples of 10 (optionally in multiples of a specified
REN-50,20	number).
RUN	Starts executing the current program, optionally starting at a specified
RUN-50	statement number.
SAV	Saves the current program in the user's library.
SCR	Erases the current program (but not the program name).
TAP	Informs system that input will now be from paper tape.
TIM	Lists terminal and account time.

EXAMPLE: A Complete BASIC Program

Program   10 LET X = 1
20 FOR Y = 1.1 TO 3.1 STEP .5
30 LET H = SQR(X↑2 + Y↑2)
40 PRINT "WHEN (X,Y) =" X;Y; "THE HYPOTENUSE IS" H
50 NEXT Y
60 END
RUN

Results   WHEN (X,Y) = 1 1.1 THE HYPOTENUSE IS 1.48661
WHEN (X,Y) = 1 1.6 THE HYPOTENUSE IS 1.8868
WHEN (X,Y) = 1 2.1 THE HYPOTENUSE IS 2.32594
WHEN (X,Y) = 1 2.6 THE HYPOTENUSE IS 2.78568
WHEN (X,Y) = 1 3.1 THE HYPOTENUSE IS 3.2573
DONE

REFERENCE TABLES

TABLE B-1. Powers of Two.

		2^N			N
				1	0
				2	1
				4	2
				8	3
				16	4
				32	5
				64	6
				128	7
				256	8
				512	9
			1	024	10
			2	048	11
			4	096	12
			8	192	13
			16	384	14
			32	768	15
			65	536	16
			131	072	17
			262	144	18
			524	288	19
		1	048	576	20
		2	097	152	21
		4	194	304	22
		8	388	608	23
		16	777	216	24
		33	554	432	25
		67	108	864	26
		134	217	728	27
		268	435	456	28
		536	870	912	29
	1	073	741	824	30
	2	147	483	648	31
	4	294	967	296	32
	8	589	934	592	33
	17	179	869	184	34
	34	359	738	368	35
	68	719	476	736	36
	137	438	953	472	37
	274	877	906	944	38
	549	755	813	888	39
1	099	511	627	776	40
2	199	023	255	552	41
4	398	046	511	104	42
8	796	093	022	208	43
17	592	186	044	416	44
35	184	372	088	832	45
70	368	744	177	664	46
140	737	488	355	328	47
281	474	976	710	656	48
562	949	953	421	312	49

TABLE B-1. Powers of Two (*Continued*).

2^N

											N
					1	125	899	906	842	624	50
					2	251	799	813	685	248	51
					4	503	599	627	370	496	52
					9	007	199	254	740	992	53
					18	014	398	509	481	984	54
					36	028	797	018	963	968	55
					72	057	594	037	927	936	56
					144	115	188	075	855	872	57
					288	230	376	151	711	744	58
					576	460	752	303	423	488	59
				1	152	921	504	606	846	976	60
				2	305	843	009	213	693	952	61
				4	611	686	018	427	387	904	62
				9	223	372	036	854	775	808	63
				18	446	744	073	709	551	616	64
				36	893	488	147	419	103	232	65
				73	786	976	294	838	206	464	66
				147	573	952	589	676	412	928	67
				295	147	905	179	352	825	856	68
				590	295	810	358	705	651	712	69
			1	180	591	620	717	411	303	424	70
			2	361	183	241	434	822	606	848	71
			4	722	366	482	869	645	213	696	72
			9	444	732	965	739	290	427	392	73
			18	889	465	931	478	580	854	784	74
			37	778	931	862	957	161	709	568	75
			75	557	863	725	914	323	419	136	76
			151	115	727	451	828	646	838	272	77
			302	231	454	903	657	293	676	544	78
			604	462	909	807	314	587	353	088	79
		1	208	925	819	614	629	174	706	176	80
		2	417	851	639	229	258	349	412	352	81
		4	835	703	278	458	516	698	824	704	82
		9	671	406	556	917	033	397	649	408	83
		19	342	813	113	834	066	795	298	816	84
		38	685	626	227	668	133	590	597	632	85
		77	371	252	455	336	267	181	195	264	86
		154	742	504	910	672	534	362	390	528	87
		309	485	009	821	345	068	724	781	056	88
		618	970	019	642	690	137	449	562	112	89
	1	237	940	039	285	380	274	899	124	224	90
	2	475	880	078	570	760	549	798	248	448	91
	4	951	760	157	141	521	099	596	496	896	92
	9	903	520	314	283	042	199	192	993	792	93
	19	807	040	628	566	084	398	385	987	584	94
	39	614	081	257	132	168	796	771	975	168	95
	79	228	162	514	264	337	593	543	950	336	96
	158	456	325	028	528	675	187	087	900	672	97
	316	912	650	057	057	350	374	175	801	344	98
	633	825	300	114	114	700	748	351	602	688	99
1	267	650	600	228	229	401	496	703	205	376	100

TABLE B-2. **Miscellaneous Tables.**

2^x IN DECIMAL

x	2^x	x	2^x	x	2^x
0.001	1.00069 33874 62581	0.01	1.00695 55500 56719	0.1	1.07177 34625 36293
0.002	1.00138 72557 11335	0.02	1.01395 94797 90029	0.2	1.14869 83549 97035
0.003	1.00208 16050 79633	0.03	1.02101 21257 07193	0.3	1.23114 44133 44916
0.004	1.00277 64359 01078	0.04	1.02811 38266 56067	0.4	1.31950 79107 72894
0.005	1.00347 17485 09503	0.05	1.03526 49238 41377	0.5	1.41421 35623 73095
0.006	1.00416 75432 38973	0.06	1.04246 57608 41121	0.6	1.51571 65665 10398
0.007	1.00486 38204 23785	0.07	1.04971 66836 23067	0.7	1.62450 47927 12471
0.008	1.00556 05803 98468	0.08	1.05701 80405 61380	0.8	1.74110 11265 92248
0.009	1.00625 78234 97782	0.09	1.06437 01824 53360	0.9	1.86606 59830 73615

$10^{\pm n}$ IN OCTAL

10^n	n	10^{-n}	10^n	n	10^{-n}
1	0	1.000 000 000 000 000 000 00	112 402 762 000	10	0.000 000 000 006 676 337 66
12	1	0.063 146 314 631 463 146 31	1 351 035 564 000	11	0.000 000 000 000 537 657 77
144	2	0.005 075 341 217 270 243 66	16 432 451 210 000	12	0.000 000 000 000 043 136 32
1 750	3	0.000 406 111 564 570 651 77	221 411 634 520 000	13	0.000 000 000 000 003 411 35
23 420	4	0.000 032 155 613 530 704 15	2 657 142 036 440 000	14	0.000 000 000 000 000 264 11
303 240	5	0.000 002 476 132 610 706 64	34 327 724 461 500 000	15	0.000 000 000 000 000 022 01
3 641 100	6	0.000 000 206 157 364 055 37	434 157 115 760 200 000	16	0.000 000 000 000 000 001 63
46 113 200	7	0.000 000 015 327 745 152 75	5 432 127 413 542 400 000	17	0.000 000 000 000 000 000 14
575 360 400	8	0.000 000 001 257 143 561 06	67 405 553 164 731 000 000	18	0.000 000 000 000 000 000 01
7 346 545 000	9	0.000 000 000 104 560 276 41			

$n \log_{10} 2$, $n \log_2 10$ IN DECIMAL

n	$n \log_{10} 2$	$n \log_2 10$	n	$n \log_{10} 2$	$n \log_2 10$
1	0.30102 99957	3.32192 80949	6	1.80617 99740	19.93156 85693
2	0.60205 99913	6.64385 61898	7	2.10720 99696	23.25349 66642
3	0.90308 99870	9.96578 42847	8	2.40823 99653	26.57542 47591
4	1.20411 99827	13.28771 23795	9	2.70926 99610	29.89735 28540
5	1.50514 99783	16.60964 04744	10	3.01029 99566	33.21928 09489

ADDITION AND MULTIPLICATION TABLES

Addition   Multiplication

Binary Scale

$$0 + 0 = 0 \qquad\qquad 0 \times 0 = 0$$
$$0 + 1 = 1 + 0 = 1 \qquad 0 \times 1 = 1 \times 0 = 0$$
$$1 + 1 = 10 \qquad\qquad 1 \times 1 = 1$$

Octal Scale

0	01	02	03	04	05	06	07	1	02	03	04	05	06	07
1	02	03	04	05	06	07	10	2	04	06	10	12	14	16
2	03	04	05	06	07	10	11	3	06	11	14	17	22	25
3	04	05	06	07	10	11	12	4	10	14	20	24	30	34
4	05	06	07	10	11	12	13	5	12	17	24	31	36	43
5	06	07	10	11	12	13	14	6	14	22	30	36	44	52
6	07	10	11	12	13	14	15	7	16	25	34	43	52	61
7	10	11	12	13	14	15	16							

MATHEMATICAL CONSTANTS IN OCTAL SCALE

$\pi = 3.11037\ 552421_8$ $\qquad e = 2.55760\ 521305_8$ $\qquad \gamma = 0.44742\ 147707_8$

$\pi^{-1} = 0.24276\ 301556_8$ $\qquad e^{-1} = 0.27426\ 530661_8$ $\qquad \ln \gamma = -0.43127\ 233602_8$

$\sqrt{\pi} = 1.61337\ 611067_8$ $\qquad \sqrt{e} = 1.51411\ 230704_8$ $\qquad \log_2 \gamma = -0.62573\ 030645_8$

$\ln \pi = 1.11206\ 404435_8$ $\qquad \log_{10} e = 0.33626\ 754251_8$ $\qquad \sqrt{2} = 1.32404\ 746320_8$

$\log_2 \pi = 1.51544\ 163223_8$ $\qquad \log_2 e = 1.34252\ 166245_8$ $\qquad \ln 2 = 0.54271\ 027760_8$

$\sqrt{10} = 3.12305\ 407267_8$ $\qquad \log_2 10 = 3.24464\ 741136_8$ $\qquad \ln 10 = 2.23273\ 067355_8$

TABLE B-3. Octal-Decimal Integer Conversion Table.

$X =$	0	1	2	3	4	5	6	7
0X	0	1	2	3	4	5	6	7
1X	8	9	10	11	12	13	14	15
2X	16	17	18	19	20	21	22	23
3X	24	25	26	27	28	29	30	31
4X	32	33	34	35	36	37	38	39
5X	40	41	42	43	44	45	46	47
6X	48	49	50	51	52	53	54	55
7X	56	57	58	59	60	61	62	63
10X	64	65	66	67	68	69	70	71
11X	72	73	74	75	76	77	78	79
12X	80	81	82	83	84	85	86	87
13X	88	89	90	91	92	93	94	95
14X	96	97	98	99	100	101	102	103
15X	104	105	106	107	108	109	110	111
16X	112	113	114	115	116	117	118	119
17X	120	121	122	123	124	125	126	127
20X	128	129	130	131	132	133	134	135
21X	136	137	138	139	140	141	142	143
22X	144	145	146	147	148	149	150	151
23X	152	153	154	155	156	157	158	159
24X	160	161	162	163	164	165	166	167
25X	168	169	170	171	172	173	174	175
26X	176	177	178	179	180	181	182	183
27X	184	185	186	187	188	189	190	191
30X	192	193	194	195	196	197	198	199
31X	200	201	202	203	204	205	206	207
32X	208	209	210	211	212	213	214	215
33X	216	217	218	219	220	221	222	223
34X	224	225	226	227	228	229	230	231
35X	232	233	234	235	236	237	238	239
36X	240	241	242	243	244	245	246	247
37X	248	249	250	251	252	253	254	255
40X	256	257	258	259	260	261	262	263
41X	264	265	266	267	268	269	270	271
42X	272	273	274	275	276	277	278	279
43X	280	281	282	283	284	285	286	287
44X	288	289	290	291	292	293	294	295
45X	296	297	298	299	300	301	302	303
46X	304	305	306	307	308	309	310	311
47X	312	313	314	315	316	317	318	319
50X	320	321	322	323	324	325	326	327
51X	328	329	330	331	332	333	334	335
52X	336	337	338	339	340	341	342	343
53X	344	345	346	347	348	349	350	351

Octal	Decimal
10000 =	4096
20000 =	8192
30000 =	12288
40000 =	16384
50000 =	20480
60000 =	24576
70000 =	28672

335

TABLE B-3. Octal-Decimal Integer Conversion Table (*Continued*).

$X =$	0	1	2	3	4	5	6	7
54X	352	353	354	355	356	357	358	359
55X	360	361	362	363	364	365	366	367
56X	368	369	370	371	372	373	374	375
57X	376	377	378	379	380	381	382	383
60X	384	385	386	387	388	389	390	391
61X	392	393	394	395	396	397	398	399
62X	400	401	402	403	404	405	406	407
63X	408	409	410	411	412	413	414	415
64X	416	417	418	419	420	421	422	423
65X	424	425	426	427	428	429	430	431
66X	432	433	434	435	436	437	438	439
67X	440	441	442	443	444	445	446	447
70X	448	449	450	451	452	453	454	455
71X	456	457	458	459	460	461	462	463
72X	464	465	466	467	468	469	470	471
73X	472	473	474	475	476	477	478	479
74X	480	481	482	483	484	485	486	487
75X	488	489	490	491	492	493	494	495
76X	496	497	498	499	500	501	502	503
77X	504	505	506	507	508	509	510	511
100X	512	513	514	515	516	517	518	519
101X	520	521	522	523	524	525	526	527
102X	528	529	530	531	532	533	534	535
103X	536	537	538	539	540	541	542	543
104X	544	545	546	547	548	549	550	551
105X	552	553	554	555	556	557	558	559
106X	560	561	562	563	564	565	566	567
107X	568	569	570	571	572	573	574	575
110X	576	577	578	579	580	581	582	583
111X	584	585	586	587	588	589	590	591
112X	592	593	594	595	596	597	598	599
113X	600	601	602	603	604	605	606	607
114X	608	609	610	611	612	613	614	615
115X	616	617	618	619	620	621	622	623
116X	624	625	626	627	628	629	630	631
117X	632	633	634	635	636	637	638	639
120X	640	641	642	643	644	645	646	647
121X	648	649	650	651	652	653	654	655
122X	656	657	658	659	660	661	662	663
123X	664	665	666	667	668	669	670	671
124X	672	673	674	675	676	677	678	679
125X	680	681	682	683	684	685	686	687
126X	688	689	690	691	692	693	694	695
127X	696	697	698	699	700	701	702	703

Octal	Decimal
100000 =	32768
200000 =	65536
300000 =	98304
400000 =	131072
500000 =	163840
600000 =	196608
700000 =	229376

$X =$	0	1	2	3	4	5	6	7
130X	704	705	706	707	708	709	710	711
131X	712	713	714	715	716	717	718	719
132X	720	721	722	723	724	725	726	727
133X	728	729	730	731	732	733	734	735
134X	736	737	738	739	740	741	742	743
135X	744	745	746	747	748	749	750	751
136X	752	753	754	755	756	757	758	759
137X	760	761	762	763	764	765	766	767
140X	768	769	770	771	772	773	774	775
141X	776	777	778	779	780	781	782	783
142X	784	785	786	787	788	789	790	791
143X	792	793	794	795	796	797	798	799
144X	800	801	802	803	804	805	806	807
145X	808	809	810	811	812	813	814	815
146X	816	817	818	819	820	821	822	823
147X	824	825	826	827	828	829	830	831
150X	832	833	834	835	836	837	838	839
151X	840	841	842	843	844	845	846	847
152X	848	849	850	851	852	853	854	855
153X	856	857	858	859	860	861	862	863
154X	864	865	866	867	868	869	870	871
155X	872	873	874	875	876	877	878	879
156X	880	881	882	883	884	885	886	887
157X	888	889	890	891	892	893	894	895
160X	896	897	898	899	900	901	902	903
161X	904	905	906	907	908	909	910	911
162X	912	913	914	915	916	917	918	919
163X	920	921	922	923	924	925	926	927
164X	928	929	930	931	932	933	934	935
165X	936	937	938	939	940	941	942	943
166X	944	945	946	947	948	949	950	951
167X	952	953	954	955	956	957	958	959
170X	960	961	962	963	964	965	966	967
171X	968	969	970	971	972	973	974	975
172X	976	977	978	979	980	981	982	983
173X	984	985	986	987	988	989	990	991
174X	992	993	994	995	996	997	998	999
175X	1000	1001	1002	1003	1004	1005	1006	1007
176X	1008	1009	1010	1011	1012	1013	1014	1015
177X	1016	1017	1018	1019	1020	1021	1022	1023
200X	1024	1025	1026	1027	1028	1029	1030	1031
201X	1032	1033	1034	1035	1036	1037	1038	1039
202X	1040	1041	1042	1043	1044	1045	1046	1047
203X	1048	1049	1050	1051	1052	1053	1054	1055
204X	1056	1057	1058	1059	1060	1061	1062	1063
205X	1064	1065	1066	1067	1068	1069	1070	1071

Octal	Decimal
1000000 =	262144
2000000 =	524288
3000000 =	786432
4000000 =	1048576
5000000 =	1310720
6000000 =	1572864
7000000 =	1835008

$X =$	0	1	2	3	4	5	6	7
206X	1072	1073	1074	1075	1076	1077	1078	1079
207X	1080	1081	1082	1083	1084	1085	1086	1087
210X	1088	1089	1090	1091	1092	1093	1094	1095
211X	1096	1097	1098	1099	1100	1101	1102	1103
212X	1104	1105	1106	1107	1108	1109	1110	1111
213X	1112	1113	1114	1115	1116	1117	1118	1119
214X	1120	1121	1122	1123	1124	1125	1126	1127
215X	1128	1129	1130	1131	1132	1133	1134	1135
216X	1136	1137	1138	1139	1140	1141	1142	1143
217X	1144	1145	1146	1147	1148	1149	1150	1151
220X	1152	1153	1154	1155	1156	1157	1158	1159
221X	1160	1161	1162	1163	1164	1165	1166	1167
222X	1168	1169	1170	1171	1172	1173	1174	1175
223X	1176	1177	1178	1179	1180	1181	1182	1183
224X	1184	1185	1186	1187	1188	1189	1190	1191
225X	1192	1193	1194	1195	1196	1197	1198	1199
226X	1200	1201	1202	1203	1204	1205	1206	1207
227X	1208	1209	1210	1211	1212	1213	1214	1215
230X	1216	1217	1218	1219	1220	1221	1222	1223
231X	1224	1225	1226	1227	1228	1229	1230	1231
232X	1232	1233	1234	1235	1236	1237	1238	1239
233X	1240	1241	1242	1243	1244	1245	1246	1247
234X	1248	1249	1250	1251	1252	1253	1254	1255
235X	1256	1257	1258	1259	1260	1261	1262	1263
236X	1264	1265	1266	1267	1268	1269	1270	1271
237X	1272	1273	1274	1275	1276	1277	1278	1279
240X	1280	1281	1282	1283	1284	1285	1286	1287
241X	1288	1289	1290	1291	1292	1293	1294	1295
242X	1296	1297	1298	1299	1300	1301	1302	1303
243X	1304	1305	1306	1307	1308	1309	1310	1311
244X	1312	1313	1314	1315	1316	1317	1318	1319
245X	1320	1321	1322	1323	1324	1325	1326	1327
246X	1328	1329	1330	1331	1332	1333	1334	1335
247X	1336	1337	1338	1339	1340	1241	1342	1343
250X	1344	1345	1346	1347	1348	1349	1350	1351
251X	1352	1353	1354	1355	1356	1357	1358	1359
252X	1360	1361	1362	1363	1364	1365	1366	1367
253X	1368	1369	1370	1371	1372	1373	1374	1375
254X	1376	1377	1378	1379	1380	1381	1382	1383
255X	1384	1385	1386	1387	1388	1389	1390	1391
256X	1392	1393	1394	1395	1396	1397	1398	1399
257X	1400	1401	1402	1403	1404	1405	1406	1407
260X	1408	1409	1410	1411	1412	1413	1414	1415
261X	1416	1417	1418	1419	1420	1421	1422	1423
262X	1424	1425	1426	1427	1428	1429	1430	1431

Octal		Decimal
10000000	=	2097152
20000000	=	4194304
30000000	=	6291456
40000000	=	8388608
50000000	=	10485760
60000000	=	12582912
70000000	=	14680064

$X =$	0	1	2	3	4	5	6	7
$263X$	1432	1433	1434	1435	1436	1437	1438	1439
$264X$	1440	1441	1442	1443	1444	1445	1446	1447
$265X$	1448	1449	1450	1451	1452	1453	1454	1455
$266X$	1456	1457	1458	1459	1460	1461	1462	1463
$267X$	1464	1465	1466	1467	1468	1469	1470	1471
$270X$	1472	1473	1474	1475	1476	1477	1478	1479
$271X$	1480	1481	1482	1483	1484	1485	1486	1487
$272X$	1488	1489	1490	1491	1492	1493	1494	1495
$273X$	1496	1497	1498	1499	1500	1501	1502	1503
$274X$	1504	1505	1506	1507	1508	1509	1510	1511
$275X$	1512	1513	1514	1515	1516	1517	1518	1519
$276X$	1520	1521	1522	1523	1524	1525	1526	1527
$277X$	1528	1529	1530	1531	1532	1533	1534	1535
$300X$	1536	1537	1538	1539	1540	1541	1542	1543
$301X$	1544	1545	1546	1547	1548	1549	1550	1551
$302X$	1552	1553	1554	1555	1556	1557	1558	1559
$303X$	1560	1561	1562	1563	1564	1565	1566	1567
$304X$	1568	1569	1570	1571	1572	1573	1574	1575
$305X$	1576	1577	1578	1579	1580	1581	1582	1583
$306X$	1584	1585	1586	1587	1588	1589	1590	1591
$307X$	1592	1593	1594	1595	1596	1597	1598	1599
$310X$	1600	1601	1602	1603	1604	1605	1606	1607
$311X$	1608	1609	1610	1611	1612	1613	1614	1615
$312X$	1616	1617	1618	1619	1620	1621	1622	1623
$313X$	1624	1625	1626	1627	1628	1629	1630	1631
$314X$	1632	1633	1634	1635	1636	1637	1638	1639
$315X$	1640	1641	1642	1643	1644	1645	1646	1647
$316X$	1648	1649	1650	1651	1652	1653	1654	1655
$317X$	1656	1657	1658	1659	1660	1661	1662	1663
$320X$	1664	1665	1666	1667	1668	1669	1670	1671
$321X$	1672	1673	1674	1675	1676	1677	1678	1679
$322X$	1680	1681	1682	1683	1684	1685	1686	1687
$323X$	1688	1689	1690	1691	1692	1693	1694	1695
$324X$	1696	1697	1698	1699	1700	1701	1702	1703
$325X$	1704	1705	1706	1707	1708	1709	1710	1711
$326X$	1712	1713	1714	1715	1716	1717	1718	1719
$327X$	1720	1721	1722	1723	1724	1725	1726	1727
$330X$	1728	1729	1730	1731	1732	1733	1734	1735
$331X$	1736	1737	1738	1739	1740	1741	1742	1743
$332X$	1744	1745	1746	1747	1748	1749	1750	1751
$333X$	1752	1753	1754	1755	1756	1757	1758	1759
$334X$	1760	1761	1762	1763	1764	1765	1766	1767
$335X$	1768	1769	1770	1771	1772	1773	1774	1775
$336X$	1776	1777	1778	1779	1780	1781	1782	1783
$337X$	1784	1785	1786	1787	1788	1789	1790	1791

Octal	Decimal
100000000 =	16777216
200000000 =	33554432
300000000 =	50331648
400000000 =	67108864
500000000 =	83886080
600000000 =	100663296
700000000 =	117440512

$X =$	0	1	2	3	4	5	6	7
340X	1792	1793	1794	1795	1796	1797	1798	1799
341X	1800	1801	1802	1803	1804	1805	1806	1807
342X	1808	1809	1810	1811	1812	1813	1814	1815
343X	1816	1817	1818	1819	1820	1821	1822	1823
344X	1824	1825	1826	1827	1828	1829	1830	1831
345X	1832	1833	1834	1835	1836	1837	1838	1839
346X	1840	1841	1842	1843	1844	1845	1846	1847
347X	1848	1849	1850	1851	1852	1853	1854	1855
350X	1856	1857	1858	1859	1860	1861	1862	1863
351X	1864	1865	1866	1867	1868	1869	1870	1871
352X	1872	1873	1874	1875	1876	1877	1878	1879
353X	1880	1881	1882	1883	1884	1885	1886	1887
354X	1888	1889	1890	1891	1892	1893	1894	1895
355X	1896	1897	1898	1899	1900	1901	1902	1903
356X	1904	1905	1906	1907	1908	1909	1910	1911
357X	1912	1913	1914	1915	1916	1917	1918	1919
360X	1920	1921	1922	1923	1924	1925	1926	1927
361X	1928	1929	1930	1931	1932	1933	1934	1935
362X	1936	1937	1938	1939	1940	1941	1942	1943
363X	1944	1945	1946	1947	1948	1949	1950	1951
364X	1952	1953	1954	1955	1956	1957	1958	1959
365X	1960	1961	1962	1963	1964	1965	1966	1967
366X	1968	1969	1970	1971	1972	1973	1974	1975
367X	1976	1977	1978	1979	1980	1981	1982	1983
370X	1984	1985	19ǝ6	1987	1988	1989	1990	1991
371X	1992	1993	1994	1995	1996	1997	1998	1999
372X	2000	2001	2002	2003	2004	2005	2006	2007
373X	2008	2009	2010	2011	2012	2013	2014	2015
374X	2016	2017	2018	2019	2020	2021	2022	2023
375X	2024	2025	2026	2027	2028	2029	2030	2031
376X	2032	2033	2034	2035	2036	2037	2038	2039
377X	2040	2041	2042	2043	2044	2045	2046	2047
400X	2048	2049	2050	2051	2052	2053	2054	2055
401X	2056	2057	2058	2059	2060	2061	2062	2063
402X	2064	2065	2066	2067	2068	2069	2070	2071
403X	2072	2073	2074	2075	2076	2077	2078	2079
404X	2080	2081	2082	2083	2084	2085	2086	2087
405X	2088	2089	2090	2091	2092	2093	2094	2095
406X	2096	2097	2098	2099	2100	2101	2102	2103
407X	2104	2105	2106	2107	2108	2109	2110	2111
410X	2112	2113	2114	2115	2116	2117	2118	2119
411X	2120	2121	2122	2123	2124	2125	2126	2127
412X	2128	2129	2130	2131	2132	2133	2134	2135
413X	2136	2137	2138	2139	2140	2141	2142	2143
414X	2144	2145	2146	2147	2148	2149	2150	2151
415X	2152	2153	2154	2155	2156	2157	2158	2159

$X =$	0	1	2	3	4	5	6	7
416X	2160	2161	2162	2163	2164	2165	2166	2167
417X	2168	2169	2170	2171	2172	2173	2174	2175
420X	2176	2177	2178	2179	2180	2181	2182	2183
421X	2184	2185	2186	2187	2188	2189	2190	2191
422X	2192	2193	2194	2195	2196	2197	2198	2199
423X	2200	2201	2202	2203	2204	2205	2206	2207
424X	2208	2209	2210	2211	2212	2213	2214	2215
425X	2216	2217	2218	2219	2220	2221	2222	2223
426X	2224	2225	2226	2227	2228	2229	2230	2231
427X	2232	2233	2234	2235	2236	2237	2238	2239
430X	2240	2241	2242	2243	2244	2245	2246	2247
431X	2248	2249	2250	2251	2252	2253	2254	2255
432X	2256	2257	2258	2259	2260	2261	2262	2263
433X	2264	2265	2266	2267	2268	2269	2270	2271
434X	2272	2273	2274	2275	2276	2277	2278	2279
435X	2280	2281	2282	2283	2284	2285	2286	2287
436X	2288	2289	2290	2291	2292	2293	2294	2295
437X	2296	2297	2298	2299	2300	2301	2302	2303
440X	2304	2305	2306	2307	2308	2309	2310	2311
441X	2312	2313	2314	2315	2316	2317	2318	2319
442X	2320	2321	2322	2323	2324	2325	2326	2327
443X	2328	2329	2330	2331	2332	2333	2334	2335
444X	2336	2337	2338	2339	2340	2341	2342	2343
445X	2344	2345	2346	2347	2348	2349	2350	2351
446X	2352	2353	2354	2355	2356	2357	2358	2359
447X	2360	2361	2362	2363	2364	2365	2366	2367
450X	2368	2369	2370	2371	2372	2373	2374	2375
451X	2376	2377	2378	2379	2380	2381	2382	2383
452X	2384	2385	2386	2387	2388	2389	2390	2391
453X	2392	2393	2394	2395	2396	2397	2398	2399
454X	2400	2401	2402	2403	2404	2405	2406	2407
455X	2408	2409	2410	2411	2412	2413	2414	2415
456X	2416	2417	2418	2419	2420	2421	2422	2423
457X	2424	2425	2426	2427	2428	2429	2430	2431
460X	2432	2433	2434	2435	2436	2437	2438	2439
461X	2440	2441	2442	2443	2444	2445	2446	2447
462X	2448	2449	2450	2451	2452	2453	2454	2455
463X	2456	2457	2458	2459	2460	2461	2462	2463
464X	2464	2465	2466	2467	2468	2469	2470	2471
465X	2472	2473	2474	2475	2476	2477	2478	2479
466X	2480	2481	2482	2483	2484	2485	2486	2487
467X	2488	2489	2490	2491	2492	2493	2494	2495
470X	2496	2497	2498	2499	2500	2501	2502	2503
471X	2504	2505	2506	2507	2508	2509	2510	2511
472X	2512	2513	2514	2515	2516	2517	2518	2519

TABLE B-3. Octal-Decimal Integer Conversion Table (*Continued*).

X =	0	1	2	3	4	5	6	7
473X	2520	2521	2522	2523	2524	2525	2526	2527
474X	2528	2529	2530	2531	2532	2533	2534	2535
475X	2536	2537	2538	2539	2540	2541	2542	2543
476X	2544	2545	2546	2547	2548	2549	2550	2551
477X	2552	2553	2554	2555	2556	2557	2558	2559
500X	2560	2561	2562	2563	2564	2565	2566	2567
501X	2568	2569	2570	2571	2572	2573	2574	2575
502X	2576	2577	2578	2579	2580	2581	2582	2583
503X	2584	2585	2586	2587	2588	2589	2590	2591
504X	2592	2593	2594	2595	2596	2597	2598	2599
505X	2600	2601	2602	2603	2604	2605	2606	2607
506X	2608	2609	2610	2611	2612	2613	2614	2615
507X	2616	2617	2618	2619	2620	2621	2622	2623
510X	2624	2625	2626	2627	2628	2629	2630	2631
511X	2632	2633	2634	2635	2636	2637	2638	2639
512X	2640	2641	2642	2643	2644	2645	2646	2647
513X	2648	2649	2650	2651	2652	2653	2654	2655
514X	2656	2657	2658	2659	2660	2661	2662	2663
515X	2664	2665	2666	2667	2668	2669	2670	2671
516X	2672	2673	2674	2675	2676	2677	2678	2679
517X	2680	2681	2682	2683	2684	2685	2686	2687
520X	2688	2689	2690	2691	2692	2693	2694	2695
521X	2696	2697	2698	2699	2700	2701	2702	2703
522X	2704	2705	2706	2707	2708	2709	2710	2711
523X	2712	2713	2714	2715	2716	2717	2718	2719
524X	2720	2721	2722	2723	2724	2725	2726	2727
525X	2728	2729	2730	2731	2732	2733	2734	2735
526X	2736	2737	2738	2739	2740	2741	2742	2743
527X	2744	2745	2746	2747	2748	2749	2750	2751
530X	2752	2753	2754	2755	2756	2757	2758	2759
531X	2760	2761	2762	2763	2764	2765	2766	2767
532X	2768	2769	2770	2771	2772	2773	2774	2775
533X	2776	2777	2778	2779	2780	2781	2782	2783
534X	2784	2785	2786	2787	2788	2789	2790	2791
535X	2792	2793	2794	2795	2796	2797	2798	2799
536X	2800	2801	2802	2803	2804	2805	2806	2807
537X	2808	2809	2810	2811	2812	2813	2814	2815
540X	2816	2817	2818	2819	2820	2821	2822	2823
541X	2824	2825	2826	2827	2828	2829	2830	2831
542X	2832	2833	2834	2835	2836	2837	2838	2839
543X	2840	2841	2842	2843	2844	2845	2846	2847
544X	2848	2849	2850	2851	2852	2853	2854	2855
545X	2856	2857	2858	2859	2860	2861	2862	2863
546X	2864	2865	2866	2867	2868	2869	2870	2871
547X	2872	2873	2874	2875	2876	2877	2878	2879

$X =$	0	1	2	3	4	5	6	7
550X	2880	2881	2882	2883	2884	2885	2886	2887
551X	2888	2889	2890	2891	2892	2893	2894	2895
552X	2896	2897	2898	2899	2900	2901	2902	2903
553X	2904	2905	2906	2907	2908	2909	2910	2911
554X	2912	2913	2914	2915	2916	2917	2918	2919
555X	2920	2921	2922	2923	2924	2925	2926	2927
556X	2928	2929	2930	2931	2932	2933	2934	2935
557X	2936	2937	2938	2939	2940	2941	2942	2943
560X	2944	2945	2946	2947	2948	2949	2950	2951
561X	2952	2953	2954	2955	2956	2957	2958	2959
562X	2960	2961	2962	2963	2964	2965	2966	2967
563X	2968	2969	2970	2971	2972	2973	2974	2975
564X	2976	2977	2978	2979	2980	2981	2982	2983
565X	2984	2985	2986	2987	2988	2989	2990	2991
566X	2992	2993	2994	2995	2996	2997	2998	2999
567X	3000	3001	3002	3003	3004	3005	3006	3007
570X	3008	3009	3010	3011	3012	3013	3014	3015
571X	3016	3017	3018	3019	3020	3021	3022	3023
572X	3024	3025	3026	3027	3028	3029	3030	3031
573X	3032	3033	3034	3035	3036	3037	3038	3039
574X	3040	3041	3042	3043	3044	3045	3046	3047
575X	3048	3049	3050	3051	3052	3053	3054	3055
576X	3056	3057	3058	3059	3060	3061	3062	3063
577X	3064	3065	3066	3067	3068	3069	3070	3071
600X	3072	3073	3074	3075	3076	3077	3078	3079
601X	3080	3081	3082	3083	3084	3085	3086	3087
602X	3088	3089	3090	3091	3092	3093	3094	3095
603X	3096	3097	3098	3099	3100	3101	3102	3103
604X	3104	3105	3106	3107	3108	3109	3110	3111
605X	3112	3113	3114	3115	3116	3117	3118	3119
606X	3120	3121	3122	3123	3124	3125	3126	3127
607X	3128	3129	3130	3131	3132	3133	3134	3135
610X	3136	3137	3138	3139	3140	3141	3142	3143
611X	3144	3145	3146	3147	3148	3149	3150	3151
612X	3152	3153	3154	3155	3156	3157	3158	3159
613X	3160	3161	3162	3163	3164	3165	3166	3167
614X	3168	3169	3170	3171	3172	3173	3174	3175
615X	3176	3177	3178	3179	3180	3181	3182	3183
616X	3184	3185	3186	3187	3188	3189	3190	3191
617X	3192	3193	3194	3195	3196	3197	3198	3199
620X	3200	3201	3202	3203	3204	3205	3206	3207
621X	3208	3209	3210	3211	3212	3213	3214	3215
622X	3216	3217	3218	3219	3220	3221	3222	3223
623X	3224	3225	3226	3227	3228	3229	3230	3231
624X	3232	3233	3234	3235	3236	3237	3238	3239
625X	3240	3241	3242	3243	3244	3245	3246	3247

X =	0	1	2	3	4	5	6	7
626X	3248	3249	3250	3251	3252	3253	3254	3255
627X	3256	3257	3258	3259	3260	3261	3262	3263
630X	3264	3265	3266	3267	3268	3269	3270	3271
631X	3272	3273	3274	3275	3276	3277	3278	3279
632X	3280	3281	3282	3283	3284	3285	3286	3287
633X	3288	3289	3290	3291	3292	3293	3294	3295
634X	3296	3297	3298	3299	3300	3301	3302	3303
635X	3304	3305	3306	3307	3308	3309	3310	3311
636X	3312	3313	3314	3315	3316	3317	3318	3319
637X	3320	3321	3322	3323	3324	3325	3326	3327
640X	3328	3329	3330	3331	3332	3333	3334	3335
641X	3336	3337	3338	3339	3340	3341	3342	3343
642X	3344	3345	3346	3347	3348	3349	3350	3351
643X	3352	3353	3354	3355	3356	3357	3358	3359
644X	3360	3361	3362	3363	3364	3365	3366	3367
645X	3368	3369	3370	3371	3372	3373	3374	3375
646X	3376	3377	3378	3379	3380	3381	3382	3383
647X	3384	3385	3386	3387	3388	3389	3390	3391
650X	3392	3393	3394	3395	3396	3397	3398	3399
651X	3400	3401	3402	3403	3404	3405	3406	3407
652X	3408	3409	3410	3411	3412	3413	3414	3415
653X	3416	3417	3418	3419	3420	3421	3422	3423
654X	3424	3425	3426	3427	3428	3429	3430	3431
655X	3432	3433	3434	3435	3436	3437	3438	3439
656X	3440	3441	3442	3443	3444	3445	3446	3447
657X	3448	3449	3450	3451	3452	3453	3454	3455
660X	3456	3457	3458	3459	3460	3461	3462	3463
661X	3464	3465	3466	3467	3468	3469	3470	3471
662X	3472	3473	3474	3475	3476	3477	3478	3479
663X	3480	3481	3482	3483	3484	3485	3486	3487
664X	3488	3489	3490	3491	3492	3493	3494	3495
665X	3496	3497	3498	3499	3500	3501	3502	3503
666X	3504	3505	3506	3507	3508	3509	3510	3511
667X	3512	3513	3514	3515	3516	3517	3518	3519
670X	3520	3521	3522	3523	3524	3525	3526	3527
671X	3528	3529	3530	3531	3532	3533	3534	3535
672X	3536	3537	3538	3539	3540	3541	3542	3543
673X	3544	3545	3546	3547	3548	3549	3550	3551
674X	3552	3553	3554	3555	3556	3557	3558	3559
675X	3560	3561	3562	3563	3564	3565	3566	3567
676X	3568	3569	3570	3571	3572	3573	3574	3575
677X	3576	3577	3578	3579	3580	3581	3582	3583
700X	3584	3585	3586	3587	3588	3589	3590	3591
701X	3592	3593	3594	3595	3596	3597	3598	3599
702X	3600	3601	3602	3603	3604	3605	3606	3607

$X =$	0	1	2	3	4	5	6	7
703X	3608	3609	3610	3611	3612	3613	3614	3615
704X	3616	3617	3618	3619	3620	3621	3622	3623
705X	3624	3625	3626	3627	3628	3629	3630	3631
706X	3632	3633	3634	3635	3636	3637	3638	3639
707X	3640	3641	3642	3643	3644	3645	3646	3647
710X	3648	3649	3650	3651	3652	3653	3654	3655
711X	3656	3657	3658	3659	3660	3661	3662	3663
712X	3664	3665	3666	3667	3668	3669	3670	3671
713X	3672	3673	3674	3675	3676	3677	3678	3679
714X	3680	3681	3682	3683	3684	3685	3686	3687
715X	3688	3689	3690	3691	3692	3693	3694	3695
716X	3696	3697	3698	3699	3700	3701	3702	3703
717X	3704	3705	3706	3707	3708	3709	3710	3711
720X	3712	3713	3714	3715	3716	3717	3718	3719
721X	3720	3721	3722	3723	3724	3725	3726	3727
722X	3728	3729	3730	3731	3732	3733	3734	3735
723X	3736	3737	3738	3739	3740	3741	3742	3743
724X	3744	3745	3746	3747	3748	3749	3750	3751
725X	3752	3753	3754	3755	3756	3757	3758	3759
726X	3760	3761	3762	3763	3764	3765	3766	3767
727X	3768	3769	3770	3771	3772	3773	3774	3775
730X	3776	3777	3778	3779	3780	3781	3782	3783
731X	3784	3785	3786	3787	3788	3789	3790	3791
732X	3792	3793	3794	3795	3796	3797	3798	3799
733X	3800	3801	3802	3803	3804	3805	3806	3807
734X	3808	3809	3810	3811	3812	3813	3814	3815
735X	3816	3817	3818	3819	3820	3821	3822	3823
736X	3824	3825	3826	3927	3828	3829	3830	3831
737X	3832	3833	3834	3835	3836	3837	3838	3839
740X	3840	3841	3842	3843	3844	3845	3846	3847
741X	3848	3849	3850	3851	3852	3853	3854	3855
742X	3856	3857	3858	3859	3860	3861	3862	3863
743X	3864	3865	3866	3867	3868	3869	3870	3871
744X	3872	3873	3874	3875	3876	3877	3878	3879
745X	3880	3881	3882	3883	3884	3885	3886	3887
746X	3888	3889	3890	3891	3892	3893	3894	3895
747X	3896	3897	3898	3899	3900	3901	3902	3903
750X	3904	3905	3906	3907	3908	3909	3910	3911
751X	3912	3913	3914	3915	3916	3917	3918	3919
752X	3920	3921	3922	3923	3924	3925	3926	3927
753X	3928	3929	3930	3931	3932	3933	3934	3935
754X	3936	3937	3938	3939	3940	3941	3942	3943
755X	3944	3945	3946	3947	3948	3949	3950	3951
756X	3952	3953	3954	3955	3956	3957	3958	3959
757X	3960	3961	3962	3963	3964	3965	3966	3967

X =	0	1	2	3	4	5	6	7
760X	3968	3969	3970	3971	3972	3973	3974	3975
761X	3976	3977	3978	3979	3980	3981	3982	3983
762X	3984	3985	3986	3987	3988	3989	3990	3991
763X	3992	3993	3994	3995	3996	3997	3998	3999
764X	4000	4001	4002	4003	4004	4005	4006	4007
765X	4008	4009	4010	4011	4012	4013	4014	4015
766X	4016	4017	4018	4019	4020	4021	4022	4023
767X	4024	4025	4026	4027	4028	4029	4030	4031
770X	4032	4033	4034	4035	4036	4037	4038	4039
771X	4040	4041	4042	4043	4044	4045	4046	4047
772X	4048	4049	4050	4051	4052	4053	4054	4055
773X	4056	4057	4058	4059	4060	4061	4062	4063
774X	4064	4065	4066	4067	4068	4069	4070	4071
775X	4072	4073	4074	4075	4076	4077	4078	4079
776X	4080	4081	4082	4083	4084	4085	4086	4087
777X	4088	4089	4090	4091	4092	4093	4094	4095

TABLE B-4. Powers of Sixteen.

16^n					n
				1	0
				16	1
				256	2
			4	096	3
			65	536	4
		1	048	576	5
		16	777	216	6
		268	435	456	7
	4	294	967	296	8
	68	719	476	736	9
1	099	511	627	776	10
17	592	186	044	416	11
281	474	976	710	656	12
4	503	599	627	370	496	13
72	057	594	037	927	936	14
1	152	921	504	606	846	976	15

Decimal Values

TABLE B-5. Octal-Decimal Fraction Conversion Table.

Octal	Decimal	Octal	Decimal	Octal	Decimal	Octal	Decimal
.000	.00000000	.061	.09570313	.142	.19140625	.223	.28710938
.001	.00195313	.062	.09765625	.143	.19335938	.224	.28906250
.002	.00390625	.063	.09960938	.144	.19531250	.225	.29101563
.003	.00585938	.064	.10156250	.145	.19726563	.226	.29296875
.004	.00781250	.065	.10351563	.146	.19921875	.227	.29492188
.005	.00976563	.066	.10546875	.147	.20117188	.230	.29687500
.006	.01171875	.067	.10742188	.150	.20312500	.231	.29882813
.007	.01367188	.070	.10937500	.151	.20507813	.232	.30078125
.010	.01562500	.071	.11132813	.152	.20703125	.233	.30273438
.011	.01757813	.072	.11328125	.153	.20898438	.234	.30468750
.012	.01953125	.073	.11523438	.154	.21093750	.235	.30664063
.013	.02148438	.074	.11718750	.155	.21289063	.236	.30859375
.014	.02343750	.075	.11914063	.156	.21484375	.237	.31054688
.015	.02539063	.076	.12109375	.157	.21679688	.240	.31250000
.016	.02734375	.077	.12304688	.160	.21875000	.241	.31445313
.017	.02929688	.100	.12500000	.161	.22070313	.242	.31640625
.020	.03125000	.101	.12695313	.162	.22265625	.243	.31835938
.021	.03320313	.102	.12890625	.163	.22460938	.244	.32031250
.022	.03515625	.103	.13085938	.164	.22656250	.245	.32226563
.023	.03710938	.104	.13281250	.165	.22851563	.246	.32421875
.024	.03906250	.105	.13476563	.166	.23046875	.247	.32617188
.025	.04101563	.106	.13671875	.167	.23242188	.250	.32812500
.026	.04296875	.107	.13867188	.170	.23437500	.251	.33007813
.027	.04492188	.110	.14062500	.171	.23632813	.252	.33203125
.030	.04687500	.111	.14257813	.172	.23828125	.253	.33398438
.031	.04882813	.112	.14453125	.173	.24023438	.254	.33593750
.032	.05078125	.113	.14648438	.174	.24218750	.255	.33789063
.033	.05273438	.114	.14843750	.175	.24414063	.256	.33984375
.034	.05468750	.115	.15039063	.176	.24609375	.257	.34179688
.035	.05664063	.116	.15234375	.177	.24804688	.260	.34375000
.036	.05859375	.117	.15429688	.200	.25000000	.261	.34570313
.037	.06054688	.120	.15625000	.201	.25195313	.262	.34765625
.040	.06250000	.121	.15820313	.202	.25390625	.263	.34960938
.041	.06445313	.122	.16015625	.203	.25585938	.264	.35156250
.042	.06640625	.123	.16210938	204	.25781250	.265	.35351563
.043	.06835938	.124	.16406250	.205	.25976563	.266	.35546875
.044	.07031250	.125	.16601563	.206	.26171875	.267	.35742188
.045	.07226563	.126	.16796875	.207	.26367188	.270	.35937500
.046	.07421875	.127	.16992188	.210	.26562500	.271	.36132813
.047	.07617188	.130	.17187500	.211	.26757813	.272	.36328125
.050	.07812500	.131	.17382813	.212	.26953125	.273	.36523438
.051	.08007813	.132	.17578125	.213	.27148438	.274	.36718750
.052	.08203125	.133	.17773438	.214	.27343750	.275	.36914063
.053	.08398438	.134	.17968750	.215	.27539063	.276	.37109375
.054	.08593750	.135	.18164063	.216	.27734375	.277	.37304688
.055	.08789063	.136	.18359375	.217	.27929688	.300	.37500000
.056	.08984375	.137	.18554688	.220	.28125000	.301	.37695313
.057	.09179688	.140	.18750000	.221	.28320313	.302	.37890625
.060	.09375000	.141	.18945313	.222	.28515625	.303	.38085938

347

Octal	Decimal	Octal	Decimal	Octal	Decimal	Octal	Decimal
.304	.38281250	.323	.41210938	.342	.44140625	.361	.47070313
.305	.38476563	.324	.41406250	.343	.44335938	.362	.47265625
.306	.38671875	.325	.41601563	.344	.44531250	.363	.47460938
.307	.38867188	.326	.41796875	.345	.44726563	.364	.47656250
.310	.39062500	.327	.41992188	.346	.44921875	.365	.47851563
.311	.39257813	.330	.42187500	.347	.45117188	.366	.48046875
.312	.39453125	.331	.42382813	.350	.45312500	.367	.48242188
.313	.39648438	.332	.42578125	.351	.45507813	.370	.48437500
.314	.39843750	.333	.42773438	.352	.45703125	.371	.48632813
.315	.40039063	.334	.42968750	.353	.45898438	.372	.48828125
.316	.40234375	.335	.43164063	.354	.46093750	.373	.49023438
.317	.40429688	.336	.43359375	.355	.46289063	.374	.49218750
.320	.40625000	.337	.43554688	.356	.46484375	.375	.49414063
.321	.40820313	.340	.43750000	.357	.46679688	.376	.49609375
.322	.41015625	.341	.43945313	.360	.46875000	.377	.49804688

Note: $(0.4)_8 = (0.5)_{10}$

therefore, for example,

$$(0.652)_8 = (0.252)_8 + (0.5)_{10}$$
$$= (0.33203125)_{10} + (0.5)_{10}$$

TABLE B-5. Octal-Decimal Fraction Conversion Table (*Continued*).

Octal	Decimal	Octal	Decimal	Octal	Decimal
.000000	.00000000	.000060	.00018311	.000140	.00036621
.000001	.00000381	.000061	.00018692	.000141	.00037003
.000002	.00000763	.000062	.00019073	.000142	.00037384
.000003	.00001144	.000063	.00019455	.000143	.00037766
.000004	.00001526	.000064	.00019836	.000144	.00038147
.000005	.00001907	.000065	.00020218	.000145	.00038528
.000006	.00002289	.000066	.00020599	.000146	.00038910
.000007	.00002670	.000067	.00020981	.000147	.00039291
.000010	.00003052	.000070	.00021362	.000150	.00039673
.000011	.00003433	.000071	.00021744	.000151	.00040054
.000012	.00003815	.000072	.00022125	.000152	.00040436
.000013	.00004196	.000073	.00022507	.000153	.00040817
.000014	.00004578	.000074	.00022888	.000154	.00041199
.000015	.00004959	.000075	.00023270	.000155	.00041580
.000016	.00005341	.000076	.00023651	.000156	.00041962
.000017	.00005722	.000077	.00024033	.000157	.00042343
.000020	.00006104	.000100	.00024414	.000160	.00042725
.000021	.00006485	.000101	.00024796	.000161	.00043106
.000022	.00006866	.000102	.00025177	.000162	.00043488
.000023	.00007248	.000103	.00025558	.000163	.00043869
.000024	.00007629	.000104	.00025940	.000164	.00044250
.000025	.00008011	.000105	.00026321	.000165	.00044632
.000026	.00008392	.000106	.00026703	.000166	.00045013
.000027	.00008774	.000107	.00027084	.000167	.00045395
.000030	.00009155	.000110	.00027466	.000170	.00045776
.000031	.00009537	.000111	.00027847	.000171	.00046158
.000032	.00009918	.000112	.00028229	.000172	.00046539
.000033	.00010300	.000113	.00028610	.000173	.00046921
.000034	.00010681	.000114	.00028992	.000174	.00047302
.000035	.00011063	.000115	.00029373	.000175	.00047684
.000036	.00011444	.000116	.00029755	.000176	.00048065
.000037	.00011826	.000117	.00030136	.000177	.00048447
.000040	.00012207	.000120	.00030519	.000200	.00048828
.000041	.00012589	.000121	.00030899	.000201	.00049210
.000042	.00012970	.000122	.00031281	.000202	.00049591
.000043	.00013351	.000123	.00031662	.000203	.00049973
.000044	.00013733	.000124	.00032043	.000204	.00050354
.000045	.00014114	.000125	.00032425	.000205	.00050735
.000046	.00014496	.000126	.00032806	.000206	.00051117
.000047	.00014877	.000127	.00033188	.000207	.00051498
.000050	.00015259	.000130	.00033569	.000210	.00051880
.000051	.00015640	.000131	.00033951	.000211	.00052261
.000052	.00016022	.000132	.00034332	.000212	.00052643
.000053	.00016403	.000133	.00034714	.000213	.00053024
.000054	.00016785	.000134	.00035095	.000214	.00053406
.000055	.00017166	.000135	.00035477	.000215	.00053787
.000056	.00017548	.000136	.00035858	.000216	.00054169
.000057	.00017929	.000137	.00036240	.000217	.00054550

TABLE B-5. Octal-Decimal Fraction Conversion Table (*Continued*).

Octal	Decimal	Octal	Decimal	Octal	Decimal
.000220	.00054932	.000302	.00074005	.000364	.00093079
.000221	.00055313	.000303	.00074387	.000365	.00093460
.000222	.00055695	.000304	.00074768	.000366	.00093842
.000223	.00056076	.000305	.00075150	.000367	.00094223
.000224	.00056458	.000306	.00075531	.000370	.00094604
.000225	.00056839	.000307	.00075912	.000371	.00094986
.000226	.00057220	.000310	.00076294	.000372	.00095367
.000227	.00057602	.000311	.00076675	.000373	.00095749
.000230	.00057983	.000312	.00077057	.000374	.00096130
.000231	.00058365	.000313	.00077438	.000375	.00096512
.000232	.00058746	.000314	.00077820	.000376	.00096893
.000233	.00059128	.000315	.00078201	.000377	.00097275
.000234	.00059509	.000316	.00078583	.000400	.00097656
.000235	.00059891	.000317	.00078964	.000401	.00098038
.000236	.00060272	.000320	.00079346	.000402	.00098419
.000237	.00060654	.000321	.00079727	.000403	.00098801
.000240	.00061035	.000322	.00080109	.000404	.00099182
.000241	.00061417	.000323	.00080490	.000405	.00099564
.000242	.00061798	.000324	.00080872	.000406	.00099945
.000243	.00062180	.000325	.00081253	.000407	.00100327
.000244	.00062561	.000326	.00081635	.000410	.00100708
.000245	.00062943	.000327	.00082016	.000411	.00101089
.000246	.00063324	.000330	.00082397	.000412	.00101471
.000247	.00063705	.000331	.00082779	.000413	.00101852
.000250	.00064087	.000332	.00083160	.000414	.00102234
.000251	.00064468	.000333	.00083542	.000415	.00102615
.000252	.00064850	.000334	.00083923	.000416	.00102997
.000253	.00065231	.000335	.00084305	.000417	.00103378
.000254	.00065613	.000336	.00084686	.000420	.00103760
.000255	.00065994	.000337	.00085068	.000421	.00104141
.000256	.00066376	.000340	.00085449	.000422	.00104523
.000257	.00066757	.000341	.00085831	.000423	.00104904
.000260	.00067139	.000342	.00086212	.000424	.00105286
.000261	.00067520	.000343	.00086594	.000425	.00105667
.000262	.00067902	.000344	.00086975	.000426	.00106049
.000263	.00068283	.000345	.00087357	.000427	.00106430
.000264	.00068665	.000346	.00087738	.000430	.00106812
.000265	.00069046	.000347	.00088120	.000431	.00107193
.000266	.00069427	.000350	.00088501	.000432	.00107574
.000267	.00069809	.000351	.00088882	.000433	.00107956
.000270	.00070190	.000352	.00089264	.000434	.00108337
.000271	.00070572	.000353	.00089645	.000435	.00108719
.000272	.00070953	.000354	.00090027	.000436	.00109100
.000273	.00071335	.000355	.00090408	.000437	.00109482
.000274	.00071716	.000356	.00090790	.000440	.00109863
.000275	.00072098	.000357	.00091171	.000441	.00110245
.000276	.00072479	.000360	.00091553	.000442	.00110626
.000277	.00072861	.000361	.00091934	.000443	.00111008
.000300	.00073242	.000362	.00092316	.000444	.00111389
.000301	.00073624	.000363	.00092697	.000445	.00111771

TABLE B-5. Octal-Decimal Fraction Conversion Table (*Continued*).

Octal	Decimal	Octal	Decimal	Octal	Decimal
.000446	.00112152	.000530	.00131226	.000612	.00150299
.000447	.00112534	.000531	.00131607	.000613	.00150681
.000450	.00112915	.000532	.00131989	.000614	.00151062
.000451	.00113297	.000533	.00132370	.000615	.00151443
.000452	.00113678	.000534	.00132751	.000616	.00151825
.000453	.00114059	.000535	.00133133	.000617	.00152206
.000454	.00114441	.000536	.00133514	.000620	.00152588
.000455	.00114822	.000537	.00133896	.000621	.00152969
.000456	.00115204	.000540	.00134277	.000622	.00153351
.000457	.00115585	.000541	.00134659	.000623	.00153732
.000460	.00115967	.000542	.00135040	.000624	.00154114
.000461	.00116348	.000543	.00135422	.000625	.00154495
.000462	.00116730	.000544	.00135803	.000626	.00154877
.000463	.00117111	.000545	.00136185	.000627	.00155258
.000464	.00117493	.000546	.00136566	.000630	.00155640
.000465	.00117874	.000547	.00136948	.000631	.00156021
.000466	.00118256	.000550	.00137329	.000632	.00156403
.000467	.00118637	.000551	.00137711	.000633	.00156784
.000470	.00119019	.000552	.00138092	.000634	.00157166
.000471	.00119400	.000553	.00138474	.000635	.00157547
.000472	.00119781	.000554	.00138855	.000636	.00157928
.000473	.00120163	.000555	.00139236	.000637	.00158310
.000474	.00120544	.000556	.00139618	.000640	.00158691
.000475	.00120926	.000557	.00139999	.000641	.00159073
.000476	.00121307	.000560	.00140381	.000642	.00159454
.000477	.00121689	.000561	.00140762	.000643	.00159836
.000500	.00122070	.000562	.00141144	.000644	.00160217
.000501	.00122452	.000563	.00141525	.000645	.00160599
.000502	.00122833	.000564	.00141907	.000646	.00160980
.000503	.00123215	.000565	.00142288	.000647	.00161362
.000504	.00123596	.000566	.00142670	.000650	.00161743
.000505	.00123978	.000567	.00143051	.000651	.00162125
.000506	.00124359	.000570	.00143433	.000652	.00162506
.000507	.00124741	.000571	.00143814	.000653	.00162888
.000510	.00125122	.000572	.00144196	.000654	.00163269
.000511	.00125504	.000573	.00144577	.000655	.00163651
.000512	.00125885	.000574	.00144958	.000656	.00164032
.000513	.00126266	.000575	.00145340	.000657	.00164413
.000514	.00126648	.000576	.00145721	.000660	.00164795
.000515	.00127029	.000577	.00146103	.000661	.00165176
.000516	.00127411	.000600	.00146484	.000662	.00165558
.000517	.00127792	.000601	.00146866	.000663	.00165939
.000520	.00128174	.000602	.00147247	.000664	.00166321
.000521	.00128555	.000603	.00147629	.000665	.00166702
.000522	.00128937	.000604	.00148010	.000666	.00167084
.000523	.00129318	.000605	.00148392	.000667	.00167465
.000524	.00129700	.000606	.00148773	.000670	.00167847
.000525	.00130081	.000607	.00149155	.000671	.00168228
.000526	.00130463	.000610	.00149536	.000672	.00168610
.000527	.00130844	.000611	.00149918	.000673	.00168991

Octal	Decimal	Octal	Decimal	Octal	Decimal
.000674	.00169373	.000723	.00178146	.000752	.00186920
.000675	.00169754	.000724	.00178528	.000753	.00187302
.000676	.00170135	.000725	.00178909	.000754	.00187683
.000677	.00170517	.000726	.00179291	.000755	.00188065
.000700	.00170898	.000727	.00179672	.000756	.00188446
.000701	.00171280	.000730	.00180054	.000757	.00188828
.000702	.00171661	.000731	.00180435	.000760	.00189209
.000703	.00172043	.000732	.00180817	.000761	.00189590
.000704	.00172424	.000733	.00181198	.000762	.00189972
.000705	.00172806	.000734	.00181580	.000763	.00190353
.000706	.00173187	.000735	.00181961	.000764	.00190735
.000707	.00173569	.000736	.00182343	.000765	.00191116
.000710	.00173950	.000737	.00182724	.000766	.00191498
.000711	.00174332	.000740	.00183105	.000767	.00191879
.000712	.00174713	.000741	.00183487	.000770	.00192261
.000713	.00175095	.000742	.00183868	.000771	.00192642
.000714	.00175476	.000743	.00184250	.000772	.00193024
.000715	.00175858	.000744	.00184631	.000773	.00193405
.000716	.00176239	.000745	.00185013	.000774	.00193787
.000717	.00176620	.000746	.00185394	.000775	.00194168
.000720	.00177002	.000747	.00185776	.000776	.00194550
.000721	.00177383	.000750	.00186157	.000777	.00194931
000722	00177765	.000751	.00186539		

TABLE B-6a. Hexadecimal Addition Table.

	1	2	3	4	5	6	7	8	9	A	B	C	D	E	F	
1	2	3	4	5	6	7	8	9	A	B	C	D	E	F	10	1
2	3	4	5	6	7	8	9	A	B	C	D	E	F	10	11	2
3	4	5	6	7	8	9	A	B	C	D	E	F	10	11	12	3
4	5	6	7	8	9	A	B	C	D	E	F	10	11	12	13	4
5	6	7	8	9	A	B	C	D	E	F	10	11	12	13	14	5
6	7	8	9	A	B	C	D	E	F	10	11	12	13	14	15	6
7	8	9	A	B	C	D	E	F	10	11	12	13	14	15	16	7
8	9	A	B	C	D	E	F	10	11	12	13	14	15	16	17	8
9	A	B	C	D	E	F	10	11	12	13	14	15	16	17	18	9
A	B	C	D	E	F	10	11	12	13	14	15	16	17	18	19	A
B	C	D	E	F	10	11	12	13	14	15	16	17	18	19	1A	B
C	D	E	F	10	11	12	13	14	15	16	17	18	19	1A	1B	C
D	E	F	10	11	12	13	14	15	16	17	18	19	1A	1B	1C	D
E	F	10	11	12	13	14	15	16	17	18	19	1A	1B	1C	1D	E
F	10	11	12	13	14	15	16	17	18	19	1A	1B	1C	1D	1E	F
	1	2	3	4	5	6	7	8	9	A	B	C	D	E	F	

TABLE B-6*b*. Hexadecimal Multiplication Table.

	1	2	3	4	5	6	7	8	9	A	B	C	D	E	F	
1	1	2	3	4	5	6	7	8	9	A	B	C	D	E	F	1
2	2	4	6	8	A	C	E	10	12	14	16	18	1A	1C	1E	2
3	3	6	9	C	F	12	15	18	1B	1E	21	24	27	2A	2D	3
4	4	8	C	10	14	18	1C	20	24	28	2C	30	34	38	3C	4
5	5	A	F	14	19	1E	23	28	2D	32	37	3C	41	46	4B	5
6	6	C	12	18	1E	24	2A	30	36	3C	42	48	4E	54	5A	6
7	7	E	15	1C	23	2A	31	38	3F	46	4D	54	5B	62	69	7
8	8	10	18	20	28	30	38	40	48	50	58	60	68	70	78	8
9	9	12	1B	24	2D	36	3F	48	51	5A	63	6C	75	7E	87	9
A	A	14	1E	28	32	3C	46	50	5A	64	6E	.78	82	8C	96	A
B	B	16	21	2C	37	42	4D	58	63	6E	79	84	8F	9A	A5	B
C	C	18	24	30	3C	48	54	60	6C	78	84	90	9C	A8	B4	C
D	D	1A	27	34	41	4E	5B	68	75	82	8F	9C	A9	B6	C3	D
E	E	1C	2A	38	46	54	62	70	7E	8C	9A	A8	B6	C4	D2	E
F	F	1E	2D	3C	4B	5A	69	78	87	96	A5	B4	C3	D2	E1	F
	1	2	3	4	5	6	7	8	9	A	B	C	D	E	F	

TABLE B-7. Teletype* Code.

Even parity bit	7-bit octal code	Character	Remarks
0	000	NUL	Null, tape feed. Repeats on Model 37. Control shift P on Model 33 and 35.
1	001	SOH	Start of heading; also SOM, start of message. Control A.
1	002	STX	Start of text; also EOA, end of address. Control B.
0	003	ETX	End of text; also EOM, end of message. Control C.
1	004	EOT	End of transmission (END); shuts off TWX machines. Control D.
0	005	ENQ	Enquiry (ENQRY); also WRU, "Who are you?" Triggers identification ("Here is . . . ") at remote station if so equipped. Control E.
0	006	ACK	Acknowledge; also RU, "Are you . . . ?" Control F.
1	007	BEL	Rings the bell. Control G.
1	010	BS	Backspace; also FEO, format effector. Backspaces some machines. Repeats on Model 37. Control H on Model 33 and 35.
0	011	HT	Horizontal tab. Control I on Model 33 and 35.
0	012	LF	Line feed or line space (NEW LINE); advances paper to next line. Repeats on Model 37. Duplicated by control J on Model 33 and 35.
1	013	VT	Vertical tab (VTAB). Control K on Model 33 and 35.
0	014	FF	Form feed to top of next page (PAGE). Control L.
1	015	CR	Carriage return to beginning of line. Control M on Model 33 and 35.
1	016	SO	Shift out; changes ribbon color to red. Control N.
0	017	SI	Shift in; changes ribbon color to black. Control O.
1	020	DLE	Data link escape. Control P (DCO).
0	021	DC1	Device control 1, turns transmitter (reader) on. Control Q (X ON).
0	022	DC2	Device control 2, turns punch or auxiliary on. Control R (TAPE, AUX ON).
1	023	DC3	Device control 3, turns transmitter (reader) off. Control S (X OFF).
0	024	DC4	Device control 4, turns punch or auxiliary off. Control T (AUX OFF).
1	025	NAK	Negative acknowledge; also ERR, error. Control U.
1	026	SYN	Synchronous idle (SYNC). Control V.
0	027	ETB	End of transmission block; also LEM, logical end of medium. Control W.
0	030	CAN	Cancel (CANCL). Control X.
1	031	EM	End of medium. Control Y.
1	032	SUB	Substitute. Control Z.
0	033	ESC	Escape, prefix. This code is also generated by control shift K on Model 33 and 35.
1	034	FS	File separator. Control shift L on Model 33 and 35.
0	035	GS	Group separator. Control shift M on Model 33 and 35.
0	036	RS	Record separator. Control shift N on Model 33 and 35.
1	037	US	Unit separator. Control shift O on Model 33 and 35.
1	040	SP	Space.
0	041	!	
0	042	"	

* Teletype is a registered trademark of the Teletype Corporation.

Even parity bit	7-bit octal code	Character	Even parity bit	7-bit octal code	Character	
1	043	#	0	116	N	
0	044	$	1	117	O	
1	045	%	0	120	P	
1	046	&	1	121	Q	
0	047	'	1	122	R	
0	050	(	0	123	S	
1	051	)	1	124	T	
1	052	*	0	125	U	
0	053	+	0	126	V	
1	054	,	1	127	W	
0	055	−	1	130	X	
0	056	.	0	131	Y	
1	057	/	0	132	Z	
0	060	Ø	1	133	[	Shift K on Model 33 and 35.
1	061	1	0	134	\	Shift L on Model 33 and 35.
1	062	2	1	135	]	Shift M on Model 33 and 35.
0	063	3	1	136	↑	
1	064	4	0	137	←	
0	065	5	0	140	'	
0	066	6	1	141	a	
1	067	7	1	142	b	
1	070	8	0	143	c	
0	071	9	1	144	d	
0	072	:	0	145	e	
1	073	;	0	146	f	
0	074	<	1	147	g	
1	075	=	1	150	h	
1	076	>	0	151	i	
0	077	?	0	152	j	
1	100	@	1	153	k	
0	101	A	0	154	l	
0	102	B	1	155	m	
1	103	C	1	156	n	
0	104	D	0	157	o	
1	105	E	1	160	p	
1	106	F	0	161	q	
0	107	G	0	162	r	
0	110	H	1	163	s	
1	111	I	0	164	t	
1	112	J	1	165	u	
0	113	K	1	166	v	
1	114	L	0	167	w	
0	115	M	0	170	x	

TABLE B-7. **Teletype Code** (*Continued*).

Even parity bit	7-bit octal code	Character	Remarks
1	171	y	
1	172	z	
0	173	{	
1	174	|	
0	175	}	
0	176	~	On early versions of the Model 33 and 35, this code may be generated by either the ALT MODE or ESC key.
1	177	DEL	Delete, rub out. Repeats on Model 37.

	Keys that generate no codes
REPT	Model 33 and 35 only: causes any other key that is struck to repeat continuously until REPT is released.
PAPER ADVANCE	Model 37 local line feed.
LOCAL RETURN	Model 37 local carriage return.
LOC LF	Model 33 and 35 local line feed.
LOC CR	Model 33 and 35 local carriage return.
INTERRUPT, BREAK	Opens the line (machine sends a continuous string of null characters).
PROCEED, BRK RLS	Break release (not applicable).
HERE IS	Transmits predetermined 20-character message.

→, −, ., =, X, x, also repeat on Model 37.

TABLE B-8. Teletype*/Paper-Tape Code.

● = HOLE PUNCHED = MARK = 1 BIT
O = NO HOLE PUNCHED = SPACE = 0 BIT

MOST SIGNIFICANT BIT
LEAST SIGNIFICANT BIT

Ctrl	@ col		SP col		Name	8	7	6	5	4	S	3	2	1
	@		SPACE		NULL (IDLE)			O	O	O		O	O	O
	A		!	*	START OF MESSAGE			O	O	O		O	O	●
	B		"	*	END OF ADDRESS (EOA)			O	O	O		O	●	O
	C		#	*	END OF MESSAGE (EOM)			O	O	O		O	●	●
	D		$	*	END OF TRANSMISSION (EOT)			O	O	O		●	O	O
	E		%	*	WHO ARE YOU (WRU)			O	O	O		●	O	●
	F		&	*	ARE YOU (RU)			O	O	O		●	●	O
	G		'	*	BELL			O	O	O		●	●	●
	H		(	*	FORMAT EFFECTOR			O	O	●		O	O	O
	I		)	*	HORIZONTAL TAB			O	O	●		O	O	●
	J		*	*	LINE FEED			O	O	●		O	●	O
	K		+	*	VERTICAL TAB			O	O	●		O	●	●
	L		,		FORM FEED			O	O	●		●	O	O
	M		–		CARRIAGE RETURN			O	O	●		●	O	●
	N		.		SHIFT OUT			O	O	●		●	●	O
	O		/		SHIFT IN			O	O	●		●	●	●
	P		0		DCO			O	●	O		O	O	O
	Q		1		READER ON			O	●	O		O	O	●
	R		2		TAPE (AUX ON)			O	●	O		O	●	O
	S		3		READER OFF			O	●	O		O	●	●
	T		4		(AUX OFF)			O	●	O		●	O	O
	U		5		ERROR			O	●	O		●	O	●
	V		6		SYNCHRONOUS IDLE			O	●	O		●	●	O
	W		7		LOGICAL END OF MEDIA			O	●	O		●	●	●
	X		8		SO			O	●	●		O	O	O
	Y		9		S1			O	●	●		O	O	●
	Z		:		S2			O	●	●		O	●	O
	[	*	;		S3			O	●	●		O	●	●
ACK	\	*	<	*	S4			O	●	●		●	O	O
ALT MODE	]	*	=	*	S5			O	●	●		●	O	●
	↑	*	>	*	S6			O	●	●		●	●	O
RUB OUT	←	*	?	*	S7			O	●	●		●	●	●

NON-TYPING
NON-TYPING

●	O	O	SAME
●	O	●	SAME
●	●	O	SAME
●	●	●	SAME

← OBTAINED WITH SHIFT KEY

* Teletype is a registered trademark of the Teletype Corporation.

TABLE B-9. ASCII/Teletypewriter/Hexadecimal Conversion Table.

Teletypewriter-tape channels 1, 2, . . . , 7 correspond to bits 0 (LSB), 1, 2, . . . , 6 of a character byte; channel 8 or bit 7 represents the parity bit. The unassigned codes are used optionally for lowercase letters.

HEX (MSD) →					8	9	A	B	C	D	E	F
(LSD)	Teletypewriter Tape Channels →			8	DEPENDS UPON PARITY							
				7	0	0	0	0	1	1	1	1
				6	0	0	1	1	0	0	1	1
				5	0	1	0	1	0	1	0	1
	4	3	2	1								
$\emptyset$	0	0	0	0	NULL	DC_0	SPACE	0	@	P		
1	0	0	0	1	SUM	X-ON	!	1	A	Q		
2	0	0	1	0	EOA	TAPE ON	"	2	B	R		
3	0	0	1	1	EOM	X-OFF	#	3	C	S		
4	0	1	0	0	EOT	TAPE OFF	$	4	D	T		
5	0	1	0	1	WRU	ERR	%	5	E	U		
6	0	1	1	0	RU	SYNC	&	6	F	V		
7	0	1	1	1	BELL	LEM	'	7	G	W		
8	1	0	0	0	FE_0	S_0	(	8	H	X		
9	1	0	0	1	HT/SK	S_1	)	9	I	Y		
A	1	0	1	0	LF	S_2	*	:	J	Z		
B	1	0	1	1	VT	S_3	+	;	K	[		
C	1	1	0	0	FF	S_4	,	<	L	\		ACK
D	1	1	0	1	CR	S_5	−	=	M	]		ALT. MODE
E	1	1	1	0	SO	S_6	.	>	N	↑		ESC
F	1	1	1	1	SI	S_7	/	?	O	←		DEL

TABLE B-10. ASCII/Card-Code Conversion Table.

Graphic	8-bit ASCII code	7-bit ASCII code	Card code	Graphic	8-bit ASCII code	7-bit ASCII code	Card code
SPACE	A0	20	0-8-2	@	C0	40	8-4
!	A1	21	12-8-7	A	C1	41	12-1
"	A2	22	8-7	B	C2	42	12-2
#	A3	23	8-3	C	C3	43	12-3
$	A4	24	11-8-3	D	C4	44	12-4
%	A5	25	0-8-4	E	C5	45	12-5
&	A6	26	12	F	C6	46	12-6
'	A7	27	8-5	G	C7	47	12-7
(	A8	28	12-8-5	H	C8	48	12-8
)	A9	29	11-8-5	I	C9	49	12-9
*	AA	2A	11-8-4	J	CA	4A	11-1
+	AB	2B	12-8-6	K	CB	4B	11-2
,	AC	2C	0-8-3	L	CC	4C	11-3
−	AD	2D	11	M	CD	4D	11-4
.	AE	2E	12-8-3	N	CE	4E	11-5
/	AF	2F	0-1	O	CF	4F	11-6
0	B0	30	0	P	D0	50	11-7
1	B1	31	1	Q	D1	51	11-8
2	B2	32	2	R	D2	52	11-9
3	B3	33	3	S	D3	53	0-2
4	B4	34	4	T	D4	54	0-3
5	B5	35	5	U	D5	55	0-4
6	B6	36	6	V	D6	56	0-5
7	B7	37	7	W	D7	57	0-6
8	B8	38	8	X	D8	58	0-7
9	B9	39	9	Y	D9	59	0-8
:	BA	3A	8-2	Z	DA	5A	0-9
;	BB	3B	11-8-6	[	DB	5B	12-8-2
<	BC	3C	12-8-4	\	DC	5C	11-8-1
=	BD	3D	8-6	]	DD	5D	11-8-2
>	BE	3E	0-8-6	↑	DE	5E	11-8-7
?	BF	3F	0-8-7	←	DF	5F	0-8-5

TABLE B-11. 7-Bit and 6-Bit "Trimmed" ASCII Codes.

Printing character	7-bit ASCII	6-bit trimmed ASCII	Printing character	7-bit ASCII	6-bit trimmed ASCII
@	100	00	(Space)	040	40
A	101	01	!	041	41
B	102	02	"	042	42
C	103	03	#	043	43
D	104	04	$	044	44
E	105	05	%	045	45
F	106	06	&	046	46
G	107	07	'	047	47
H	110	10	(	050	50
I	111	11	)	051	51
J	112	12	*	052	52
K	113	13	+	053	53
L	114	14	'	054	54
M	115	15	−	055	55
N	116	16	.	056	56
O	117	17	/	057	57
P	120	20	0	060	60
Q	121	21	1	061	61
R	122	22	2	062	62
S	123	23	3	063	63
T	124	24	4	064	64
U	125	25	5	065	65
V	126	26	6	066	66
W	127	27	7	067	67
X	130	30	8	070	70
Y	131	31	9	071	71
Z	132	32	:*	072	72
[*	133	33	;	073	73
\	134	34	<	074	74
]*	135	35	=	075	75
↑*	136	36	>	076	76
← *	137	37	?	077	77
Null	000				
Horizontal Tab	011				
Line Feed	012				
Vertical Tab	013				
Form Feed	014				
Carriage Return	015				
Rubout	177				

TABLE B-12.   Table of Powers of 10_{16}.

10^n				n	10^{-n}				
			1	0	1.0000	0000	0000	0000	
			A	1	0.1999	9999	9999	999A	
			64	2	0.28F5	C28F	5C28	F5C3	$\times\ 16^{-1}$
			3E8	3	0.4189	374B	C6A7	EF9E	$\times\ 16^{-2}$
			2710	4	0.68DB	8BAC	710C	B296	$\times\ 16^{-3}$
		1	86A0	5	0.A7C5	AC47	1B47	8423	$\times\ 16^{-4}$
		F	4240	6	0.10C6	F7A0	B5ED	8D37	$\times\ 16^{-4}$
		98	9680	7	0.1AD7	F29A	BCAF	4858	$\times\ 16^{-5}$
		5F5	E100	8	0.2AF3	1DC4	6118	73BF	$\times\ 16^{-6}$
		3B9A	CA00	9	0.44B8	2FA0	9B5A	52CC	$\times\ 16^{-7}$
	2	540B	E400	10	0.6DF3	7F67	5EF6	EADF	$\times\ 16^{-8}$
	17	4876	E800	11	0.AFEB	FF0B	CB24	AAFF	$\times\ 16^{-9}$
	E8	D4A5	1000	12	0.1197	9981	2DEA	1119	$\times\ 16^{-9}$
	918	4E72	A000	13	0.1C25	C268	4976	81C2	$\times\ 16^{-10}$
	5AF3	107A	4000	14	0.2D09	370D	4257	3604	$\times\ 16^{-11}$
3	8D7E	A4C6	8000	15	0.480E	BE7B	9D58	566D	$\times\ 16^{-12}$
23	8652	6FC1	0000	16	0.734A	CA5F	6226	F0AE	$\times\ 16^{-13}$
163	4578	5D8A	0000	17	0.B877	AA32	36A4	B449	$\times\ 16^{-14}$
DE0	B6B3	A764	0000	18	0.1272	5DD1	D243	ABA1	$\times\ 16^{-14}$
8AC7	2304	89E8	0000	19	0.1D83	C94F	B6D2	AC35	$\times\ 16^{-15}$

TABLE B-13.   Hexadecimal-Decimal Integer Conversion.

Hexadecimal	Decimal	Hexadecimal	Decimal
01 000	4 096	20 000	131 072
02 000	8 192	30 000	196 608
03 000	12 288	40 000	262 144
04 000	16 384	50 000	327 680
05 000	20 480	60 000	393 216
06 000	24 576	70 000	458 752
07 000	28 672	80 000	524 288
08 000	32 768	90 000	589 824
09 000	36 864	A0 000	655 360
0A 000	40 960	B0 000	720 896
0B 000	45 056	C0 000	786 432
0C 000	49 152	D0 000	851 968
0D 000	53 248	E0 000	917 504
0E 000	57 344	F0 000	983 040
0F 000	61 440	100 000	1 048 576
10 000	65 536	200 000	2 097 152
11 000	69 632	300 000	3 145 728
12 000	73 728	400 000	4 194 304
13 000	77 824	500 000	5 242 880
14 000	81 920	600 000	6 291 456
15 000	86 016	700 000	7 340 032
16 000	90 112	800 000	8 388 608
17 000	94 208	900 000	9 437 184
18 000	98 304	A00 000	10 485 760
19 000	102 400	B00 000	11 534 336
1A 000	106 496	C00 000	12 582 912
1B 000	110 592	D00 000	13 631 488
1C 000	114 688	E00 000	14 680 064
1D 000	118 784	F00 000	15 728 640
1E 000	122 880	1 000 000	16 777 216
1F 000	126 976	2 000 000	33 554 432

TABLE B-13. Hexadecimal-Decimal Integer Conversion (*Continued*).

	0	1	2	3	4	5	6	7	8	9	A	B	C	D	E	F
000	0000	0001	0002	0003	0004	0005	0006	0007	0008	0009	0010	0011	0012	0013	0014	0015
010	0016	0017	0018	0019	0020	0021	0022	0023	0024	0025	0026	0027	0028	0029	0030	0031
020	0032	0033	0034	0035	0036	0037	0038	0039	0040	0041	0042	0043	0044	0045	0046	0047
030	0048	0049	0050	0051	0052	0053	0054	0055	0056	0057	0058	0059	0060	0061	0062	0063
040	0064	0065	0066	0067	0068	0069	0070	0071	0072	0073	0074	0075	0076	0077	0078	0079
050	0080	0081	0082	0083	0084	0085	0086	0087	0088	0089	0090	0091	0092	0093	0094	0095
060	0096	0097	0098	0099	0100	0101	0102	0103	0104	0105	0106	0107	0108	0109	0110	0111
070	0112	0113	0114	0115	0116	0117	0118	0119	0120	0121	0122	0123	0124	0125	0126	0127
080	0128	0129	0130	0131	0132	0133	0134	0135	0136	0137	0138	0139	0140	0141	0142	0143
090	0144	0145	0146	0147	0148	0149	0150	0151	0152	0153	0154	0155	0156	0157	0158	0159
0A0	0160	0161	0162	0163	0164	0165	0166	0167	0168	0169	0170	0171	0172	0173	0174	0175
0B0	0176	0177	0178	0179	0180	0181	0182	0183	0184	0185	0186	0187	0188	0189	0190	0191
0C0	0192	0193	0194	0195	0196	0197	0198	0199	0200	0201	0202	0203	0204	0205	0206	0207
0D0	0208	0209	0210	0211	0212	0213	0214	0215	0216	0217	0218	0219	0220	0221	0222	0223
0E0	0224	0225	0226	0227	0228	0229	0230	0231	0232	0233	0234	0235	0236	0237	0238	0239
0F0	0240	0241	0242	0243	0244	0245	0246	0247	0248	0249	0250	0251	0252	0253	0254	0255
100	0256	0257	0258	0259	0260	0261	0262	0263	0264	0265	0266	0267	0268	0269	0270	0271
110	0272	0273	0274	0275	0276	0277	0278	0279	0280	0281	0282	0283	0284	0285	0286	0287
120	0288	0289	0290	0291	0292	0293	0294	0295	0296	0297	0298	0299	0300	0301	0302	0303
130	0304	0305	0306	0307	0308	0309	0310	0311	0312	0313	0314	0315	0316	0317	0318	0319
140	0320	0321	0322	0323	0324	0325	0326	0327	0328	0329	0330	0331	0332	0333	0334	0335
150	0336	0337	0338	0339	0340	0341	0342	0343	0344	0345	0346	0347	0348	0349	0350	0351
160	0352	0353	0354	0355	0356	0357	0358	0359	0360	0361	0362	0363	0364	0365	0366	0367
170	0368	0369	0370	0371	0372	0373	0374	0375	0376	0377	0378	0379	0380	0381	0382	0383
180	0384	0385	0386	0387	0388	0389	0390	0391	0392	0393	0394	0395	0396	0397	0398	0399
190	0400	0401	0402	0403	0404	0405	0406	0407	0408	0409	0410	0411	0412	0413	0414	0415

TABLE B-13. Hexadecimal-Decimal Integer Conversion (*Continued*).

	0	1	2	3	4	5	6	7	8	9	A	B	C	D	E	F
1A0	0416	0417	0418	0419	0420	0421	0422	0423	0424	0425	0426	0427	0428	0429	0430	0431
1B0	0432	0433	0434	0435	0436	0437	0438	0439	0440	0441	0442	0443	0444	0445	0446	0447
1C0	0448	0449	0450	0451	0452	0453	0454	0455	0456	0457	0458	0459	0460	0461	0462	0463
1D0	0464	0465	0466	0467	0468	0469	0470	0471	0472	0473	0474	0475	0476	0477	0478	0479
1E0	0480	0481	0482	0483	0484	0485	0486	0487	0488	0489	0490	0491	0492	0493	0494	0495
1F0	0496	0497	0498	0499	0500	0501	0502	0503	0504	0505	0506	0507	0508	0509	0510	0511
200	0512	0513	0514	0515	0516	0517	0518	0519	0520	0521	0522	0523	0524	0525	0526	0527
210	0528	0529	0530	0531	0532	0533	0534	0535	0536	0537	0538	0539	0540	0541	0542	0543
220	0544	0545	0546	0547	0548	0549	0550	0551	0552	0553	0554	0555	0556	0557	0558	0559
230	0560	0561	0562	0563	0564	0565	0566	0567	0568	0569	0570	0571	0572	0573	0574	0575
240	0576	0577	0578	0579	0580	0581	0582	0583	0584	0585	0586	0587	0588	0589	0590	0591
250	0592	0593	0594	0595	0596	0597	0598	0599	0600	0601	0602	0603	0604	0605	0606	0607
260	0608	0609	0610	0611	0612	0613	0614	0165	0616	0617	0618	0619	0620	0621	0622	0623
270	0624	0625	0626	0627	0628	0629	0630	0631	0632	0633	0634	0635	0636	0637	0638	0639
280	0640	0641	0642	0643	0644	0645	0646	0647	0648	0649	0650	0651	0652	0653	0654	0655
290	0656	0657	0658	0659	0660	0661	0662	0663	0664	0665	0666	0667	0668	0669	0670	0671
2A0	0672	0673	0674	0675	0676	0677	0678	0679	0680	0681	0682	0683	0684	0685	0686	0687
2B0	0688	0689	0690	0691	0692	0693	0694	0695	0696	0697	0698	0699	0700	0701	0702	0703
2C0	0704	0705	0706	0707	0708	0709	0710	0711	0712	0713	0714	0715	0716	0717	0718	0719
2D0	0720	0721	0722	0723	0724	0725	0726	0727	0728	0729	0730	0731	0732	0733	0734	0735
2E0	0736	0737	0738	0739	0740	0741	0742	0743	0744	0745	0746	0747	0748	0749	0750	0751
2F0	0752	0753	0754	0755	0756	0757	0758	0759	0760	0761	0762	0763	0764	0765	0766	0767
300	0768	0769	0770	0771	0772	0773	0774	0775	0776	0777	0778	0779	0780	0781	0782	0783
310	0784	0785	0786	0787	0788	0789	0790	0791	0792	0793	0794	0795	0796	0797	0798	0799
320	0800	0801	0802	0803	0804	0805	0806	0807	0808	0809	0810	0811	0812	0813	0814	0185
330	0816	0817	0818	0819	0820	0821	0822	0823	0824	0825	0826	0827	0828	0829	0830	0831

	0	1	2	3	4	5	6	7	8	9	A	B	C	D	E	F
340	0832	0833	0834	0835	0836	0837	0838	0839	0840	0841	0842	0843	0844	0845	0846	0847
350	0848	0849	0850	0851	0852	0853	0854	0855	0856	0857	0858	0859	0860	0861	0862	0863
360	0864	0865	0866	0867	0868	0869	0870	0871	0872	0873	0874	0875	0876	0877	0878	0879
370	0880	0881	0882	0883	0884	0885	0886	0887	0888	0889	0890	0891	0892	0893	0894	0895
380	0896	0897	0898	0899	0900	0901	0902	0903	0904	0905	0906	0907	0908	0909	0910	0911
390	0912	0913	0914	0915	0916	0917	0918	0919	0920	0921	0922	0923	0924	0925	0926	0927
3A0	0928	0929	0930	0931	0932	0933	0934	0935	0936	0937	0938	0939	0940	0941	0942	0943
3B0	0944	0945	0946	0947	0948	0949	0950	0951	0952	0953	0954	0955	0956	0957	0958	0959
3C0	0960	0961	0962	0963	0964	0965	0966	0967	0968	0969	0970	0971	0972	0973	0974	0975
3D0	0976	0977	0978	0979	0980	0981	0982	0983	0984	0985	0986	0987	0988	0989	0990	0991
3E0	0992	0993	0994	0995	0996	0997	0998	0999	1000	1001	1002	1003	1004	1005	1006	1007
3F0	1008	1009	1100	1011	1012	1013	1014	1015	1016	1017	1018	1019	1020	1021	1022	1023
400	1024	1025	1026	1027	1028	1029	1030	1031	1032	1033	1034	1035	1036	1037	1038	1039
410	1040	1041	1042	1043	1044	1045	1046	1047	1048	1049	1050	1051	1052	1053	1054	1055
420	1056	1057	1058	1059	1060	1061	1062	1063	1064	1065	1066	1067	1068	1069	1070	1071
430	1072	1073	1074	1075	1076	1077	1078	1079	1080	1081	1082	1083	1084	1085	1086	1087
440	1088	1089	1090	1091	1092	1093	1094	1095	1096	1097	1098	1099	1100	1101	1102	1103
450	1104	1105	1106	1107	1108	1109	1110	1111	1112	1113	1114	1115	1116	1117	1118	1119
460	1120	1121	1122	1123	1124	1125	1126	1127	1128	1129	1130	1131	1132	1133	1134	1135
470	1136	1137	1138	1139	1140	1141	1142	1143	1144	1145	1146	1147	1148	1149	1150	1151
480	1152	1153	1154	1155	1156	1157	1158	1159	1160	1161	1162	1163	1164	1165	1166	1167
490	1168	1169	1170	1171	1172	1173	1174	1175	1176	1177	1178	1179	1180	1181	1182	1183
4A0	1184	1185	1186	1187	1188	1189	1190	1191	1192	1193	1194	1195	1196	1197	1198	1199
4B0	1200	1201	1202	1203	1204	1205	1206	1207	1208	1209	1210	1211	1212	1213	1214	1215
4C0	1216	1217	1218	1219	1220	1221	1222	1223	1224	1225	1226	1227	1228	1229	1230	1231
4D0	1232	1233	1234	1235	1236	1237	1238	1239	1240	1241	1242	1243	1244	1245	1246	1247
4E0	1248	1249	1250	1251	1525	1253	1254	1255	1256	1257	1258	1259	1260	1261	1262	1263
4F0	1264	1265	1266	1267	1268	1269	1270	1271	1272	1273	1274	1275	1276	1277	1278	1279

TABLE B-13. Hexadecimal-Decimal Integer Conversion (*Continued*).

	0	1	2	3	4	5	6	7	8	9	A	B	C	D	E	F
500	1280	1281	1282	1283	1284	1285	1286	1287	1288	1289	1290	1291	1292	1293	1294	1295
510	1296	1297	1298	1299	1300	1301	1302	1303	1304	1305	1306	1307	1308	1309	1310	1311
520	1312	1313	1314	1315	1316	1317	1318	1319	1320	1321	1322	1323	1324	1325	1326	1327
530	1328	1329	1330	1331	1332	1333	1334	1335	1336	1337	1338	1339	1340	1341	1342	1343
540	1344	1345	1346	1347	1348	1349	1350	1351	1352	1353	1354	1355	1356	1357	1358	1359
550	1360	1361	1362	1363	1364	1365	1366	1367	1368	1369	1370	1371	1372	1373	1374	1375
560	1376	1377	1378	1379	1380	1381	1382	1383	1384	1385	1386	1387	1388	1389	1390	1391
570	1392	1393	1394	1395	1396	1397	1398	1399	1400	1401	1402	1403	1404	1405	1406	1407
580	1408	1409	1410	1411	1412	1413	1414	1415	1416	1417	1418	1419	1420	1421	1422	1423
590	1424	1425	1426	1427	1428	1429	1430	1431	1432	1433	1434	1435	1436	1437	1438	1439
5A0	1440	1441	1442	1443	1444	1445	1446	1447	1448	1449	1450	1451	1452	1453	1454	1455
5B0	1456	1457	1458	1459	1460	1461	1462	1463	1464	1465	1466	1467	1468	1469	1470	1471
5C0	1472	1473	1474	1475	1476	1477	1478	1479	1480	1481	1482	1483	1484	1485	1486	1487
5D0	1488	1489	1490	1491	1492	1493	1494	1495	1496	1497	1498	1499	1500	1501	1502	1503
5E0	1504	1505	1506	1507	1508	1509	1510	1511	1512	1513	1514	1515	1516	1517	1518	1519
5F0	1520	1521	1522	1523	1524	1525	1526	1527	1528	1529	1530	1531	1532	1533	1534	1535
600	1536	1537	1538	1539	1540	1541	1542	1543	1544	1545	1546	1547	1548	1549	1550	1551
610	1552	1553	1554	1555	1556	1557	1558	1559	1560	1561	1562	1563	1564	1565	1566	1567
620	1568	1569	1570	1571	1572	1573	1574	1575	1576	1577	1578	1579	1580	1581	1582	1583
630	1584	1585	1586	1587	1588	1589	1590	1591	1592	1593	1594	1595	1596	1597	1598	1599
640	1600	1601	1602	1603	1604	1605	1606	1607	1608	1609	1610	1611	1612	1613	1614	1615
650	1616	1617	1618	1619	1620	1621	1622	1623	1624	1625	1626	1627	1628	1629	1630	1631
660	1632	1633	1634	1635	1636	1637	1638	1639	1640	1641	1642	1643	1644	1645	1646	1647
670	1648	1649	1650	1651	1652	1653	1654	1655	1656	1657	1658	1659	1660	1661	1662	1663
680	1664	1665	1666	1667	1668	1669	1670	1671	1672	1673	1674	1675	1676	1677	1678	1679
690	1680	1681	1682	1683	1684	1685	1686	1687	1688	1689	1690	1691	1692	1693	1694	1695

6A0	1696	1697	1698	1699	1700	1701	1702	1703	1704	1705	1706	1707	1708	1709	1710	1711
6B0	1712	1713	1714	1715	1716	1717	1718	1719	1720	1721	1722	1723	1724	1725	1726	1727
6C0	1728	1729	1730	1731	1732	1733	1734	1735	1736	1737	1738	1739	1740	1741	1742	1743
6D0	1744	1745	1746	1747	1748	1749	1750	1751	1752	1753	1754	1755	1756	1757	1758	1759
6E0	1760	1761	1762	1763	1764	1765	1766	1767	1768	1769	1770	1771	1772	1773	1774	1775
6F0	1776	1777	1778	1779	1780	1781	1782	1783	1784	1785	1786	1787	1788	1789	1790	1791
700	1792	1793	1794	1795	1796	1797	1798	1799	1800	1801	1802	1803	1804	1805	1806	1807
710	1808	1809	1810	1811	1812	1813	1814	1815	1816	1817	1818	1819	1820	1821	1822	1823
720	1824	1825	1826	1827	1828	1829	1830	1831	1832	1833	1834	1835	1836	1837	1838	1839
730	1840	1841	1842	1843	1844	1845	1846	1847	1848	1849	1850	1851	1852	1853	1854	1855
740	1856	1857	1858	1859	1860	1861	1862	1863	1864	1865	1866	1867	1868	1869	1870	1871
750	1872	1873	1874	1875	1876	1877	1878	1879	1880	1881	1882	1883	1884	1885	1886	1887
760	1888	1889	1890	1891	1892	1893	1894	1895	1896	1897	1898	1899	1900	1901	1902	1903
770	1904	1905	1906	1907	1908	1909	1910	1911	1912	1913	1914	1915	1916	1917	1918	1919
780	1920	1921	1922	1923	1924	1925	1926	1927	1928	1929	1930	1931	1932	1933	1934	1935
790	1936	1937	1938	1939	1940	1941	1942	1943	1944	1945	1946	1947	1948	1949	1950	1951
7A0	1952	1953	1954	1955	1956	1957	1958	1959	1960	1961	1962	1963	1964	1965	1966	1967
7B0	1968	1969	1970	1971	1972	1973	1974	1975	1976	1977	1978	1979	1980	1981	1982	1983
7C0	1984	1985	1986	1987	1988	1989	1990	1991	1992	1993	1994	1995	1996	1997	1998	1999
7D0	2000	2001	2002	2003	2004	2005	2006	2007	2008	2009	2010	2011	2012	2013	2014	2015
7E0	2016	2017	2018	2019	2020	2021	2022	2023	2024	2025	2026	2027	2028	2029	2030	2031
7F0	2032	2033	2034	2035	2036	2037	2038	2039	2040	2041	2042	2043	2044	2045	2046	2047
800	2048	2049	2050	2051	2052	2053	2054	2055	2056	2057	2058	2059	2060	2061	2062	2063
810	2064	2065	2066	2067	2068	2069	2070	2071	2072	2073	2074	2075	2076	2077	2078	2079
820	2080	2081	2082	2083	2084	2085	2086	2087	2088	2089	2090	2091	2092	2093	2094	2095
830	2096	2097	2098	2099	2100	2101	2102	2103	2104	2105	2106	2107	2108	2109	2110	2111
840	2112	2113	2114	2115	2116	2117	2118	2119	2120	2121	2122	2123	2124	2125	2126	2127
850	2128	2129	2130	2131	2132	2133	2134	2135	2136	2137	2138	2139	2140	2141	2142	2143
860	2144	2145	2146	2147	2148	2149	2150	2151	2152	2153	2154	2155	2156	2157	2158	2159
870	2160	2161	2162	2163	2164	2165	2166	2167	2168	2169	2170	2171	2172	2173	2174	2175

TABLE B-13. Hexadecimal-Decimal Integer Conversion (*Continued*).

	0	1	2	3	4	5	6	7	8	9	A	B	C	D	E	F
880	2176	2177	2178	2179	2180	2181	2182	2183	2184	2185	2186	2187	2188	2189	2190	2191
890	2192	2193	2194	2195	2196	2197	2198	2199	2200	2201	2202	2203	2204	2205	2206	2207
8A0	2208	2209	2210	2211	2212	2213	2214	2215	2216	2217	2218	2219	2220	2221	2222	2223
8B0	2224	2225	2226	2227	2228	2229	2230	2231	2232	2233	2234	2235	2236	2237	2238	2239
8C0	2240	2241	2242	2243	2244	2245	2246	2247	2248	2249	2250	2251	2252	2253	2254	2255
8D0	2256	2257	2258	2259	2260	2261	2262	2263	2264	2265	2266	2267	2268	2269	2270	2271
8E0	2272	2273	2274	2275	2276	2277	2278	2279	2280	2281	2282	2283	2284	2285	2286	2287
8F0	2288	2289	2290	2291	2292	2293	2294	2295	2296	2297	2298	2299	2300	2301	2302	2303
900	2304	2305	2306	2307	2308	2309	2310	2311	2312	2313	2314	2315	2316	2317	2318	2319
910	2320	2321	2322	2323	2324	2325	2326	2327	2328	2329	2330	2331	2332	2333	2334	2335
920	2336	2337	2338	2339	2340	2341	2342	2343	2344	2345	2346	2347	2348	2349	2350	2351
930	2352	2353	2354	2355	2356	2357	2358	2359	2360	2361	2362	2363	2364	2365	2366	2367
940	2368	2369	2370	2371	2372	2373	2374	2375	2376	2377	2378	2379	2380	2381	2382	2383
950	2384	2385	2386	2387	2388	2389	2390	2391	2392	2393	2394	2395	2396	2397	2398	2399
960	2400	2401	2402	2403	2404	2405	2406	2407	2408	2409	2410	2411	2412	2413	2414	2415
970	2416	2417	2418	2419	2420	2421	2422	2423	2424	2425	2426	2427	2428	2429	2430	2431
980	2432	2433	2434	2435	2436	2437	2438	2439	2440	2441	2442	2443	2444	2445	2446	2447
990	2448	2449	2450	2451	2452	2453	2454	2455	2456	2457	0458	2459	2460	2461	2462	2463
9A0	2464	2465	2466	2467	2468	2469	2470	2471	2472	2473	2474	2475	2476	2477	2478	2479
9B0	2480	2481	2482	2483	2484	2485	2486	2487	2488	2489	2490	2491	2492	2493	2494	2495
9C0	2496	2497	2498	2499	2500	2501	2502	2503	2504	2505	2506	2507	2508	2509	2510	2511
9D0	2512	2513	2514	2515	2516	2517	2518	2519	2520	2521	2522	2523	2524	2525	2526	2527
9E0	2528	2529	2530	2531	2532	2533	2534	2535	2536	2537	2538	2539	2540	2541	2542	2543
9F0	2544	2545	2546	2547	2548	2549	2550	2551	2552	2553	2554	2555	2556	2557	2558	2559
A00	2560	2561	2562	2563	2564	2565	2566	2567	2568	2569	2570	2571	2572	2573	2574	2575

A10	2576	2577	2578	2579	2580	2581	2582	2583	2584	2585	2586	2587	2588	2589	2590	2591
A20	2592	2593	2594	2595	2596	2597	2598	2599	2600	2601	2602	2603	2604	2605	2606	2607
A30	2608	2609	2610	2611	2612	2613	2614	2615	2616	2617	2618	2619	2620	2621	2622	2623
A40	2624	2625	2626	2627	2628	2629	2630	2631	2632	2633	2634	2635	2636	2637	2638	2639
A50	2640	2641	2642	2643	2644	2645	2646	2647	2648	2649	2650	2651	2652	2653	2654	2655
A60	2656	2657	2658	2659	2660	2661	2662	2663	2664	2665	2666	2667	2668	2669	2670	2671
A70	2672	2673	2674	2675	2676	2677	2678	2679	2680	2681	2682	2683	2684	2685	2686	2687
A80	2688	2689	2690	2691	2692	2693	2694	2695	2696	2697	2698	2699	2700	2701	2702	2703
A90	2704	2705	2706	2707	2708	2709	2710	2711	2712	2713	2714	2715	2716	2717	2718	2719
AA0	2720	2721	2722	2723	2724	2725	2726	2727	2728	2729	2730	2731	2732	2733	2734	2735
AB0	2736	2737	2738	2739	2740	2741	2742	2743	2744	2745	2746	2747	2748	2749	2750	2751
AC0	2752	2753	2754	2755	2756	2757	2758	2759	2760	2761	2762	2763	2764	2765	2766	2767
AD0	2768	2769	2770	2771	2772	2773	2774	2775	2776	2777	2778	2779	2780	2781	2782	2783
AE0	2784	2785	2786	2787	2788	2789	2790	2791	2792	2793	2794	2795	2796	2797	2798	2799
AF0	2800	2801	2802	2803	2804	2805	2806	2807	2808	2809	2810	2811	2812	2813	2814	2815
B00	2816	2817	2818	2819	2820	2821	2822	2823	2824	2825	2826	2827	2828	2829	2830	2831
B10	2832	2833	2834	2835	2836	2837	2838	2839	2840	2841	2842	2843	2844	2845	2846	2847
B20	2848	2849	2850	2851	2852	2853	2854	2855	2856	2857	2858	2859	2860	2861	2862	2863
B30	2864	2865	2866	2867	2868	2869	2870	2871	2872	2873	2874	2875	2876	2877	2878	2879
B40	2880	2881	2882	2883	2884	2885	2886	2887	2888	2889	2890	2891	2892	2893	2894	2895
B50	2896	2897	2898	2899	2900	2901	2902	2903	2904	2905	2906	2907	2908	2909	2910	2911
B60	2912	2913	2914	2915	2916	2917	2918	2919	2920	2921	2922	2923	2924	2925	2926	2927
B70	2928	2929	2930	2931	2932	2933	2934	2935	2936	2937	2938	2939	2940	2941	2942	2943
B80	2944	2945	2946	2947	2948	2949	2950	2951	2952	2953	2954	2955	2956	2957	2958	2959
B90	2960	2961	2962	2963	2964	2965	2966	2967	2968	2969	2970	2971	2972	2973	2974	2975
BA0	2976	2977	2978	2979	2980	2981	2982	2983	2984	2985	2986	2987	2988	2989	2990	2991
BB0	2992	2993	2994	2995	2996	2997	2998	2999	3000	3001	3002	3003	3004	3005	3006	3007
BC0	3008	3009	3010	3011	3012	3013	3014	3015	3016	3017	3018	3019	3020	3021	3022	3023
BD0	3024	3025	3026	3027	3028	3029	3030	3031	3032	3033	3034	3035	3036	3037	3038	3039

TABLE B-13. Hexadecimal-Decimal Integer Conversion (*Continued*).

	0	1	2	3	4	5	6	7	8	9	A	B	C	D	E	F
BE0	3040	3041	3042	3043	3044	3045	3046	3047	3048	3049	3050	3051	3052	3053	3054	3055
BF0	3056	3057	3058	3059	3060	3061	3062	3063	3064	3065	3066	3067	3068	3069	3070	3071
C00	3072	3073	3074	3075	3076	3077	3078	3079	3080	3081	3082	3083	3084	3085	3086	3087
C10	3088	3089	3090	3091	3092	3093	3094	3095	3096	3097	3098	3099	3100	3101	3102	3103
C20	3104	3105	3106	3107	3108	3109	3110	3111	3112	3113	3114	3115	3116	3117	3118	3119
C30	3120	3121	3122	3123	3124	3125	3126	3127	3128	3129	3130	3131	3132	3133	1334	3135
C40	3136	3137	3138	3139	3140	3141	3142	3143	3144	3145	3146	3147	3148	3149	3150	3151
C50	3152	3153	3154	3155	3156	3157	3158	3159	3160	3161	3162	3163	3164	3165	3166	3167
C60	3168	3169	3170	3171	3172	3173	3174	3175	3176	3177	3178	3179	3180	3181	3182	3183
C70	3184	3185	3186	3187	3188	3189	3190	3191	3192	3193	3194	3195	3196	3197	3198	3199
C80	3200	3201	3202	3203	3204	3205	3206	3207	3208	3209	3210	3211	3212	3213	3214	3215
C90	3216	3217	3218	3219	3220	3221	3222	3223	3224	3225	3226	3227	3228	3229	3230	3231
CA0	3232	3233	3234	3235	3236	3237	3238	3239	3240	3241	3242	3243	3244	3245	3246	3247
CB0	3248	3249	3250	3251	3252	3253	3254	3255	3256	3257	3258	3259	3260	3261	3262	3263
CC0	3264	3265	3266	3267	3268	3269	3270	3271	3272	3273	3274	3275	3276	3277	3278	3279
CD0	3280	3281	3282	3283	3284	3285	3286	3287	3288	3289	3290	3291	3292	3293	3294	3295
CE0	3296	3297	3298	3299	3300	3301	3302	3303	3304	3305	3306	3307	3308	3309	3310	3311
CF0	3312	3313	3314	3315	3316	3317	3318	3319	3320	3321	3322	3323	3324	3325	3326	3327
D00	3328	3329	3330	3331	3332	3333	3334	3335	3336	3337	3338	3339	3340	3341	3342	3343
D10	3344	3345	3346	3347	3348	3349	3350	3351	3352	3353	3354	3355	3356	3357	3358	3359
D20	3360	3361	3362	3363	3364	3365	3366	3367	3368	3369	3370	3371	3372	3373	3374	3375
D30	3376	3377	3378	3379	3380	3381	3382	3383	3384	3385	3386	3387	3388	3389	3390	3391
D40	3392	3393	3394	3395	3396	3397	3398	3399	3400	3401	3402	3403	3404	3405	3406	3407
D50	3408	3409	3410	3411	3412	3413	3414	3415	3416	3417	3418	3419	3420	3421	3422	3423
D60	3424	3425	3426	3427	3428	3429	3430	3431	3432	3433	3434	3435	3436	3437	3438	3439
D70	3440	3441	3442	3443	3444	3445	3446	3447	3448	3449	3450	3451	3452	3453	3454	3455

	0	1	2	3	4	5	6	7	8	9	A	B	C	D	E	F
D80	3456	3457	3458	3459	3460	3461	3462	3463	3464	3465	3466	3467	3468	3469	3470	3471
D90	3472	3473	3474	3475	3476	3477	3478	3479	3480	3481	3482	3483	3484	3485	3486	3487
DA0	3488	3489	3490	3491	3492	3493	3494	3495	3496	3497	3498	3499	3500	3501	3502	3503
DB0	3504	3505	3506	3507	3508	3509	3510	3511	3512	3513	3514	3515	3516	3517	3518	3519
DC0	3520	3521	3522	3523	3524	3525	3526	3527	3528	3529	3530	3531	3532	3533	3534	3535
DD0	3536	3537	3538	3539	3540	3541	3542	3543	3544	3545	3546	3547	3548	3549	3550	3551
DE0	3552	3553	3554	3555	3556	3557	3558	3559	3560	3561	3562	3563	3564	3565	3566	3567
DF0	3568	3569	3570	3571	3572	3573	3574	3575	3576	3577	3578	3579	3580	3581	3582	3583
E00	3584	3585	3586	3587	3588	3589	3590	3591	3592	3593	3594	3595	3596	3597	3598	3599
E10	3600	3601	3602	3603	3604	3605	3606	3607	3608	3609	3610	3611	3612	3613	3614	3615
E20	3616	3617	3618	3619	3620	3621	3622	3623	3624	3625	3626	3627	3628	3629	3630	3631
E30	3632	3633	3634	3635	3636	3637	3638	3639	3640	3641	3642	3643	3644	3645	3646	3647
E40	3648	3649	3650	3651	3652	3653	3654	3655	3656	3657	3658	3659	3660	3661	3662	3663
E50	3664	3665	3666	3667	3668	3669	3670	3671	3672	3673	3674	3675	3676	3677	3678	3679
E60	3680	3681	3682	3683	3684	3685	3686	3687	3688	3689	3690	3691	3692	3693	3694	3695
E70	3696	3697	3698	3699	3700	3701	3702	3703	3704	3705	3706	3707	3708	3709	3710	3711
E80	3712	3713	3714	3715	3716	3717	3718	3719	3720	3721	3722	3723	3724	3725	3726	3727
E90	3728	3729	3730	3731	3732	3733	3734	3735	3736	3737	3738	3739	3740	3741	3742	3743
EA0	3744	3745	3746	3747	3748	3749	3750	3751	3752	3753	3754	3755	3756	3757	3758	3759
EB0	3760	3761	3762	3763	3764	3765	3766	3767	3768	3769	3770	3771	3772	3773	3774	3775
EC0	3776	3777	3778	3779	3780	3781	3782	3783	3784	3785	3786	3787	3788	3789	3790	3791
ED0	3792	3793	3794	3795	3796	3797	3798	3799	3800	3801	3802	3803	3804	3805	3806	3807
EE0	3808	3809	3810	3811	3812	3813	3814	3815	3816	3817	3818	3819	3820	3821	3822	3823
EF0	3824	3825	3826	3827	3828	3829	3830	3831	3832	3833	3834	3835	3836	3837	3838	3839
F00	3840	3841	3842	3843	3844	3845	3846	3847	3848	3849	3850	3851	3852	3853	3854	3855
F10	3856	3857	3858	3859	3860	3861	3862	3863	3864	3865	3866	3867	3868	3869	3870	3871
F20	3872	3873	3874	3875	3876	3877	3878	3879	3880	3881	3882	3883	3884	3885	3886	3887
F30	3888	3889	3890	3891	3892	3893	3894	3895	3896	3897	3898	3899	3900	3901	3902	3903
F40	3904	3905	3906	3907	3908	3909	3910	3911	3912	3913	3914	3915	3916	3917	3918	3919

TABLE B-13. Hexadecimal-Decimal Integer Conversion (*Continued*).

	0	1	2	3	4	5	6	7	8	9	A	B	C	D	E	F
F50	3920	3921	3922	3923	3924	3925	3926	3927	3928	3929	3930	3931	3932	3933	3934	3935
F60	3936	3937	3938	3939	3940	3941	3942	3943	3944	3945	3946	3947	3948	3949	3950	3951
F70	3952	3953	3954	3955	3956	3957	3958	3959	3960	3961	3962	3963	3964	3965	3966	3967
F80	3968	3969	3970	3971	3972	3973	3974	3975	3976	3977	3978	3979	3980	3981	3982	3983
F90	3984	3985	3986	3987	3988	3989	3990	3991	3992	3993	3994	3995	3996	3997	3998	3999
FA0	4000	4001	4002	4003	4004	4005	4006	4007	4008	4009	4010	4011	4012	4013	4014	4015
FB0	4016	4017	4018	4019	4020	4021	4022	4023	4024	4025	4026	4027	4028	4029	4030	4031
FC0	4032	4033	4034	4035	4036	4037	4038	4039	4040	4041	4042	4043	4044	4045	4046	4047
FD0	4048	4049	4050	4051	4052	4053	4054	4055	4056	4057	4058	4059	4060	4061	4062	4063
FE0	4064	4065	4066	4067	4068	4069	4070	4071	4072	4073	4074	4075	4076	4077	4078	4079
FF0	4080	4081	4082	4083	4084	4085	4086	4087	4088	4089	4090	4091	4092	4093	4094	4095

TABLE B-14. Hexadecimal-Decimal Fraction Conversion.

Hexadecimal	Decimal	Hexadecimal	Decimal	Hexadecimal	Decimal	Hexadecimal	Decimal
.00 00 00 00	.00000 00000	.40 00 00 00	.25000 00000	.80 00 00 00	.50000 00000	.C0 00 00 00	.75000 00000
.01 00 00 00	.00390 62500	.41 00 00 00	.25390 62500	.81 00 00 00	.50390 62500	.C1 00 00 00	.75390 62500
.02 00 00 00	.00781 25000	.42 00 00 00	.25781 25000	.82 00 00 00	.50781 25000	.C2 00 00 00	.75781 25000
.03 00 00 00	.01171 87500	.43 00 00 00	.26171 87500	.83 00 00 00	.51171 87500	.C3 00 00 00	.76171 87500
.04 00 00 00	.01562 50000	.44 00 00 00	.26562 50000	.84 00 00 00	.51562 50000	.C4 00 00 00	.76562 50000
.05 00 00 00	.01953 12500	.45 00 00 00	.26953 12500	.85 00 00 00	.51953 12500	.C5 00 00 00	.76953 12500
.06 00 00 00	.02343 75000	.46 00 00 00	.27343 75000	.86 00 00 00	.52343 75000	.C6 00 00 00	.77343 75000
.07 00 00 00	.02734 37500	.47 00 00 00	.27734 37500	.87 00 00 00	.52734 37500	.C7 00 00 00	.77734 37500
.08 00 00 00	.03125 00000	.48 00 00 00	.28125 00000	.88 00 00 00	.53125 00000	.C8 00 00 00	.78125 00000
.09 00 00 00	.03515 62500	.49 00 00 00	.28515 62500	.89 00 00 00	.53515 62500	.C9 00 00 00	.78515 62500
.0A 00 00 00	.03906 25000	.4A 00 00 00	.28906 25000	.8A 00 00 00	.53906 25000	.CA 00 00 00	.78906 25000
.0B 00 00 00	.04296 87500	.4B 00 00 00	.29296 87500	.8B 00 00 00	.54296 87500	.CB 00 00 00	.79296 87500
.0C 00 00 00	.04687 50000	.4C 00 00 00	.29687 50000	.8C 00 00 00	.54687 50000	.CC 00 00 00	.79687 50000
.0D 00 00 00	.05078 12500	.4D 00 00 00	.30078 12500	.8D 00 00 00	.55078 12500	.CD 00 00 00	.80078 12500
.0E 00 00 00	.05468 75000	.4E 00 00 00	.30468 75000	.8E 00 00 00	.55468 75000	.CE 00 00 00	.80468 75000
.0F 00 00 00	.05859 37500	.4F 00 00 00	.30859 37500	.8F 00 00 00	.55859 37500	.CF 00 00 00	.80859 37500
.10 00 00 00	.06250 00000	.50 00 00 00	.31250 00000	.90 00 00 00	.56250 00000	.D0 00 00 00	.81250 00000
.11 00 00 00	.06640 62500	.51 00 00 00	.31640 62500	.91 00 00 00	.56640 62500	.D1 00 00 00	.81640 62500
.12 00 00 00	.07031 25000	.52 00 00 00	.32031 25000	.92 00 00 00	.57031 25000	.D2 00 00 00	.82031 25000
.13 00 00 00	.07421 87500	.53 00 00 00	.32421 87500	.93 00 00 00	.57421 87500	.D3 00 00 00	.82421 87500
.14 00 00 00	.07812 50000	.54 00 00 00	.32812 50000	.94 00 00 00	.57812 50000	.D4 00 00 00	.82812 50000
.15 00 00 00	.08203 12500	.55 00 00 00	.33203 12500	.95 00 00 00	.58203 12500	.D5 00 00 00	.83203 12500
.16 00 00 00	.08593 75000	.56 00 00 00	.33593 75000	.96 00 00 00	.58593 75000	.D6 00 00 00	.83593 75000
.17 00 00 00	.08984 37500	.57 00 00 00	.33984 37500	.97 00 00 00	.58984 37500	.D7 00 00 00	.83984 37500
.18 00 00 00	.09375 00000	.58 00 00 00	.34375 00000	.98 00 00 00	.59375 00000	.D8 00 00 00	.84375 00000
.19 00 00 00	.09765 62500	.59 00 00 00	.34765 62500	.99 00 00 00	.59765 62500	.D9 00 00 00	.84765 62500
.1A 00 00 00	.10156 25000	.5A 00 00 00	.35156 25000	.9A 00 00 00	.60156 25000	.DA 00 00 00	.85156 25000
.1B 00 00 00	.10546 87500	.5B 00 00 00	.35546 87500	.9B 00 00 00	.60546 87500	.DB 00 00 00	.85546 87500
.1C 00 00 00	.10937 50000	.5C 00 00 00	.35937 50000	.9C 00 00 00	.60937 50000	.DC 00 00 00	.85937 50000
.1D 00 00 00	.11328 12500	.5D 00 00 00	.36328 12500	.9D 00 00 00	.61328 12500	.DD 00 00 00	.86328 12500
.1E 00 00 00	.11718 75000	.5E 00 00 00	.36718 75000	.9E 00 00 00	.61718 75000	.DE 00 00 00	.86718 75000
.1F 00 00 00	.12109 37500	.5F 00 00 00	.37109 37500	.9F 00 00 00	.62109 37500	.DF 00 00 00	.87109 37500

TABLE B-14. Hexadecimal-Decimal Fraction Conversion (Continued).

Hexadecimal	Decimal	Hexadecimal	Decimal	Hexadecimal	Decimal	Hexadecimal	Decimal
.20 00 00 00	.12500 00000	.60 00 00 00	.37500 00000	.A0 00 00 00	.62500 00000	.E0 00 00 00	.87500 00000
.21 00 00 00	.12890 62500	.61 00 00 00	.37890 62500	.A1 00 00 00	.62890 62500	.E1 00 00 00	.87890 62500
.22 00 00 00	.13281 25000	.62 00 00 00	.38281 25000	.A2 00 00 00	.63281 25000	.E2 00 00 00	.88281 25000
.23 00 00 00	.13671 87500	.63 00 00 00	.38671 87500	.A3 00 00 00	.63671 87500	.E3 00 00 00	.88671 87500
.24 00 00 00	.14062 50000	.64 00 00 00	.39062 50000	.A4 00 00 00	.64062 50000	.E4 00 00 00	.89062 50000
.25 00 00 00	.14453 12500	.65 00 00 00	.39453 12500	.A5 00 00 00	.64453 12500	.E5 00 00 00	.89453 12500
.26 00 00 00	.14843 75000	.66 00 00 00	.39843 75000	.A6 00 00 00	.64843 75000	.E6 00 00 00	.89843 75000
.27 00 00 00	.15234 37500	.67 00 00 00	.40234 37500	.A7 00 00 00	.65234 37500	.E7 00 00 00	.90234 37500
.28 00 00 00	.15625 00000	.68 00 00 00	.40625 00000	.A8 00 00 00	.65625 00000	.E8 00 00 00	.90625 00000
.29 00 00 00	.16015 62500	.69 00 00 00	.41015 62500	.A9 00 00 00	.66015 62500	.E9 00 00 00	.91015 62500
.2A 00 00 00	.16406 25000	.6A 00 00 00	.41406 25000	.AA 00 00 00	.66406 25000	.EA 00 00 00	.91406 25000
.2B 00 00 00	.16796 87500	.6B 00 00 00	.41796 87500	.AB 00 00 00	.66796 87500	.EB 00 00 00	.91796 87500
.2C 00 00 00	.17187 50000	.6C 00 00 00	.42187 50000	.AC 00 00 00	.67187 50000	.EC 00 00 00	.92187 50000
.2D 00 00 00	.17578 12500	.6D 00 00 00	.42578 12500	.AD 00 00 00	.67578 12500	.ED 00 00 00	.92578 12500
.2E 00 00 00	.17968 75000	.6E 00 00 00	.42968 75000	.AE 00 00 00	.67968 75000	.EE 00 00 00	.92968 75000
.2F 00 00 00	.18359 37500	.6F 00 00 00	.43359 37500	.AF 00 00 00	.68359 37500	.EF 00 00 00	.93359 37500
.30 00 00 00	.18750 00000	.70 00 00 00	.43750 00000	.B0 00 00 00	.68750 00000	.F0 00 00 00	.93750 00000
.31 00 00 00	.19140 62500	.71 00 00 00	.44140 62500	.B1 00 00 00	.69140 62500	.F1 00 00 00	.94140 62500
.32 00 00 00	.19531 25000	.72 00 00 00	.44531 25000	.B2 00 00 00	.69531 25000	.F2 00 00 00	.94531 25000
.33 00 00 00	.19921 87500	.73 00 00 00	.44921 87500	.B3 00 00 00	.69921 87500	.F3 00 00 00	.94921 87500
.34 00 00 00	.20312 50000	.74 00 00 00	.45312 50000	.B4 00 00 00	.70312 50000	.F4 00 00 00	.95312 50000
.35 00 00 00	.20703 12500	.75 00 00 00	.45703 12500	.B5 00 00 00	.70703 12500	.F5 00 00 00	.95703 12500
.36 00 00 00	.21093 75000	.76 00 00 00	.46093 75000	.B6 00 00 00	.71093 75000	.F6 00 00 00	.96093 75000
.37 00 00 00	.21484 37500	.77 00 00 00	.46484 37500	.B7 00 00 00	.71484 37500	.F7 00 00 00	.96484 37500
.38 00 00 00	.21875 00000	.78 00 00 00	.46875 00000	.B8 00 00 00	.71875 00000	.F8 00 00 00	.96875 00000
.39 00 00 00	.22265 62500	.79 00 00 00	.47265 62500	.B9 00 00 00	.72265 62500	.F9 00 00 00	.97265 62500
.3A 00 00 00	.22656 25000	.7A 00 00 00	.47656 25000	.BA 00 00 00	.72656 25000	.FA 00 00 00	.97656 25000
.3B 00 00 00	.23046 87500	.7B 00 00 00	.48046 87500	.BB 00 00 00	.73046 87500	.FB 00 00 00	.98046 87500
.3C 00 00 00	.23437 50000	.7C 00 00 00	.48437 50000	.BC 00 00 00	.73437 50000	.FC 00 00 00	.98437 50000
.3D 00 00 00	.23828 12500	.7D 00 00 00	.48828 12500	.BD 00 00 00	.73828 12500	.FD 00 00 00	.98828 12500
.3E 00 00 00	.24218 75000	.7E 00 00 00	.49218 75000	.BE 00 00 00	.74218 75000	.FE 00 00 00	.99218 75000
.3F 00 00 00	.24609 37500	.7F 00 00 00	.49609 37500	.BF 00 00 00	.74609 37500	.FF 00 00 00	.99609 37500

Index	Value	Index	Value	Index	Value	Index	Value
.00 00 00 00	.00000 00000	.00 40 00 00	.00097 65625	.00 80 00 00	.00195 31250	.00 C0 00 00	.00292 96875
.00 01 00 00	.00001 52587	.00 41 00 00	.00099 18212	.00 81 00 00	.00196 83837	.00 C1 00 00	.00294 49462
.00 02 00 00	.00003 05175	.00 42 00 00	.00100 70800	.00 82 00 00	.00198 36425	.00 C2 00 00	.00296 02050
.00 03 00 00	.00004 57763	.00 43 00 00	.00102 23388	.00 83 00 00	.00199 89013	.00 C3 00 00	.00297 54638
.00 04 00 00	.00006 10351	.00 44 00 00	.00103 75976	.00 84 00 00	.00201 41601	.00 C4 00 00	.00299 07226
.00 05 00 00	.00007 62939	.00 45 00 00	.00105 28564	.00 85 00 00	.00202 94189	.00 C5 00 00	.00300 59814
.00 06 00 00	.00009 15527	.00 46 00 00	.00106 81152	.00 86 00 00	.00204 46777	.00 C6 00 00	.00302 12402
.00 07 00 00	.00010 68115	.00 47 00 00	.00108 33740	.00 87 00 00	.00205 99365	.00 C7 00 00	.00303 64990
.00 08 00 00	.00012 20703	.00 48 00 00	.00109 86328	.00 88 00 00	.00207 51953	.00 C8 00 00	.00305 17578
.00 09 00 00	.00013 73291	.00 49 00 00	.00111 38916	.00 89 00 00	.00209 04541	.00 C9 00 00	.00306 70166
.00 0A 00 00	.00015 25878	.00 4A 00 00	.00112 91503	.00 8A 00 00	.00210 57128	.00 CA 00 00	.00308 22753
.00 0B 00 00	.00016 78466	.00 4B 00 00	.00114 44091	.00 8B 00 00	.00212 09716	.00 CB 00 00	.00309 75341
.00 0C 00 00	.00018 31054	.00 4C 00 00	.00115 96679	.00 8C 00 00	.00213 62304	.00 CC 00 00	.00311 27929
.00 0D 00 00	.00019 83642	.00 4D 00 00	.00117 49267	.00 8D 00 00	.00215 14892	.00 CD 00 00	.00312 80517
.00 0E 00 00	.00021 36230	.00 4E 00 00	.00119 01855	.00 8E 00 00	.00216 67480	.00 CE 00 00	.00314 33105
.00 0F 00 00	.00022 88818	.00 4F 00 00	.00120 54443	.00 8F 00 00	.00218 20068	.00 CF 00 00	.00315 85693
.00 10 00 00	.00024 41406	.00 50 00 00	.00122 07031	.00 90 00 00	.00219 72656	.00 D0 00 00	.00317 38281
.00 11 00 00	.00025 93994	.00 51 00 00	.00123 59619	.00 91 00 00	.00221 25244	.00 D1 00 00	.00318 90869
.00 12 00 00	.00027 46582	.00 52 00 00	.00125 12207	.00 92 00 00	.00222 77832	.00 D2 00 00	.00320 43457
.00 13 00 00	.00028 99169	.00 53 00 00	.00126 64794	.00 93 00 00	.00224 30419	.00 D3 00 00	.00321 96044
.00 14 00 00	.00030 51757	.00 54 00 00	.00128 17382	.00 94 00 00	.00225 83007	.00 D4 00 00	.00323 48632
.00 15 00 00	.00032 04345	.00 55 00 00	.00129 69970	.00 95 00 00	.00227 35595	.00 D5 00 00	.00325 01220
.00 16 00 00	.00033 56933	.00 56 00 00	.00131 22558	.00 96 00 00	.00228 88183	.00 D6 00 00	.00326 53808
.00 17 00 00	.00035 09521	.00 57 00 00	.00132 75146	.00 97 00 00	.00230 40771	.00 D7 00 00	.00328 06396
.00 18 00 00	.00036 62109	.00 58 00 00	.00134 27734	.00 98 00 00	.00231 93359	.00 D8 00 00	.00329 58984
.00 19 00 00	.00038 14697	.00 59 00 00	.00135 80322	.00 99 00 00	.00233 45947	.00 D9 00 00	.00331 11572
.00 1A 00 00	.00039 67285	.00 5A 00 00	.00137 32910	.00 9A 00 00	.00234 98535	.00 DA 00 00	.00332 64160
.00 1B 00 00	.00041 19873	.00 5B 00 00	.00138 85498	.00 9B 00 00	.00236 51123	.00 DB 00 00	.00334 16748
.00 1C 00 00	.00042 72460	.00 5C 00 00	.00140 38085	.00 9C 00 00	.00238 03710	.00 DC 00 00	.00335 69335
.00 1D 00 00	.00044 25048	.00 5D 00 00	.00141 90673	.00 9D 00 00	.00239 56298	.00 DD 00 00	.00337 21923
.00 1E 00 00	.00045 77636	.00 5E 00 00	.00143 43261	.00 9E 00 00	.00241 08886	.00 DE 00 00	.00338 74511
.00 1F 00 00	.00047 30224	.00 5F 00 00	.00144 95849	.00 9F 00 00	.00242 61474	.00 DF 00 00	.00340 27099
.00 20 00 00	.00048 82812	.00 60 00 00	.00146 48437	.00 A0 00 00	.00244 14062	.00 E0 00 00	.00341 79687
.00 21 00 00	.00050 35400	.00 61 00 00	.00148 01025	.00 A1 00 00	.00245 66650	.00 E1 00 00	.00343 32275
.00 22 00 00	.00051 87988	.00 62 00 00	.00149 53613	.00 A2 00 00	.00247 19238	.00 E2 00 00	.00344 84863

TABLE B-14. Hexadecimal-Decimal Fraction Conversion (Continued).

Hexadecimal	Decimal	Hexadecimal	Decimal	Hexadecimal	Decimal	Hexadecimal	Decimal
.00 23 00 00	.00053 40576	.00 63 00 00	.00151 06201	.00 A3 00 00	.00248 71826	.00 E3 00 00	.00346 37451
.00 24 00 00	.00054 93164	.00 64 00 00	.00152 58789	.00 A4 00 00	.00250 24414	.00 E4 00 00	.00347 90039
.00 25 00 00	.00056 45751	.00 65 00 00	.00154 11376	.00 A5 00 00	.00251 77001	.00 E5 00 00	.00349 42626
.00 26 00 00	.00057 98339	.00 66 00 00	.00155 63964	.00 A6 00 00	.00253 29589	.00 E6 00 00	.00350 95214
.00 27 00 00	.00059 50927	.00 67 00 00	.00157 16552	.00 A7 00 00	.00254 82177	.00 E7 00 00	.00352 47802
.00 28 00 00	.00061 03515	.00 68 00 00	.00158 69140	.00 A8 00 00	.00256 34765	.00 E8 00 00	.00354 00390
.00 29 00 00	.00062 56103	.00 69 00 00	.00160 21728	.00 A9 00 00	.00257 87353	.00 E9 00 00	.00355 52978
.00 2A 00 00	.00064 08691	.00 6A 00 00	.00161 74316	.00 AA 00 00	.00259 39941	.00 EA 00 00	.00357 05566
.00 2B 00 00	.00065 61279	.00 6B 00 00	.00163 26904	.00 AB 00 00	.00260 92529	.00 EB 00 00	.00358 58154
.00 2C 00 00	.00067 13867	.00 6C 00 00	.00164 79492	.00 AC 00 00	.00262 45117	.00 EC 00 00	.00360 10742
.00 2D 00 00	.00068 66455	.00 6D 00 00	.00166 32080	.00 AD 00 00	.00263 97705	.00 ED 00 00	.00361 63330
.00 2E 00 00	.00070 19042	.00 6E 00 00	.00167 84667	.00 AE 00 00	.00265 50292	.00 EE 00 00	.00363 15917
.00 2F 00 00	.00071 71630	.00 6F 00 00	.00169 37255	.00 AF 00 00	.00267 02880	.00 EF 00 00	.00364 68505
.00 30 00 00	.00073 24218	.00 70 00 00	.00170 89843	.00 B0 00 00	.00268 55468	.00 F0 00 00	.00366 21093
.00 31 00 00	.00074 76806	.00 71 00 00	.00172 42431	.00 B1 00 00	.00270 08056	.00 F1 00 00	.00367 73681
.00 32 00 00	.00076 29394	.00 72 00 00	.00173 95019	.00 B2 00 00	.00271 60644	.00 F2 00 00	.00369 26269
.00 33 00 00	.00077 81982	.00 73 00 00	.00175 47607	.00 B3 00 00	.00273 13232	.00 F3 00 00	.00370 78857
.00 34 00 00	.00079 34570	.00 74 00 00	.00177 00195	.00 B4 00 00	.00274 65820	.00 F4 00 00	.00372 31445
.00 35 00 00	.00080 87158	.00 75 00 00	.00178 52783	.00 B5 00 00	.00276 18408	.00 F5 00 00	.00373 84033
.00 36 00 00	.00082 39746	.00 76 00 00	.00180 05371	.00 B6 00 00	.00277 70996	.00 F6 00 00	.00375 36621
.00 37 00 00	.00083 92333	.00 77 00 00	.00181 57958	.00 B7 00 00	.00279 23583	.00 F7 00 00	.00376 89208
.00 38 00 00	.00085 44921	.00 78 00 00	.00183 10546	.00 B8 00 00	.00280 76171	.00 F8 00 00	.00378 41796
.00 39 00 00	.00086 97509	.00 79 00 00	.00184 63134	.00 B9 00 00	.00282 28759	.00 F9 00 00	.00379 94384
.00 3A 00 00	.00088 50097	.00 7A 00 00	.00186 15722	.00 BA 00 00	.00283 81347	.00 FA 00 00	.00381 46972
.00 3B 00 00	.00090 02685	.00 7B 00 00	.00187 68310	.00 BB 00 00	.00285 33935	.00 FB 00 00	.00382 99560
.00 3C 00 00	.00091 55273	.00 7C 00 00	.00189 20898	.00 BC 00 00	.00286 86523	.00 FC 00 00	.00384 52148
.00 3D 00 00	.00093 07861	.00 7D 00 00	.00190 73486	.00 BD 00 00	.00288 39111	.00 FD 00 00	.00386 04736
.00 3E 00 00	.00094 60449	.00 7E 00 00	.00192 26074	.00 BE 00 00	.00289 91699	.00 FE 00 00	.00387 57324
.00 3F 00 00	.00096 13037	.00 7F 00 00	.00193 78662	.00 BF 00 00	.00291 44287	.00 FF 00 00	.00389 09912
.00 00 00 00	.00000 00000	.00 00 40 00	.00000 38146	.00 00 80 00	.00000 76293	.00 00 C0 00	.00001 14440
.00 00 01 00	.00000 00596	.00 00 41 00	.00000 38743	.00 00 81 00	.00000 76889	.00 00 C1 00	.00001 15036

.00 00 02 00	.00000 01192		.00 00 42 00	.00000 39339		.00 00 82 00	.00000 77486		.00 00 C2 00	.00001 15633
.00 00 03 00	.00000 01788		.00 00 43 00	.00000 39935		.00 00 83 00	.00000 78082		.00 00 C3 00	.00001 16229
.00 00 04 00	.00000 02384		.00 00 44 00	.00000 40531		.00 00 84 00	.00000 78678		.00 00 C4 00	.00001 16825
.00 00 05 00	.00000 02980		.00 00 45 00	.00000 41127		.00 00 85 00	.00000 79274		.00 00 C5 00	.00001 17421
.00 00 06 00	.00000 03576		.00 00 46 00	.00000 41723		.00 00 86 00	.00000 79870		.00 00 C6 00	.00001 18017
.00 00 07 00	.00000 04172		.00 00 47 00	.00000 42319		.00 00 87 00	.00000 80466		.00 00 C7 00	.00001 18613
.00 00 08 00	.00000 04768		.00 00 48 00	.00000 42915		.00 00 88 00	.00000 81062		.00 00 C8 00	.00001 19209
.00 00 09 00	.00000 05364		.00 00 49 00	.00000 43511		.00 00 89 00	.00000 81658		.00 00 C9 00	.00001 19805
.00 00 0A 00	.00000 05960		.00 00 4A 00	.00000 44107		.00 00 8A 00	.00000 82254		.00 00 CA 00	.00001 20401
.00 00 0B 00	.00000 06556		.00 00 4B 00	.00000 44703		.00 00 8B 00	.00000 82850		.00 00 CB 00	.00001 20997
.00 00 0C 00	.00000 07152		.00 00 4C 00	.00000 45299		.00 00 8C 00	.00000 83446		.00 00 CC 00	.00001 21593
.00 00 0D 00	.00000 07748		.00 00 4D 00	.00000 45895		.00 00 8D 00	.00000 84042		.00 00 CD 00	.00001 22189
.00 00 0E 00	.00000 08344		.00 00 4E 00	.00000 46491		.00 00 8E 00	.00000 84638		.00 00 CE 00	.00001 22785
.00 00 0F 00	.00000 08940		.00 00 4F 00	.00000 47087		.00 00 8F 00	.00000 85234		.00 00 CF 00	.00001 23381
.00 00 10 00	.00000 09536		.00 00 50 00	.00000 47683		.00 00 90 00	.00000 85830		.00 00 D0 00	.00001 23977
.00 00 11 00	.00000 10132		.00 00 51 00	.00000 48279		.00 00 91 00	.00000 86426		.00 00 D1 00	.00001 24573
.00 00 12 00	.00000 10728		.00 00 52 00	.00000 48875		.00 00 92 00	.00000 87022		.00 00 D2 00	.00001 25169
.00 00 13 00	.00000 11324		.00 00 53 00	.00000 49471		.00 00 93 00	.00000 87618		.00 00 D3 00	.00001 25765
.00 00 14 00	.00000 11920		.00 00 54 00	.00000 50067		.00 00 94 00	.00000 88214		.00 00 D4 00	.00001 26361
.00 00 15 00	.00000 12516		.00 00 55 00	.00000 50663		.00 00 95 00	.00000 88810		.00 00 D5 00	.00001 26957
.00 00 16 00	.00000 13113		.00 00 56 00	.00000 51259		.00 00 96 00	.00000 89406		.00 00 D6 00	.00001 27553
.00 00 17 00	.00000 13709		.00 00 57 00	.00000 51856		.00 00 97 00	.00000 90003		.00 00 D7 00	.00001 28149
.00 00 18 00	.00000 14305		.00 00 58 00	.00000 52452		.00 00 98 00	.00000 90599		.00 00 D8 00	.00001 28746
.00 00 19 00	.00000 14901		.00 00 59 00	.00000 53048		.00 00 99 00	.00000 91195		.00 00 D9 00	.00001 29342
.00 00 1A 00	.00000 15497		.00 00 5A 00	.00000 53644		.00 00 9A 00	.00000 91791		.00 00 DA 00	.00001 29938
.00 00 1B 00	.00000 16093		.00 00 5B 00	.00000 54240		.00 00 9B 00	.00000 92387		.00 00 DB 00	.00001 30534
.00 00 1C 00	.00000 16689		.00 00 5C 00	.00000 54836		.00 00 9C 00	.00000 92983		.00 00 DC 00	.00001 31130
.00 00 1D 00	.00000 17285		.00 00 5D 00	.00000 55432		.00 00 9D 00	.00000 93579		.00 00 DD 00	.00001 31726
.00 00 1E 00	.00000 17881		.00 00 5E 00	.00000 56028		.00 00 9E 00	.00000 94175		.00 00 DE 00	.00001 32322
.00 00 1F 00	.00000 18477		.00 00 5F 00	.00000 56624		.00 00 9F 0	.00000 94771		.00 00 DF 00	.00001 32918
.00 00 20 00	.00000 19073		.00 00 60 00	.00000 57220		.00 00 A0 00	.00000 95367		.00 00 E0 00	.00001 33514
.00 00 21 00	.00000 19669		.00 00 61 00	.00000 57816		.00 00 A1 00	.00000 95963		.00 00 E1 00	.00001 34110
.00 00 22 00	.00000 20265		.00 00 62 00	.00000 58412		.00 00 A2 00	.00000 96559		.00 00 E2 00	.00001 34706
.00 00 23 00	.00000 20861		.00 00 63 00	.00000 59008		.00 00 A3 00	.00000 97155		.00 00 E3 00	.00001 35302
.00 00 24 00	.00000 21457		.00 00 64 00	.00000 59604		.00 00 A4 00	.00000 97751		.00 00 E4 00	.00001 35898

TABLE B-14. Hexadecimal-Decimal Fraction Conversion (*Continued*).

Hexadecimal	Decimal	Hexadecimal	Decimal	Hexadecimal	Decimal	Hexadecimal	Decimal
.00 00 25 00	.00000 22053	.00 00 65 00	.00000 60200	.00 00 A5 00	.00000 98347	.00 00 E5 00	.00001 36494
.00 00 26 00	.00000 22649	.00 00 66 00	.00000 60796	.00 00 A6 00	.00000 98943	.00 00 E6 00	.00001 37090
.00 00 27 00	.00000 23245	.00 00 67 00	.00000 61392	.00 00 A7 00	.00000 99539	.00 00 E7 00	.00001 37686
.00 00 28 00	.00000 23841	.00 00 68 00	.00000 61988	.00 00 A8 00	.00001 00135	.00 00 E8 00	.00001 38282
.00 00 29 00	.00000 24437	.00 00 69 00	.00000 62584	.00 00 A9 00	.00001 00731	.00 00 E9 00	.00001 38878
.00 00 2A 00	.00000 25033	.00 00 6A 00	.00000 63180	.00 00 AA 00	.00001 01327	.00 00 EA 00	.00001 39474
.00 00 2B 00	.00000 25629	.00 00 6B 00	.00000 63776	.00 00 AB 00	.00001 01923	.00 00 EB 00	.00001 40070
.00 00 2C 00	.00000 26226	.00 00 6C 00	.00000 64373	.00 00 AC 00	.00001 02519	.00 00 EC 00	.00001 40666
.00 00 2D 00	.00000 26822	.00 00 6D 00	.00000 64969	.00 00 AD 00	.00001 03116	.00 00 ED 00	.00001 41263
.00 00 2E 00	.00000 27418	.00 00 6E 00	.00000 65565	.00 00 AE 00	.00001 03712	.00 00 EE 00	.00001 41859
.00 00 2F 00	.00000 28014	.00 00 6F 00	.00000 66161	.00 00 AF 00	.00001 04308	.00 00 EF 00	.00001 42455
.00 00 30 00	.00000 28610	.00 00 70 00	.00000 66757	.00 00 B0 00	.00001 04904	.00 00 F0 00	.00001 43051
.00 00 31 00	.00000 29206	.00 00 71 00	.00000 67353	.00 00 B1 00	.00001 05500	.00 00 F1 00	.00001 43647
.00 00 32 00	.00000 29802	.00 00 72 00	.00000 67949	.00 00 B2 00	.00001 06096	.00 00 F2 00	.00001 44243
.00 00 33 00	.00000 30398	.00 00 73 00	.00000 68545	.00 00 B3 00	.00001 06692	.00 00 F3 00	.00001 44839
.00 00 34 00	.00000 30994	.00 00 74 00	.00000 69141	.00 00 B4 00	.00001 07288	.00 00 F4 00	.00001 45435
.00 00 35 00	.00000 31590	.00 00 75 00	.00000 69737	.00 00 B5 00	.00001 07884	.00 00 F5 00	.00001 46031
.00 00 36 00	.00000 32186	.00 00 76 00	.00000 70333	.00 00 B6 00	.00001 08480	.00 00 F6 00	.00001 46627
.00 00 37 00	.00000 32782	.00 00 77 00	.00000 70929	.00 00 B7 00	.00001 09076	.00 00 F7 00	.00001 47223
.00 00 38 00	.00000 33378	.00 00 78 00	.00000 71525	.00 00 B8 00	.00001 09672	.00 00 F8 00	.00001 47819
.00 00 39 00	.00000 33974	.00 00 79 00	.00000 72121	.00 00 B9 00	.00001 10268	.00 00 F9 00	.00001 48415
.00 00 3A 00	.00000 34570	.00 00 7A 00	.00000 72717	.00 00 BA 00	.00001 10864	.00 00 FA 00	.00001 49011
.00 00 3B 00	.00000 35166	.00 00 7B 00	.00000 73313	.00 00 BB 00	.00001 11460	.00 00 FB 00	.00001 49607
.00 00 3C 00	.00000 35762	.00 00 7C 00	.00000 73909	.00 00 BC 00	.00001 12056	.00 00 FC 00	.00001 50203
.00 00 3D 00	.00000 36358	.00 00 7D 00	.00000 74505	.00 00 BD 00	.00001 12652	.00 00 FD 00	.00001 50799
.00 00 3E 00	.00000 36954	.00 00 7E 00	.00000 75101	.00 00 BE 00	.00001 13248	.00 00 FE 00	.00001 51395
.00 00 3F 00	.00000 37550	.00 00 7F 00	.00000 75697	.00 00 BF 00	.00001 13844	.00 00 FF 00	.00001 51991
.00 00 00 00	.00000 00000	.00 00 00 40	.00000 00149	.00 00 00 80	.00000 00298	.00 00 00 C0	.00000 00447
.00 00 00 01	.00000 00002	.00 00 00 41	.00000 00151	.00 00 00 81	.00000 00300	.00 00 00 C1	.00000 00449
.00 00 00 02	.00000 00004	.00 00 00 42	.00000 00153	.00 00 00 82	.00000 00302	.00 00 00 C2	.00000 00451

Hexadecimal	Fraction	Hexadecimal	Fraction	Hexadecimal	Fraction	Hexadecimal	Fraction
00 00 00 03	.00000 00006	00 00 00 43	.00000 00155	00 00 00 83	.00000 00305	00 00 00 C3	.00000 00454
00 00 00 04	.00000 00009	00 00 00 44	.00000 00158	00 00 00 84	.00000 00307	00 00 00 C4	.00000 00456
00 00 00 05	.00000 00011	00 00 00 45	.00000 00160	00 00 00 85	.00000 00309	00 00 00 C5	.00000 00458
00 00 00 06	.00000 00013	00 00 00 46	.00000 00162	00 00 00 86	.00000 00311	00 00 00 C6	.00000 00461
00 00 00 07	.00000 00016	00 00 00 47	.00000 00165	00 00 00 87	.00000 00314	00 00 00 C7	.00000 00463
00 00 00 08	.00000 00018	00 00 00 48	.00000 00167	00 00 00 88	.00000 00316	00 00 00 C8	.00000 00465
00 00 00 09	.00000 00020	00 00 00 49	.00000 00169	00 00 00 89	.00000 00318	00 00 00 C9	.00000 00467
00 00 00 0A	.00000 00023	00 00 00 4A	.00000 00172	00 00 00 8A	.00000 00321	00 00 00 CA	.00000 00470
00 00 00 0B	.00000 00025	00 00 00 4B	.00000 00174	00 00 00 8B	.00000 00323	00 00 00 CB	.00000 00472
00 00 00 0C	.00000 00027	00 00 00 4C	.00000 00176	00 00 00 8C	.00000 00325	00 00 00 CC	.00000 00474
00 00 00 0D	.00000 00030	00 00 00 4D	.00000 00179	00 00 00 8D	.00000 00328	00 00 00 CD	.00000 00477
00 00 00 0E	.00000 00032	00 00 00 4E	.00000 00181	00 00 00 8E	.00000 00330	00 00 00 CE	.00000 00479
00 00 00 0F	.00000 00034	00 00 00 4F	.00000 00183	00 00 00 8F	.00000 00332	00 00 00 CF	.00000 00481
00 00 00 10	.00000 00037	00 00 00 50	.00000 00186	00 00 00 90	.00000 00335	00 00 00 D0	.00000 00484
00 00 00 11	.00000 00039	00 00 00 51	.00000 00188	00 00 00 91	.00000 00337	00 00 00 D1	.00000 00486
00 00 00 12	.00000 00041	00 00 00 52	.00000 00190	00 00 00 92	.00000 00339	00 00 00 D2	.00000 00488
00 00 00 13	.00000 00044	00 00 00 53	.00000 00193	00 00 00 93	.00000 00342	00 00 00 D3	.00000 00491
00 00 00 14	.00000 00046	00 00 00 54	.00000 00195	00 00 00 94	.00000 00344	00 00 00 D4	.00000 00493
00 00 00 15	.00000 00048	00 00 00 55	.00000 00197	00 00 00 95	.00000 00346	00 00 00 D5	.00000 00495
00 00 00 16	.00000 00051	00 00 00 56	.00000 00200	00 00 00 96	.00000 00349	00 00 00 D6	.00000 00498
00 00 00 17	.00000 00053	00 00 00 57	.00000 00202	00 00 00 97	.00000 00351	00 00 00 D7	.00000 00500
00 00 00 18	.00000 00055	00 00 00 58	.00000 00204	00 00 00 98	.00000 00353	00 00 00 D8	.00000 00502
00 00 00 19	.00000 00058	00 00 00 59	.00000 00207	00 00 00 99	.00000 00356	00 00 00 D9	.00000 00505
00 00 00 1A	.00000 00060	00 00 00 5A	.00000 00209	00 00 00 9A	.00000 00358	00 00 00 DA	.00000 00507
00 00 00 1B	.00000 00062	00 00 00 5B	.00000 00211	00 00 00 9B	.00000 00360	00 00 00 DB	.00000 00509
00 00 00 1C	.00000 00065	00 00 00 5C	.00000 00214	00 00 00 9C	.00000 00363	00 00 00 DC	.00000 00512
00 00 00 1D	.00000 00067	00 00 00 5D	.00000 00216	00 00 00 9D	.00000 00365	00 00 00 DD	.00000 00514
00 00 00 1E	.00000 00069	00 00 00 5E	.00000 00218	00 00 00 9E	.00000 00367	00 00 00 DE	.00000 00516
00 00 00 1F	.00000 00072	00 00 00 5F	.00000 00221	00 00 00 9F	.00000 00370	00 00 00 DF	.00000 00519
00 00 00 20	.00000 00074	00 00 00 60	.00000 00223	00 00 00 A0	.00000 00372	00 00 00 E0	.00000 00521
00 00 00 21	.00000 00076	00 00 00 61	.00000 00225	00 00 00 A1	.00000 00374	00 00 00 E1	.00000 00523
00 00 00 22	.00000 00079	00 00 00 62	.00000 00228	00 00 00 A2	.00000 00377	00 00 00 E2	.00000 00526
00 00 00 23	.00000 00081	00 00 00 63	.00000 00230	00 00 00 A3	.00000 00379	00 00 00 E3	.00000 00528
00 00 00 24	.00000 00083	00 00 00 64	.00000 00232	00 00 00 A4	.00000 00381	00 00 00 E4	.00000 00530
00 00 00 25	.00000 00086	00 00 00 65	.00000 00235	00 00 00 A5	.00000 00384	00 00 00 E5	.00000 00533

TABLE B-14. Hexadecimal-Decimal Fraction Conversion (Continued).

Hexadecimal	Decimal	Hexadecimal	Decimal	Hexadecimal	Decimal	Hexadecimal	Decimal
.00 00 00 26	.00000 00088	.00 00 00 66	.00000 00237	.00 00 00 A6	.00000 00386	.00 00 00 E6	.00000 00535
.00 00 00 27	.00000 00090	.00 00 00 67	.00000 00239	.00 00 00 A7	.00000 00388	.00 00 00 E7	.00000 00537
.00 00 00 28	.00000 00093	.00 00 00 68	.00000 00242	.00 00 00 A8	.00000 00391	.00 00 00 E8	.00000 00540
.00 00 00 29	.00000 00095	.00 00 00 69	.00000 00244	.00 00 00 A9	.00000 00393	.00 00 00 E9	.00000 00542
.00 00 00 2A	.00000 00097	.00 00 00 6A	.00000 00246	.00 00 00 AA	.00000 00395	.00 00 00 EA	.00000 00544
.00 00 00 2B	.00000 00100	.00 00 00 6B	.00000 00249	.00 00 00 AB	.00000 00398	.00 00 00 EB	.00000 00547
.00 00 00 2C	.00000 00102	.00 00 00 6C	.00000 00251	.00 00 00 AC	.00000 00400	.00 00 00 EC	.00000 00549
.00 00 00 2D	.00000 00104	.00 00 00 6D	.00000 00253	.00 00 00 AD	.00000 00402	.00 00 00 ED	.00000 00551
.00 00 00 2E	.00000 00107	.00 00 00 6E	.00000 00256	.00 00 00 AE	.00000 00405	.00 00 00 EE	.00000 00554
.00 00 00 2F	.00000 00109	.00 00 00 6F	.00000 00258	.00 00 00 AF	.00000 00407	.00 00 00 EF	.00000 00556
.00 00 00 30	.00000 00111	.00 00 00 70	.00000 00260	.00 00 00 B0	.00000 00409	.00 00 00 F0	.00000 00558
.00 00 00 31	.00000 00114	.00 00 00 71	.00000 00263	.00 00 00 B1	.00000 00412	.00 00 00 F1	.00000 00561
.00 00 00 32	.00000 00116	.00 00 00 72	.00000 00265	.00 00 00 B2	.00000 00414	.00 00 00 F2	.00000 00563
.00 00 00 33	.00000 00118	.00 00 00 73	.00000 00267	.00 00 00 B3	.00000 00416	.00 00 00 F3	.00000 00565
.00 00 00 34	.00000 00121	.00 00 00 74	.00000 00270	.00 00 00 B4	.00000 00419	.00 00 00 F4	.00000 00568
.00 00 00 35	.00000 00123	.00 00 00 75	.00000 00272	.00 00 00 B5	.00000 00421	.00 00 00 F5	.00000 00570
.00 00 00 36	.00000 00125	.00 00 00 76	.00000 00274	.00 00 00 B6	.00000 00423	.00 00 00 F6	.00000 00572
.00 00 00 37	.00000 00128	.00 00 00 77	.00000 00277	.00 00 00 B7	.00000 00426	.00 00 00 F7	.00000 00575
.00 00 00 38	.00000 00130	.00 00 00 78	.00000 00279	.00 00 00 B8	.00000 00428	.00 00 00 F8	.00000 00577
.00 00 00 39	.00000 00132	.00 00 00 79	.00000 00281	.00 00 00 B9	.00000 00430	.00 00 00 F9	.00000 00579
.00 00 00 3A	.00000 00135	.00 00 00 7A	.00000 00284	.00 00 00 BA	.00000 00433	.00 00 00 FA	.00000 00582
.00 00 00 3B	.00000 00137	.00 00 00 7B	.00000 00286	.00 00 00 BB	.00000 00435	.00 00 00 FB	.00000 00584
.00 00 00 3C	.00000 00139	.00 00 00 7C	.00000 00288	.00 00 00 BC	.00000 00437	.00 00 00 FC	.00000 00586
.00 00 00 3D	.00000 00142	.00 00 00 7D	.00000 00291	.00 00 00 BD	.00000 00440	.00 00 00 FD	.00000 00589
.00 00 00 3E	.00000 00144	.00 00 00 7E	.00000 00293	.00 00 00 BE	.00000 00442	.00 00 00 FE	.00000 00591
.00 00 00 3F	.00000 00146	.00 00 00 7F	.00000 00295	.00 00 00 BF	.00000 00444	.00 00 00 FF	.00000 00593

INDEX

References in the index are to section numbers. Note that section numbers are displayed at the top of text pages for convenient reference.